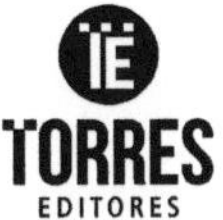

TORRES
EDITORES

Persona Art Honours
Published by Contemporary Art Station

Publisher
ICM Gestora Cultural, SL
Paseo de Gracia 95, 5º-1ª
08008 Barcelona
Spain

ISBN: 978-84-10291-78-2
DL: GR 1436-2024

Library of Congress Cataloging-in-Publication Data
Persona Art Honours / Contemporary Art Station.
Includes bibliographical references and index.
ISBN 978-84-10291-78-2

Printed in Spain, EU.

First Edition, 2024

Publisher's Contact Information:
Contemporary Art Station
contact@contemporaryartstation.com
www.contemporaryartstation.com

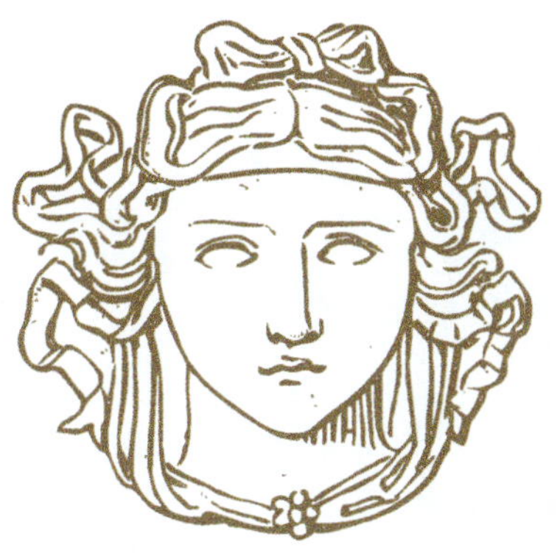

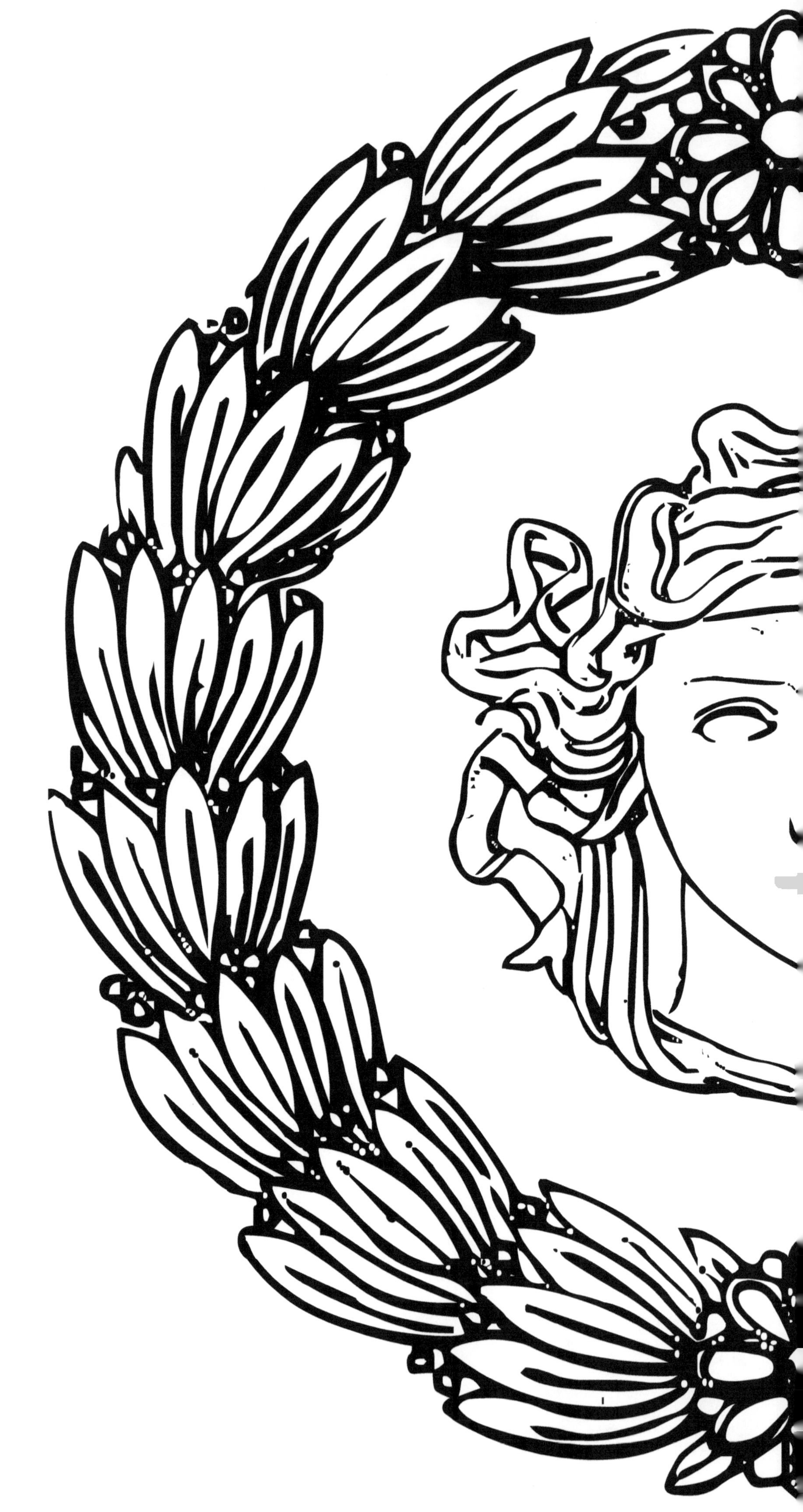

PERSONA

ART HONOURS

· MMXXIV ·

Contemporary Art Station

The Persona Art Honours stands as a distinguished accolade, awarded annually to a select group of artists who demonstrate exceptional creativity, vision, and individuality. This prestigious recognition by Contemporary Art Station seeks to celebrate those artists who possess not only a mastery of their craft but also a distinctive artistic language and personal signature that set them apart in the contemporary art world.

In today's global art market, where trends come and go, it is the artist's unique voice that resonates through time. The history of art is filled with examples of masters who transcended their era— not merely through the subjects they explored but through the originality and innovation in how they conveyed their ideas. These trailblazers left lasting imprints on art history, altering the course of artistic expression.

The Persona Art Honours pays tribute to those contemporary artists who embody this spirit of innovation and authenticity, marking their work with a signature style that defies convention and elevates the art world. Each honoree is recognized not just for what they say but for how they say it—through a powerful visual language that continues to inspire, challenge, and captivate audiences across the globe.

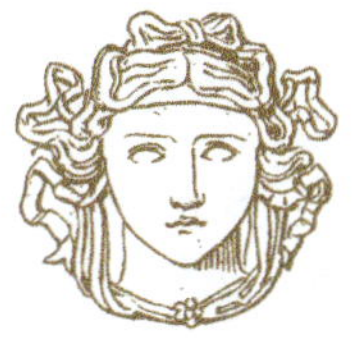

Ambro Louwe

Andrea Gendusa

Annemarie Ambrosoli

Annette Tan

Antoine Khanji

Aomi Kikuchi

Britta Ortiz

Bruce Cowell

Celine Chan

Daniel Grannan

Daniel McKinley

Dina Klumbys

Elise Bikker, Ph.D.

Eriko Kaniwa

Evaldas Gulbinas

Fine Art by AnnaK

Frédéric Steinlaender

GAYLE PRINTZ, A WORLD MASTER ARTIST

Gabriel Helou

Georg Douglas

Gregory Logan Dunn

Gunilla Daga

Henrik Saar

Ivan Kanchev

JOANNA

Jane Gottlieb

Jehan Ali

Jeong-Ah Zhang

Jette van der Lende

Josef Weidner

Judith Dupree Beale

Julie Reby Waas

Karin Monschauer

Kat Kleinman

Katja Lührs

Kenan K.

Kyunghee Lee

Lode Coen

Marcel Jomphe

Maurizio D'Andrea

Mari Winkler Solberg

Maria Stella Polce

Marianne Charlotte Mylonas-Svikovsky

Marie Ghislaine Beaucé

Marlene Jorge

Marta Carceller

Michel Audebert

Misa Aihara

Mitchell Gibson

Nancy Anne Woolf-Pettyjohn

Nashīnasu ナシーナス

Natalie Egger

Paul Hartel

Peter Wall

Pompeyo Curbelo Martin

Prudence Au

Ramón Rivas

Raúl Vega

Riitta Hellén-Vuoti

Roanne Corteza

Roxana Werner

Shiri Achu

Simon Darling

Sonia Roseval

Sotaro Takanami

Sylvia Kölbl

Symona Colina

Tamara Michel

Toti Cuesta

Ursa Schoepper

Varda Breger

Vinci Weng

Wendy Cohen

Wendy Leyten

William Prior

Xiaorui Zhong

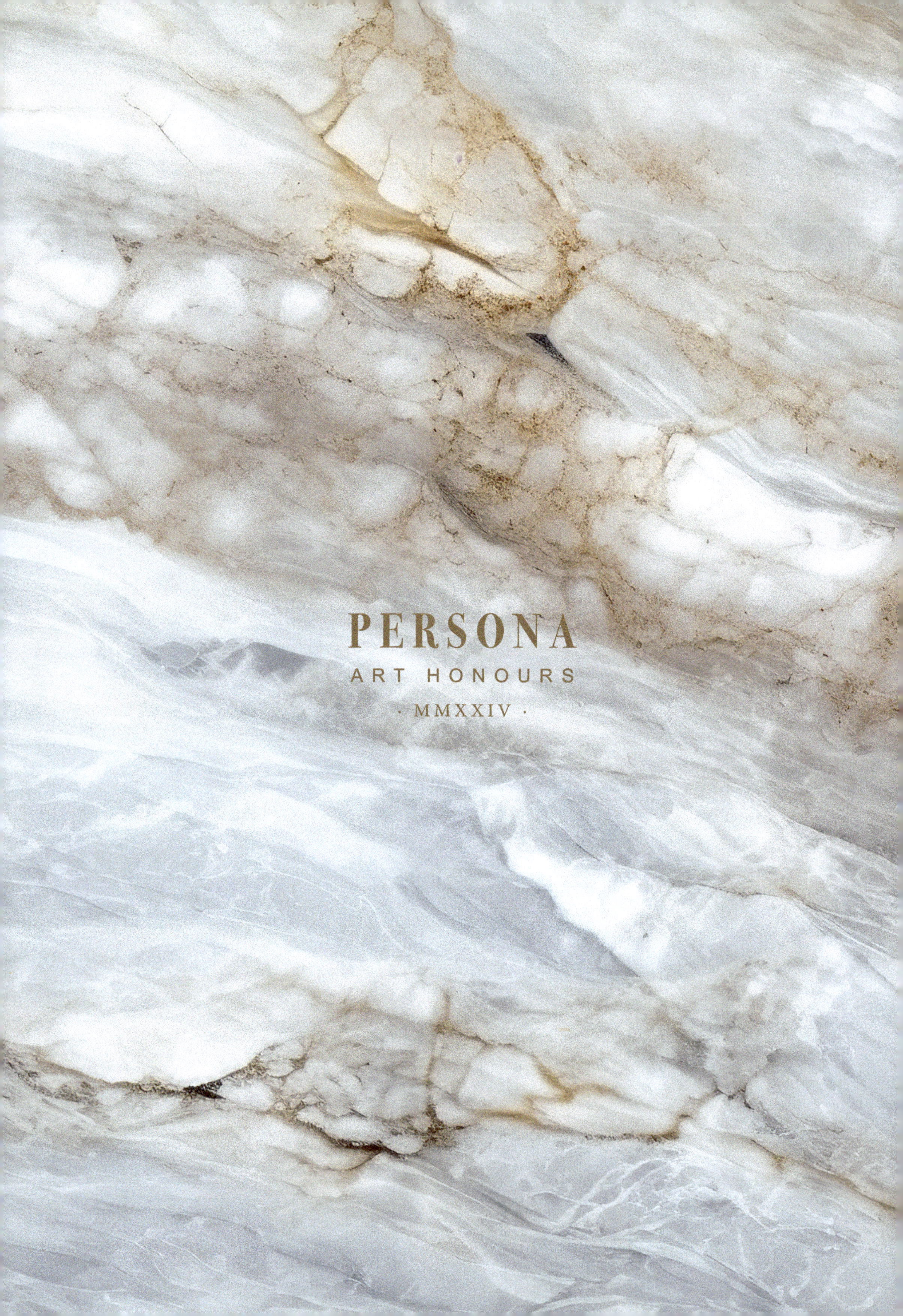

PERSONA
ART HONOURS
· MMXXIV ·

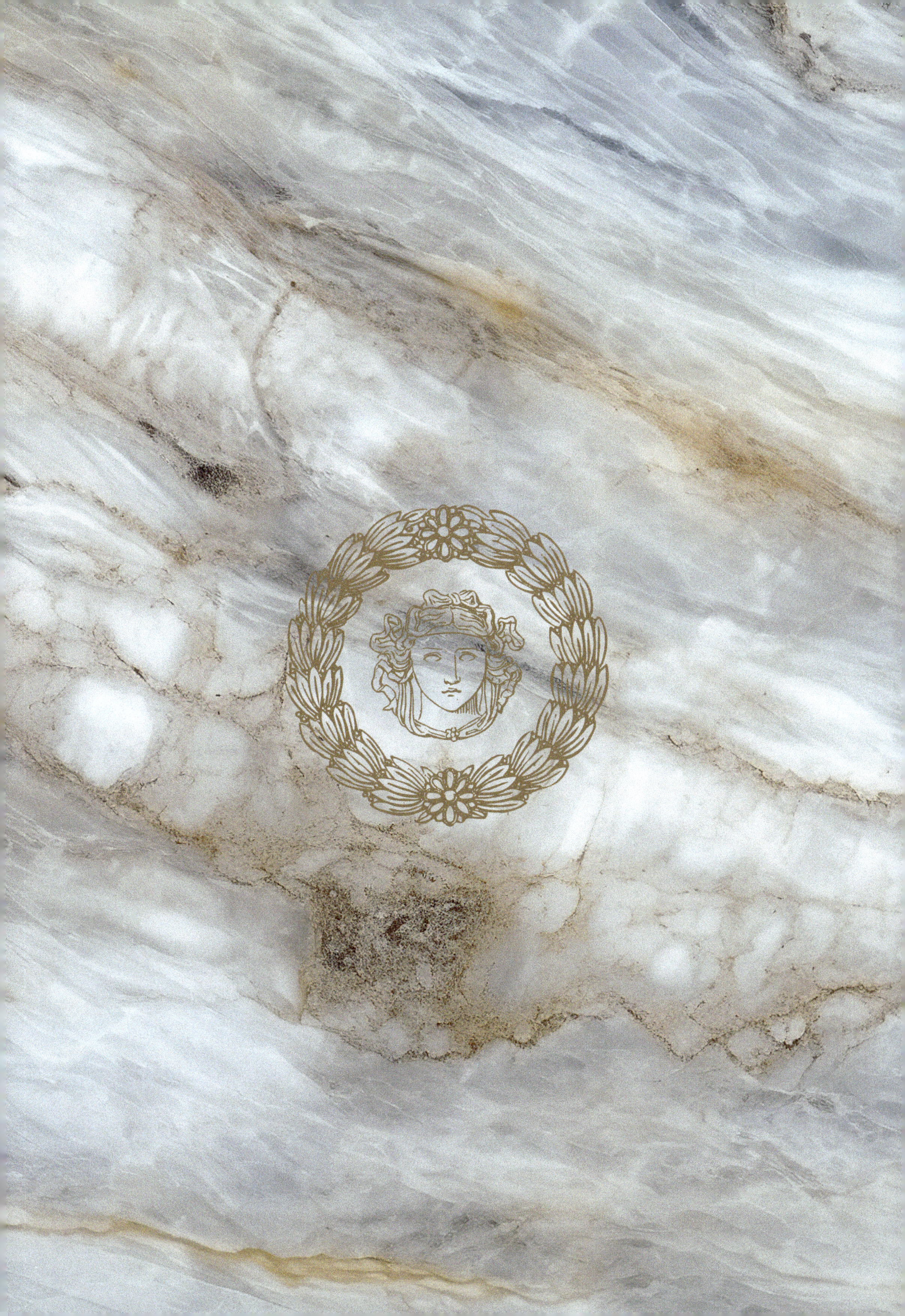

Ambro

ambrolouwe.com

A painting is not reality, but a translation of the experience of it. Which can be done in numerous ways. I enjoy playing with forms and colours. Expression in sculpture, in painting, in writing poems or stage play etcetera show the reflection of how one sees the world. For me it is showing my admiration for beauty, search for truth and the strong belief in the possibility of development. Thus, to perform and dream of nobility of the spirit. In an atmosphere, where one feels secure, new ideas and relations can flourish. So, I encourage and invite people around me to express themselves and recognize their ability do so. Sometimes in competition, but also just for the experience as such. The story of Adam and Eve for me is a glorious story of the start of enlightenment, the first steps of conscious growth. Courage against fear and uncertainty. The search for and struggle for truth and human civilisation. Again, we are in a paradise and just took a bite of the apple. We can't go back. Do we have the courage to take the next steps into a new reality and let go of many old patterns and ideas and redefine our identity?

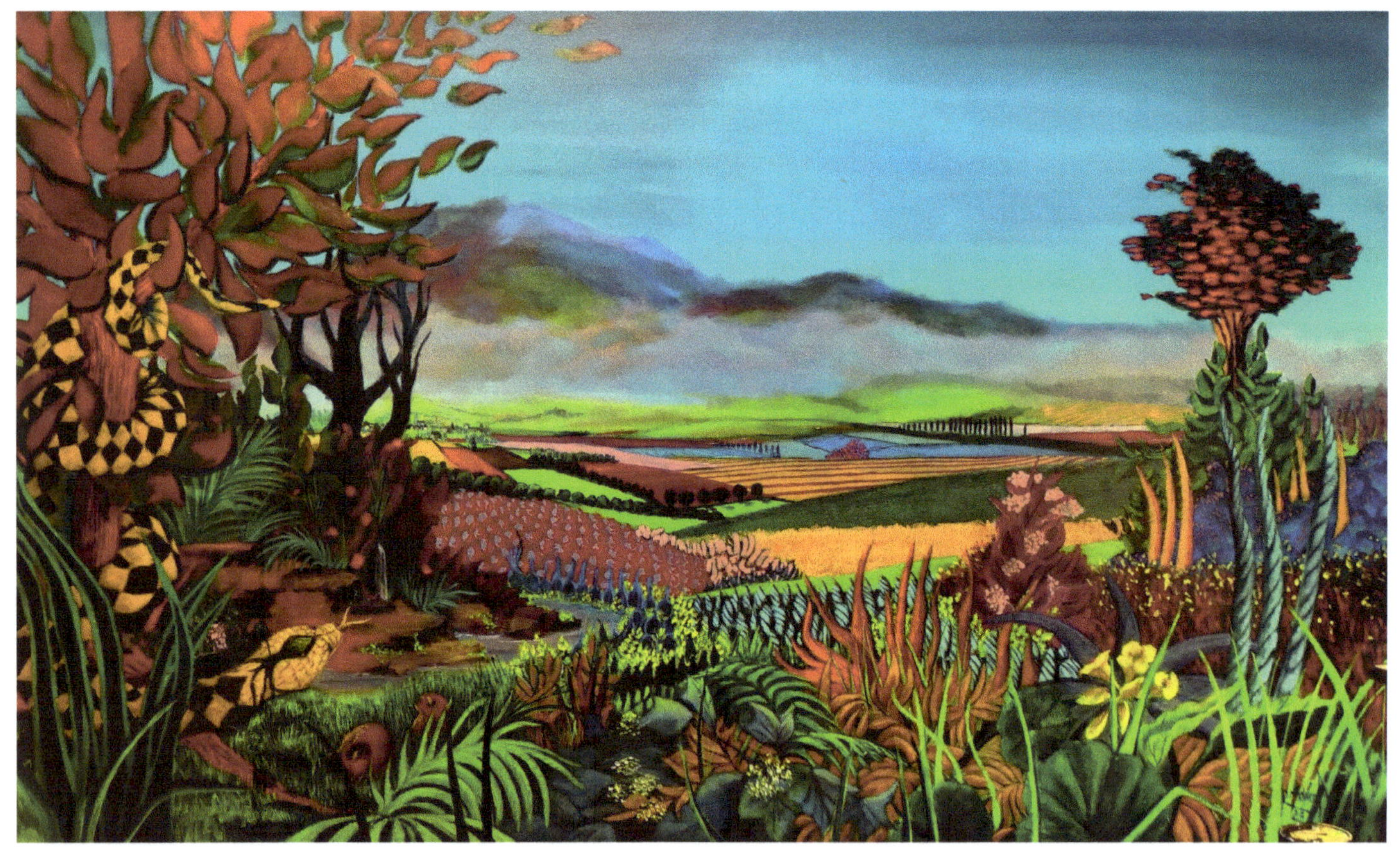

Just Left Paradise

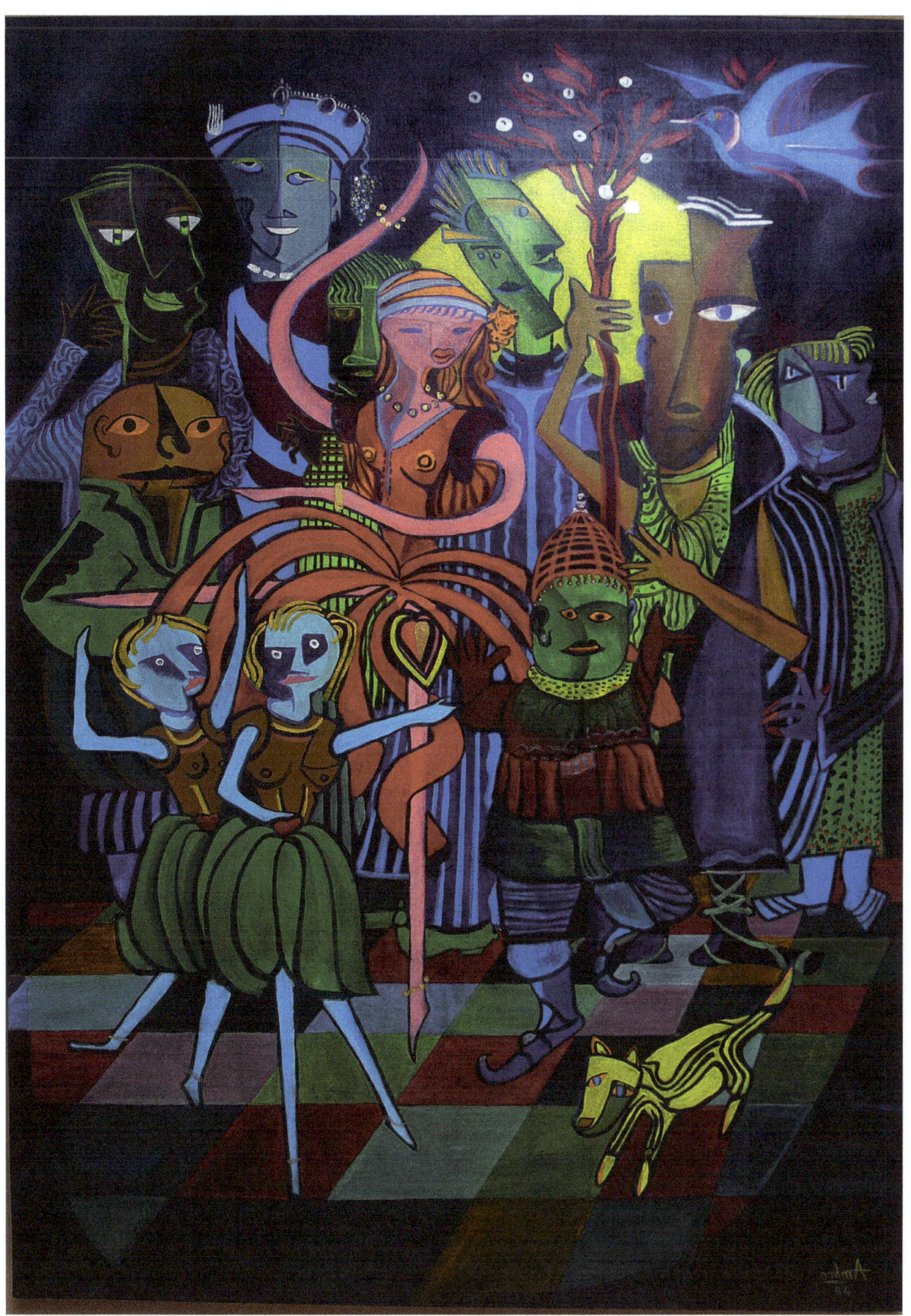

Carnaval

Andrea Gendusa

framelightstudio.art

Andrea Gendusa's artistic journey blends traditional and digital mediums, creating captivating and thought-provoking art. His work merges conventional and contemporary styles, resulting in a seamless union of form and technology. In 2019, Gendusa founded Frame Light Studio, where commercial and personal projects come together through the alchemy of form and light, creating narratives that transcend the tangible and invite viewers into contemplative realms. At the core of Gendusa's philosophy is a deep intention to communicate the essence of humanity, urging viewers toward self-discovery. His

art, through the interplay of technology, aesthetics, and a belief in beauty's transformative power serves as a conduit for profound human connection. Gendusa's pieces are not just visual spectacles but profound invitations to explore human existence. His careful use of light and form guides viewers on a contemplative journey, encouraging engagement with the inherent beauty of our collective consciousness. As a contemporary artist, he uses visual storytelling to illuminate a deeper understanding of our shared existence.

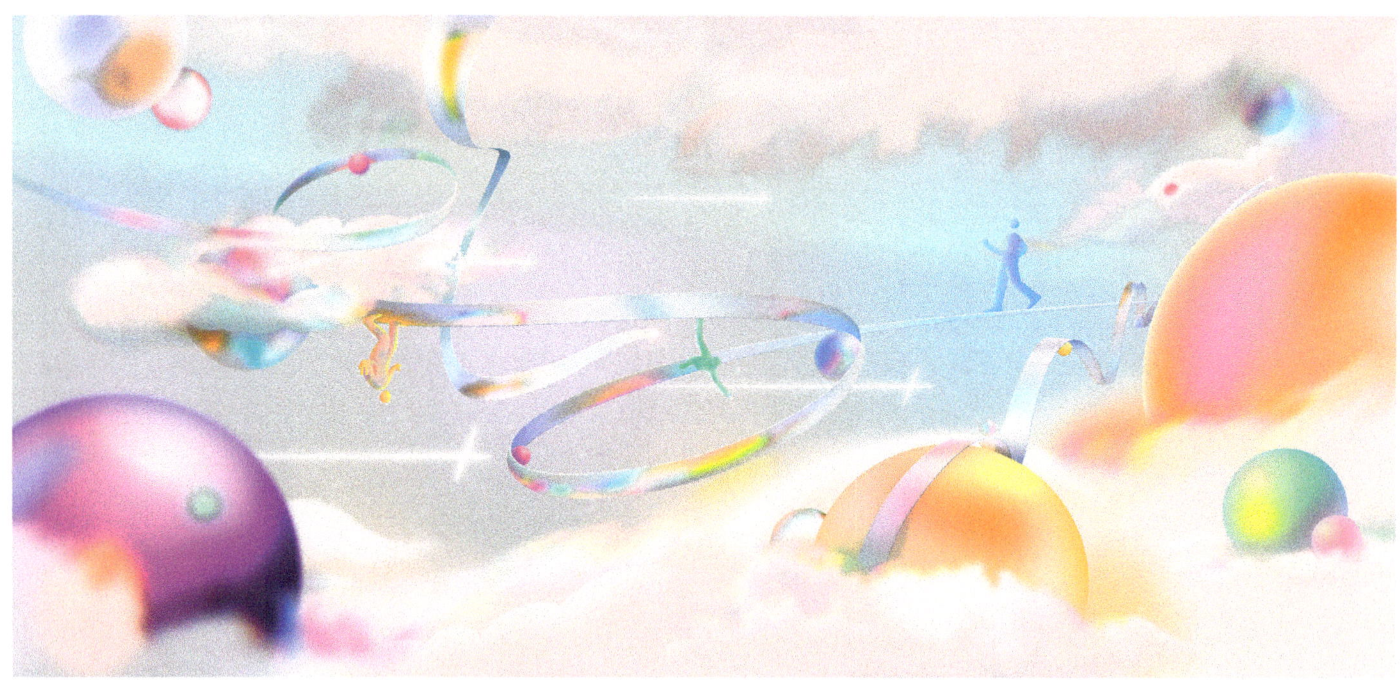

Quantum Trail

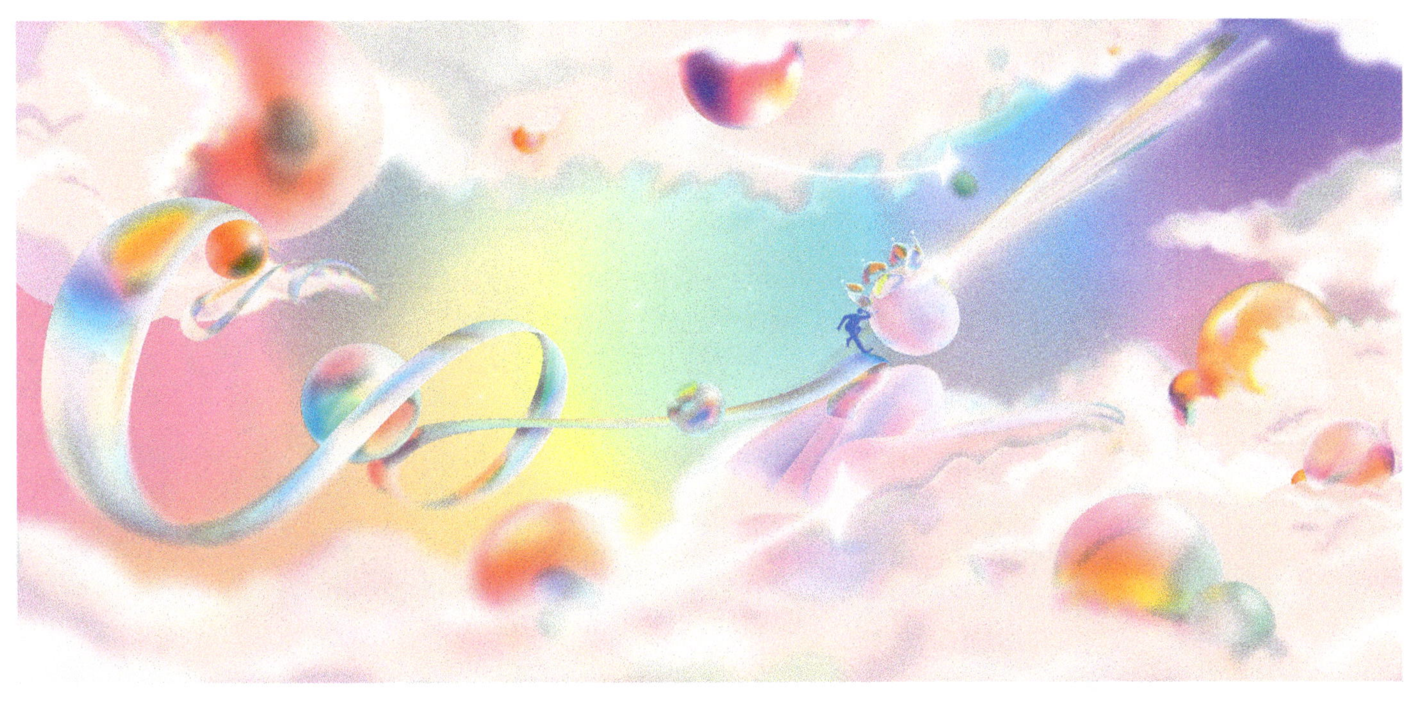

Through Essence, Into Infinity

Annemarie Ambrosoli

ambrosoliartist.com/en-gb

My artistic journey is a continual exploration of universal themes such as human connection, emotion, and movement. Through my work, I strive to distill the essence of these themes into visual narratives that resonate universally. I am fascinated by the complexities of human relationships and the depths of emotions that shape our experiences. Using a palette of vibrant colors and dynamic compositions, I aim to evoke the richness and diversity of these human experiences. Each brushstroke and color choice is deliberate, seeking to convey layers of meaning and emotion. My approach often involves abstracting forms and figures to their essential elements, allowing viewers to interpret and connect with the artwork on a personal level. By stripping away unnecessary details, I focus on capturing the essence of gestures, expressions, and interactions that define human connections. The interplay of light and shadow, texture and space, plays a crucial role in creating depth and atmosphere in my paintings. These elements enhance the narrative, inviting viewers to explore the intricate layers of meaning embedded within each piece. Ultimately, my goal as an artist is to create work that sparks introspection and dialogue, transcending cultural and linguistic boundaries. I invite viewers to immerse themselves in the emotional work I create, where colors and forms intertwine to tell stories of human experience and resilience. Through art, I aim to foster empathy, understanding, and a deeper appreciation for the beauty of our shared humanity.

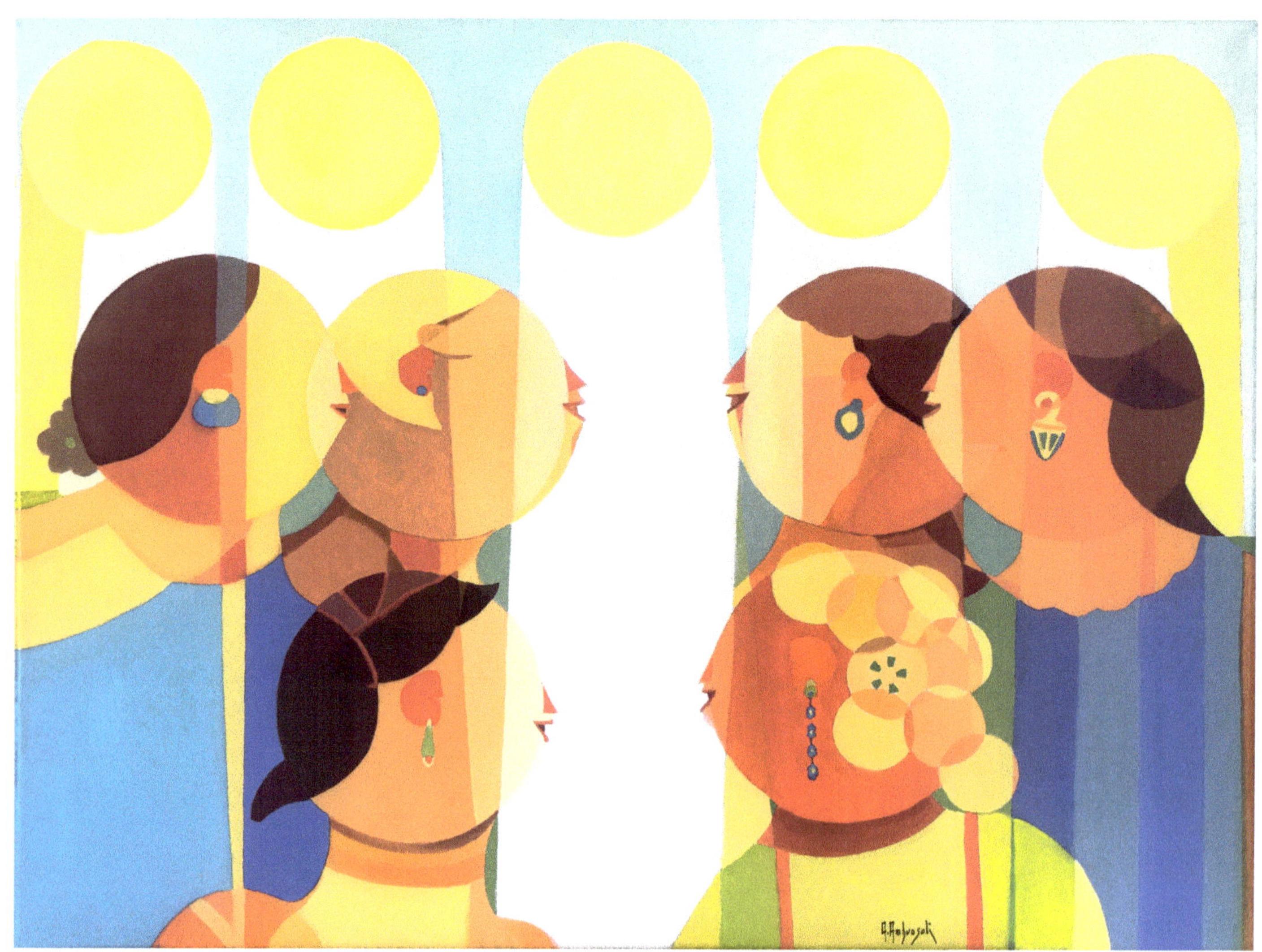

Profiles in Light, 2024, 60x80 cm, oil on canvas

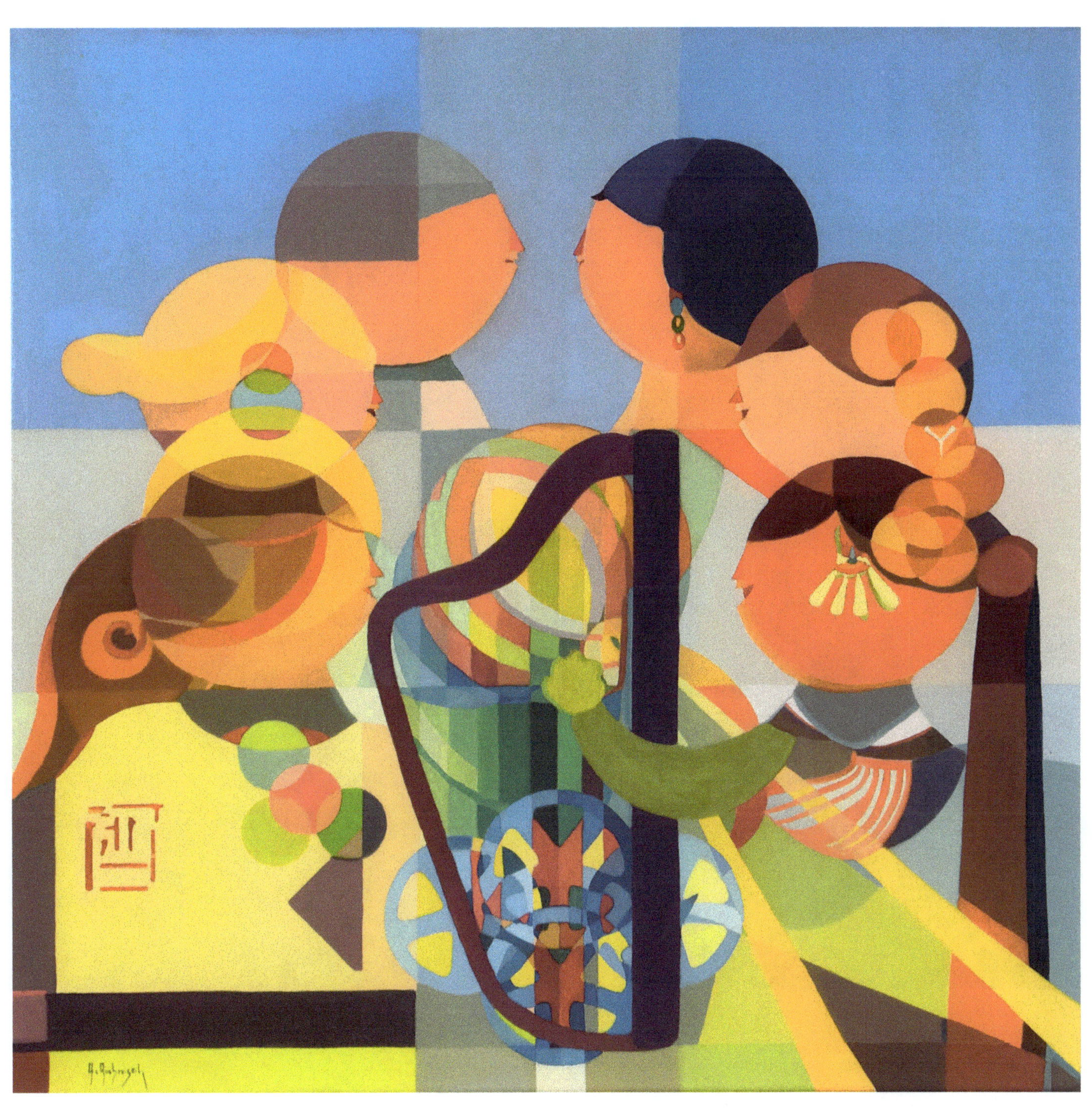

Harp Harmony, 2024, 80x80 cm, oil on canvas

Annette Tan

annettetan.com

Born in China, living in California, Annette took interest in painting in the mid 1990's. A passion for painting has led to a prolific body of colorful landscape and floral. Her inspiration comes from the works of old masters. Annette has had numerous group exhibitions in the US and in France, Italy, Hong Kong and Japan. She is in the 2021 Edition of Who's Who in America.

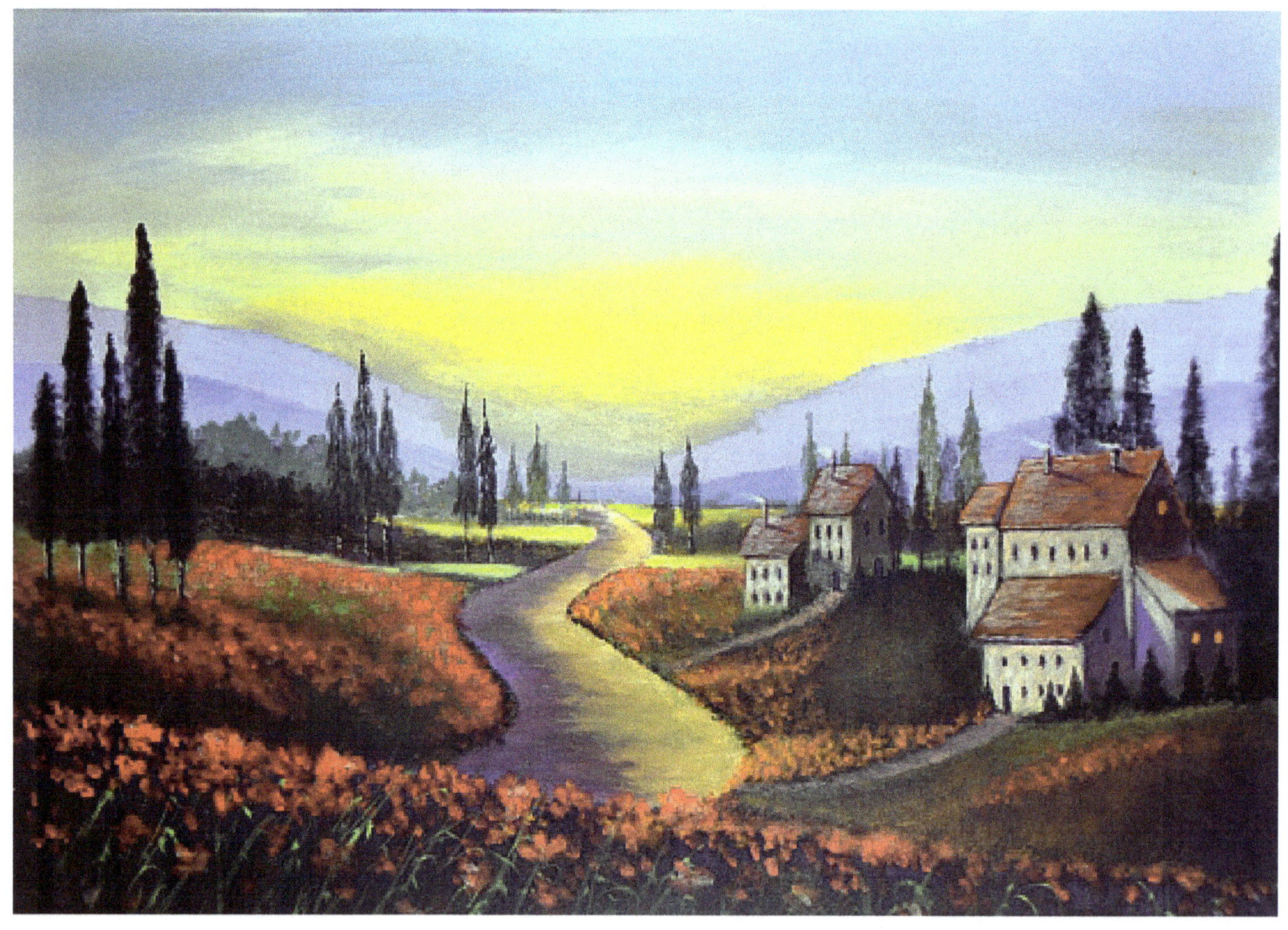

Italian Village

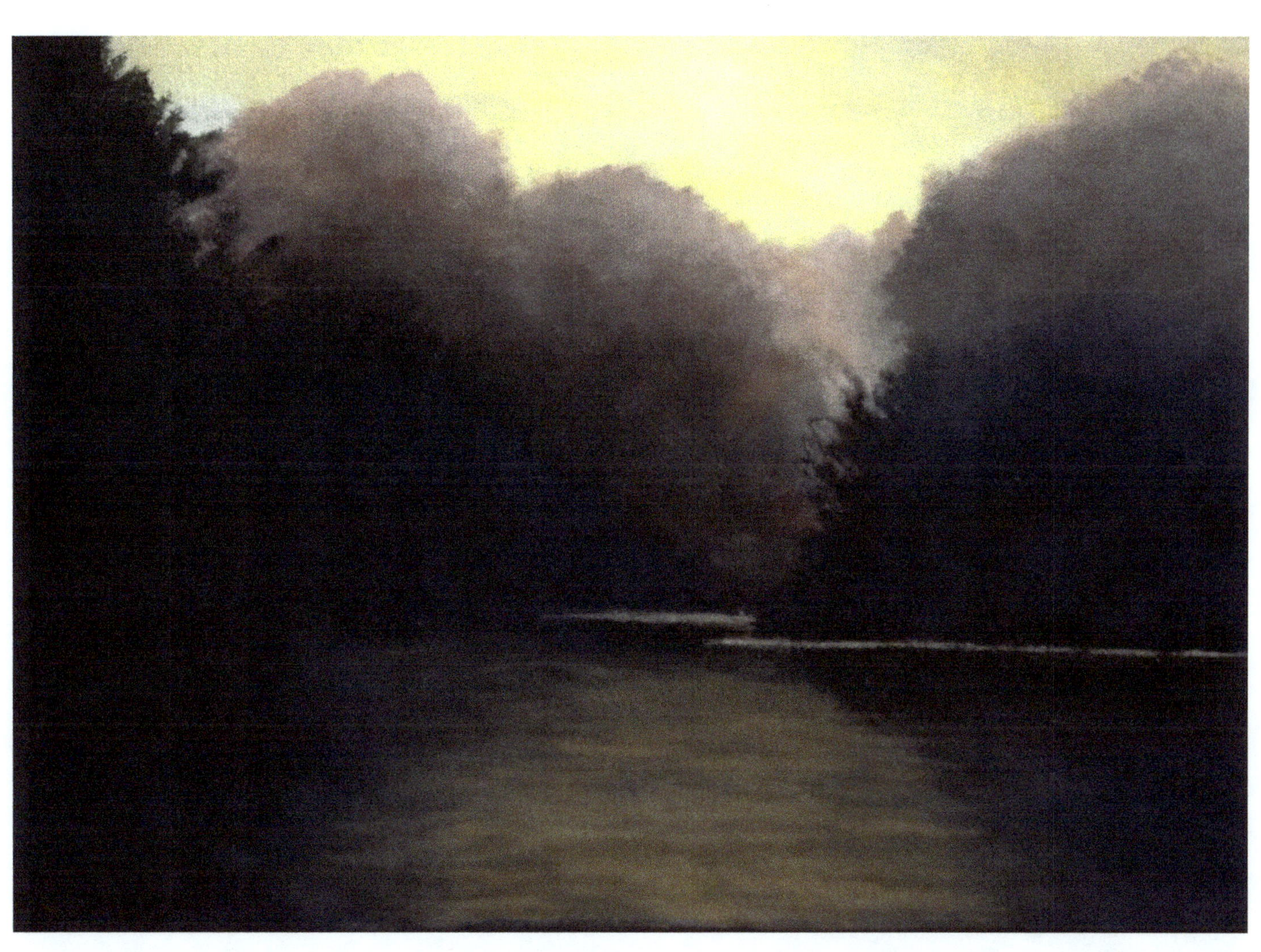

Misty River

Antoine Khanji

artogalleria.com/en/artist/antoine-khanji

Antoine's art is a dynamic exploration of form and color, designed to ignite a sense of wonder in those who experience it. Using a mixture of acrylics and a palette knife, he crafts striking abstract pieces that showcase the beauty of organic shapes and vibrant hues. Drawing inspiration from the natural world, Antoine layers his paintings with intricate mark making and captivating textures, resulting in a visual feast for the eyes. Each artwork is a reflection of his deep love for the artistic process and a heartfelt invitation for viewers to pause and appreciate the magic of existence. In a world that often feels chaotic, Antoine's art provides a moment of serenity and connection with the boundless beauty that surrounds us.

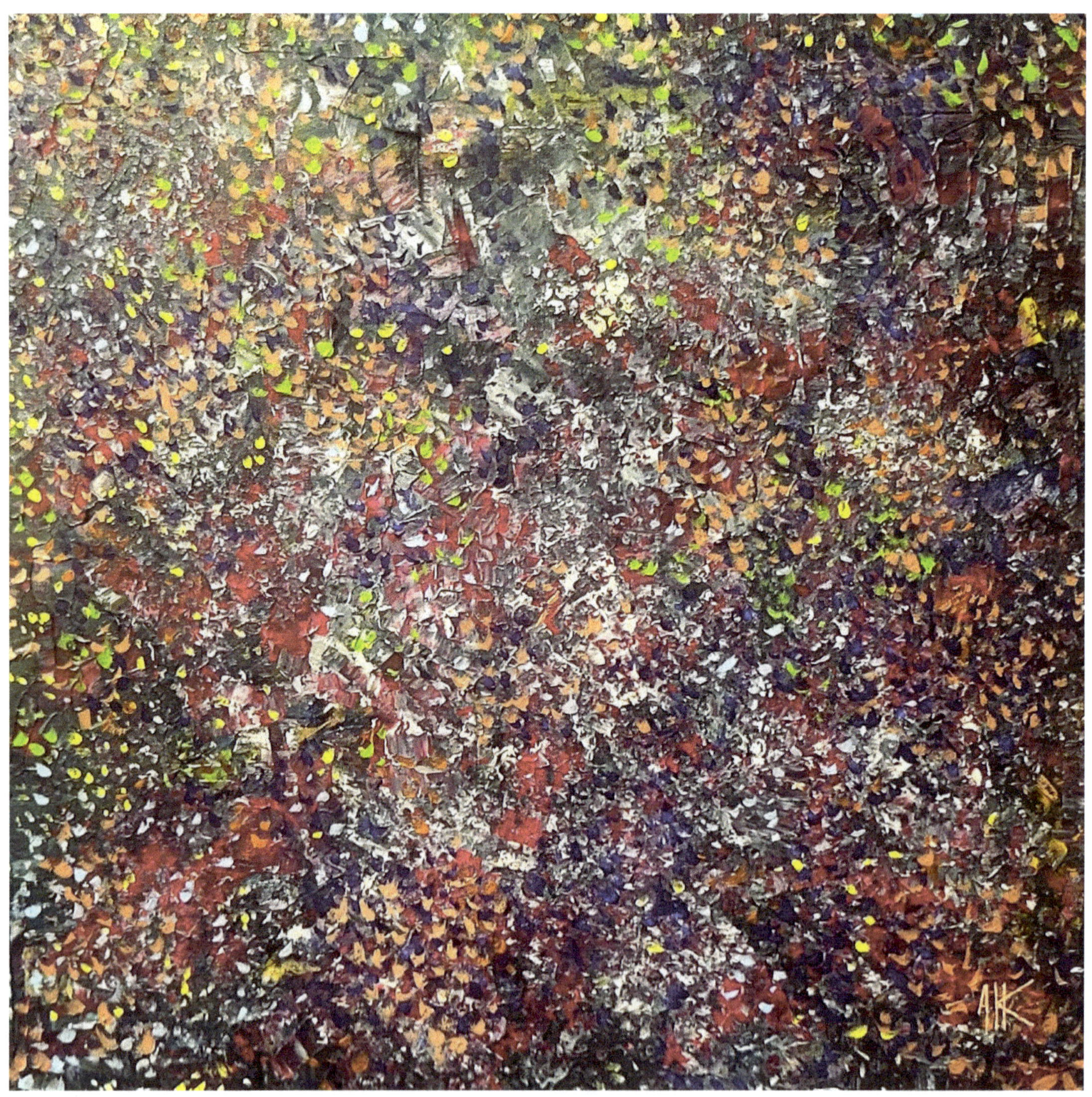

Dare to Dream

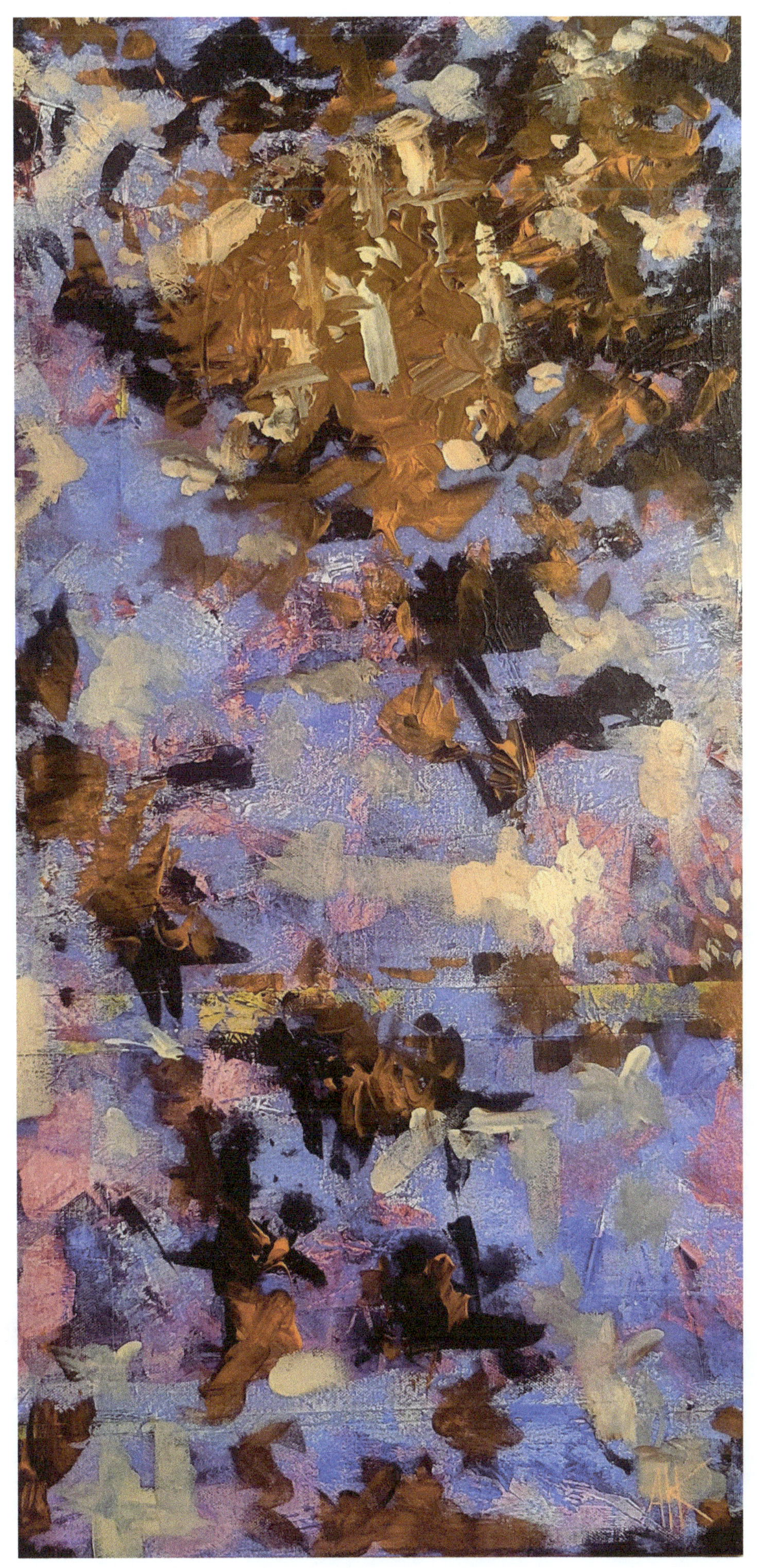

Chromatic Dance of the Subconscious

Aomi Kikuchi

aomikikuchi.com

Buddha preached that "By understanding and accepting the impermanence and insubstantiality of this world, we can control our cravings and alleviate suffering." I am inspired by his philosophy and the Japanese aesthetics of Wabi-Sabi (imperfection) and mono no a-wa-re (compassionate heart). Through my artwork, I convey that compassion is a meaningful solution to alleviating cravings. I focus on personal desires and suffering, and on people and things that are forced to suffer in order to satisfy the greed of others. Fear and disgust are also causes of suffering. I work to help people let go of negative emotions by finding new perspectives and turning negative emotions into positive ones. I am a multidisciplinary artist primarily focused on "Art Povera", an anti-hierarchical approach. I incorporate everyday goods and humble materials into 2D/3D works such as sculptures, clothing, and objects. By utilizing materials that were previously discarded or thought to have no value, and infusing them with new perspectives and meaning, we can advance the idea that anything in daily life can be used as material for art. This idea leads to creating works with less environmental impact. While studying academic art, I also followed my own curiosity and learned craft techniques. They include dressmaking, kimono dyeing, dyeing in general, ceramics, ceramic painting, Japanese embroidery, knitting, weaving, and Urushi-lacquer. In addition to continuously examining the difference between art and craft and the potential of craft as an artistic expression, I would like to pursue innovative art without being bound by preconceived notions.

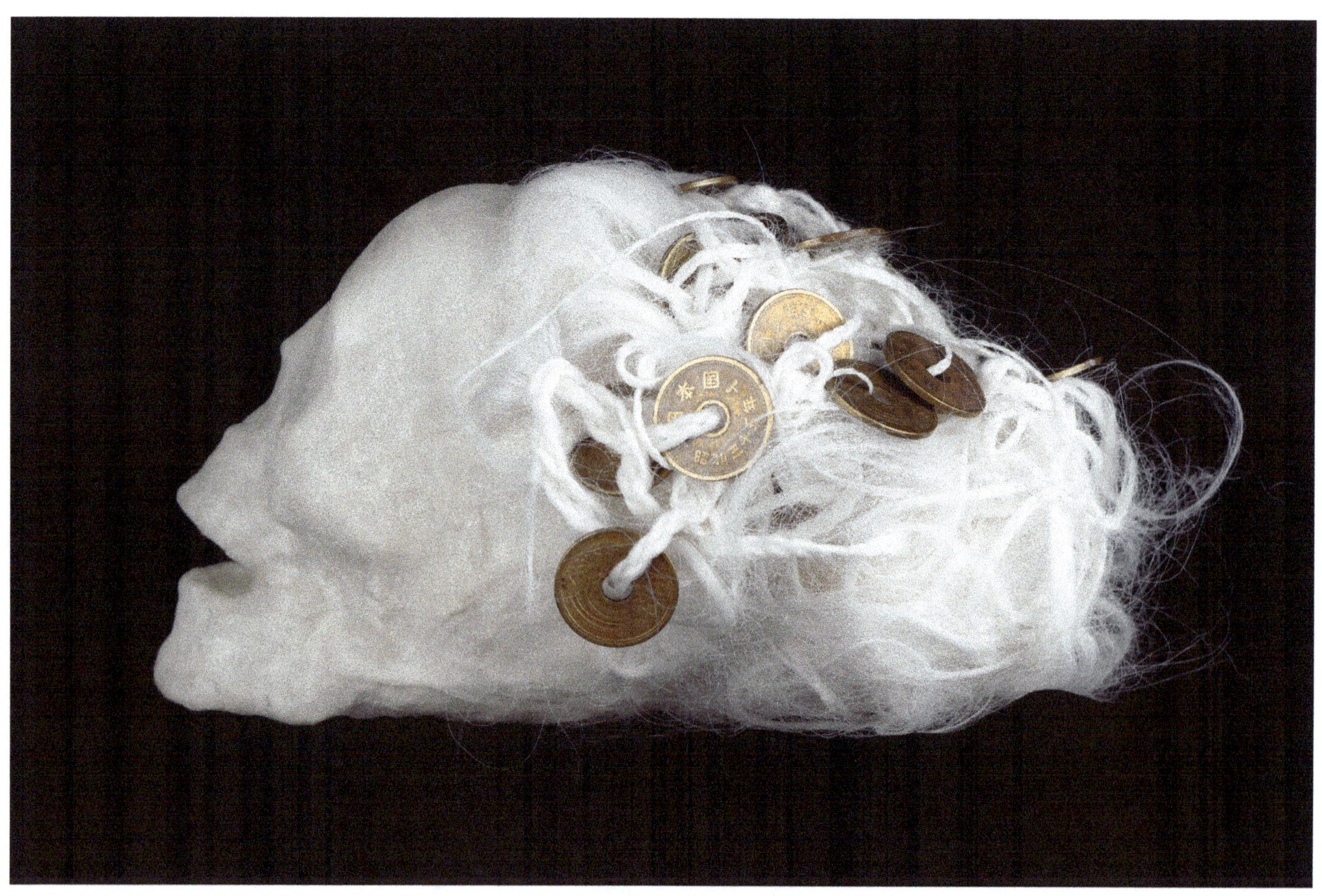

Woman 2023

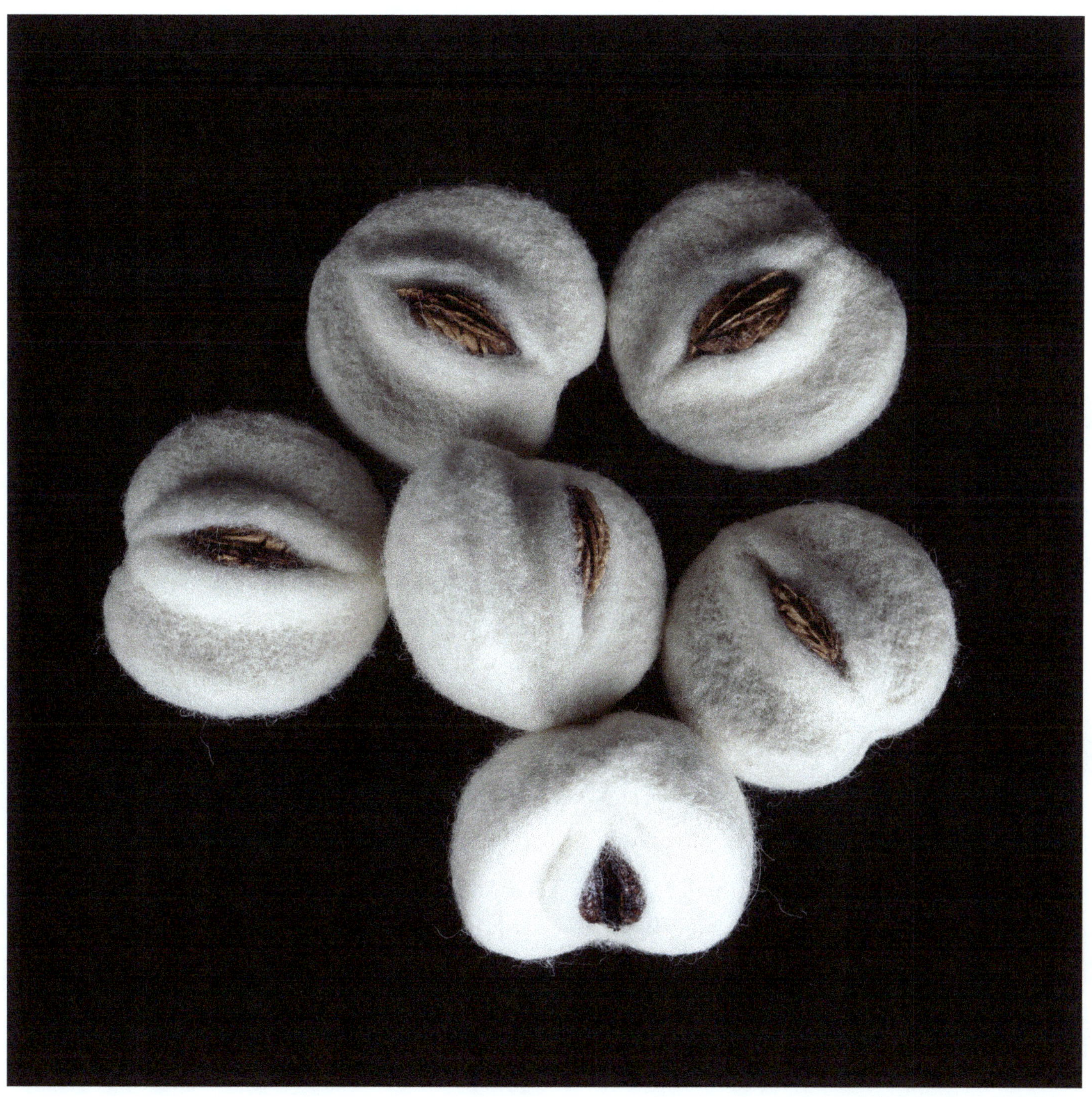

Six Peaches

Britta Ortiz

britta-ortiz.dk

Man is only one species among many thousands here on earth. We dominate many regions, but we can only survive if we learn to respect all other species, as we are all dependent on each other. Man is his own worst enemy, as we believe that we are superior to all other species. We are in some areas, but far from all. The challenge is that we view all other species from our own perspective and are not aware that other species are adapted exactly to the life they live. That is why we are also often surprised when we find out what knowledge other species have, and again we compare them with our own knowledge, as when we e.g. learns that a crow has the intelligence of a 2-3 year old child. By respecting and recognizing that other beings are just as important as us, we can live in harmony with other beings and nature and experience how magnificent the earth is. Man is only a small piece, and we are reminded of that when nature rages. Man is capable of destroying himself, but the earth will endure. By taking care of the earth and making room for other beings, man will also benefit himself.

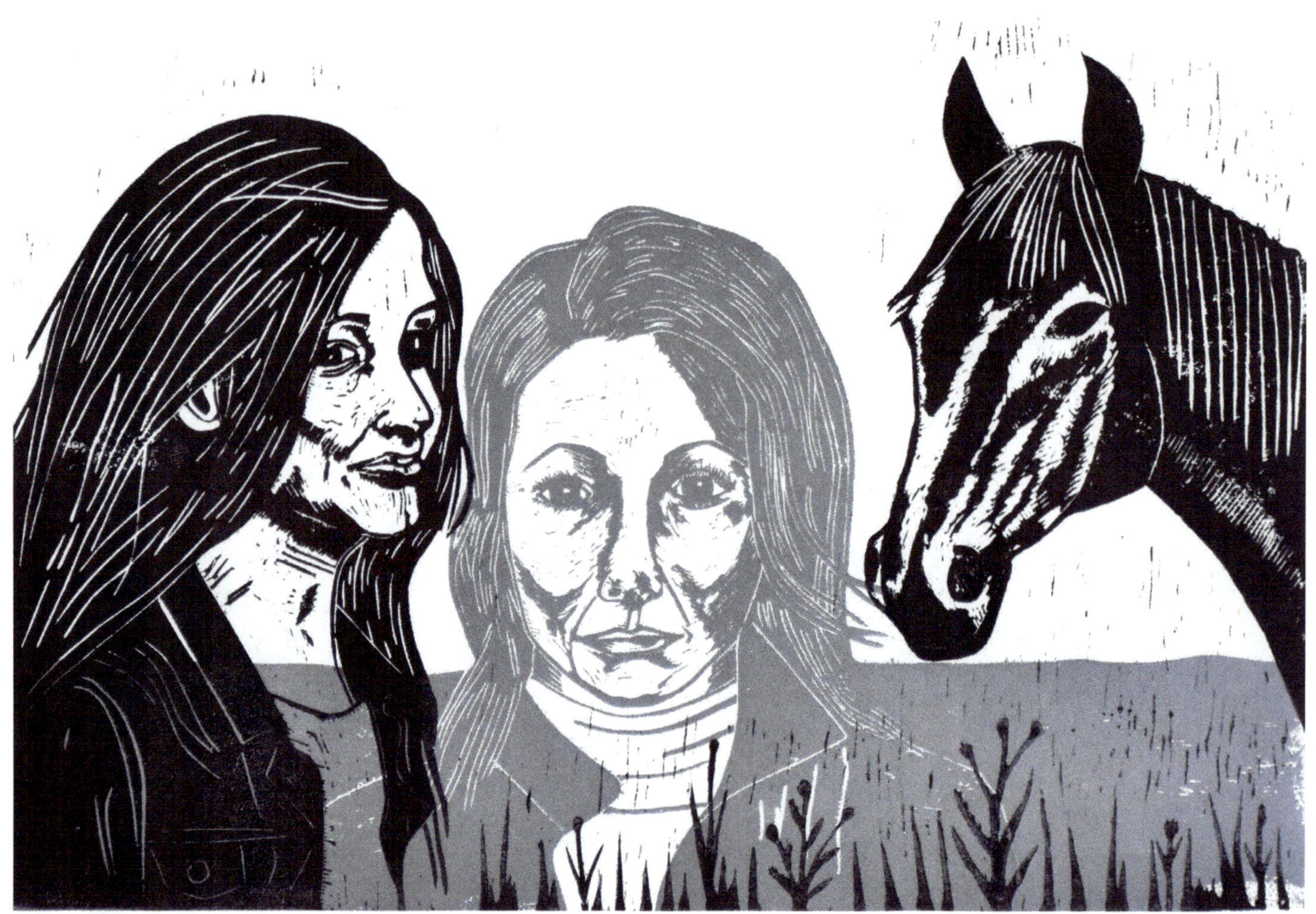

The horse girls

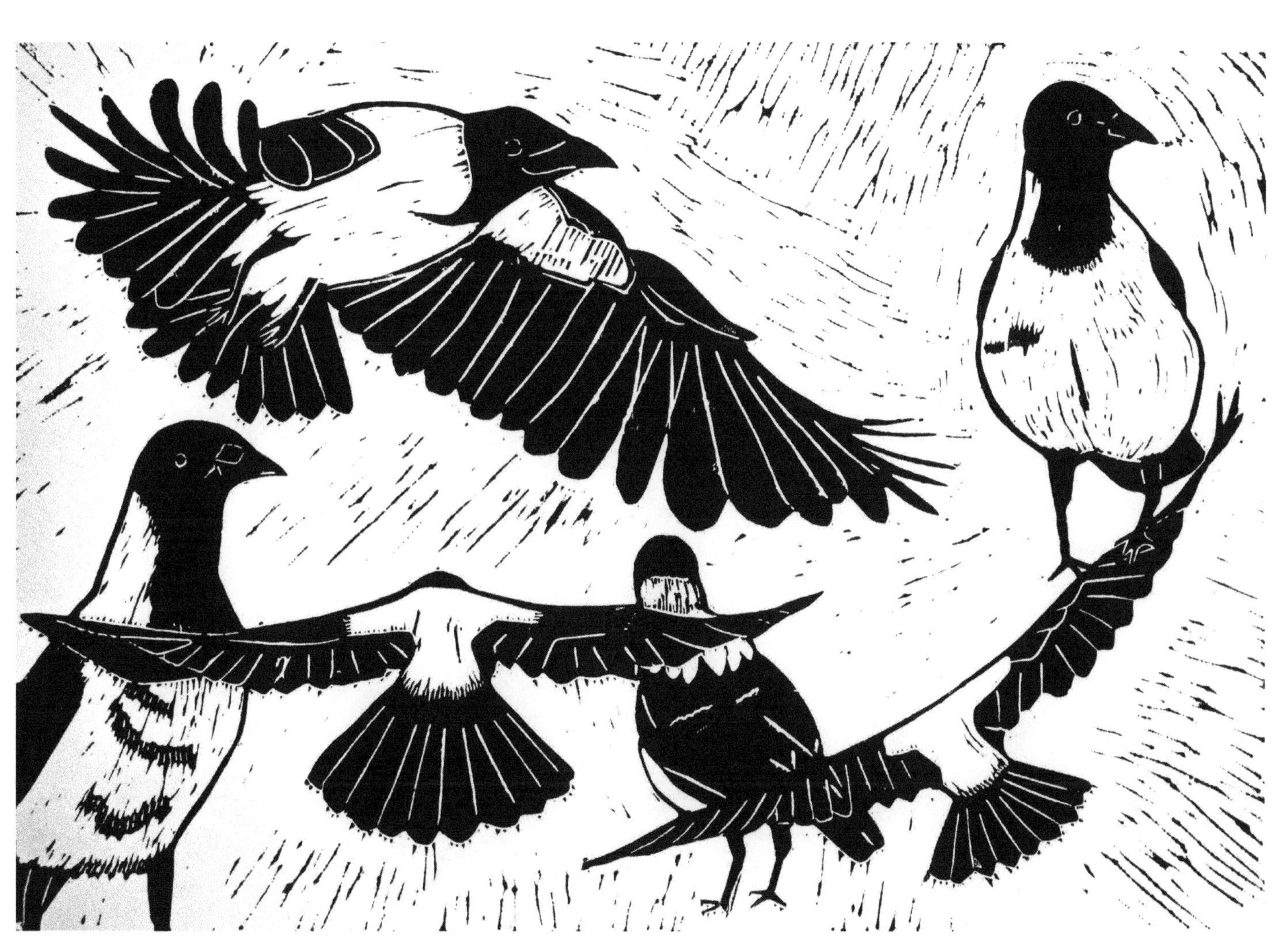

Flying intelligence

Bruce Cowell

brccow.wixsite.com/fine-art-photography

In Fine-Art Photography the subject of a photograph becomes metaphorical. Even though it's a real subject existing in the real world it speaks of something much deeper, more important and touches upon human emotions in ways that only the visual arts can do. Photographs can cross into a whole other realm and become iconic, subjective and eternal. They speak of eternal truths that are as recognisable today as they were a thousand years ago. To name those truths would be to limit them but every human understands instinctively what they are. Language, culture, lifestyle, distance, do not limit that understanding. Photography speaks at a human level and all humans understand it. What matters is that it speaks to us at a deeply human level about those things that are most important to us and touches our emotions. Love and connection are enduring themes that run through my work. This is because I see them as the primary motivators in our lives. They are our constant everyday link with eternity. My view is that fine-art photography exists to capture the eternal in the everyday. Those moments that transcend time and place and link us to the universe. I create part of the image and the viewer completes it by applying their own unique viewpoint that is informed by their own life experience. My images should not be viewed as finished works but as artworks we can complete together.

In that is the heart and soul of of photography.

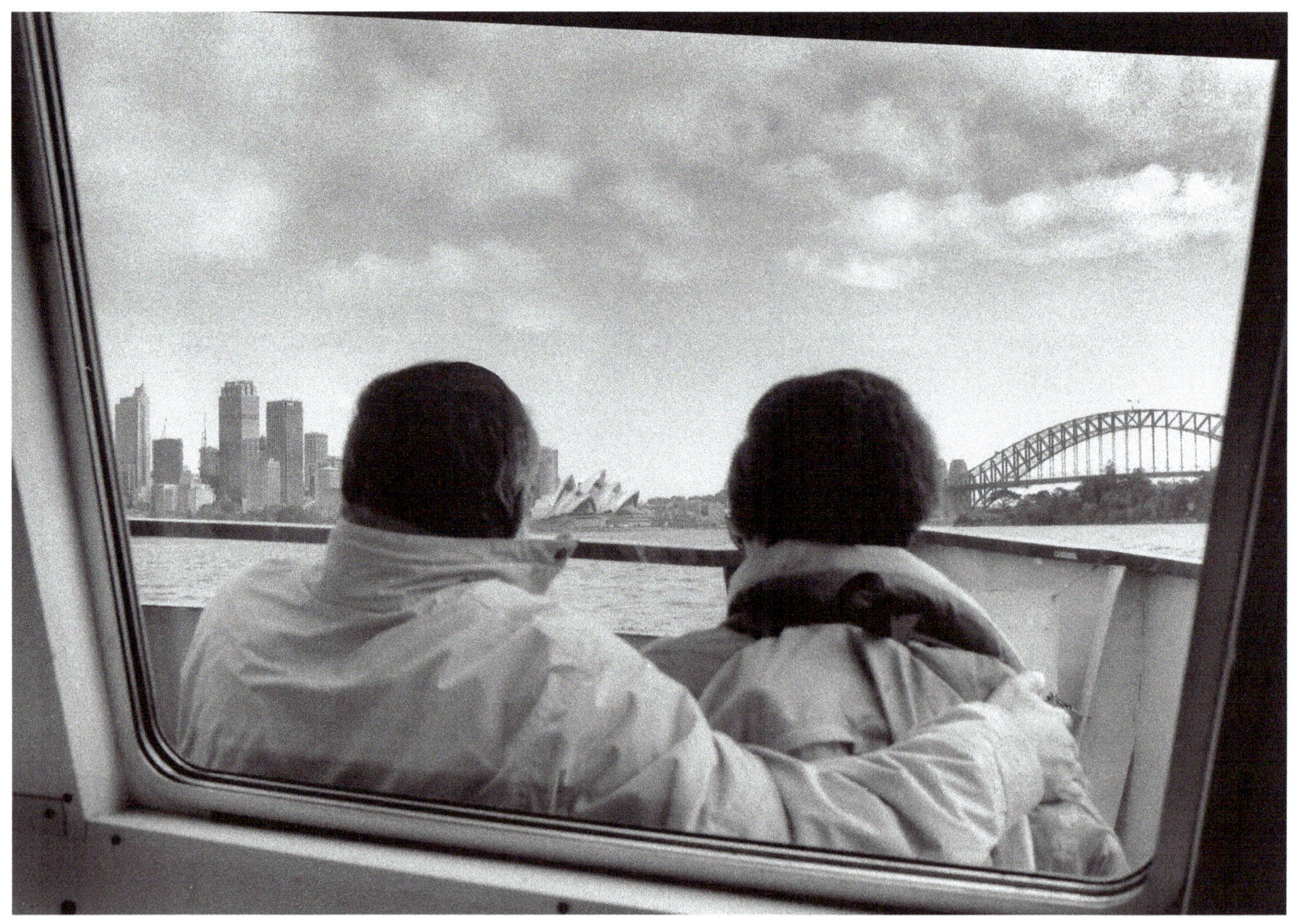

Sydney Ferry

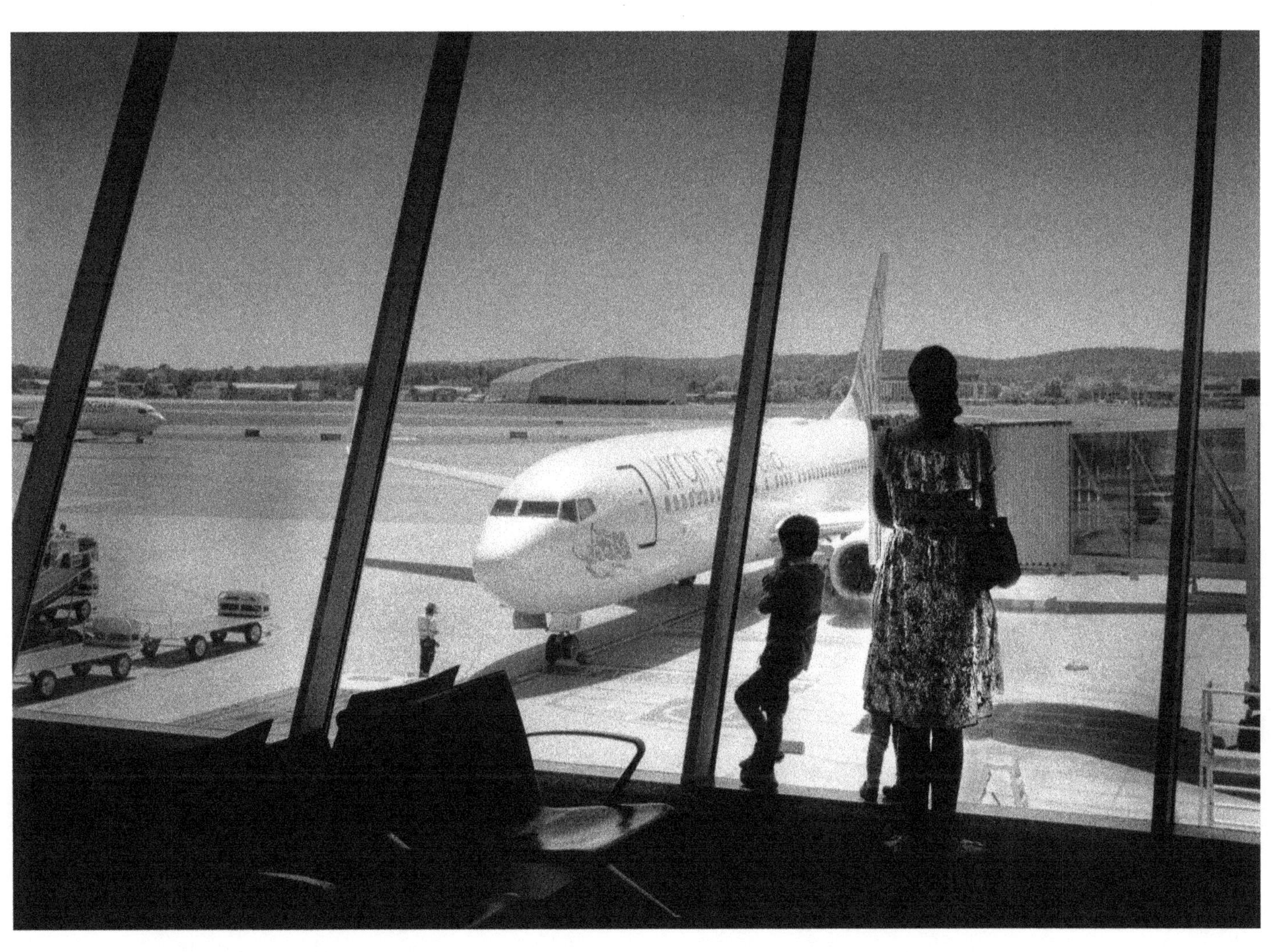

Canberra Airport

Celine Chan

celinechanwy.wixsite.com/celinechanart

Celine Chen is a novel artist in Hong Kong. She studied in Canada and further her studies in design at the Chinese University of Hong Kong. Inspired by the Russian paper quilling master Yulia Brodskaya, Celine never stopped practising and devoted herself ardently to the creation of paper quilling art. Her artworks have a strong personality, with gorgeous integration of Oriental culture. She is one of the few Asian artists engaged in the creation of paper quilling. Her works are glamorous and trendy, always demonstrating her passion for life and beauty. Her works are collected by many local and international celebrities.

The reason Celine likes doing paper quilling artwork is because she feels calm and at peace when she focuses on pasting those paper pieces to the composition carefully. Paper quilling definitely needs a lot of patience and perseverance to complete. It is a very difficult process and it is such an unforgiving art form. But on the other hand, it gives people enormous satisfaction and a sense of fulfilment after finishing making the whole artwork.

She wants to express the psychological side of human beings and the attitude of how people face problems through her artworks, giving them the power to be more resilient to difficulties. Also, she believes that the power of love can break through the gap of light leakage in the darkness, therefore, she wants her viewers to feel that positive spirit towards life.

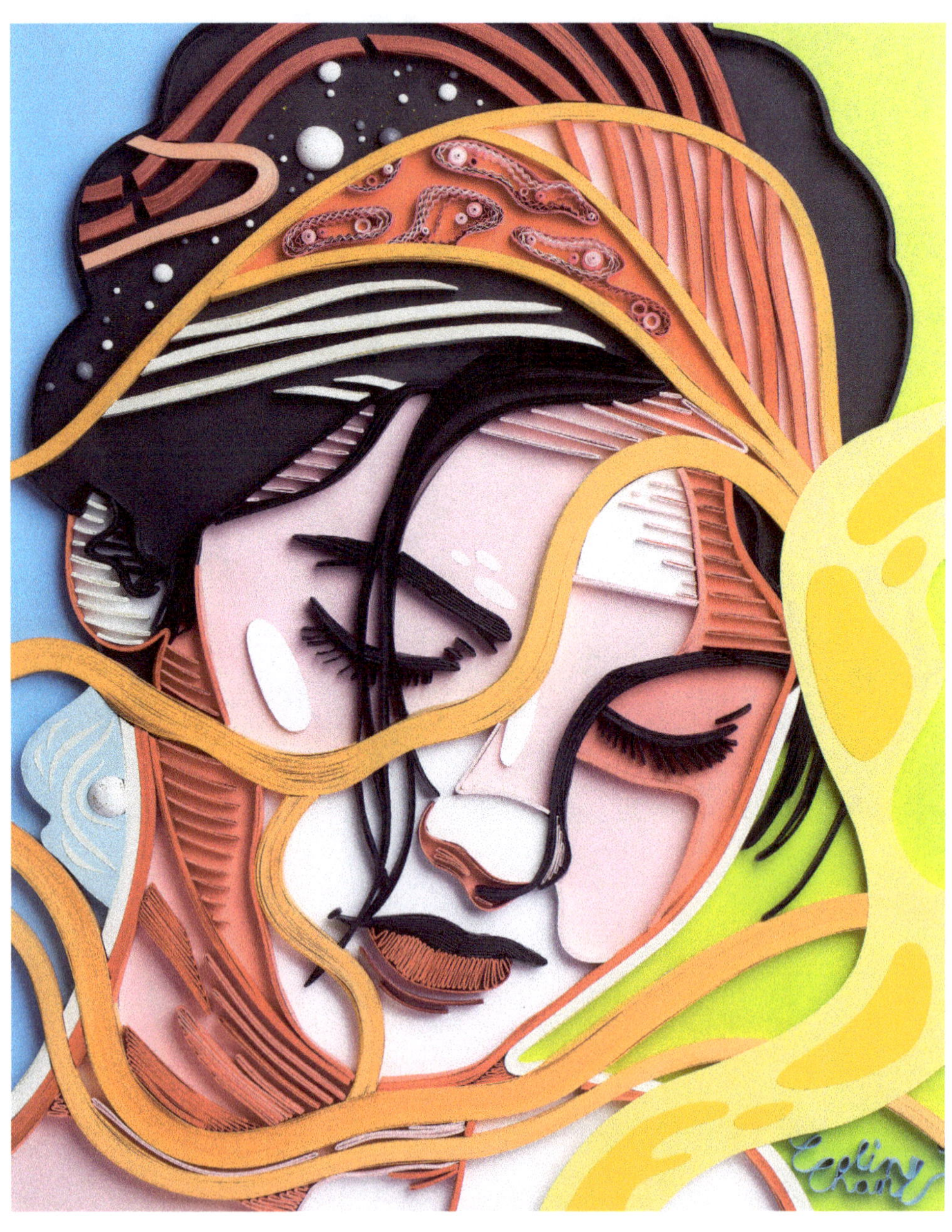

Aphrodite

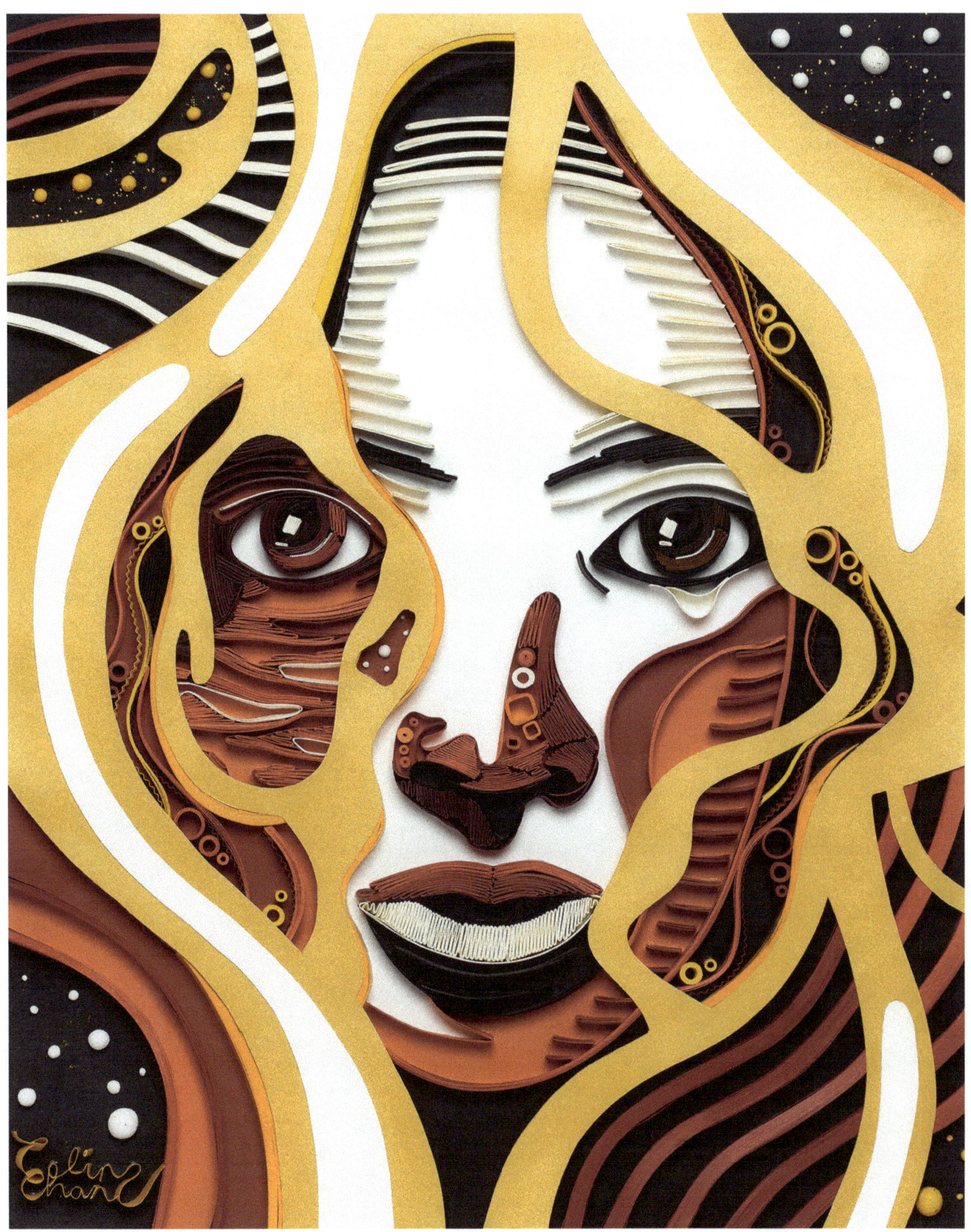

Persephone

Daniel Grannan

dangrannan.com

Daniel Grannan was born in Flagstaff Arizona in 1956 and lives in Page Springs Arizona. He studied art at the College of San Mateo in California. He is a graduate of the Famous Artist school. Grannan has had numerous expeditions in the U.S.A. and a group participation in the United Arab Emirates. His work is in many private and corporate collections. Daniel is also an awarded artist. " My paintings are are inspired by nature/our environment.

Creating paintings with strong compositions, colors and techniques that are artistically important and inspirational is my goal". "Good or great art to me has to have a strong division of space that holds the viewers interest with colors and textures that complement the composition. Using only colors, texture and the composition with no subject matter is the greatest challenge to me".

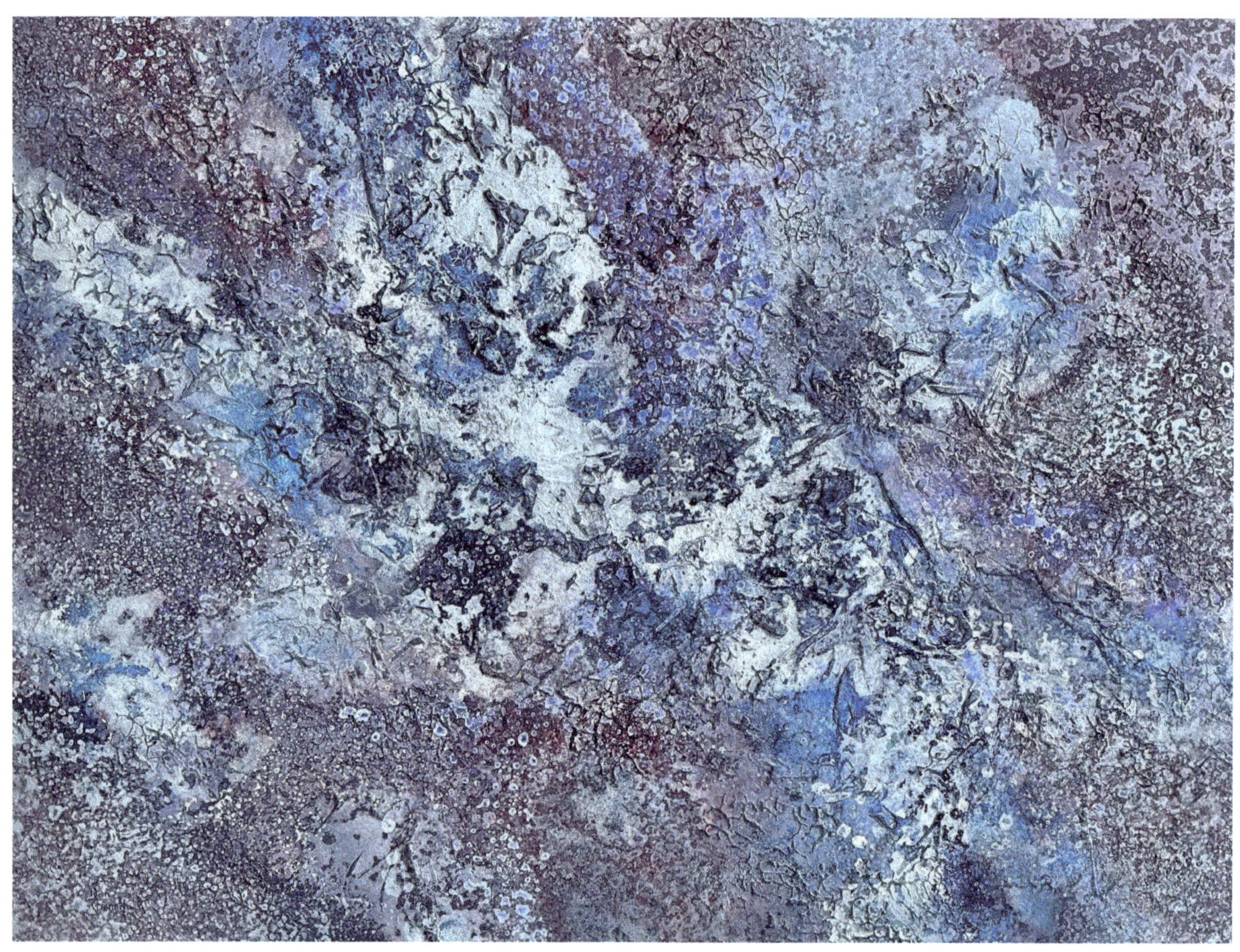

Manifestation LG 5

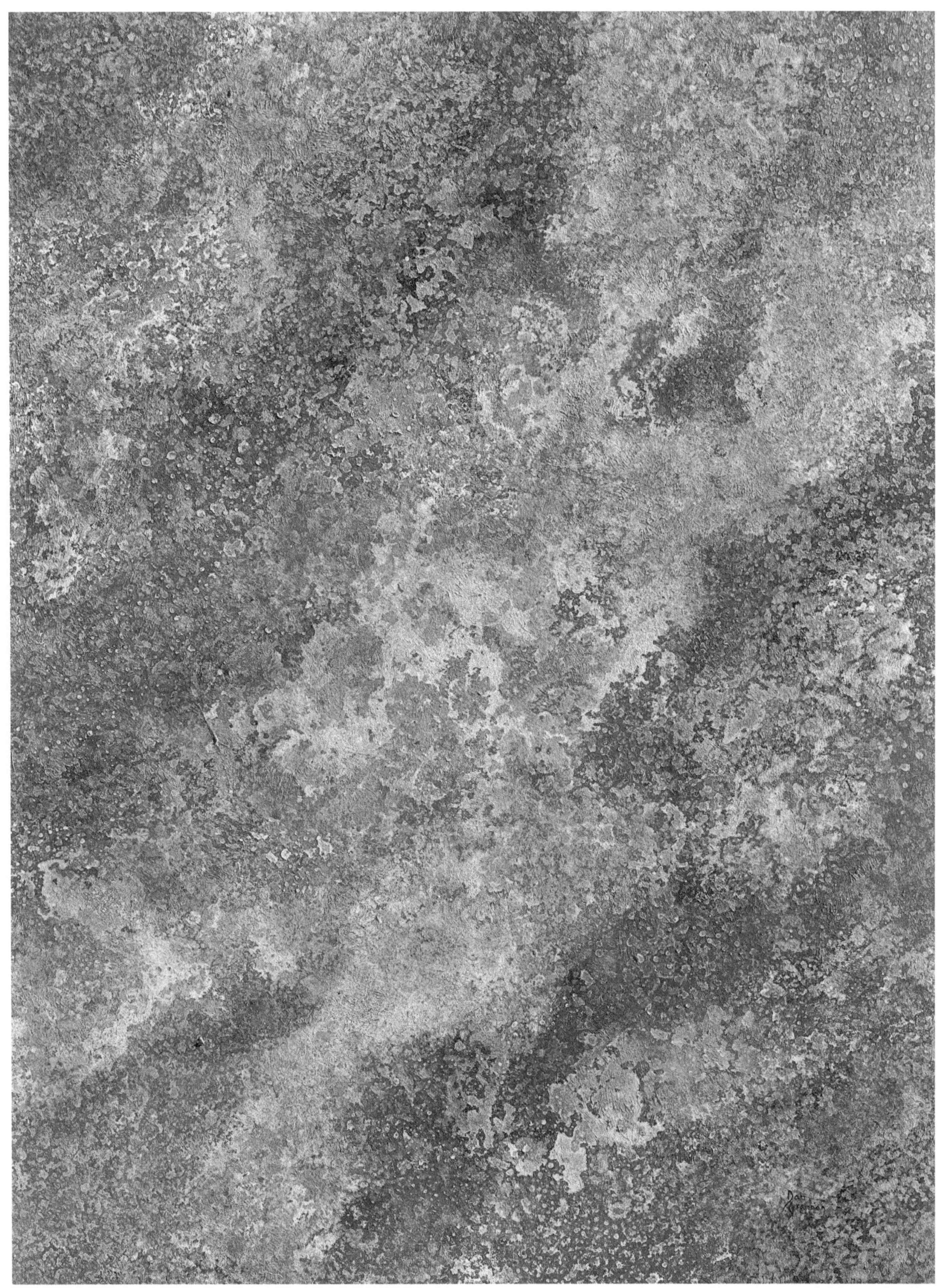

Manifestation LG 6

Daniel McKinley

mybio.art/daniel-mckinley

What inspires me most is my love of all things art. The creative process drives me. Sitting in front of an empty canvas, knowing that the possibilities are endless. I cannot call myself a traditional artist who spends a lot of time making sketches before starting a painting. I sketch directly on the canvas. I call it having a conversation with the canvas. It may start with a chair, or a flower, or a doorway, and then it all comes down to what if. There is a lot of push and pull. Addition and subtraction, until the canvas is filled and I am ready to paint. I then have a general idea of where the painting is going from there, as if the painting is in control of me and I allow it to speak to me. When I paint I use mostly transparent paints and I paint in layers. I have to allow the paint to dry, which is why I usually paint two to three paintings a time. I find that I have to end the painting if I find myself working and reworking the same area for too long.The painting then tells me that it is done, and I have to let it go. Upon looking at it months later there are many times that I can honestly not remember the process at all. This is what inspires me to continue.

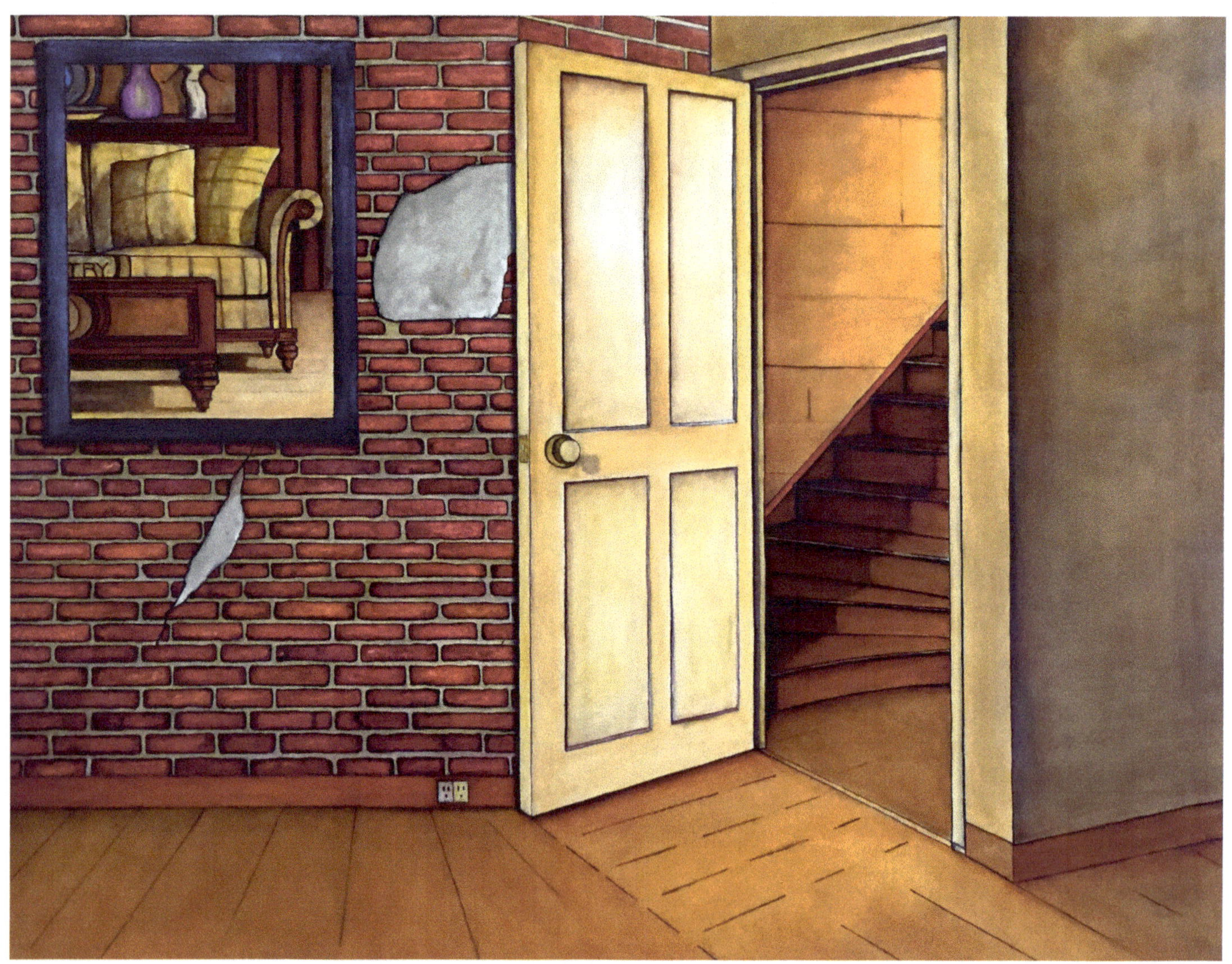

An Invitation to Ascend

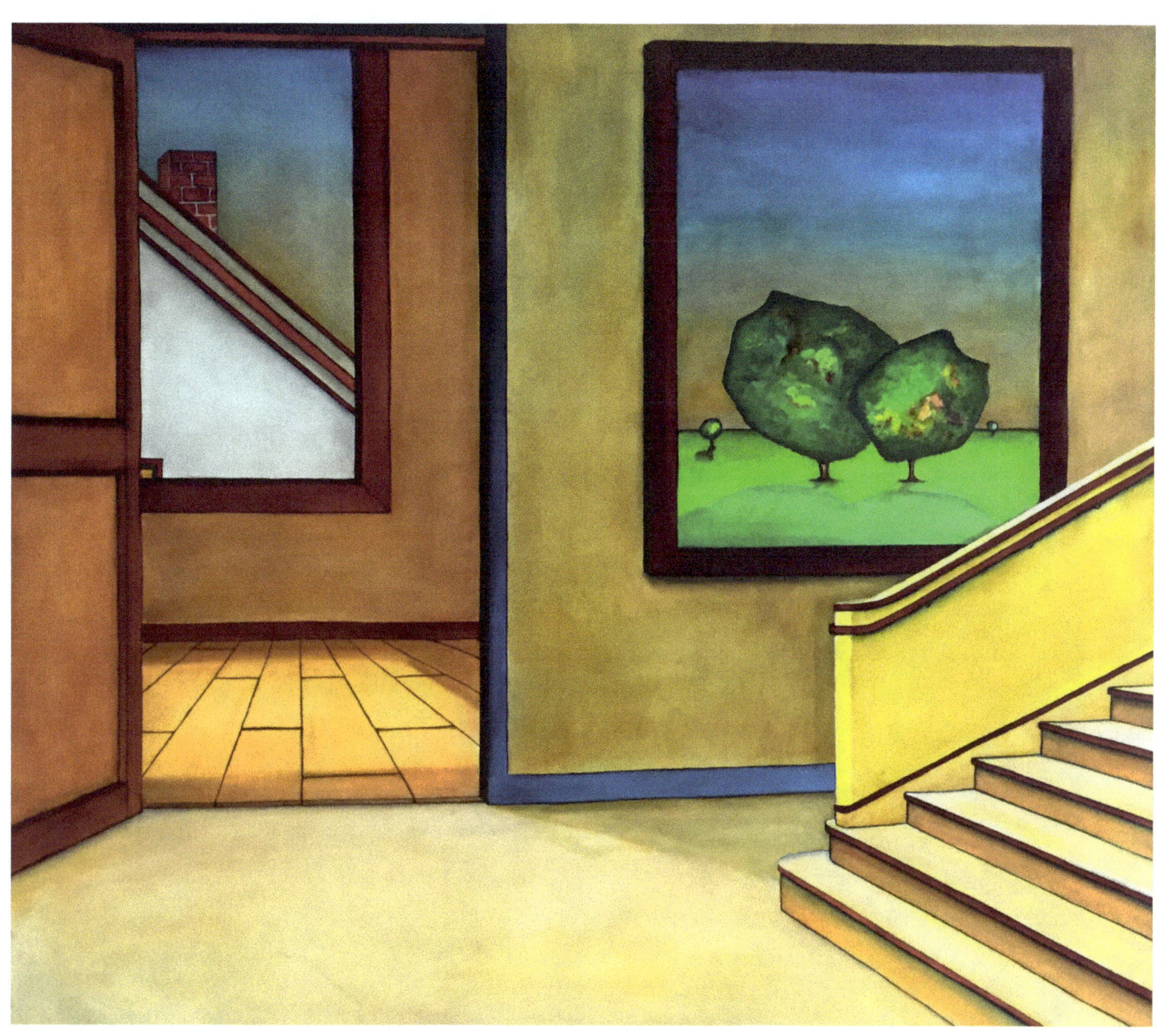

An Empty Room

Dina Klumbys

dinaklumbysart.com

Dina is a self-taught artist from South London, infuses her pieces with a contemporary twist on laid-back simplicity. Drawing from her childhood in Lithuania, particular in Kaunas, nature`s beauty and vibrant colours saturate her work. For Dina, painting is a poetic expression and a form of meditation - a profound connection to her soul`s language through colour. Her art spans abstract realism and animal portraiture, reflecting her diverse inspirations and personal journey.

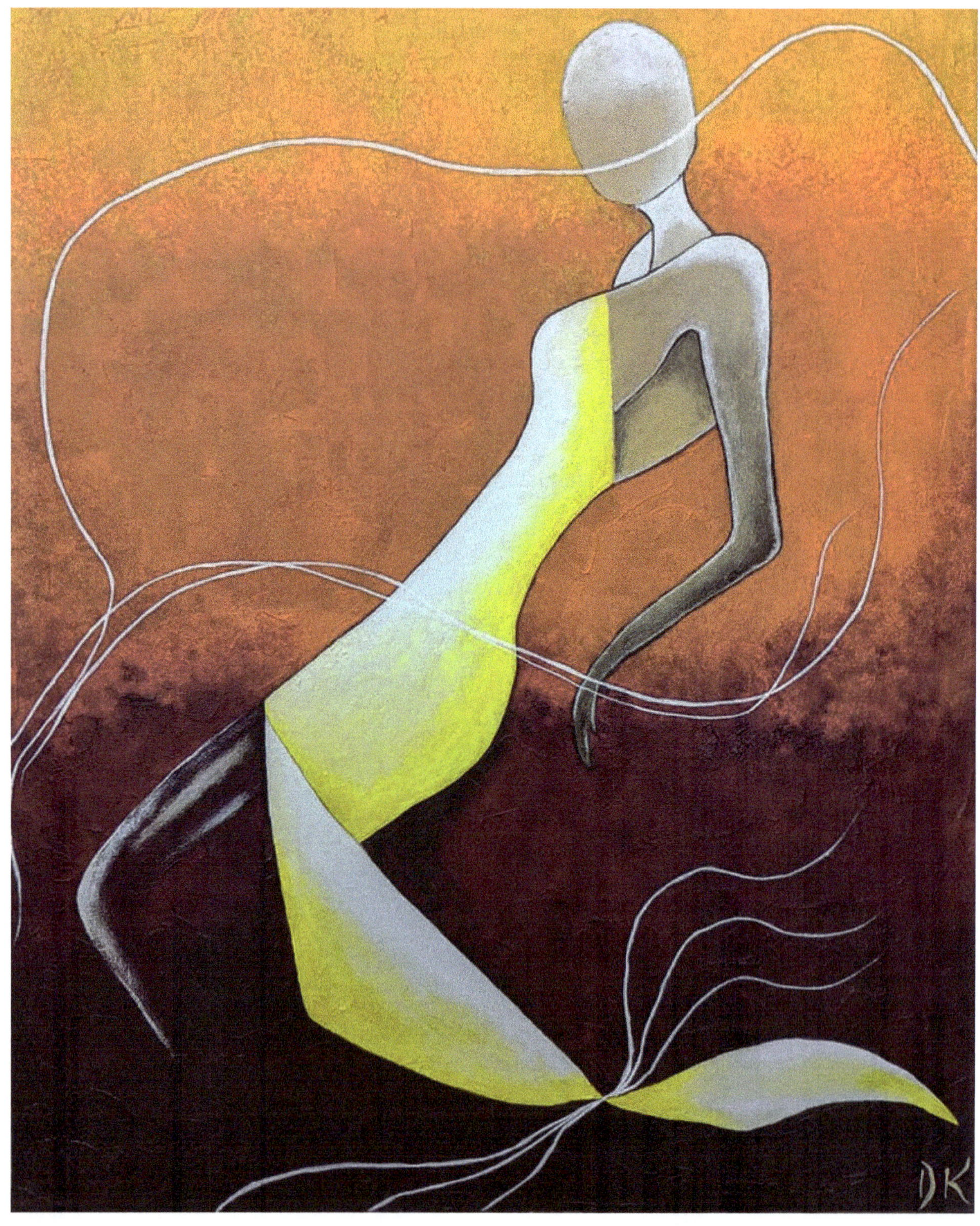

The Dance of Life

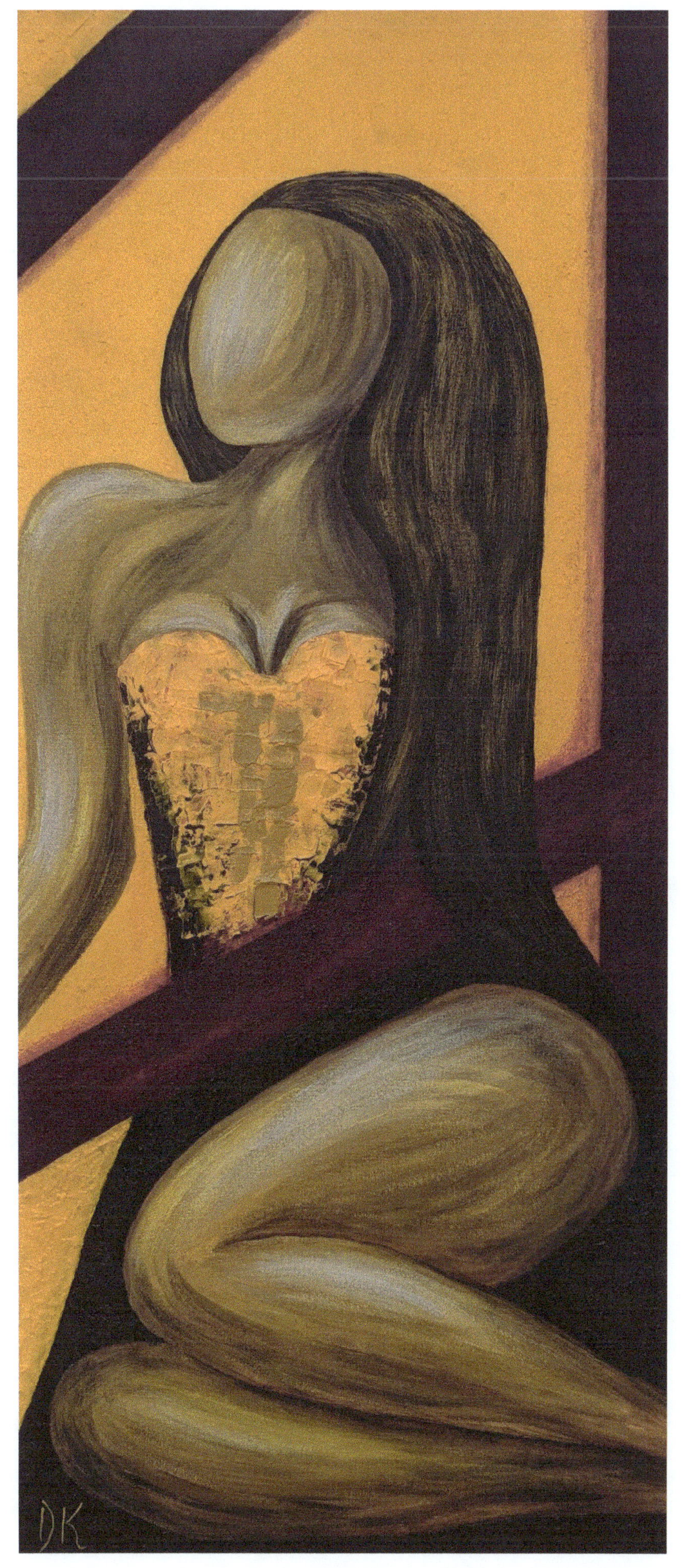

Liberation

Elise Bikker, Ph.D.

elisebikkerartist.co.uk

Elise Bikker is a visual artist originally from the Netherlands and now based in the United Kingdom. She regards herself as a visual storyteller. Her latest pastel drawings accompany a body of creative texts she is currently working on, exploring the emotions resulting from the inevitable passing of time and the transience of existence: loss, grief, isolation, the power of memory, and man's desire to find his place in the universe. Elise is interested in what the analytical psychologist Carl Jung (1875-1961) defined as the "shadow": the repressed parts of the unconscious mind that remain hidden to ourselves. In her recent work, this shadow takes the form of machines, hybrid creatures, or an ancient, solitary figure visiting places from his past. The abandoned places in which this figure finds himself symbolise these unexplored parts of the psyche and man's search to know himself. In her visual language, regarding the transgressing of existential boundaries and the question of what constitutes "life," Elise draws from her Ph.D. in English on the representation of intelligent machines in nineteenth-century fiction (University of York, 2023), as well as art history, mythology, folklore, literature, alchemical symbolism, and other allegorical narratives. Elise's sometimes magic-realist, sometimes darkly romantic imagery is everything but devoid of hope: she emphasises the strength and resilience of the human spirit and poses love, curiosity, and the transformative creative process – with the immortal Muse as its personification – as means to circumvent the decay imposed by time, i.e. as meaningful antidotes to suffering.

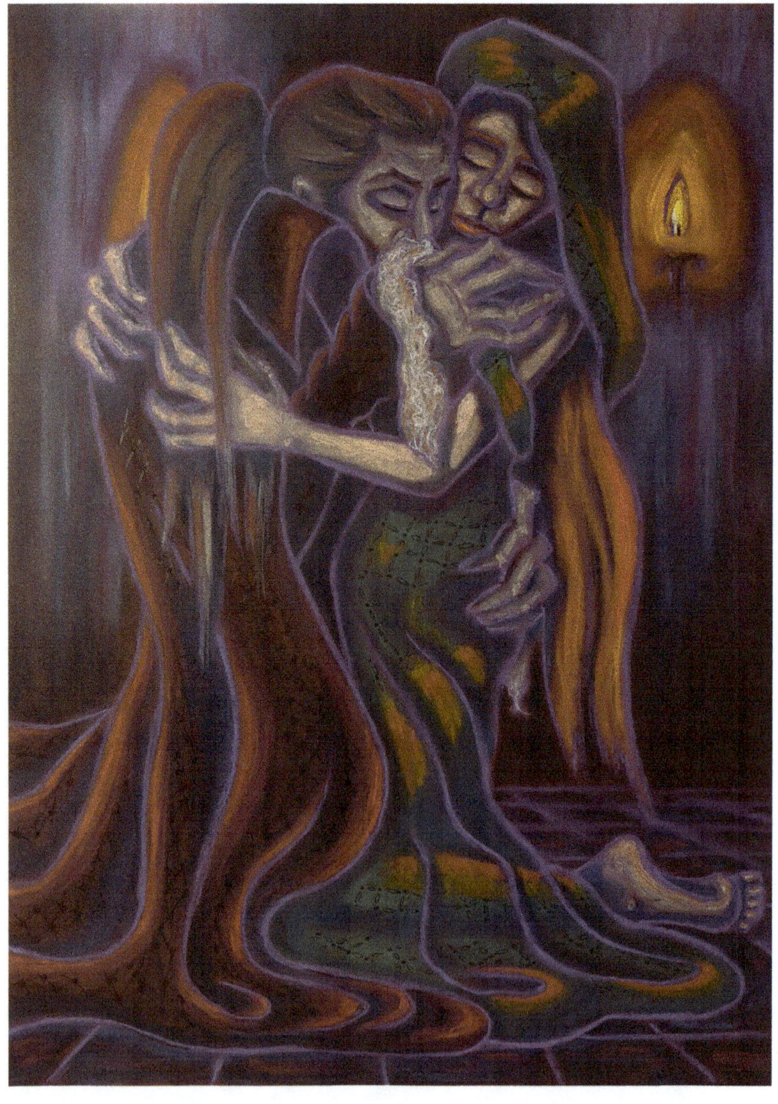

The Kiss

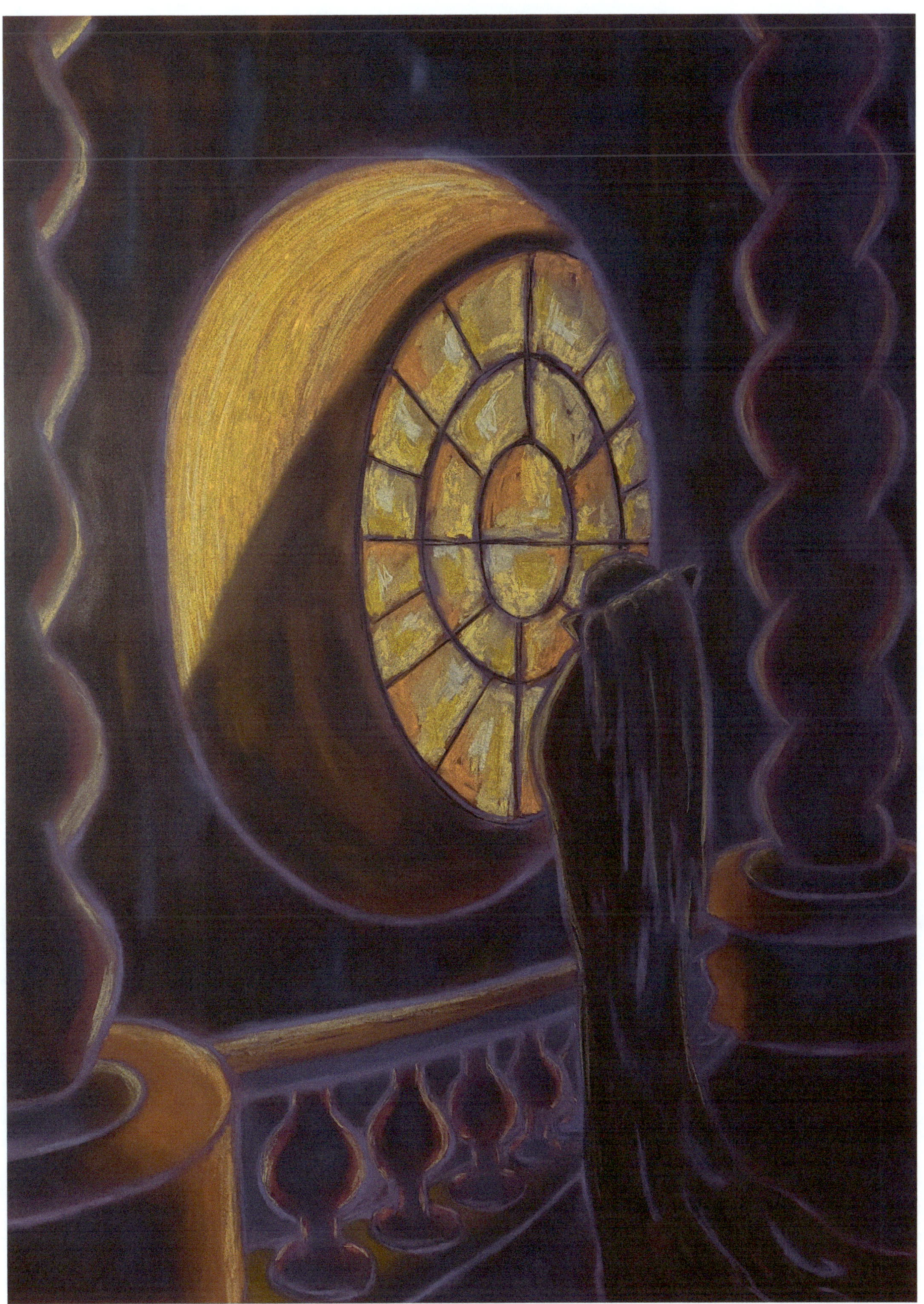

First Light

Eriko Kaniwa

sensegraphia.jp

Just as there are infinite gradations between the light and shadow that make up the essence of photography, are there not also infinite forms that exist between living and non-living (organic and inorganic) The more I photograph nature, the more I wonder, how can we, today, perceive these in-between forms. Even today, many landscapes exist in Japan that symbolize nature worship. Extending from north to south in a long, thin constellation of islands, the Japanese archipelago is blessed with four distinct seasons and an abundance of fresh water, mountains, and sea. Here, appreciating the beauty of nature is a cultural tradition. I am affectionately proud of the values that have flourished within this natural context: the wabi-sabi aesthetic of imperfection and impermanence; the

pursuit of subtle grace; the awareness that humans are a part of nature and are deeply entwined with its dynamics, both consciously and unconsciously. I wonder if this philosophical culture, characterized by empathy with nature, evolved not first and foremost from the natural landscape itself, but rather from the contemplation and perspectives of those who viewed it. The continuous world of living and inanimate, three-dimensional and four-dimensional, visible and invisible, the reality in which we now live, allows for transcendental analogies between the macro and the micro. And this is where I believe the essence of 'abstraction' resides, and it is my job to represent it.

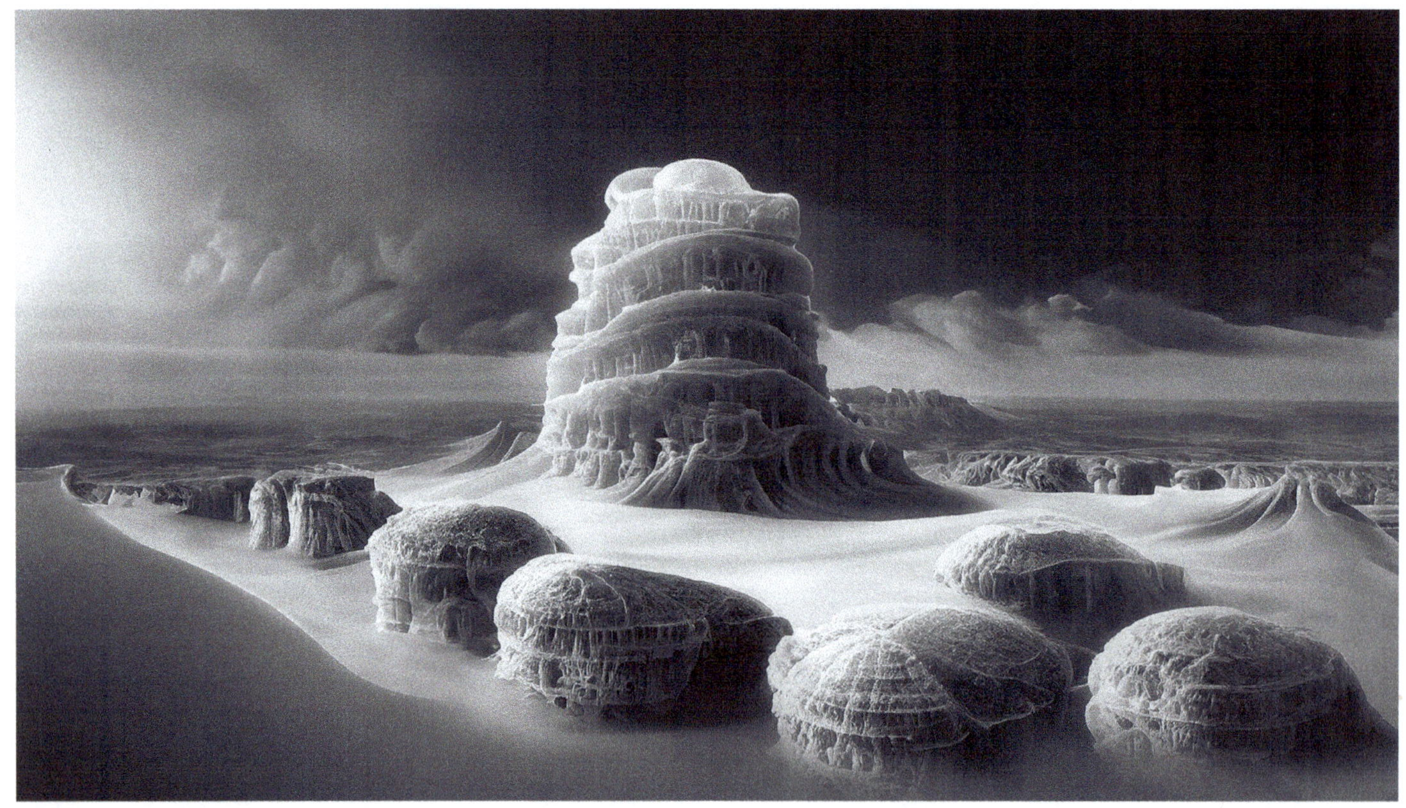

Visionary Scape #1

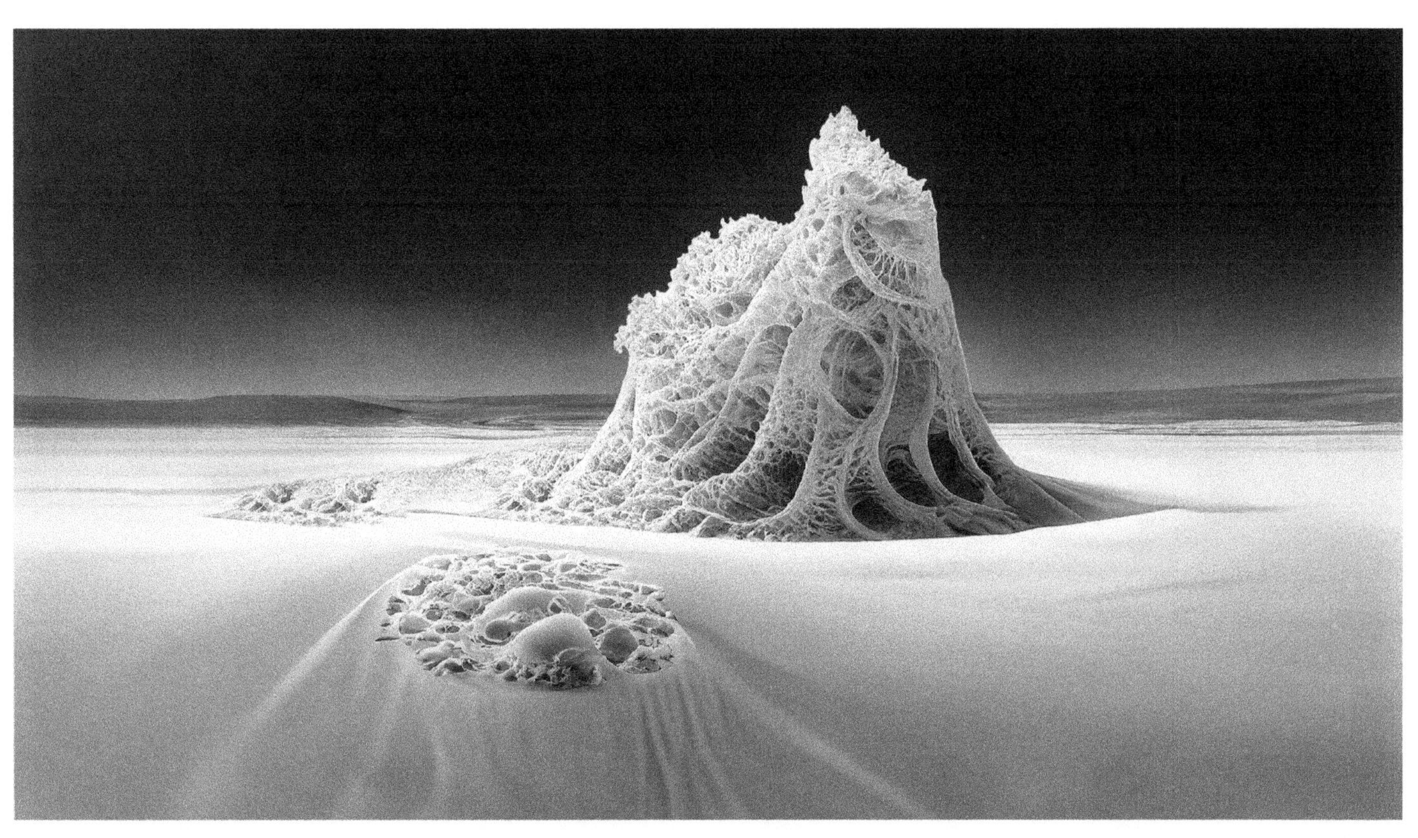

Visionary Scape #2

Evaldas Gulbinas

evaldasgulbinas.co.uk

Art practice goes through sculpture, tattoos, paintings, digital drawings, drawings, installations and mixed media work. It plays a big role, for expression. Tattooing gives the taste of today's society. As, there seen so much different of people to talk to. From the art side, picking up different styles and techniques of tattooing. Often, just to tattoo is not enough and need to do sculptures, paintings, installations and mixed media work to express thoughts better and not get bored. Ideas comes from daily life and surroundings. Usually, inspiration comes from anything. It's like observes, circulates and combines thoughts in the head. Big part does- how materials and idea merge, communicates and fights each other. The definition of material communicates to the idea's depth. Going deep down to the idea- there is always you can find the material, which connects and makes the conversation to it. Some times making art from the simplest materials as possible, but the ideas plays the role- to show that the art could be anything if you change and inject the story behind. Exploring themes of social change, freedom, conflict, people's emotions , adversity and daily life stories. As well, has the philosophical, consider life ideas. Some of art practice can be romantic, funny and aggressive. It's how the minds and emotions plays the role- goes through art. Drawing and painting 2D and 3D art, gives opportunity to play and develop skills. Most art done by digging into the context of own created world.

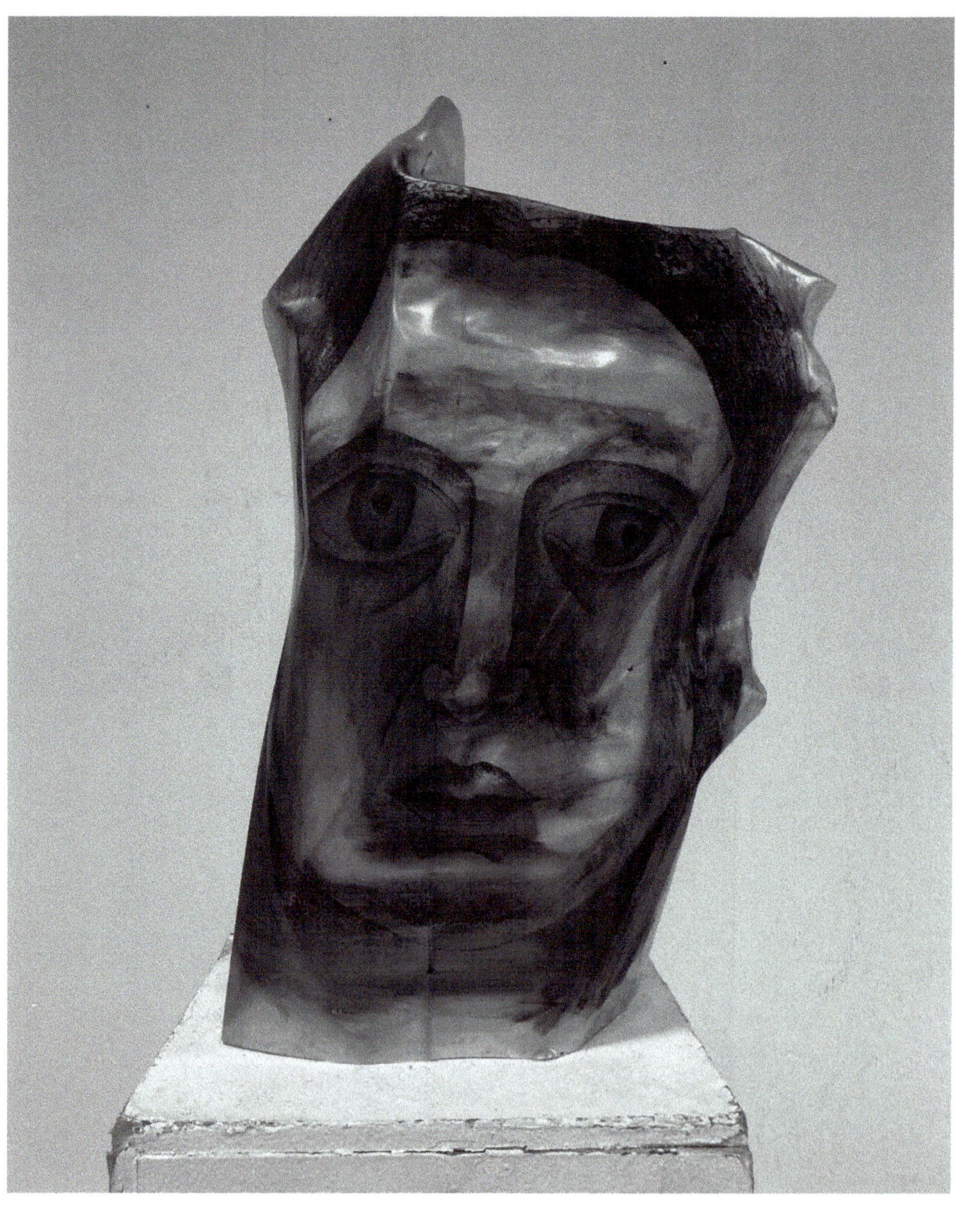

Melancholy

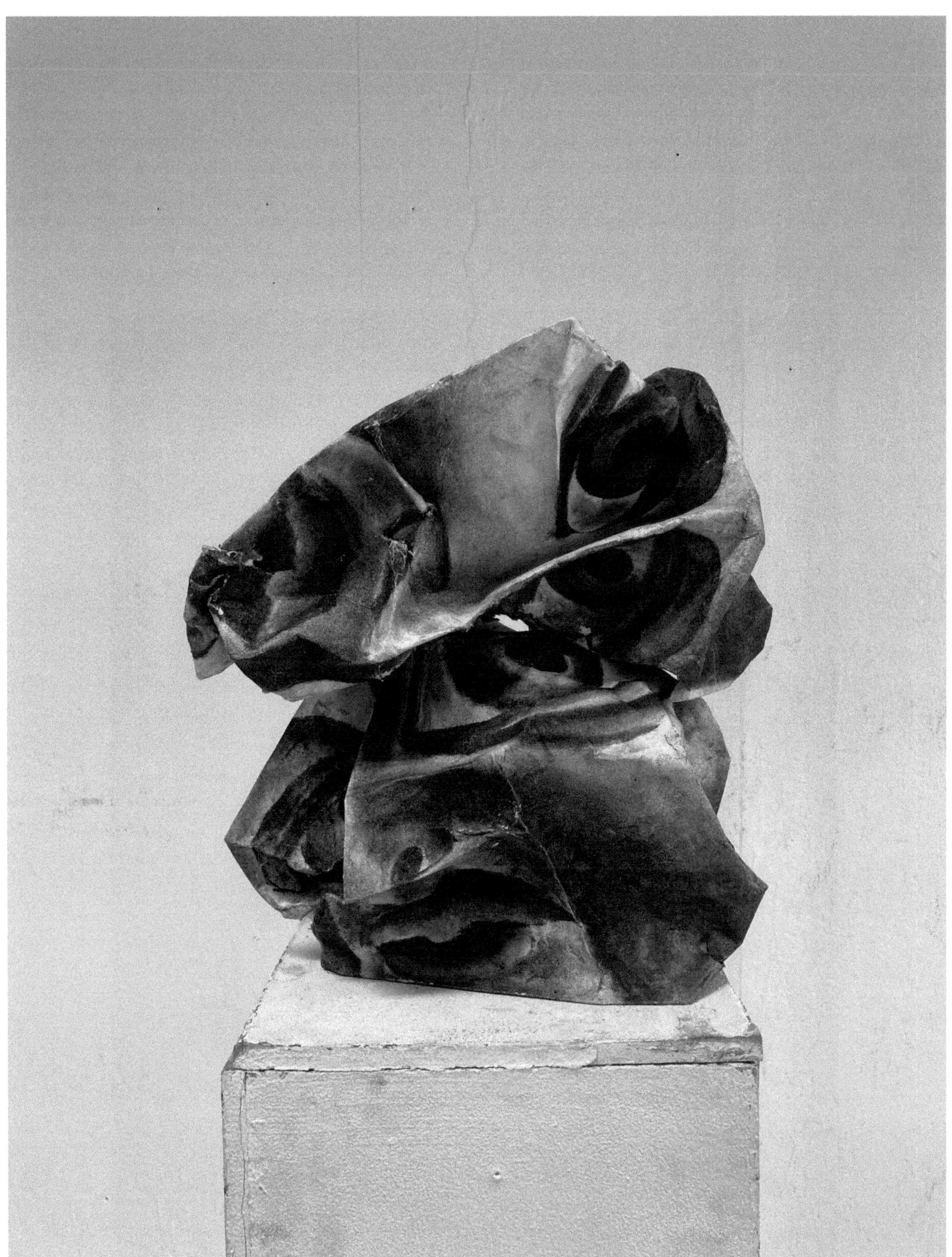

Confused connection

Fine Art by AnnaK

instagram.com/fineartbyannak

Born in Australia in 1962, AnnaK reflects on the unexpected twists of life that led her to embrace a renewed passion for art at the age of 60. Beginning with tentative explorations into drawing in 2019, AnnaK's artistic journey took flight in 2022 when her creative pursuits blossomed into a nightly ritual, expanding to encompass every available moment. In 2023, AnnaK made the bold decision to pursue art as a full-time career, embracing her identity as an artist with unwavering determination. Rooted in self-acceptance and a lifelong acknowledgment of her artistic essence, AnnaK approaches her craft with humor, resilience, and an unwavering commitment to joy. She has a deep love and respect of natural beauty in any form. AnnaK is fascinated and awed by the natural world which also includes the human form. Blessed to live in a country, Australia, with so much natural beauty, she combines this element with a personal evolution in self-awareness together with a love of colour and detail as the sources of inspiration.

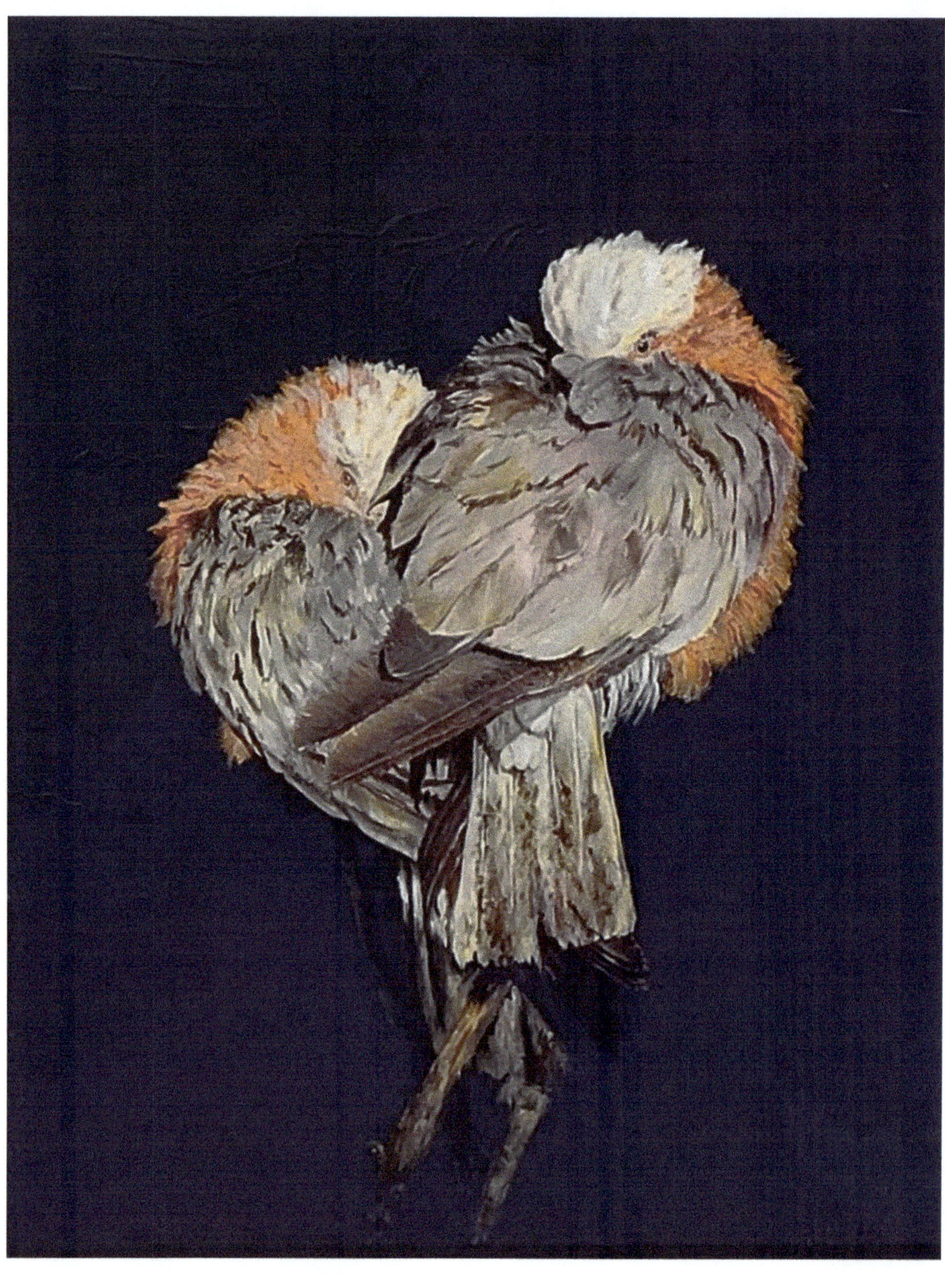

Love at Sunset - Galahs

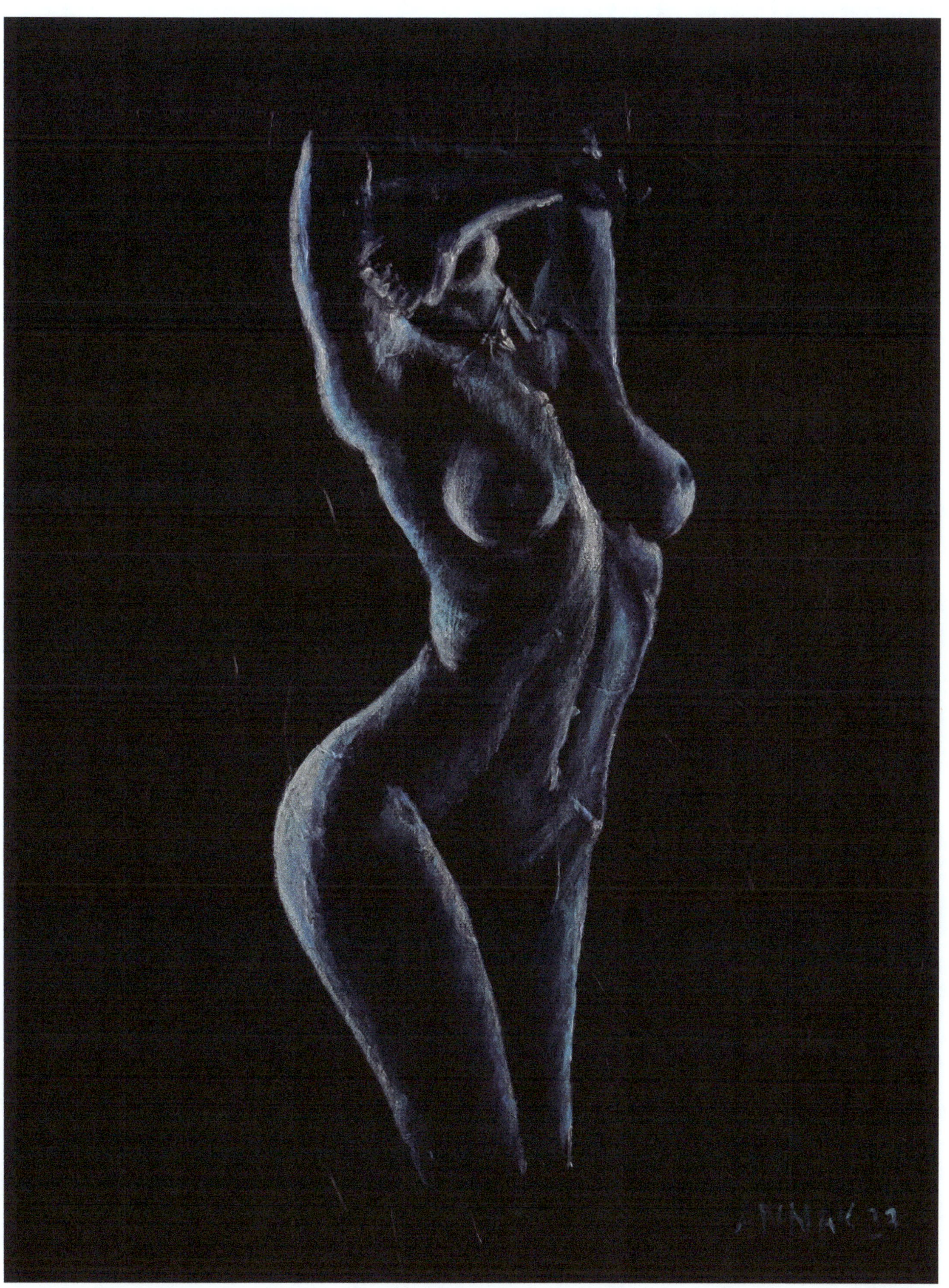

The Light in the Shadow - Truth

Frédéric Steinlaender

frederic-steinlaender.fr

Frédéric STEINLAENDER, born in Haguenau, artist painter for more than 30 years, offers astonishing paintings in which nature with infinite beauty is his field of research. Personal touch: the defined brush strokes allow the color to breathe to release an elegant and poetic composition of reality onto the support. Frédéric has exhibited his works in numerous personal and collective exhibitions in galleries around the world and many awards mark his career. He is also a painting animator in associations such as the ALC in Gumbrechtshoffen, Brumath and in Mertzwiller (Northern Vosges Regional Nature Park, Alsace – France).

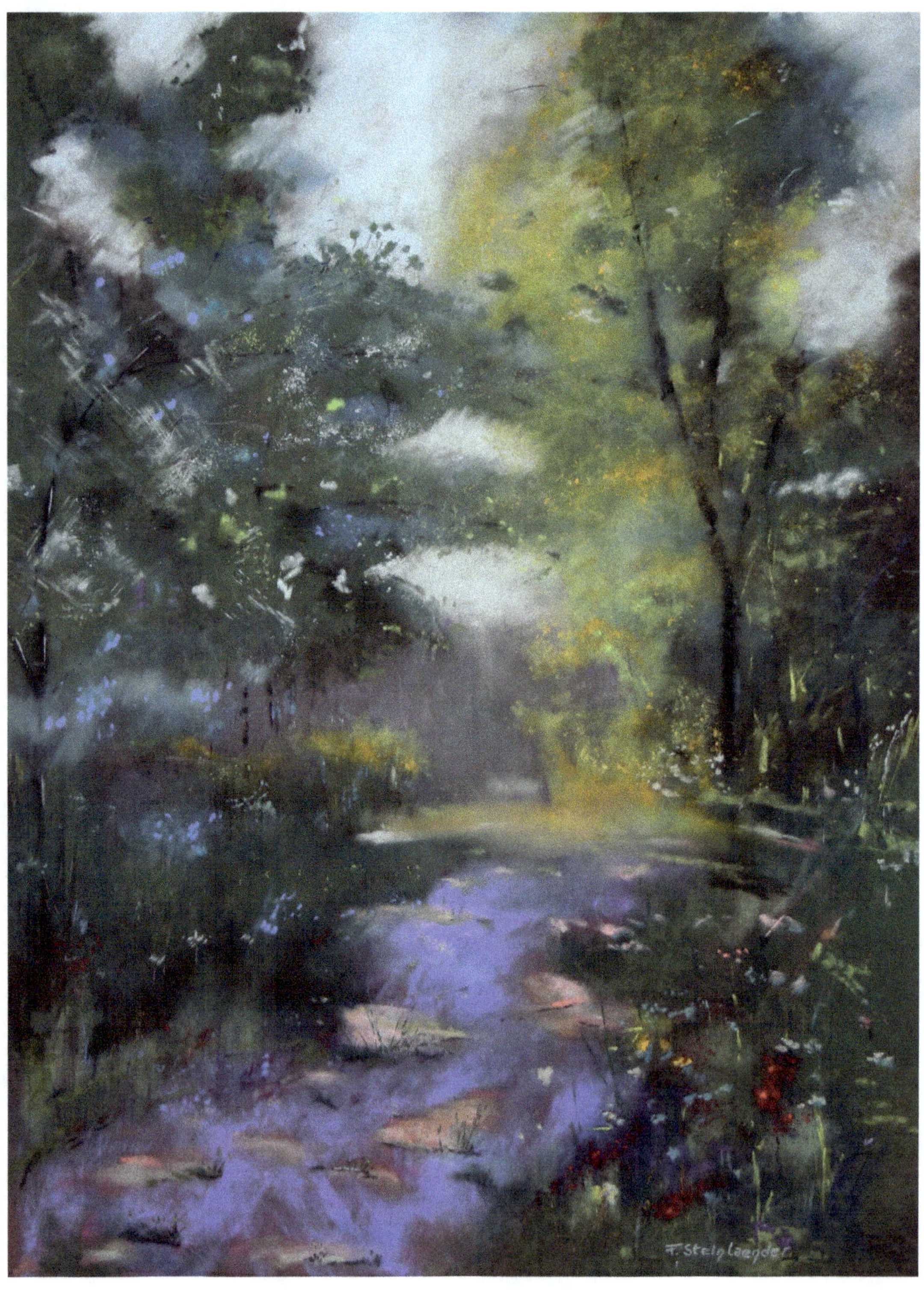

Jeux de lumières

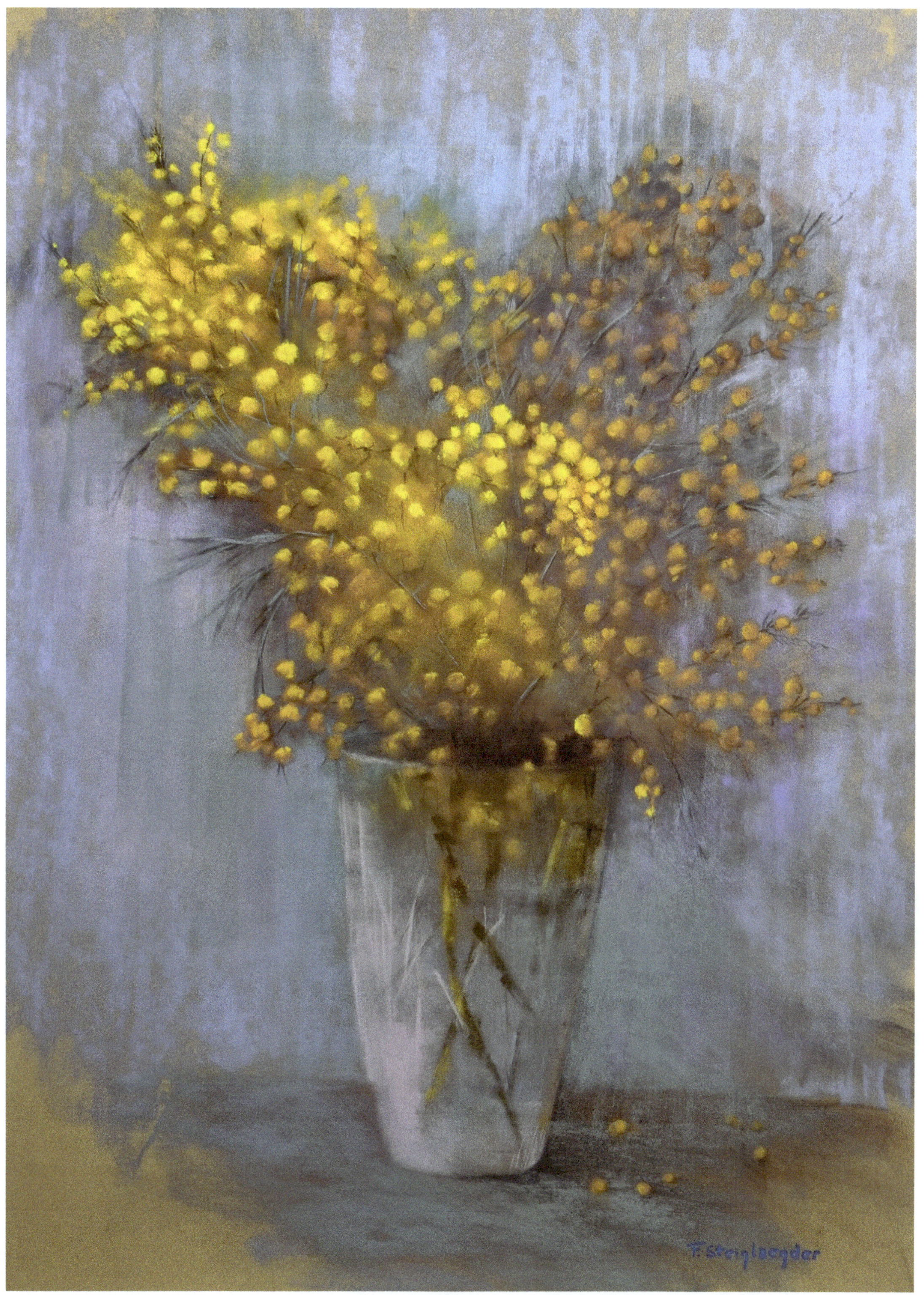

Mimosas

GAYLE PRINTZ, A WORLD MASTER ARTIST

GaylePrintz.com

Art is a universal language. It transcends boundaries. It allows us to communicate, find meaning, and experience life together. In May of 2020, I picked up my first paintbrush to reflect upon the beauty remaining in a world darkened by the pandemic. I now have a portfolio in which every painting is an international award winner said to create an intrigue and value that differs from anything yet seen in the art world. It is my hope that by translating the colors of my world into the universal language of art, I can help promote unity and inspire all people to celebrate the beauty in life. Allow your imagination to be the lens through which to find meaning in my work. For when you embrace the unfamiliar, there is a richness and tranquility that can fill your soul. And, I hope, my artwork fills yours.

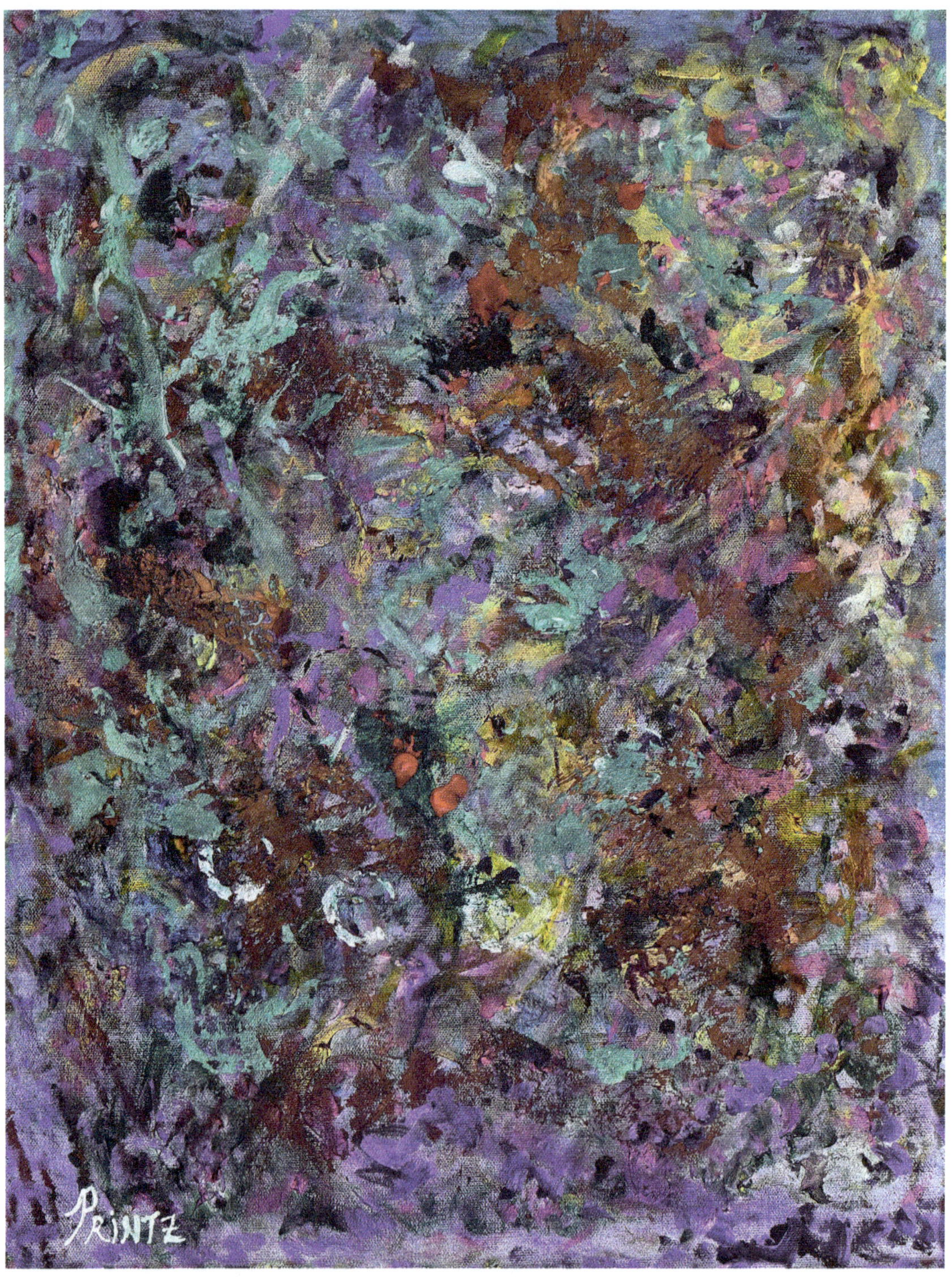

Peace

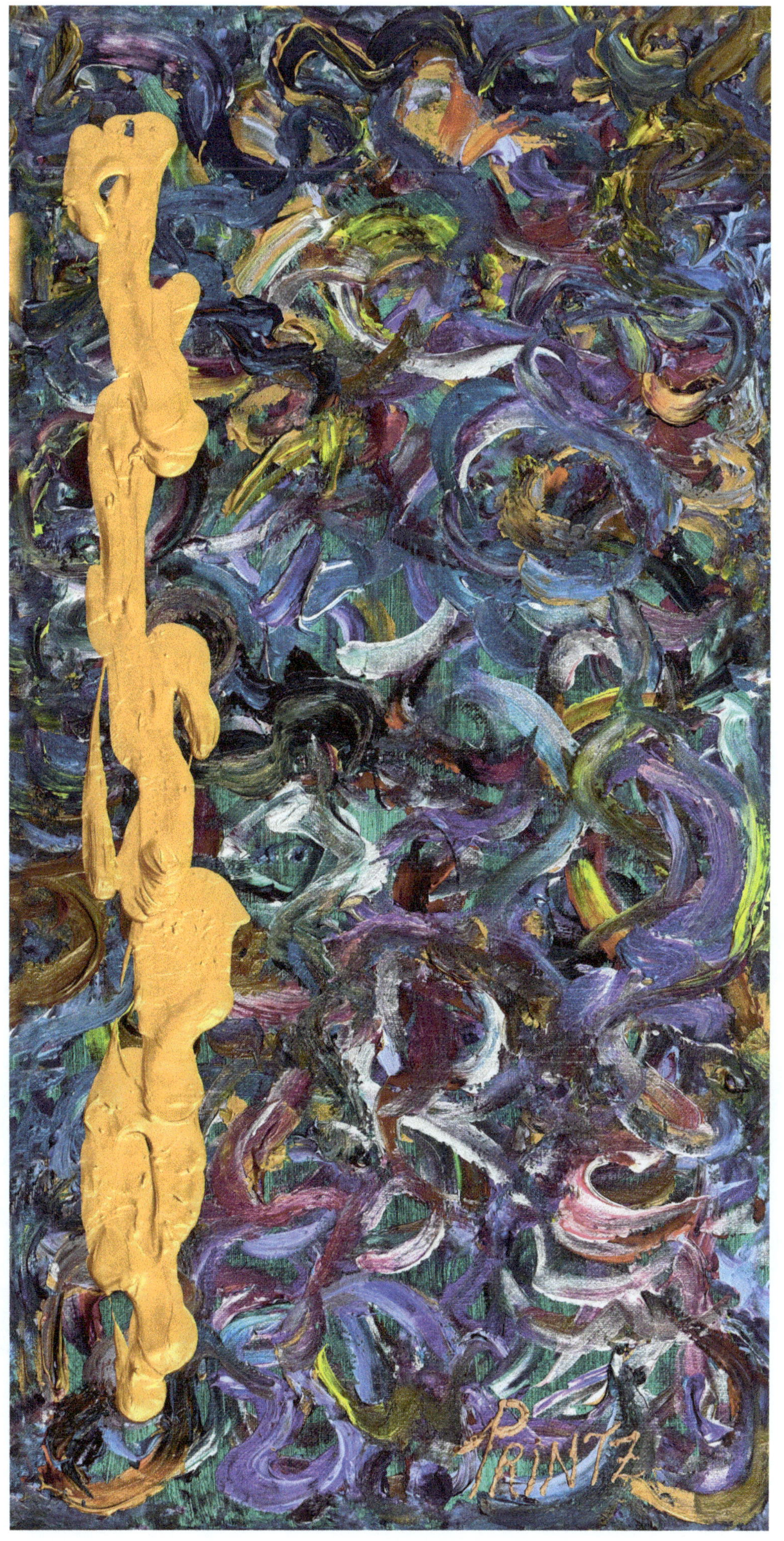

Harmony

Gabriel Helou

gabrielhelouphotography.com

I'm a Jerusalem-based award-winning fine art photographer, inspired by the beauty and rich culture of my home City - Jerusalem. I have a particular passion for cityscape and landscape photography. To me, photography is about feelings where I convey mine without words. Also, it's about discovery of interesting things in life; historical places and beauty of nature to share with those who appreciate them. It adds joy to my heart seeing my artwork hanging on people's walls. My photography work has been exhibited in international art exhibitions and published in art magazines.

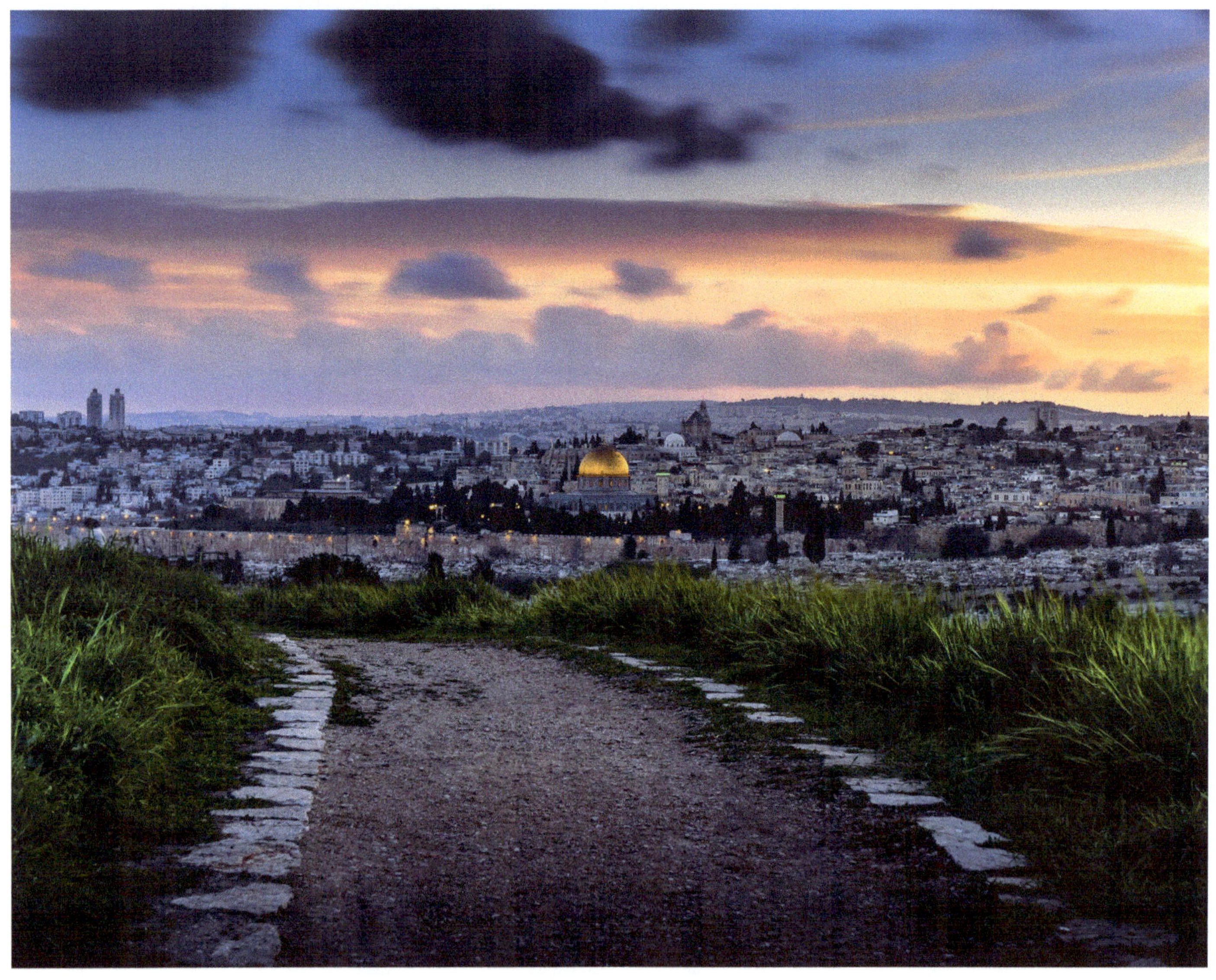

The Road to Jerusalem

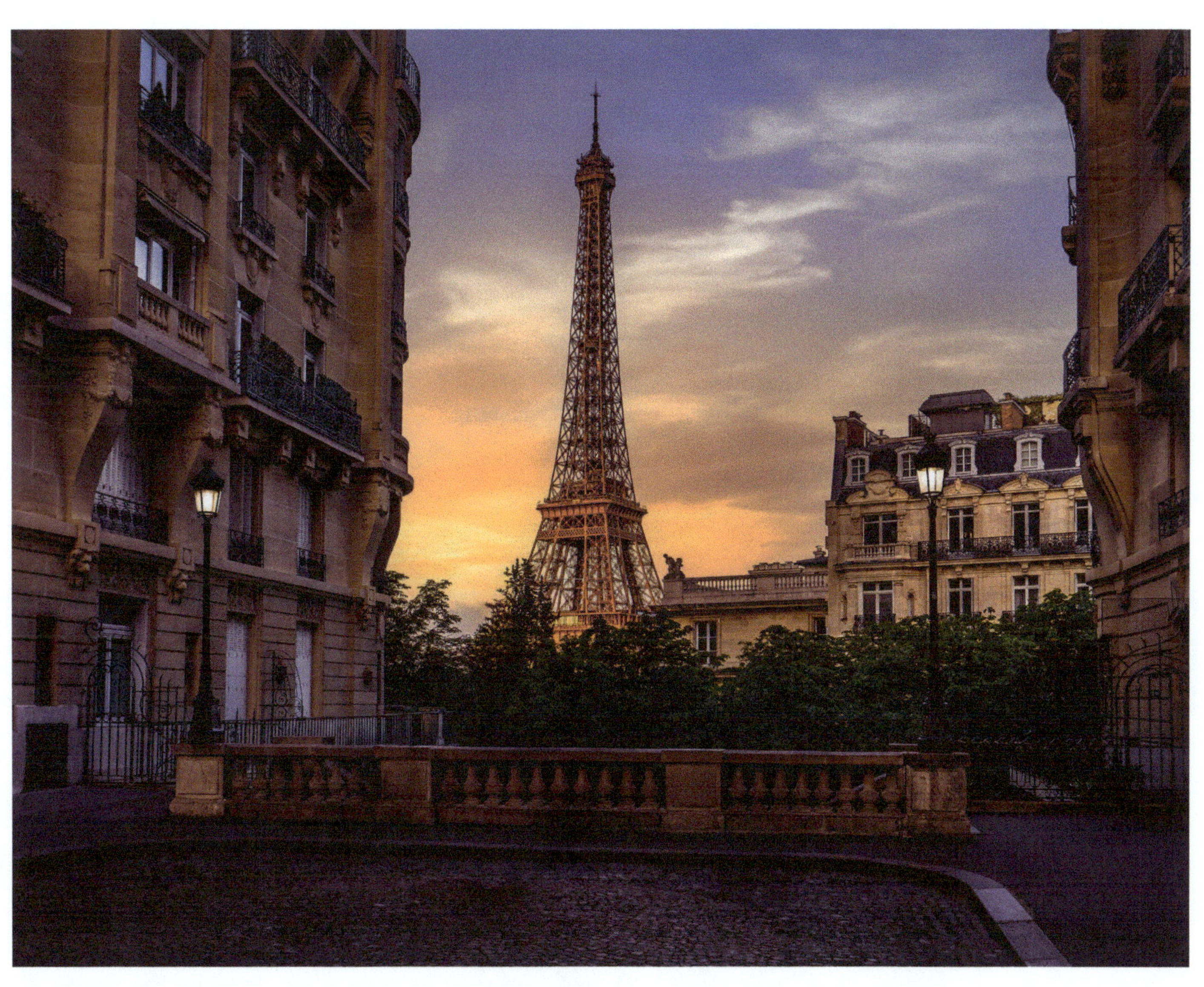

Eiffel Tower, Paris

Georg Douglas

artgeorg.com

I like my paintings to be strong, whether from colour, form or something else. I want them to invoke an immediate reaction, either confronting the viewers or drawing them in to the work. They appeal to the emotions and create an atmosphere. The world of flowers and Irish dance have been my inspiration for some time. My flower inspired paintings use strong colours and form and I also extend the field of view by incorporating microscopic and molecular elements, reflecting on my scientific training. I like to obfuscate by ignoring scale and jumbling elements which I feel comes closer to the complexity of nature itself than depicted in realistic painting, while at the same time moving my work more towards the abstract. My paintings are joyful and celebrate the complexity and beauty of nature.

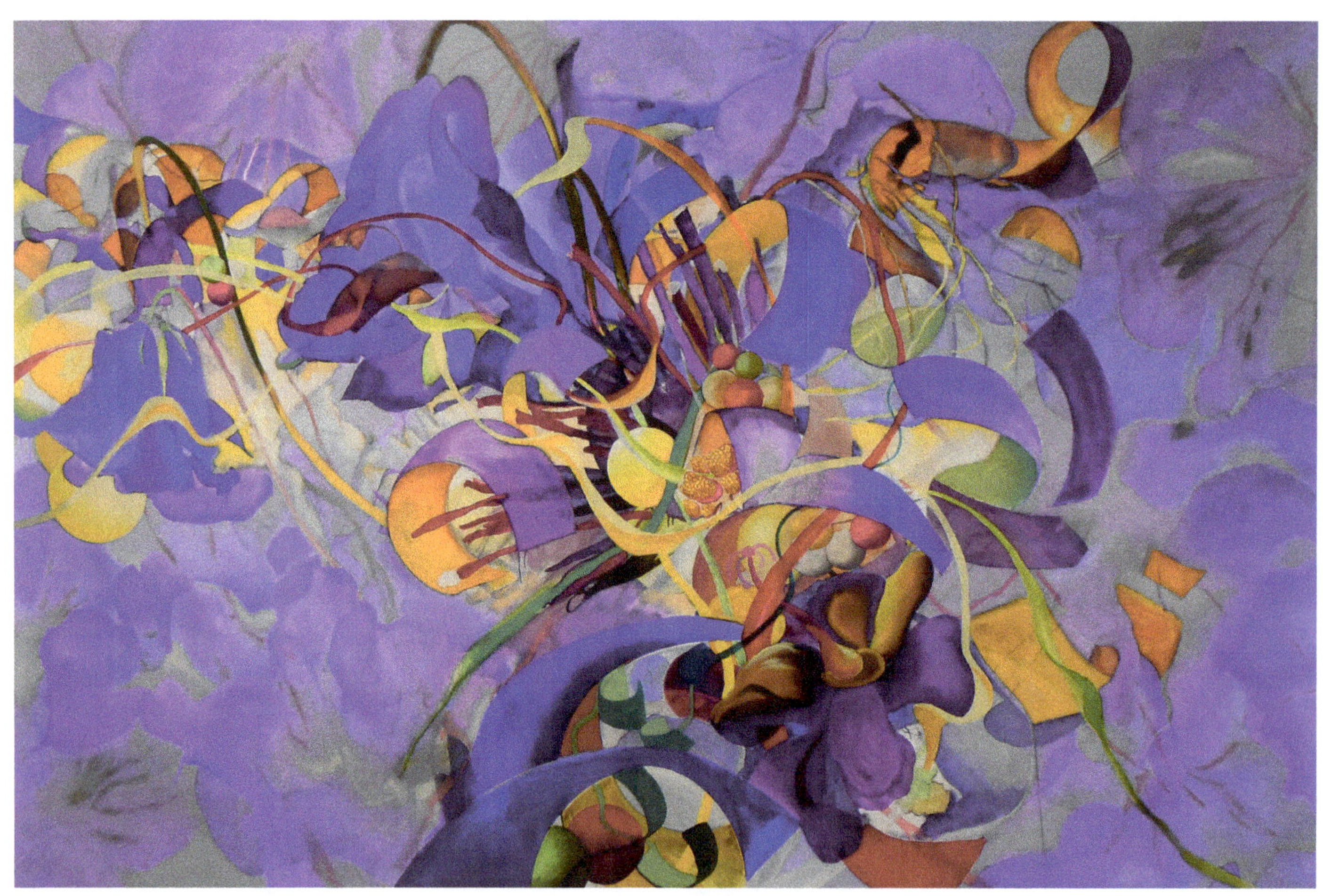

Blue flowers

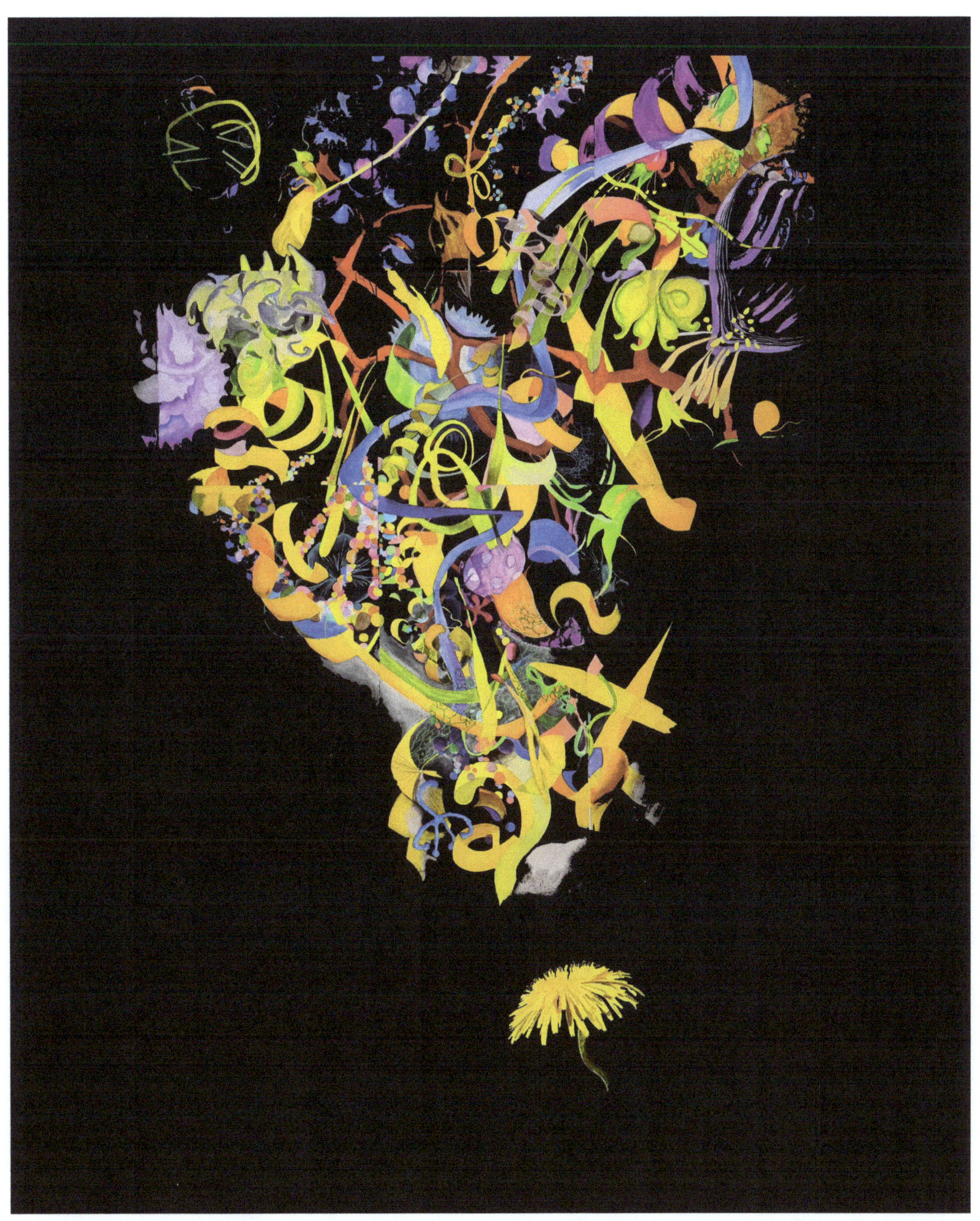

The making of a dandelion

Gregory Logan Dunn

gldunnart.com

All my paintings are about color and form. The meaning behind this color and form is not defined until the event of painting. I don't start with a preconceived idea. I don't do drawings or sketches. But in the beginning, middle and late stages of the painting I spend extensive time visualizing each layer in terms of its color, transparency, and consistency; and how they will interact with previous and future applications. I'm always looking for movement in the painting. I'm trying to create motion in a rending space. I think this is a reflection of my mind. I'm a bipolar artist, and I imagine the far reaches of my mind pulling at one another from opposite hemispheres. I'm looking for marks that do not reveal or betray the artists hand. I'm looking for color that is intense but sublime. I want to sculpt an ethereal space from the paint. Titling the painting is to divine its true nature, to find its true name. It might be a thought or a phrase, a line deciphered from a poem mostly written in color and form. They are songs lamenting humanity and grieving a dying world. They are longing for cosmogenesis, for spiritual enlightenment and the depravity of psychosis. Call and response for the lost transcript of a dream.

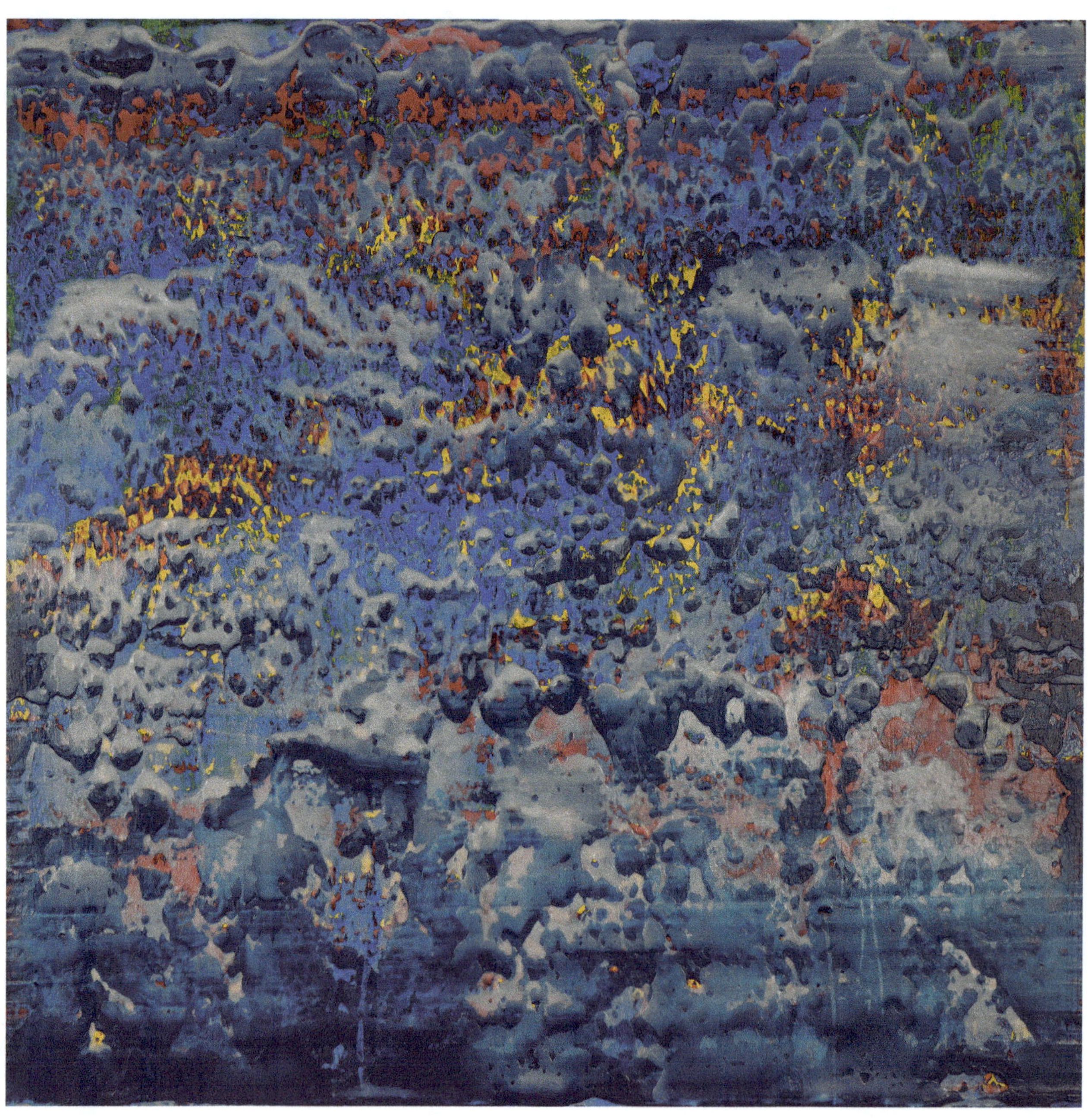

Demons Begone

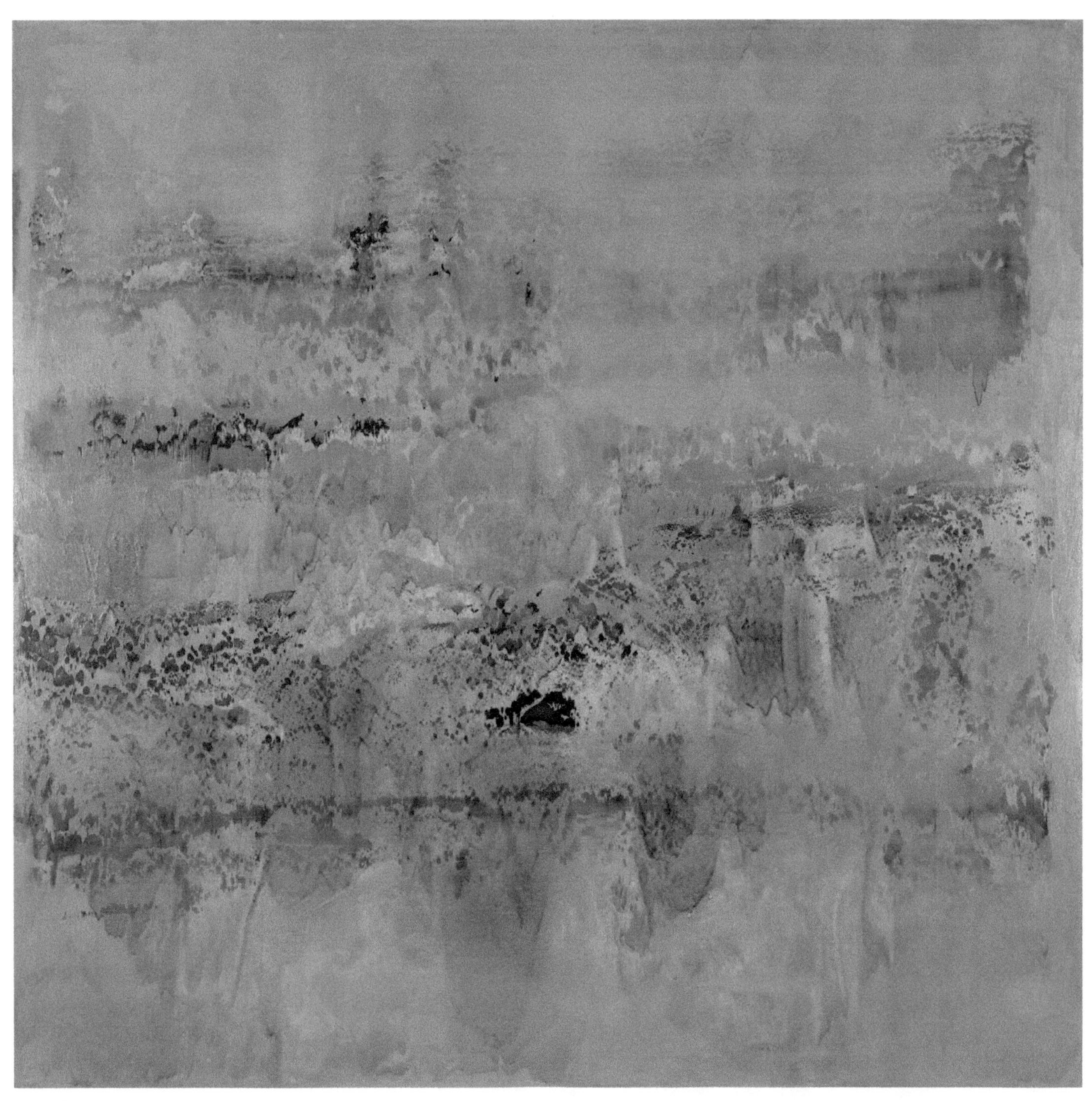

Seraphim

Gunilla Daga

gunilladaga.se

Living in Stockholm, Sweden, Gunilla Daga produces art which, in John Austin's words, is "drawn out of private experience, reaches out in universal terms to touch everyone on different levels." Her use of earth tones and primitive shapes reveal a sensitive delicacy. Daga mixes red iron oxide, bone black and titanium white to achieve a sophisticated pattern that produces an organic aesthetic. Daga's paintings are connected to each other, each image being born from the previous and forming a series of works where the artist investigates not only the nature of the materials at hand but seems to push each shape to take different forms and each time, bring forward a new vocabulary. Daga studied at Konstfack University College of Arts, Crafts and Design, Gerlesborgsskolan in Bohuslän and in Stockholm. She is a member of Swedish Artists' National Organization, IAA International Association of Art. She has exhibited in Finland, Paris, Italy, Poland, New York, Norway, Slovenia, and Sweden. She has been an Artist in Residence at NARS Foundation, Brooklyn, New York 2016 and where she has returned for studio work. Daga had a personal show at Artifact Gallery in Lower East Side, New York 2015 and has participated with Artifact at SCOPE Miami and Monaco Yacht Show 2019. Exhibited at Art Expo NY, LA ArtFair, and Spectrum Miami with ArtUpClose. Her art has been featured on Times Square Billboards 2014 with SeeMe and received the ArtSlant Showcase Prize in 2012. Exhibited with Contemporary Art Station and ArtboxProjects in several countries.

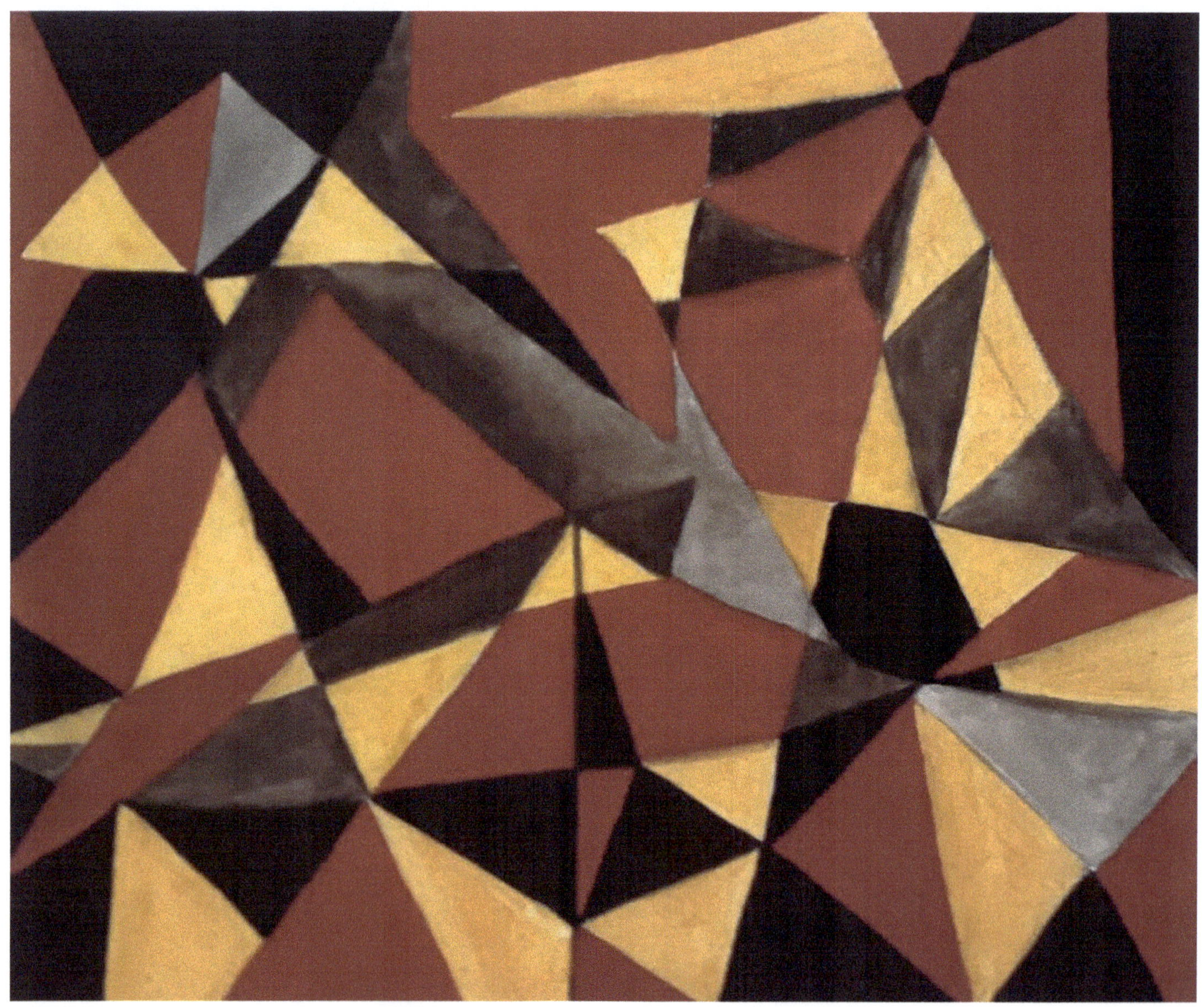

Early bird

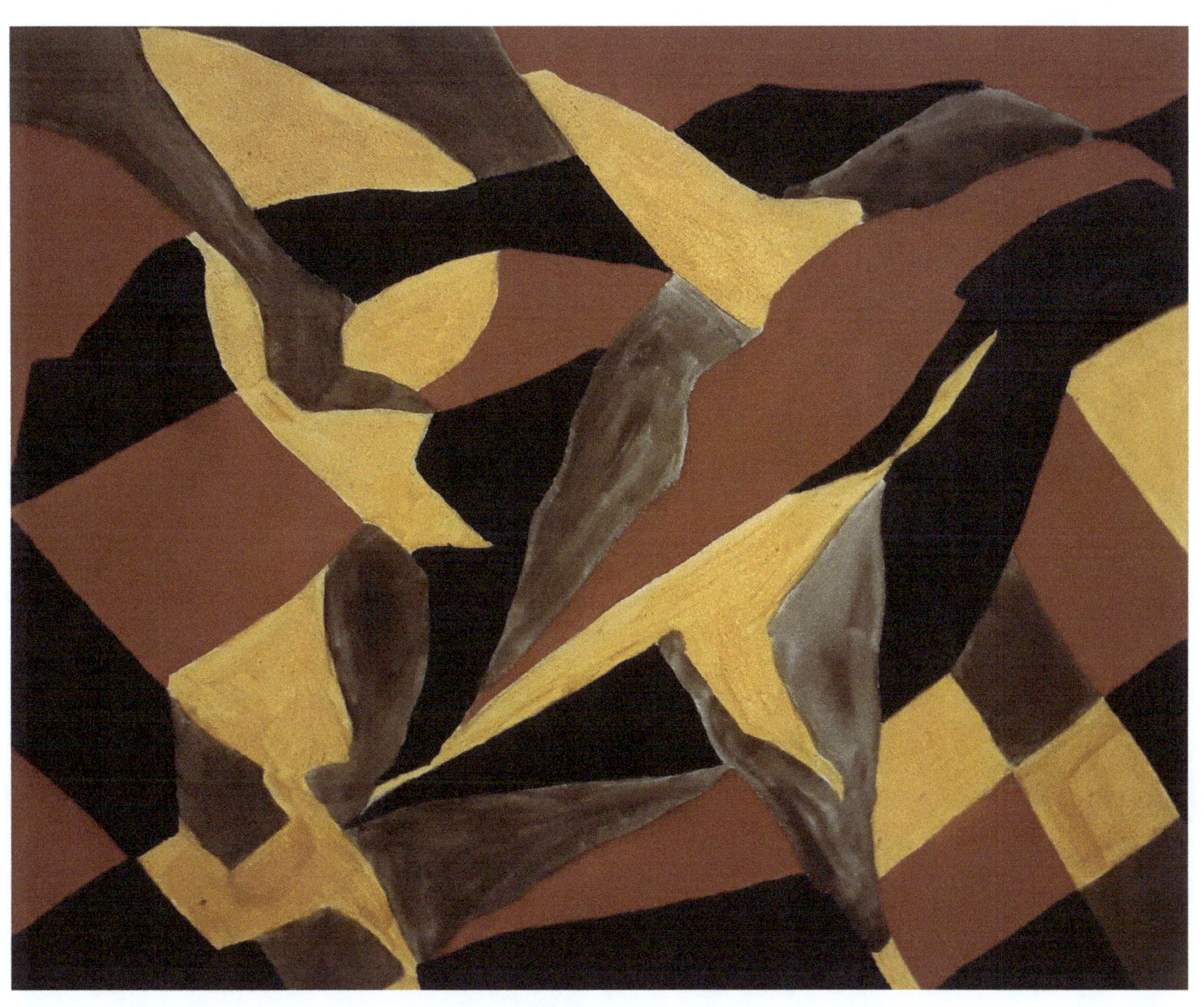

Moonlight in the garden

Henrik Saar

henriksaar.dk

I paint, what I am, as I am, what I pant. I work from out an existentially point of view in my artworks. I seek to keep focus on common human issues, and express these in simplified expressions, which may seem to be roughly expressed, but then again, very fine and precise.

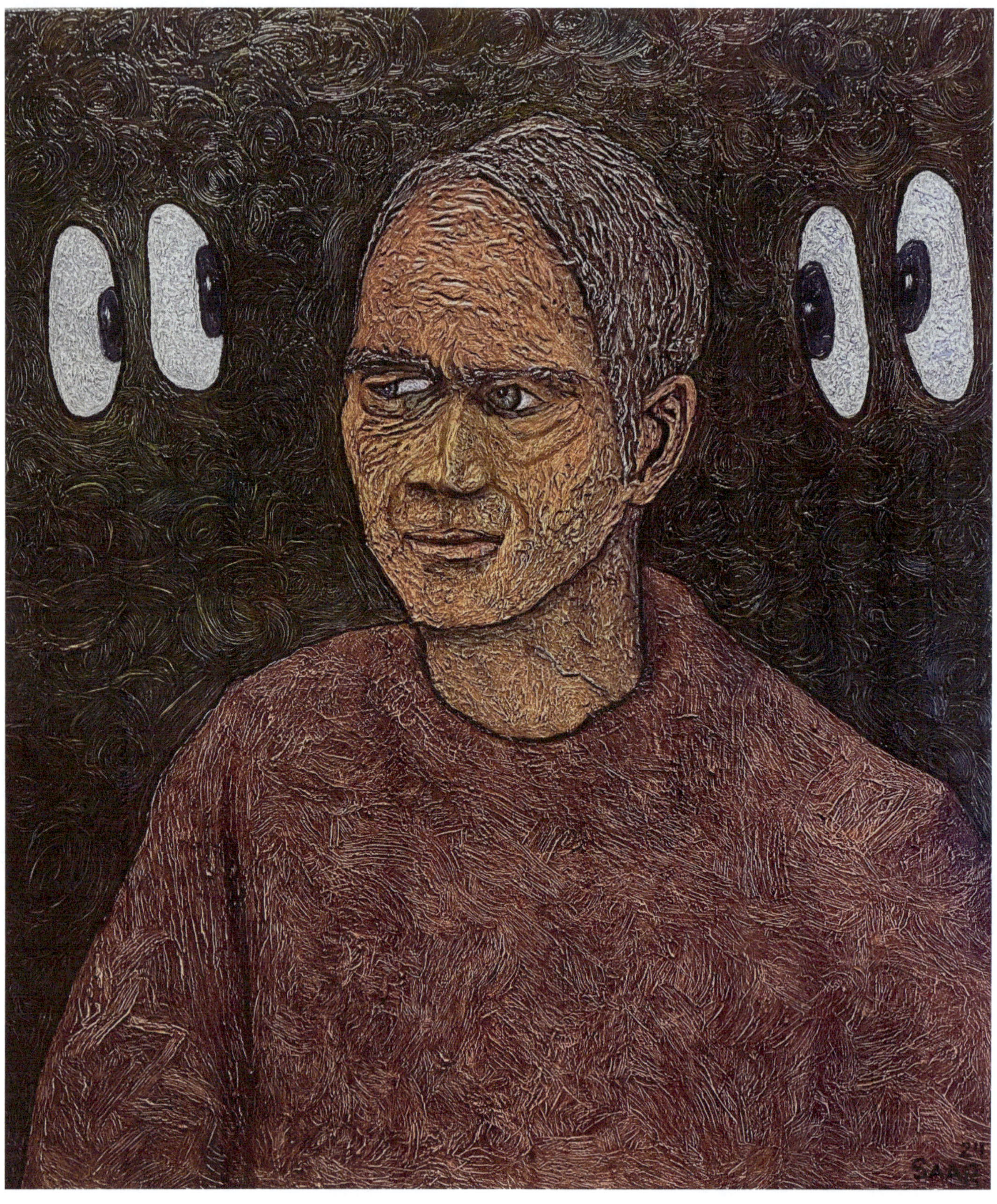

"Between two views" - Oil on canvas 70 x 60 cm. 2023

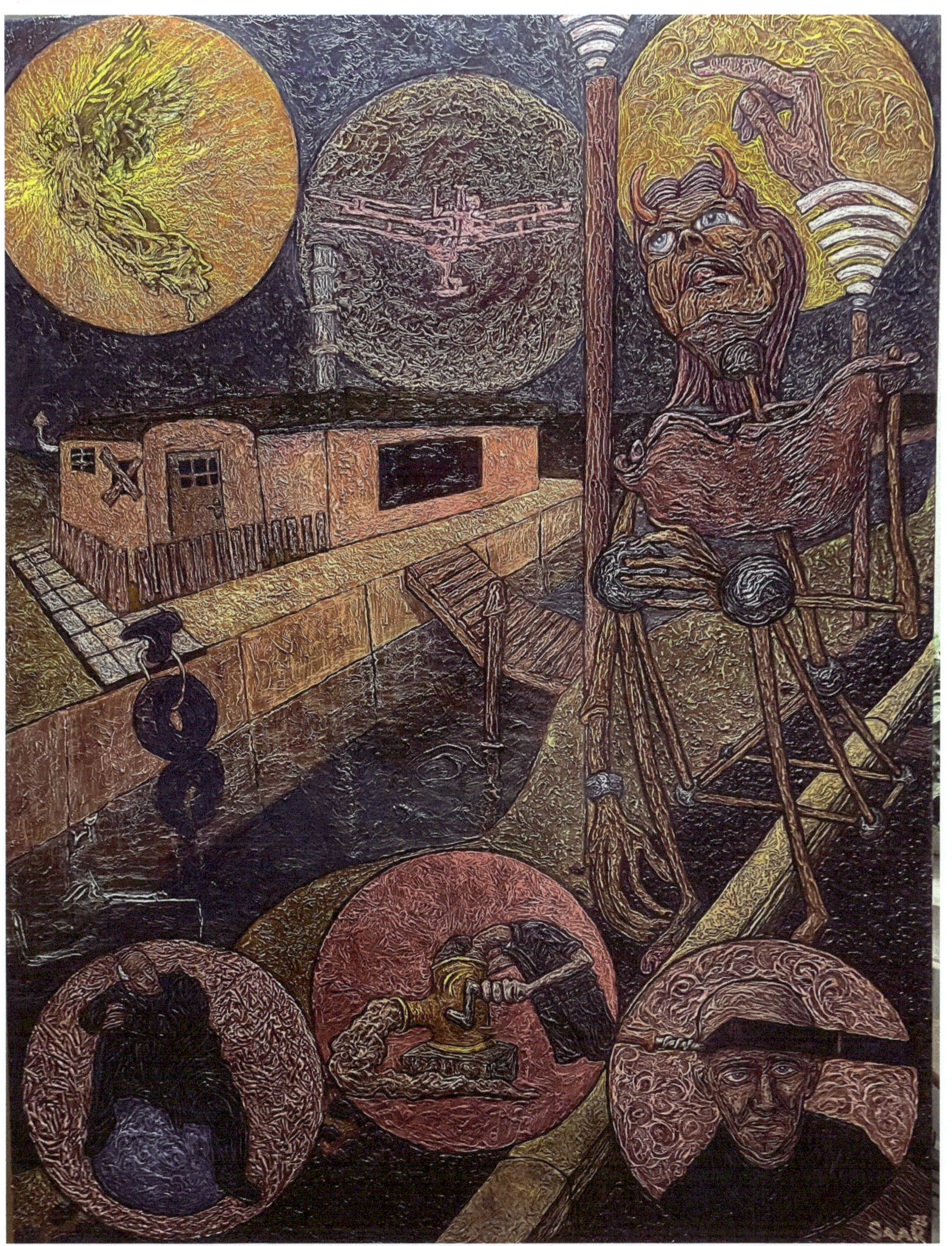

"Where am I and where am I heading" - Oil on canvas 130 x 96 cm 2024

Ivan Kanchev

instagram.com/ivan_kanchev

I try to create new synthetic forms with original language and technique of expression. In search of a new universality and the total work, I assimilate different epochs (from prehistory to the contemporary) and different types of art (painting, sculpture, installation, ceramics, graphics, drawing, mosaic, architecture, photography...). In a global perspective I present the development of civilization with its contradictions in social, political and philosophical terms. At the center is the small, naked and defenseless man who is searching for happiness. At the base is prehistory - with its universal principles. The vessel viewed in the broadest sense. The vessel with its universal form, which collects and conserves...

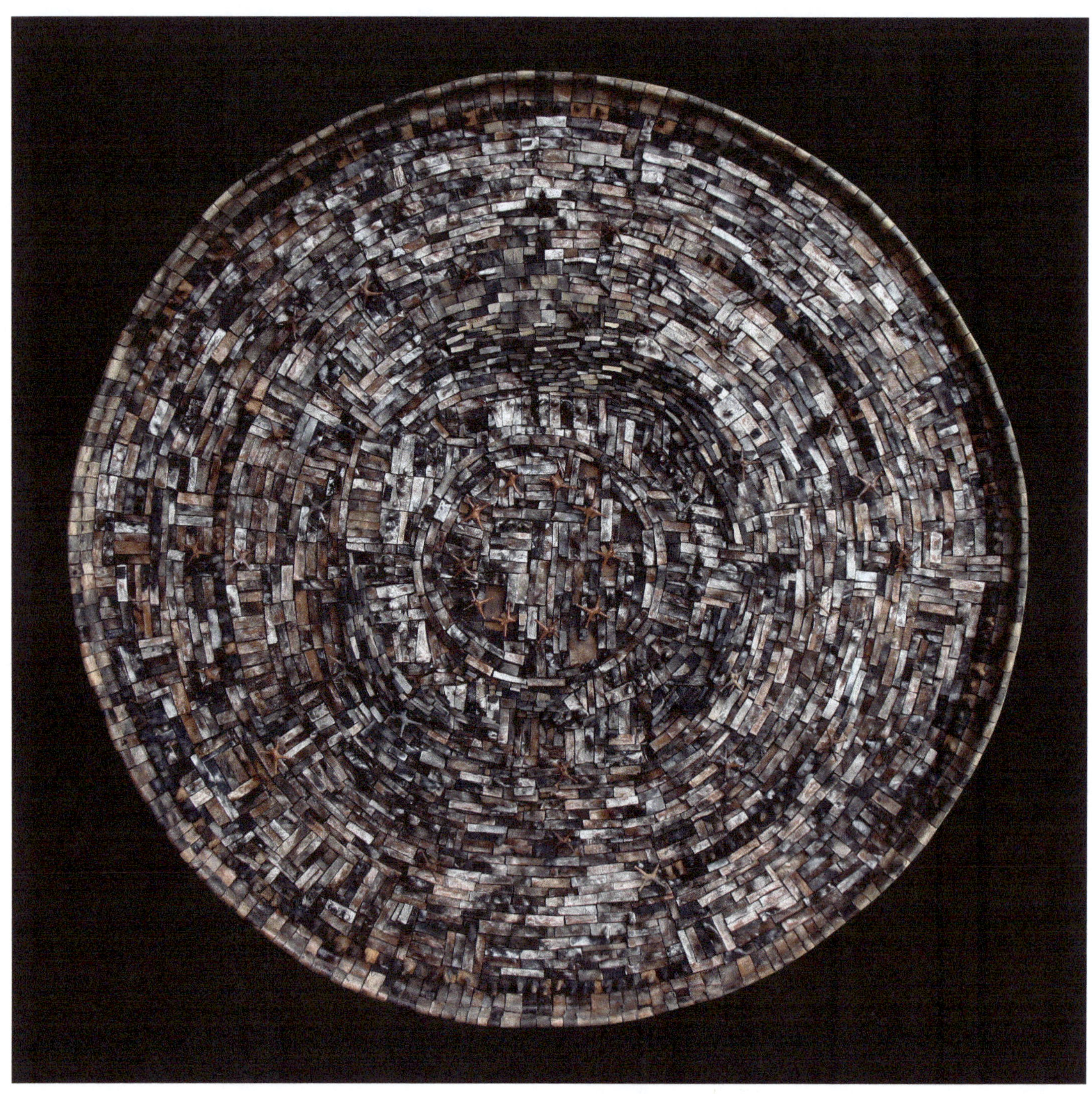

Plate - Why? (Cycle Man, where are you ? Night Visions). Red clay, engobe, glaze, soot, polyurethane, wooden base, 132x132x8 cm, 2023

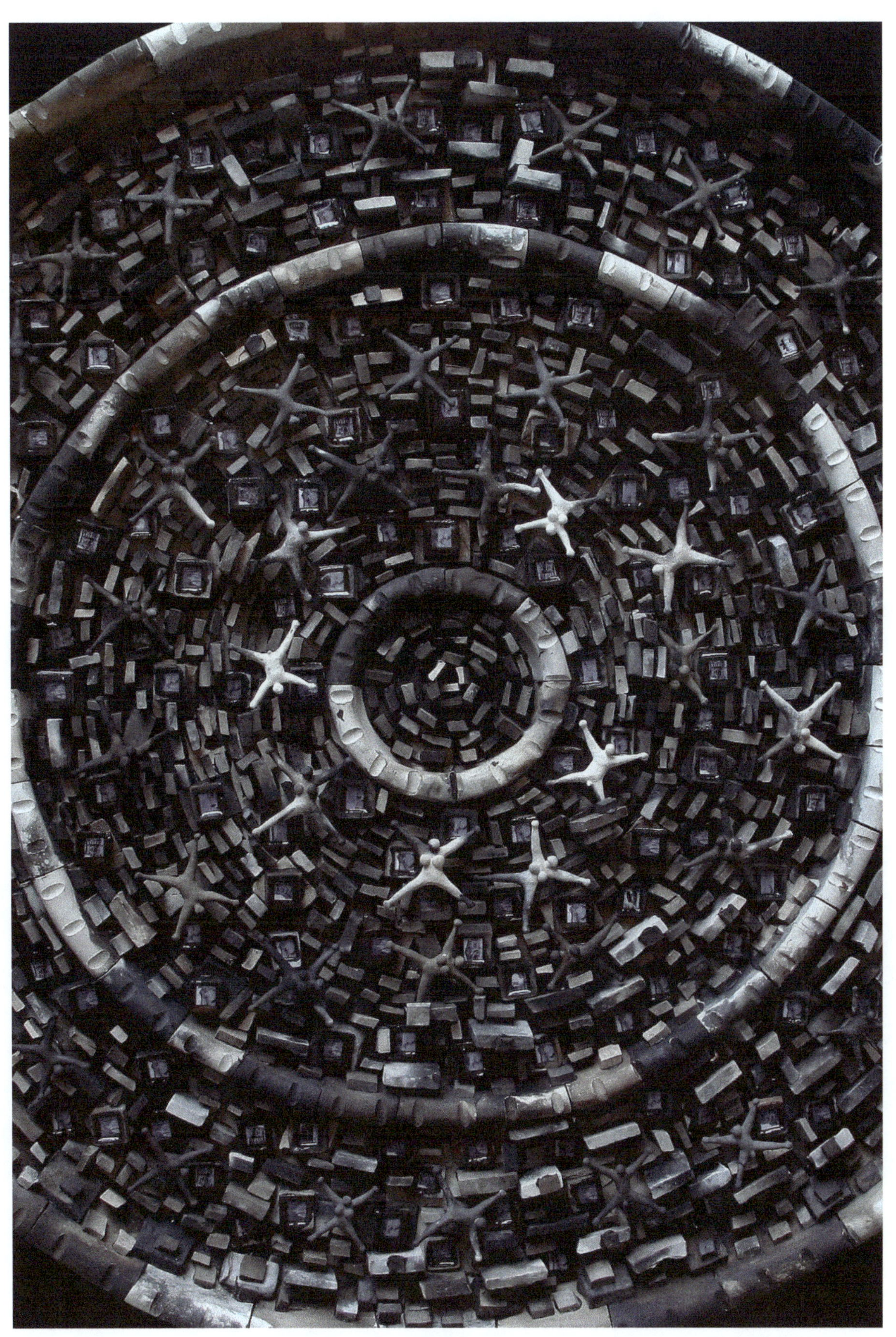

Plate - Panic (Cycle Man, where are you ? Night Visions). White clay, soot, resin, photo, polyurethane, 80x80x7 cm, 2023

JOANNA

joannanouveaustudio.co.uk

Joanna is a contemporary ink artist based in Sheffield, UK, inspired and influenced by the surrealistic approach of Salvador Dali and M.C. Escher. She is dedicated to working with abstract, fantasy pieces and aims to explore the beauty of the human spirit through her art. Joanna mainly works with black and white pen and ink drawings as well as acrylic painting, resulting in dramatic and surrealistic compositions that evoke an intricate, mysterious world. As an artist, she believes in using complex lines to create powerful concepts. Her work is driven by a passion to capture the underlying beauty and energy of things by honing into the fundamental line, exploring the limitless possibilities of the imagination. Her drawing doesn't reference recognisable form. The results are deconstructed to the extent that meaning is shifted and possible interpretation becomes multifaceted. By manipulating the viewer to create confusion, she creates intense personal moments masterfully created by means of rules and omissions, acceptance and refusal, luring the viewer round and round in circles. By applying abstraction, she often creates several practically identical works, upon which thoughts that have apparently just been developed are manifested: notes are made and then crossed out again, 'mistakes' are repeated. Her works are on the one hand touchingly beautiful, on the other hand painfully attractive. Again and again, the artist leaves us orphaned with a mix of conflicting feelings and thoughts.

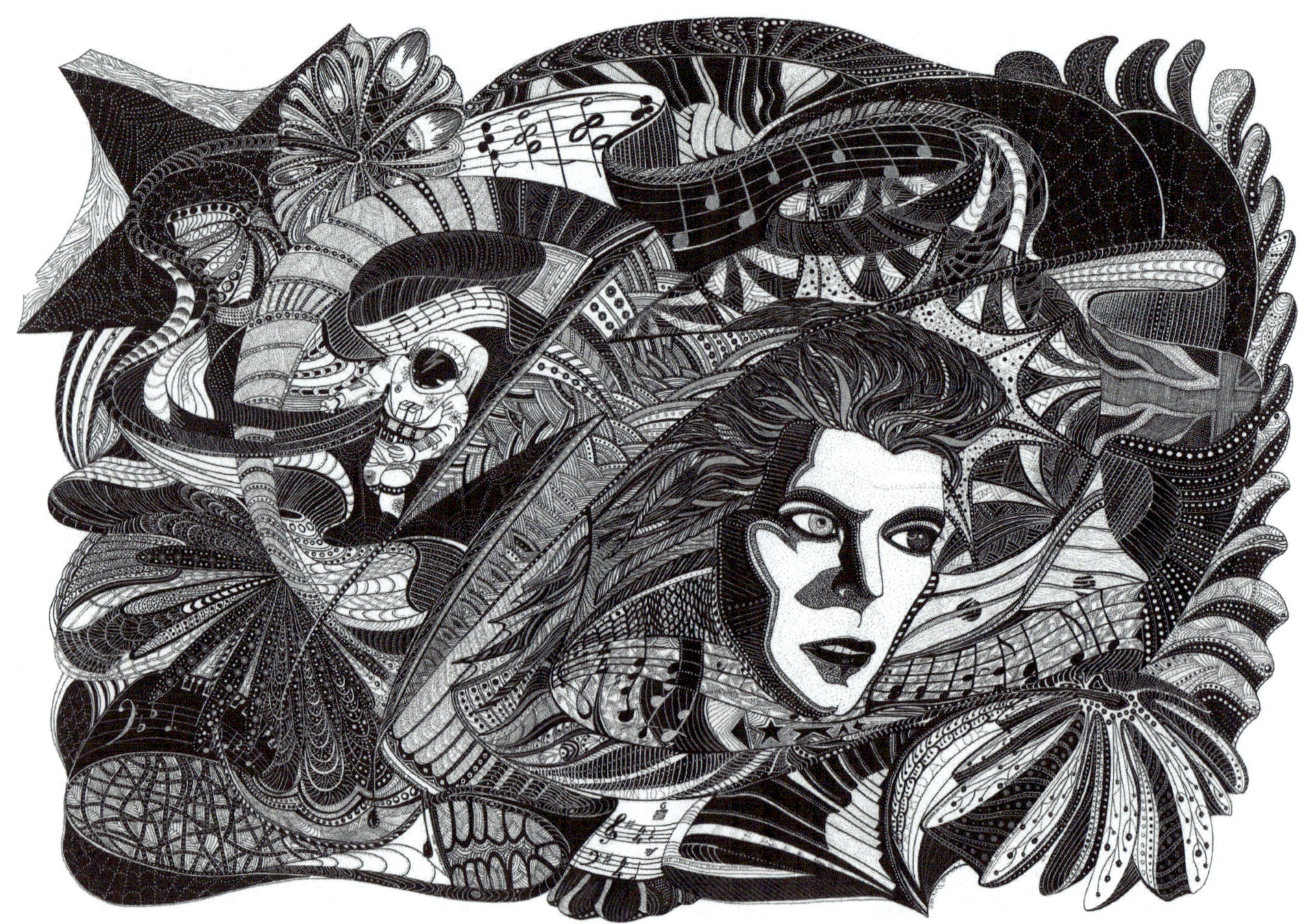

Bowie

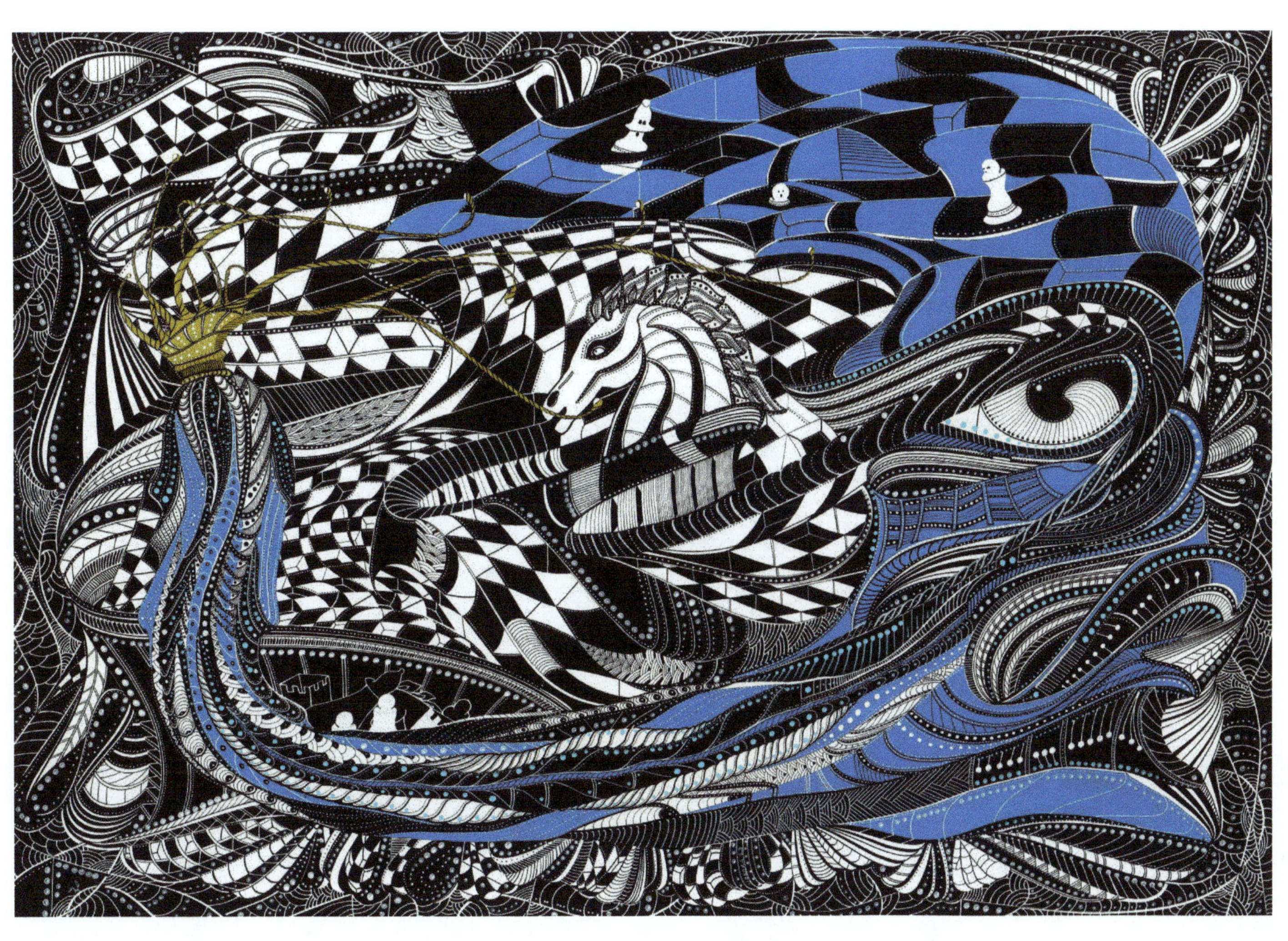

Queen's Gambit

Jane Gottlieb

janegottlieb.com

I have been expressing my joy of art since childhood. I scan my hand-painted prints and my library of 35mm Kodachrome color transparencies taken over 50 years years, and paint, collage and enhance them with Photoshop, creating a wonderful new magical reality.

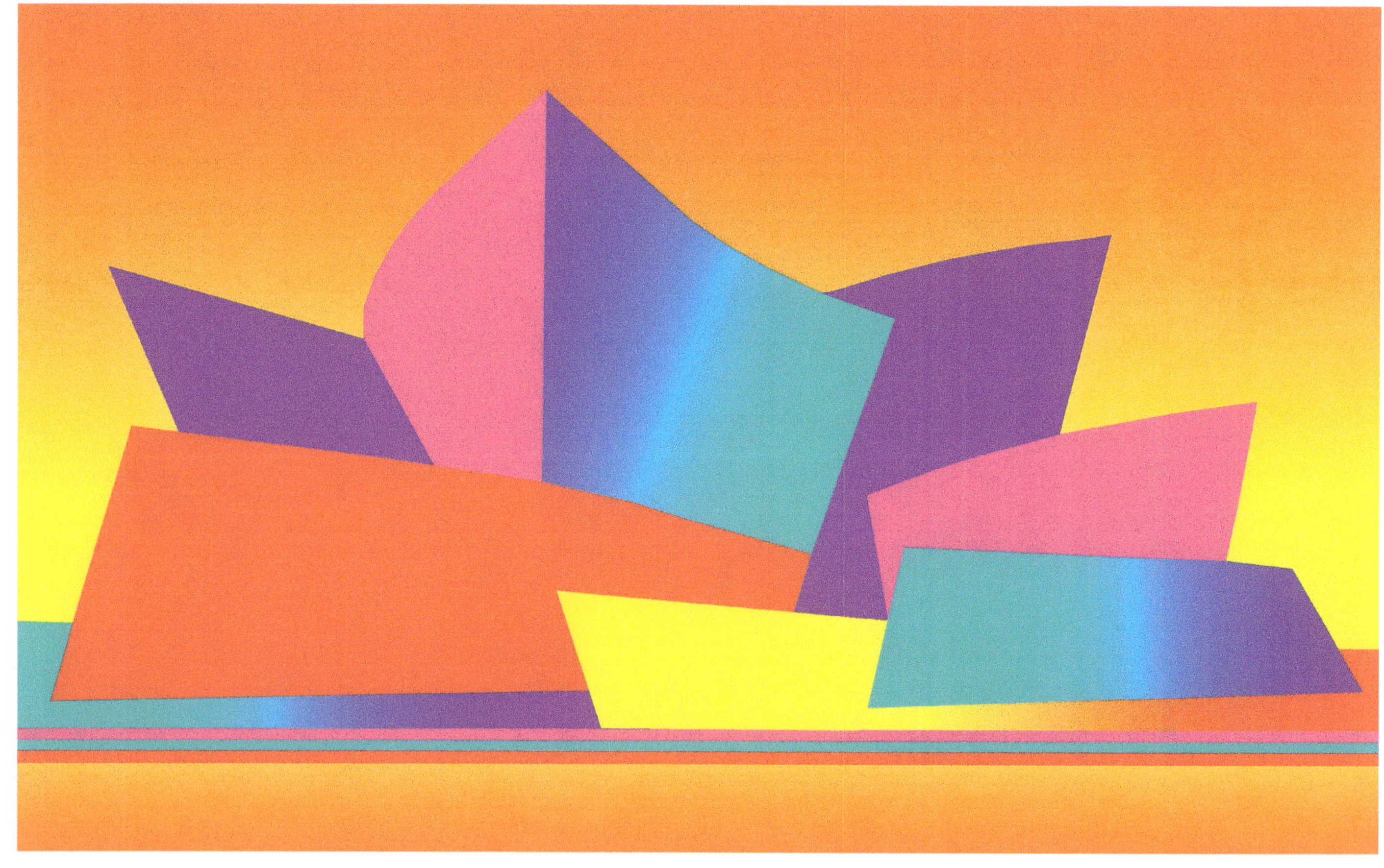

Wonderland

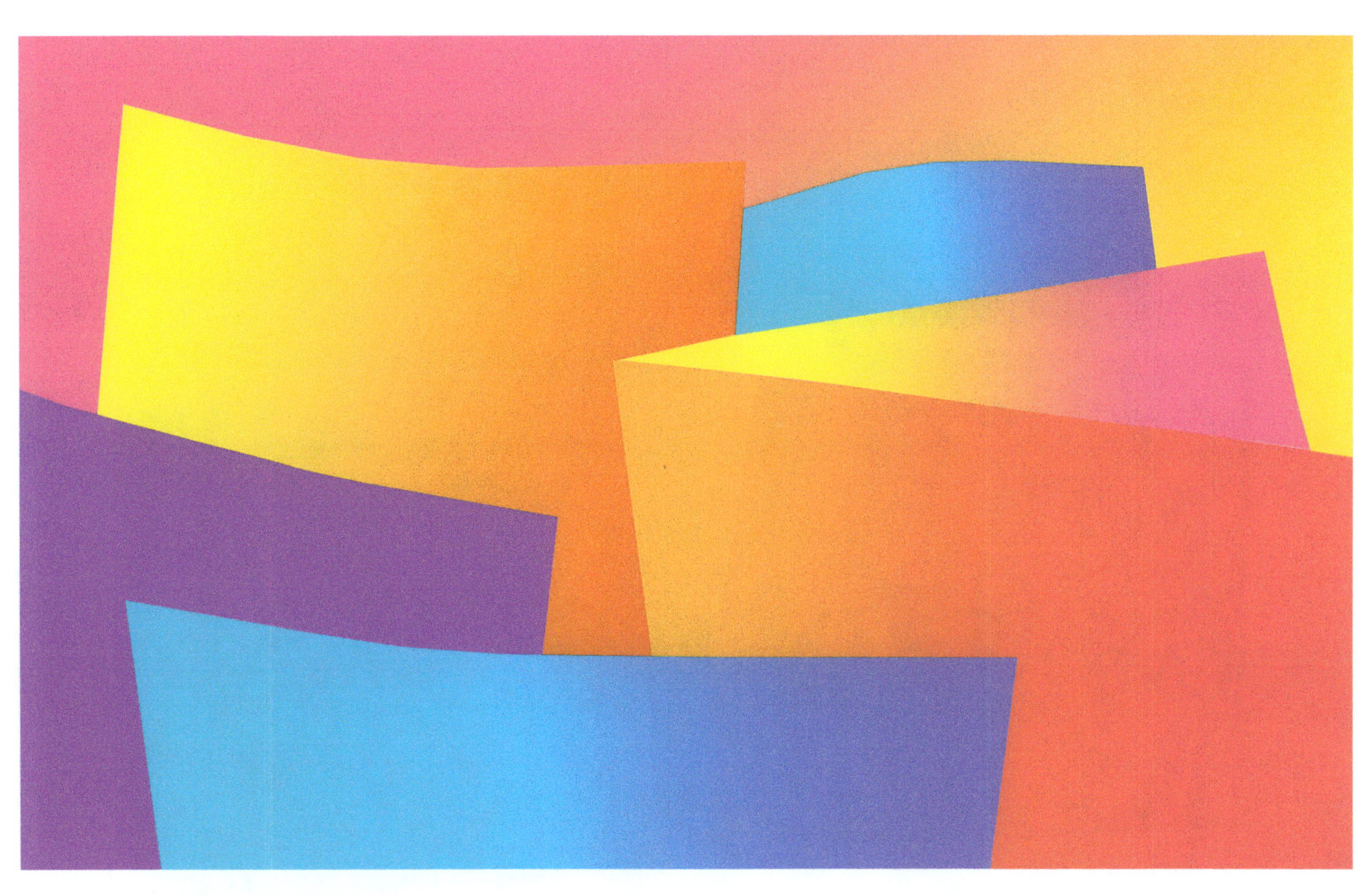

Shape of Things

Jehan Ali

f-nan.com

"I am here and there, at the undulating indents, contriving a thought, sinking in it deeply, to resurface on a paper before it extinguishes in the charcoaled heap. Or blend it brightly on a more rigid or softer surface. I like to seize fleeting moments and depict them. It begins blurry then focused. Sometimes it starts with a word, sometimes with an image and manifolds from within to outwards, or vice versa. Different angles give different perspectives. It captivates me to look through the multifarious reflections of a kaleidoscope. Where time, light, vibrant colours, various patterns and events, change constantly, with every rotation and twist. As nothing is stable in this life, but the truth, it impels me: The purpose of life is to seek the truth… the more you head away from it, the more it gets distorted… Distorted patterns are intolerable, neither harmonious, nor peaceful, and not even funny like carnival mirrors. From the havoc, I gather shreds, strips, and pieces, press them gently, stitch them. They coagulate at their borders, layers coalesce, unite and heal to whole. The chaos is calmed but stillness is temporary. Repeat: Movement either deliberate or rapid, is needed, for a new beginning."

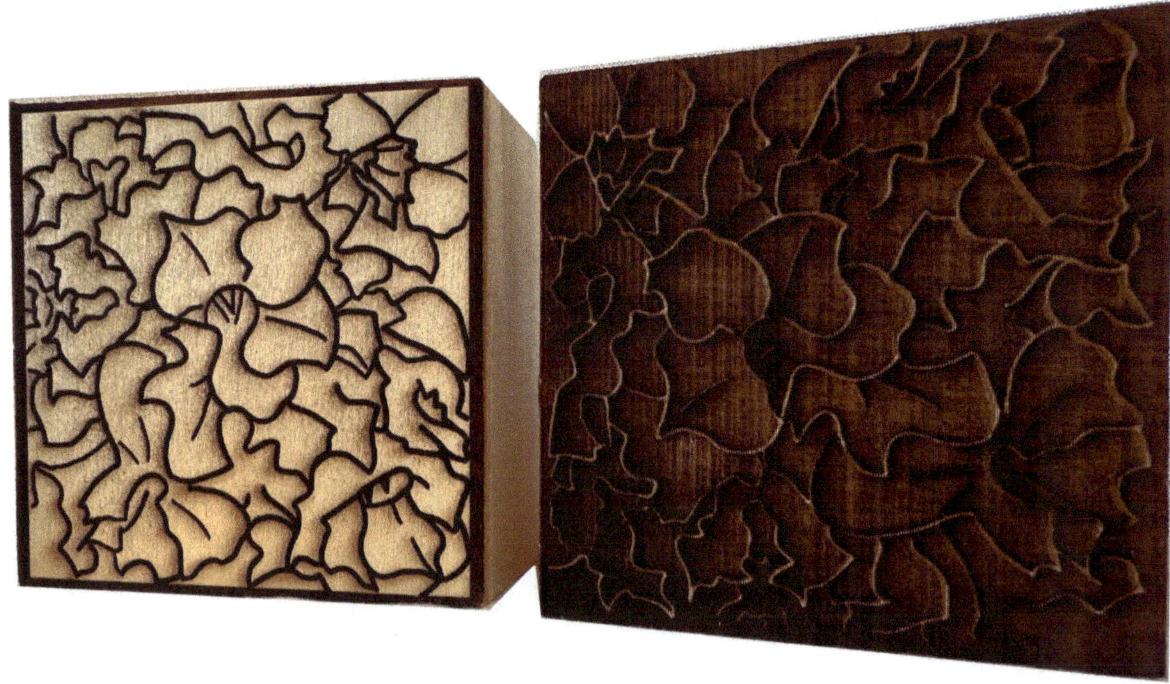

*Desert Rose I & II, laser cut basswood block, 10.2 * 10.2 * 5 cm, 2023.*

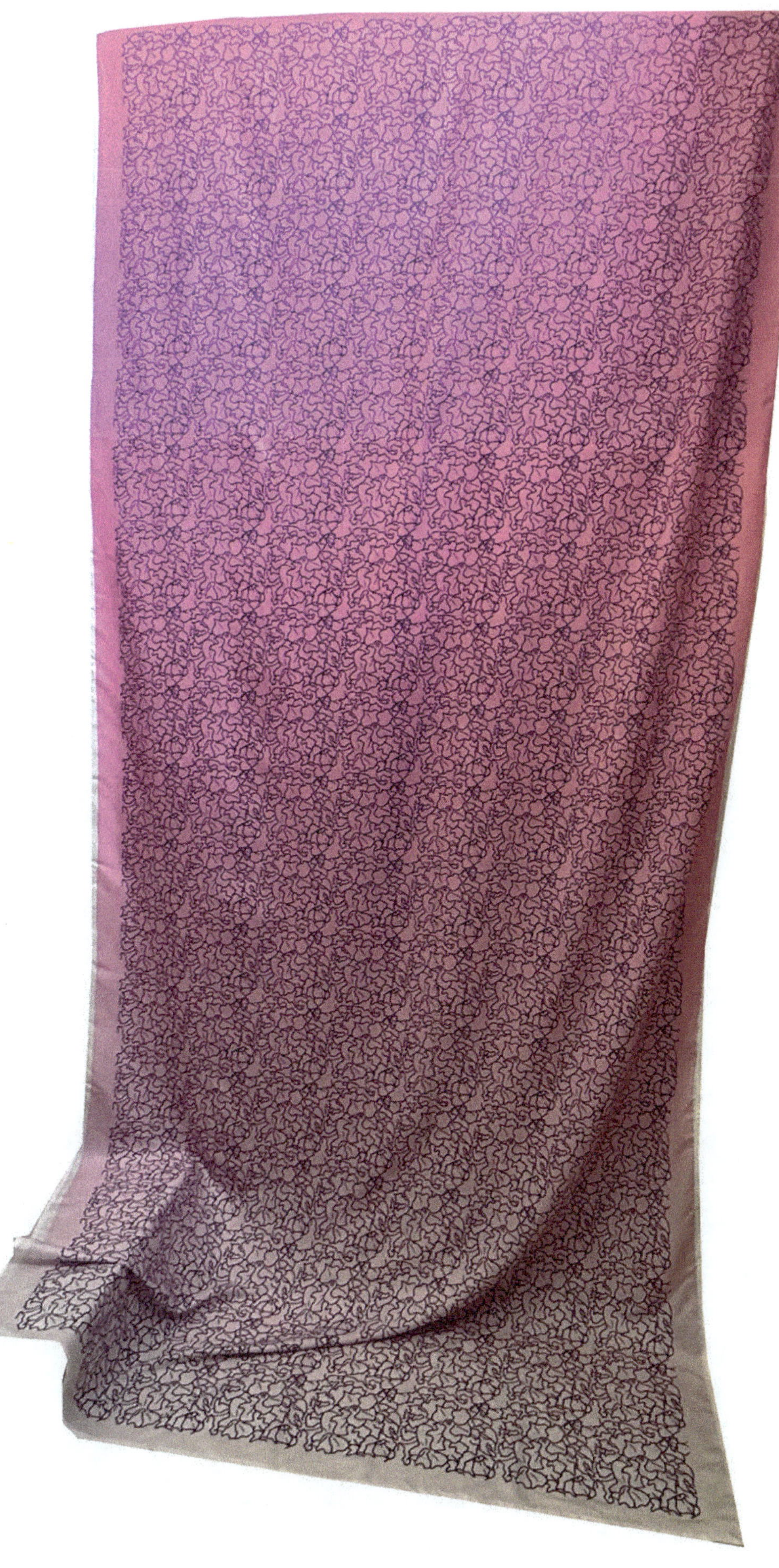

*Desert Rose Drape, Vegan Silk, 300 * 145 cm, 2024.*

Jeong-Ah Zhang

jeongahzhang.com

My life and art are based on my own philosophical thoughts and experiences. I am interested in the philosophy of immanence and transcendence on all beings, And this means that I try to focus on the essence of life by establishing core values, and at the same time, sublimate it into my works. I look at the relationship between human and nature and the universe from a very broader perspective. I think all thoughts and consciousness are breath, The breath is the switch between the conscious and the subconscious mind, It's a connected cycle of creation and extinction. And It's a soul resonance beyond the time frame. I try to listen to all the conceptions of all things, have an open mind and remember what resonates.

Therefore, my surrealism is simply is not just an exploration of the unconscious. It's a question of will and philosophy, constant introspection. I value awakening and balance, and try to embody the meaning of existence and non-existence, and the nature of things in an implicit and artistic way. My art is intended to make the viewers think, but my delivery is intended to make the viewers listen to their own inner voice. It makes people, including myself, think beyond reality and into the essence of reality. As I look back on that afternoon so long ago that presented my life, When remembering the experience of seeing the interconnected nature of all things.. The flash point of all creation in the present moment is immortality.

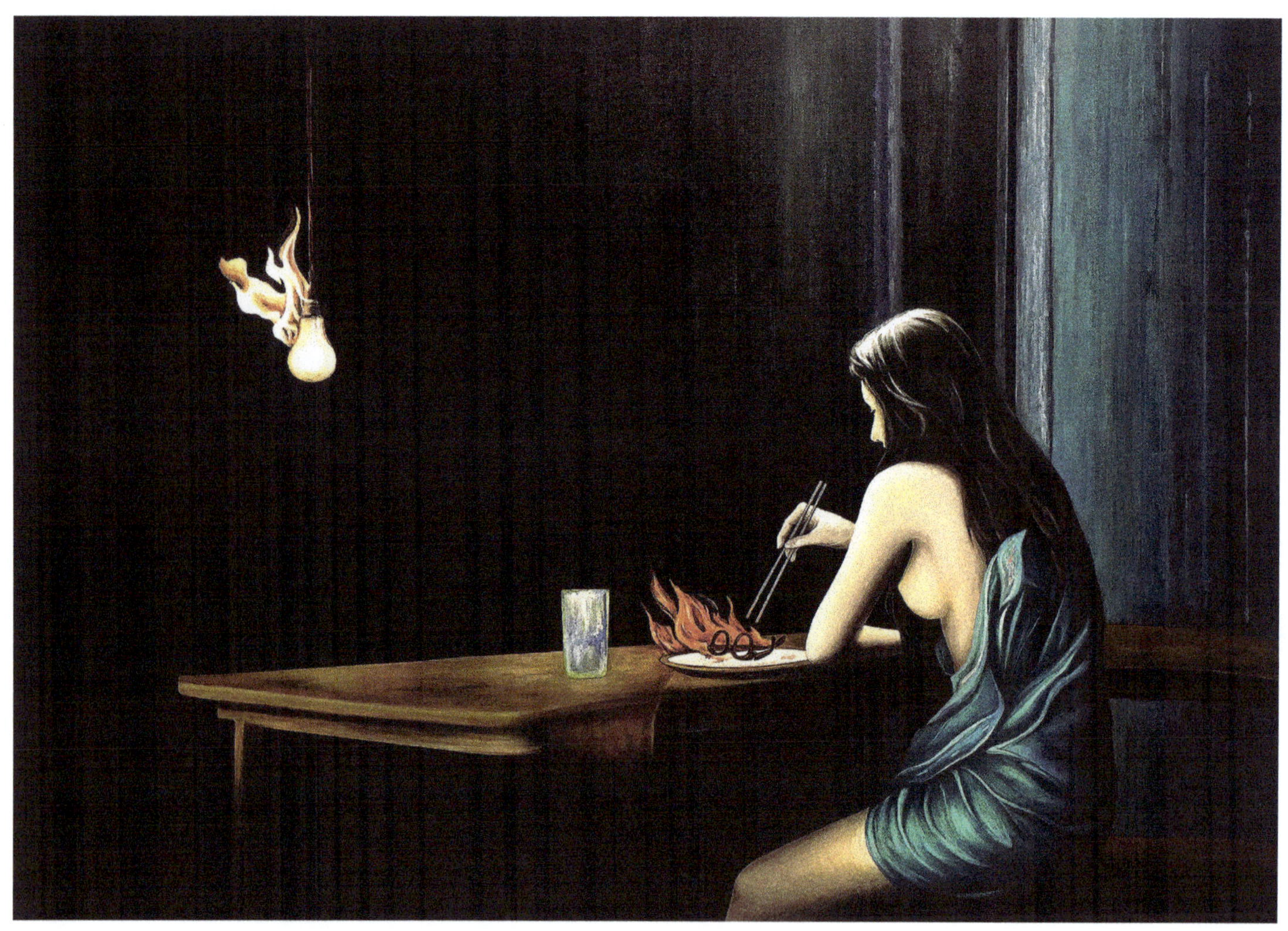

A Quiet Meal

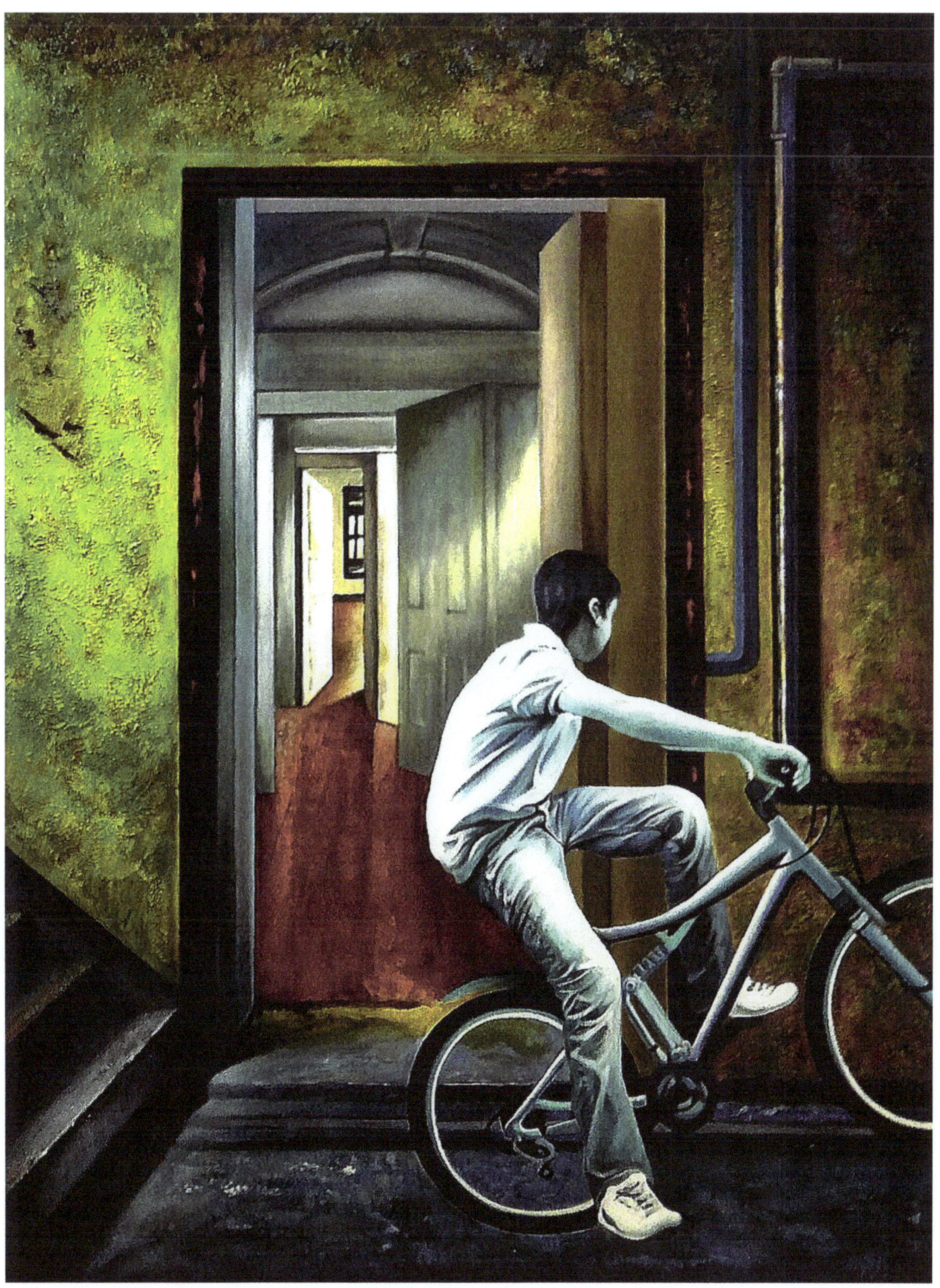

Repetition of The phenomenon

Jette van der Lende

jette.no

My paintings tell stories by focusing on what is important in life - humour, social, political and personal issues that affect us all. I portray objects that symbolize these issues, combined in purposeful ways, now often against wooden backgrounds, as I give complete attention on the objects, I like to show the wood as a frame of nature. Even though certain subject matters and the circumstances or situations they represent may be difficult for some to contemplate, I seek the beauty within them regardless. By painting portraits of common things, I remove all connotations that may relate to specific people, places or times. It is the universality of these symbols and what they represent that is significant-- to all of us, no matter who we are. At the same time, I paint in such a way that these compositions can be taken entirely at face value and appreciated on purely aesthetic terms, as classic representational still-lifes, without the necessity of referencing anything beyond that. But the invitation is always extended to explore as deeply and thoughtfully as one might wish.

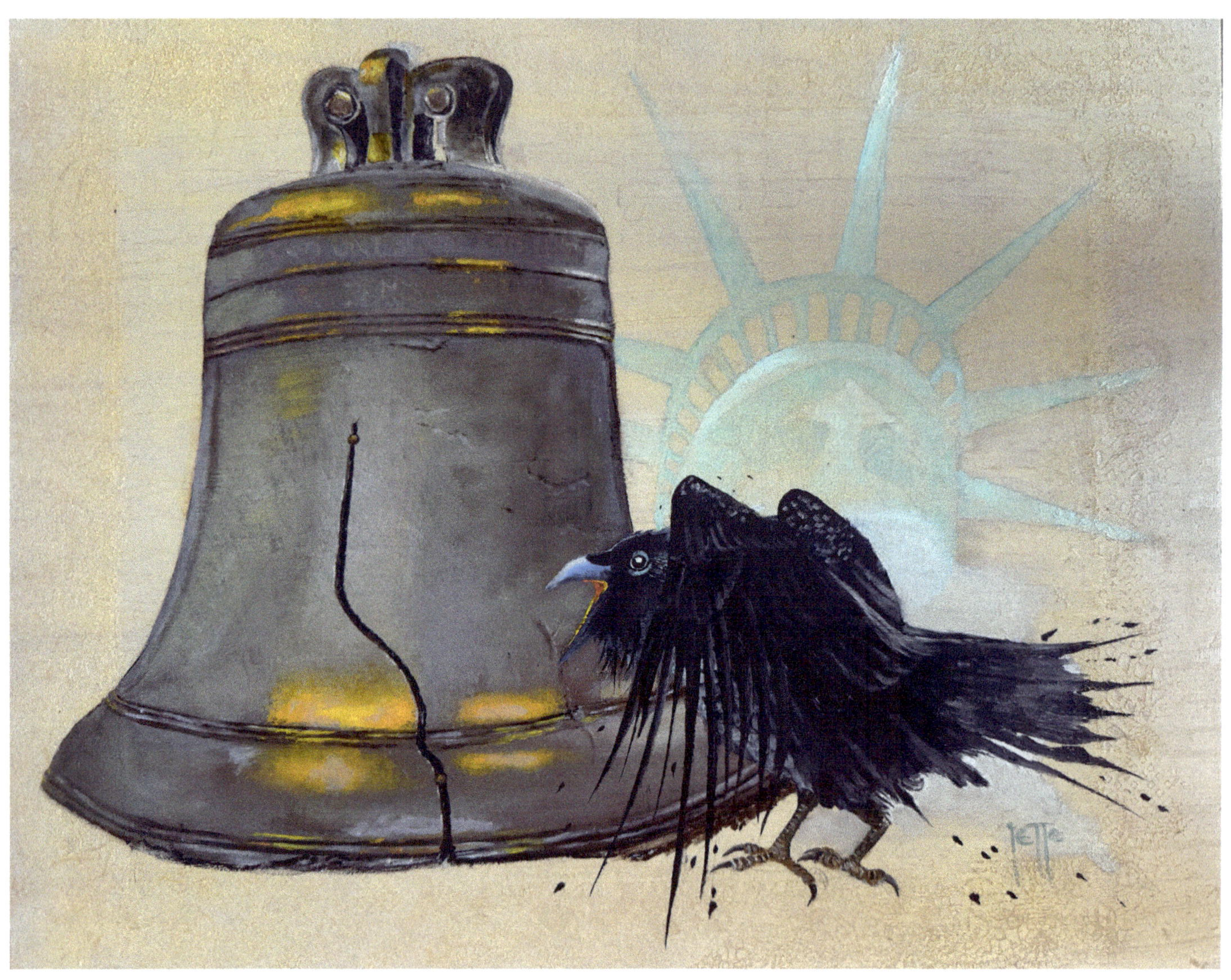

Our Fragile Freedom

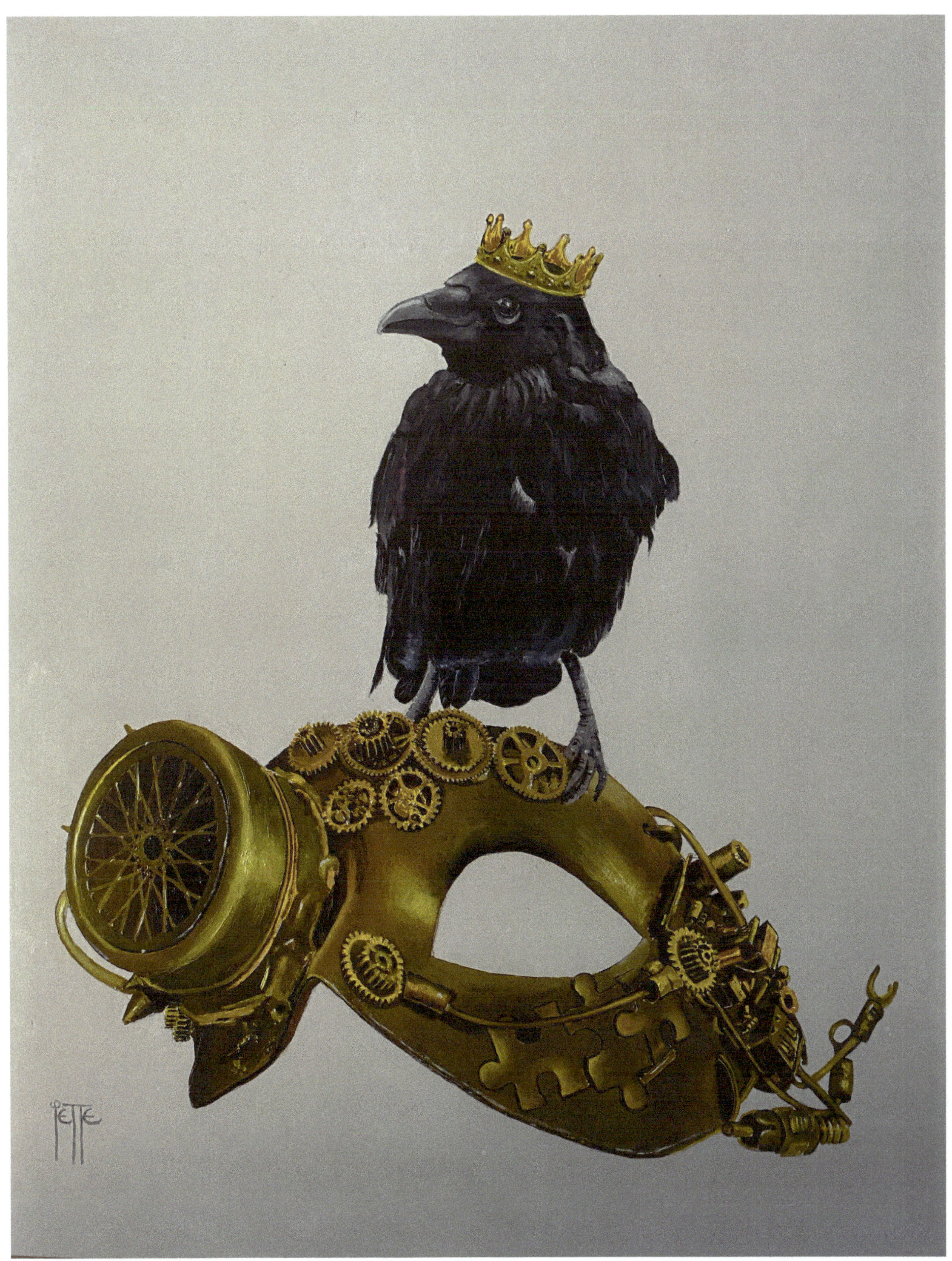

Hugin's Omen

Josef Weidner

josef-weidner.de

Kein Künstler ist vom Himmel gefallen, der nicht durch
Fleiß, Übung und Individualität glänzte.

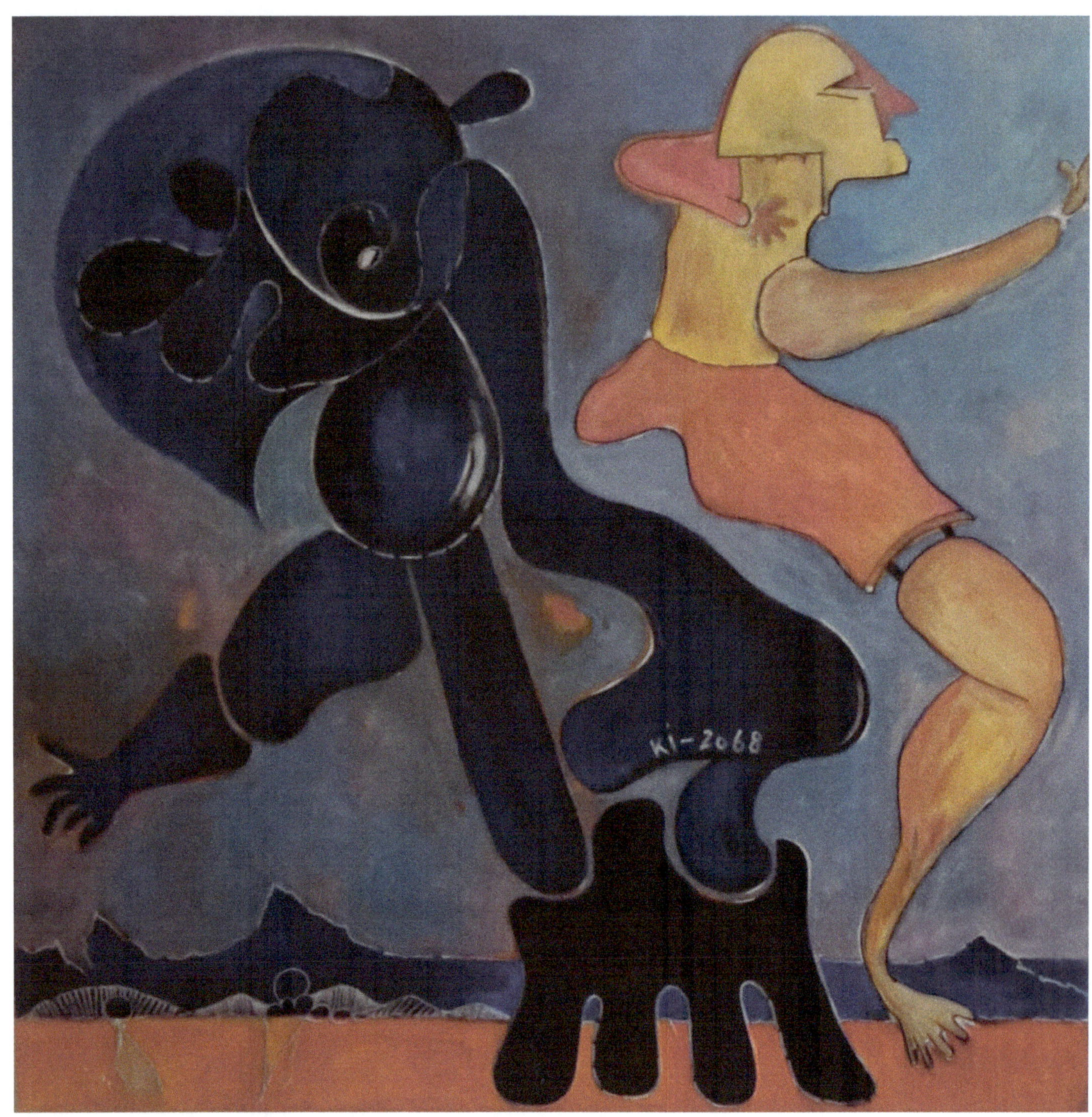

KI 2068

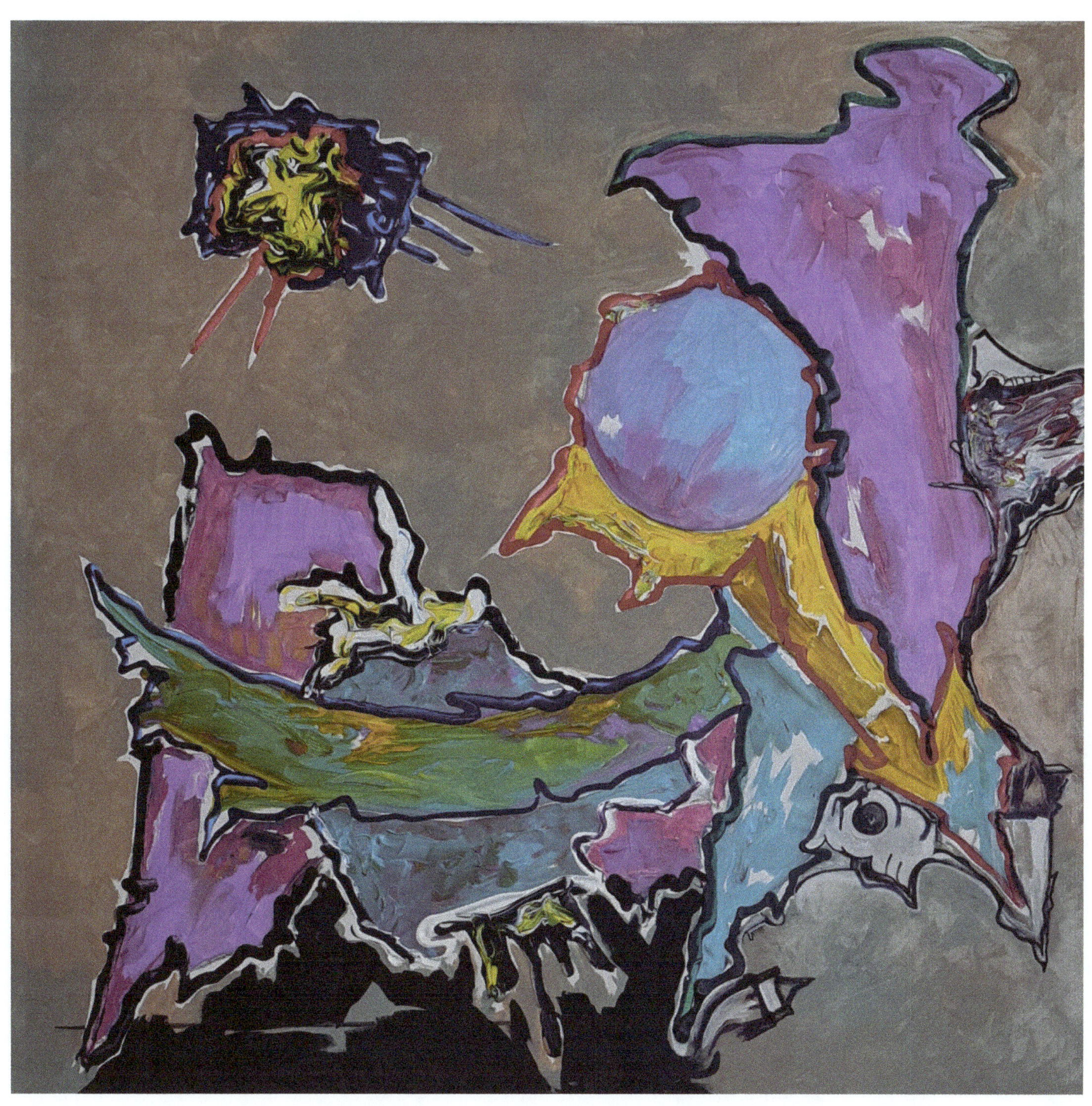

The Dancer 2

Judith Dupree Beale

jdbeale.com

Creating visual work remains life confirming. The process of mark making is akin to breathing for many who attempt to say what they have to say on paper, canvas or any other support. For me, the need to express interior thoughts, feelings and interpretations of experiences in an expressive manner has kept me working all these many years. The process is sustenance.

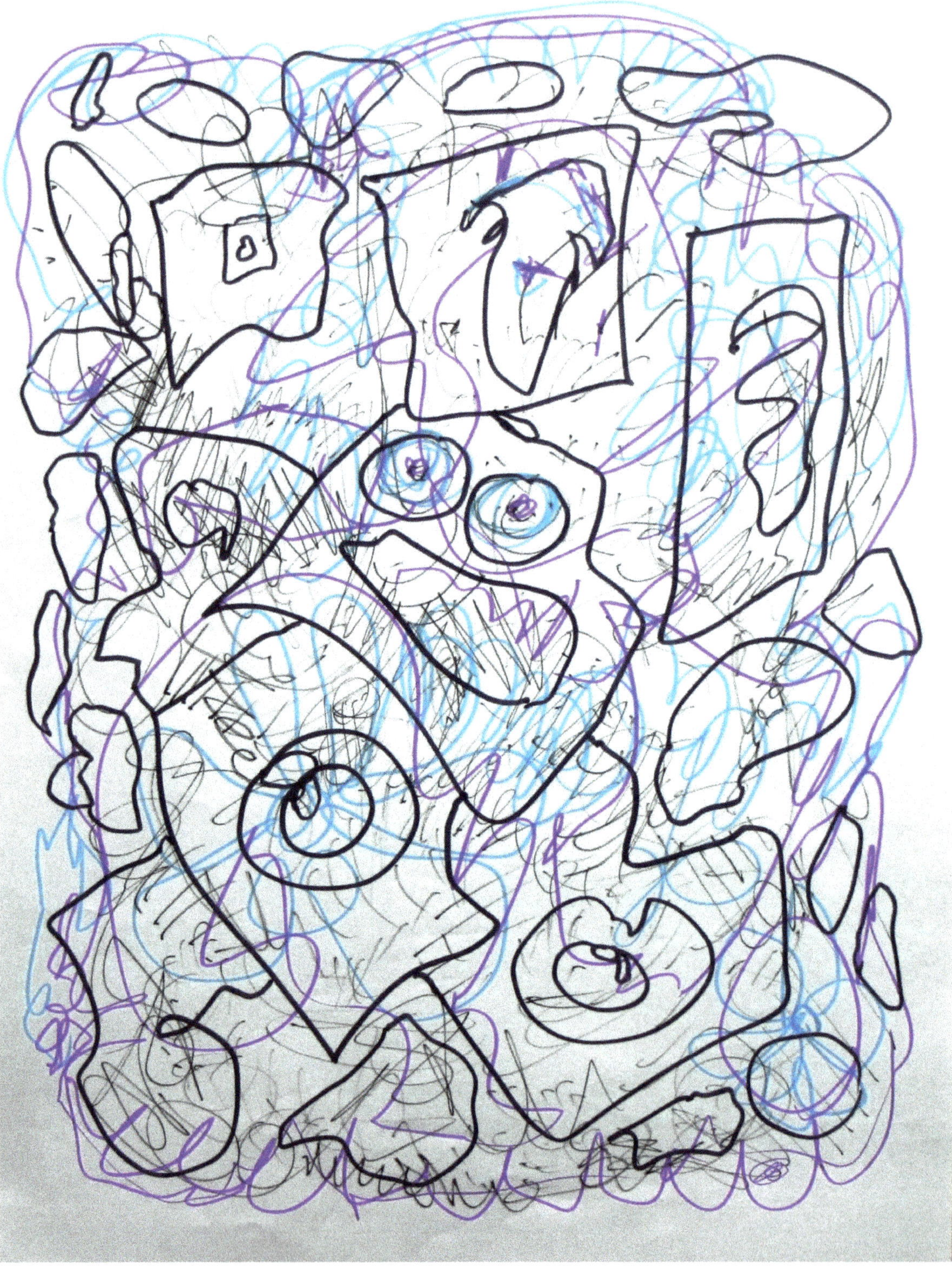

Mark Maker Abstract 9143

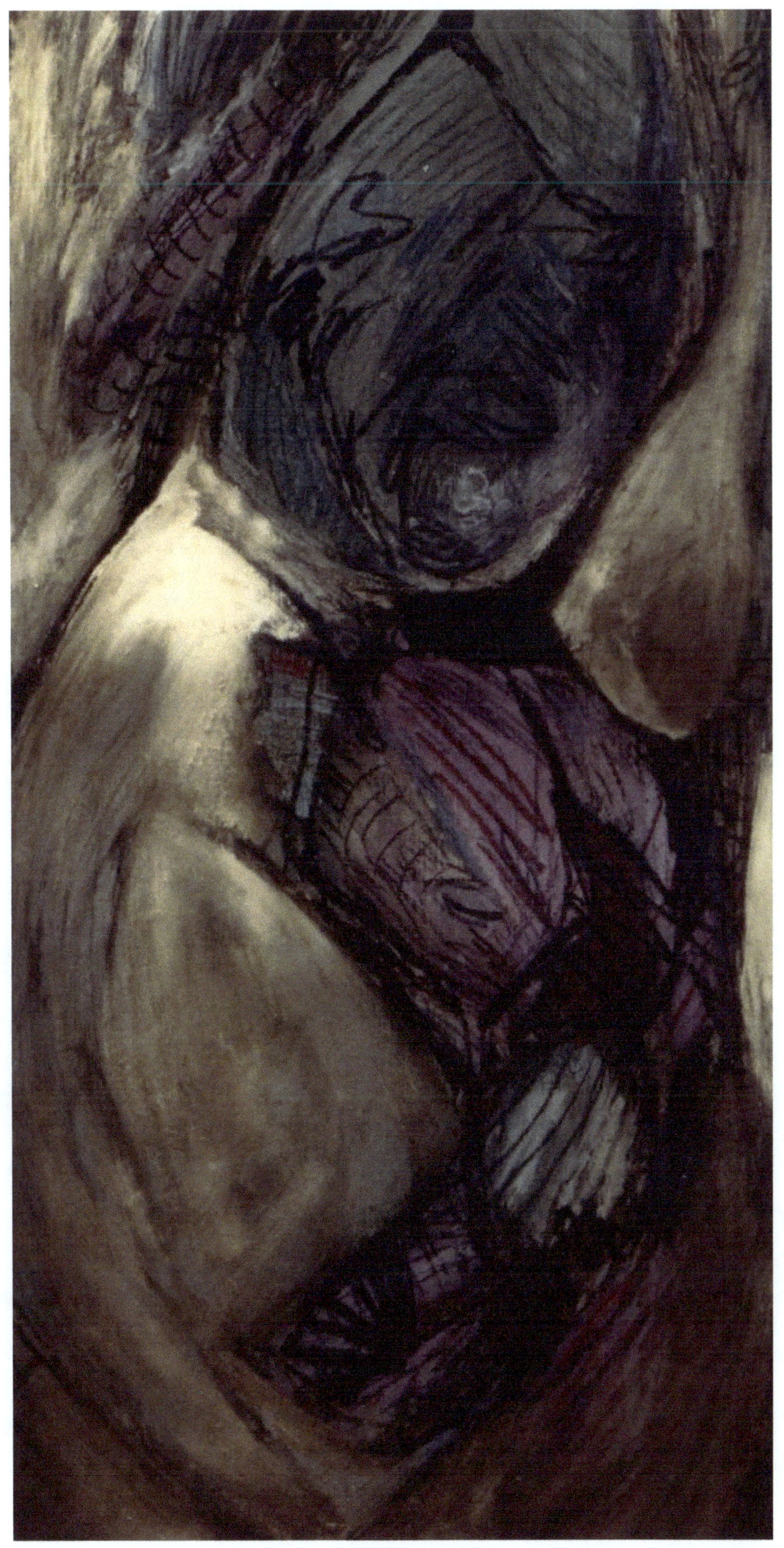

Fertility Figure

Julie Reby Waas

instagram.com/intuitive.abstract.art

My elaborate acrylic and watercolor drawings, and acrylic paintings, take shape instinctively. My process is a spiritual experience guided by my heart and intuition. When I create, I shut out the rational side of my brain and let the subconscious and intuitive voice speak through my hand and onto the paper. I often start with a simple idea, such as vines, hearts, and geometric forms, and let the outline take shape organically. Sometimes, in the case of my Rubik's Cubism series, I use my love of geometry and the randomness of the Rubik's Cube to inspire me. I trust my intuition and enjoy the thrill of seeing where it will take me. I use many recurring symbols in my work: vines, Venn diagrams, and geometric & jigsaw puzzle-like designs. To me, these symbols represent friendship, connection, common ground, and fragments coming together to create a bigger picture, which all relate to my belief that everything and everyone is interrelated in some way, and when we come together in friendship and strength we create a beautiful tapestry. I want my pieces to brighten my viewers' lives, make them pause in their busy life, and bring a smile to their face.

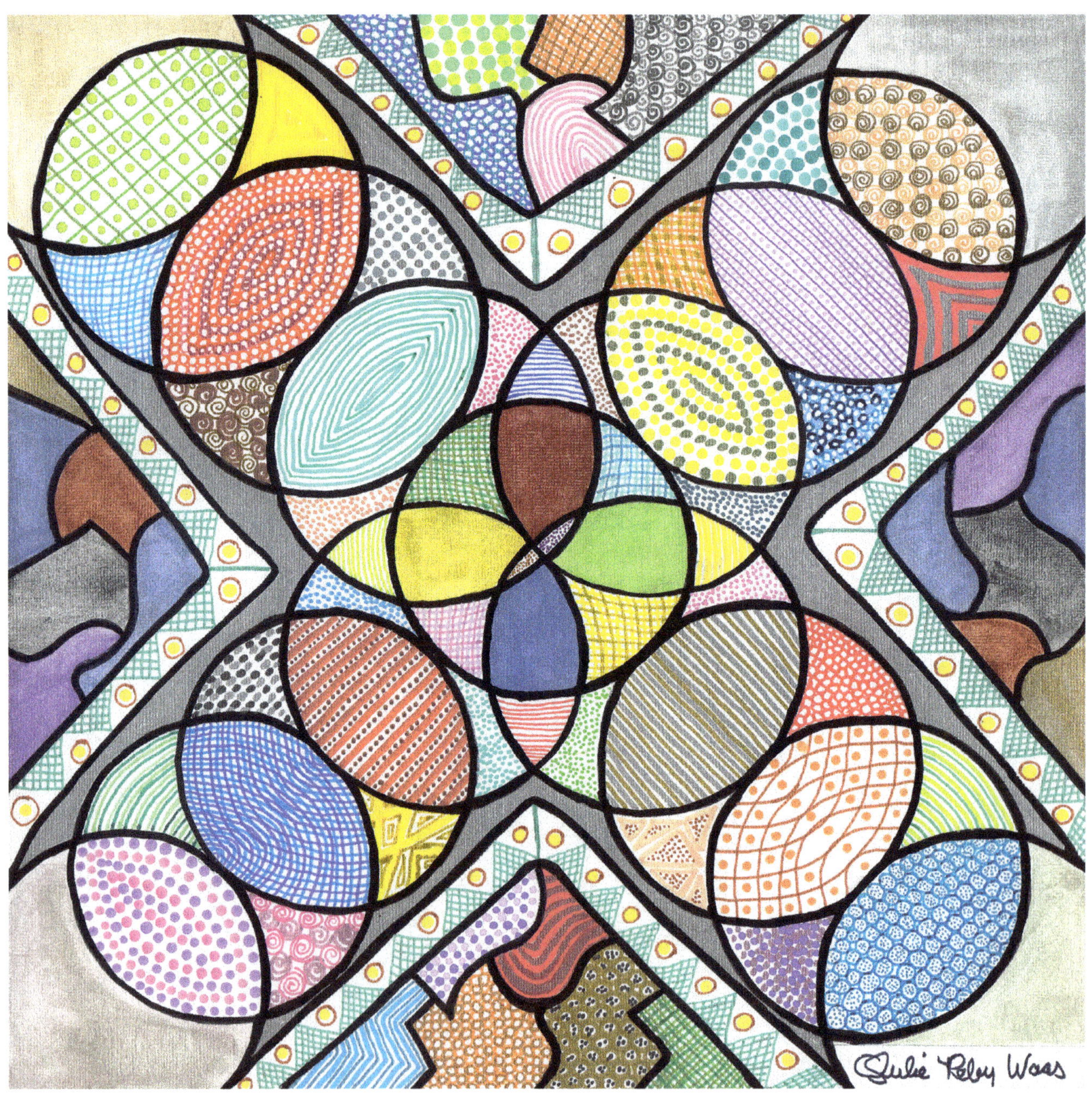

Intersection

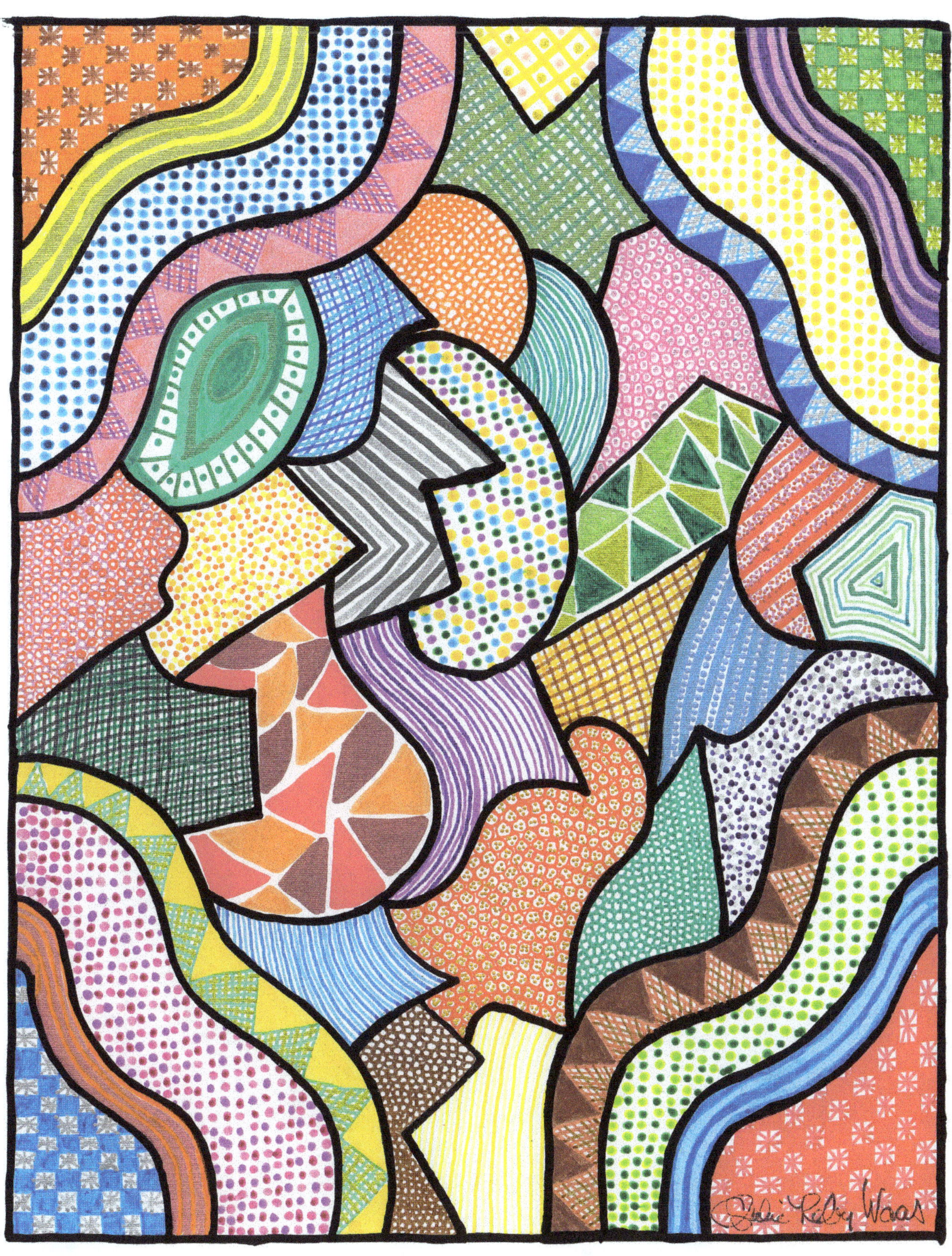

Jigsaw

Karin Monschauer

karinmonschauer.ch

It all started thanks to the embroidery technique that allowed me, over the years, to develop a personal visual and practical connection between colors and shapes. Digital art is undoubtedly the medium that allows me to reach an expressive thought rich in geometric figures, always placed in harmony with different chromatic shades. From the contemporary I combine, thanks to the computer technology, structures dear to the geometry and colors with always pulsating nuances. In this way, the universes that I am going to determine, constantly stimulate me at the artistic level and arise from the study of past civilizations together with their architectures. For example: the tradition of the ancient carpet, the history of the pre-Columbian Native Americans such as the Mayas, the Aztecs and the Incas, the Indo-European cultures such as the Byzantine empire up to the African peoples. I combine all that has existed in millennia of human history with contemporary taste. My artistic research, which is completed with a predilection for the Dutch engraver / graphic designer Maurits Cornelis Escher and mathematics, aims to communicate positive feelings such as serenity, happiness and tranquility. My personal compositional verve is experiencing a very fruitful creative moment, allowing me a constant, almost inexhaustible, creation of colors and geometric figures.

My Art simply wants to be a cultivated and enjoyable fun, aiming only at the soul of the people who are in front of my works. My abstraction and dynamism live in continuous processing for weaving compositions that are constantly in motion.

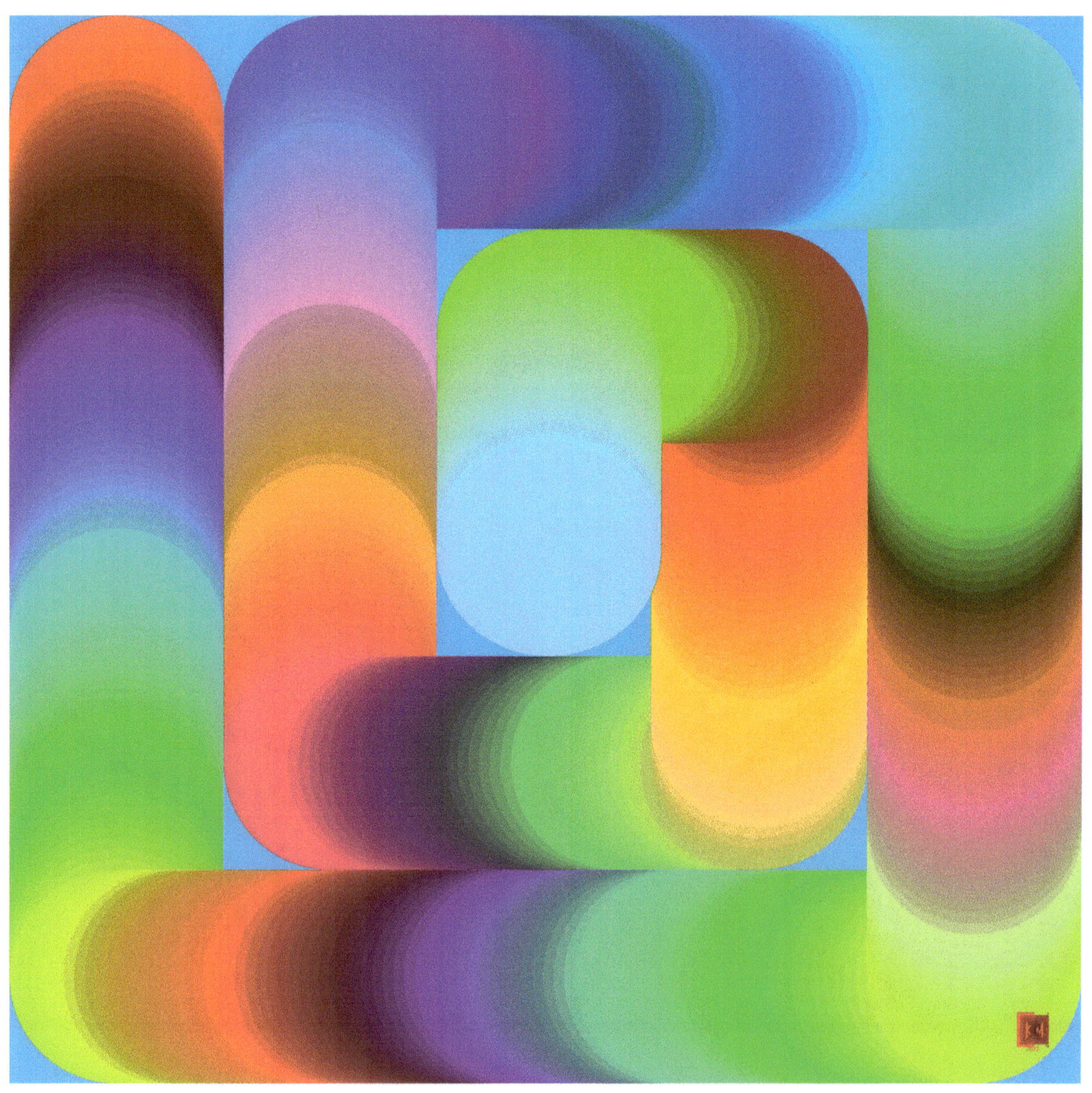

Spirale quadrata

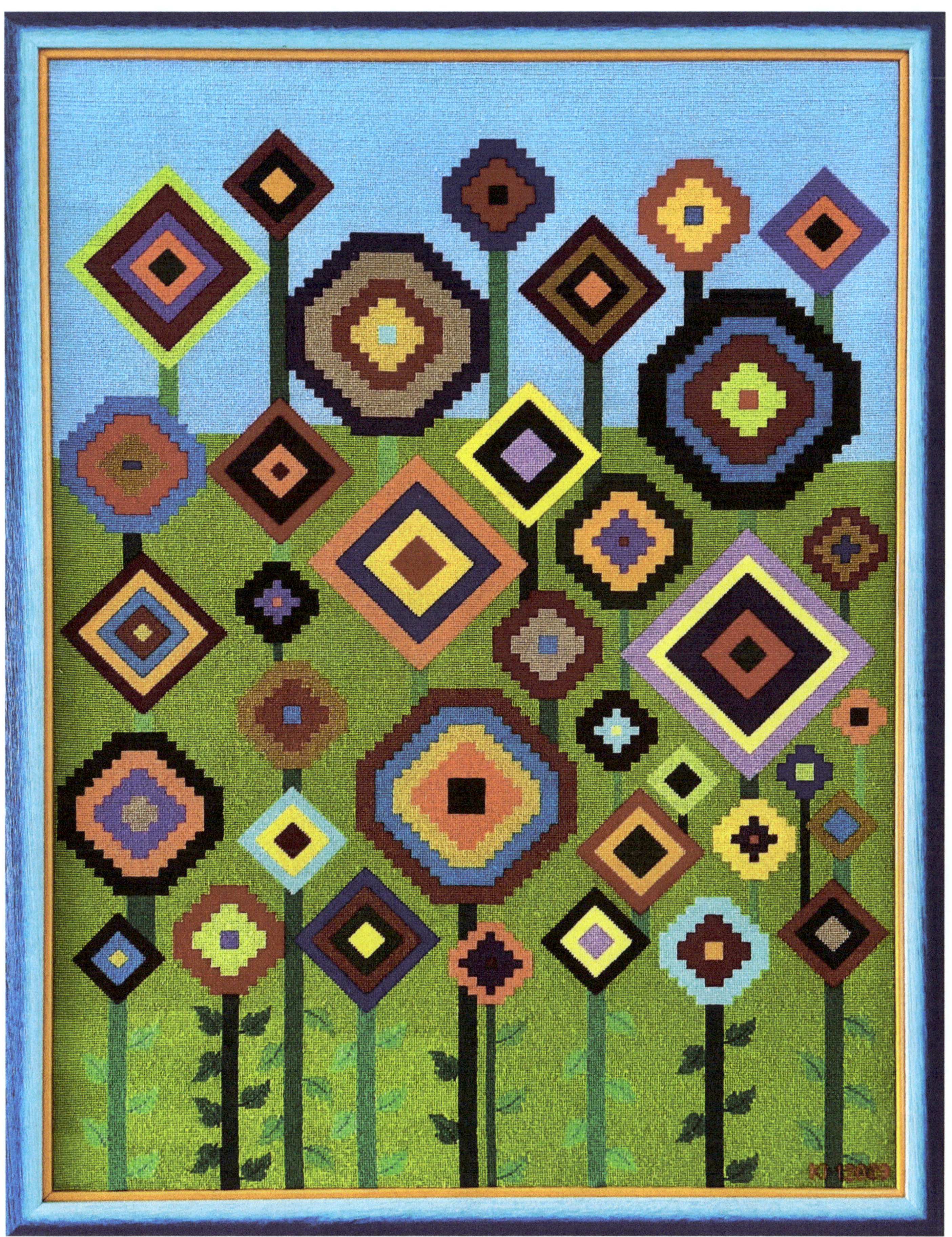

Fiori autunnali

Kat Kleinman

katkleinmanart.com

Art allows me an avenue to express my hope for the world. I am a photographer and collage artist, focusing on unique floral collages, as well as leaf and succulent compositions, because they symbolize my enthusiasm for using color to bring about positive changes, starting from within. The intention of my work has always been to make people feel better, even for a moment. I often use dozens of flowers in a single floral collage, a process that is both meditative and inspirational. The beauty of a floral collage represents healing, because fractions of color combine to create a new cohesive form. I am dedicated to creating art inspired by compassion, meditation and hope.

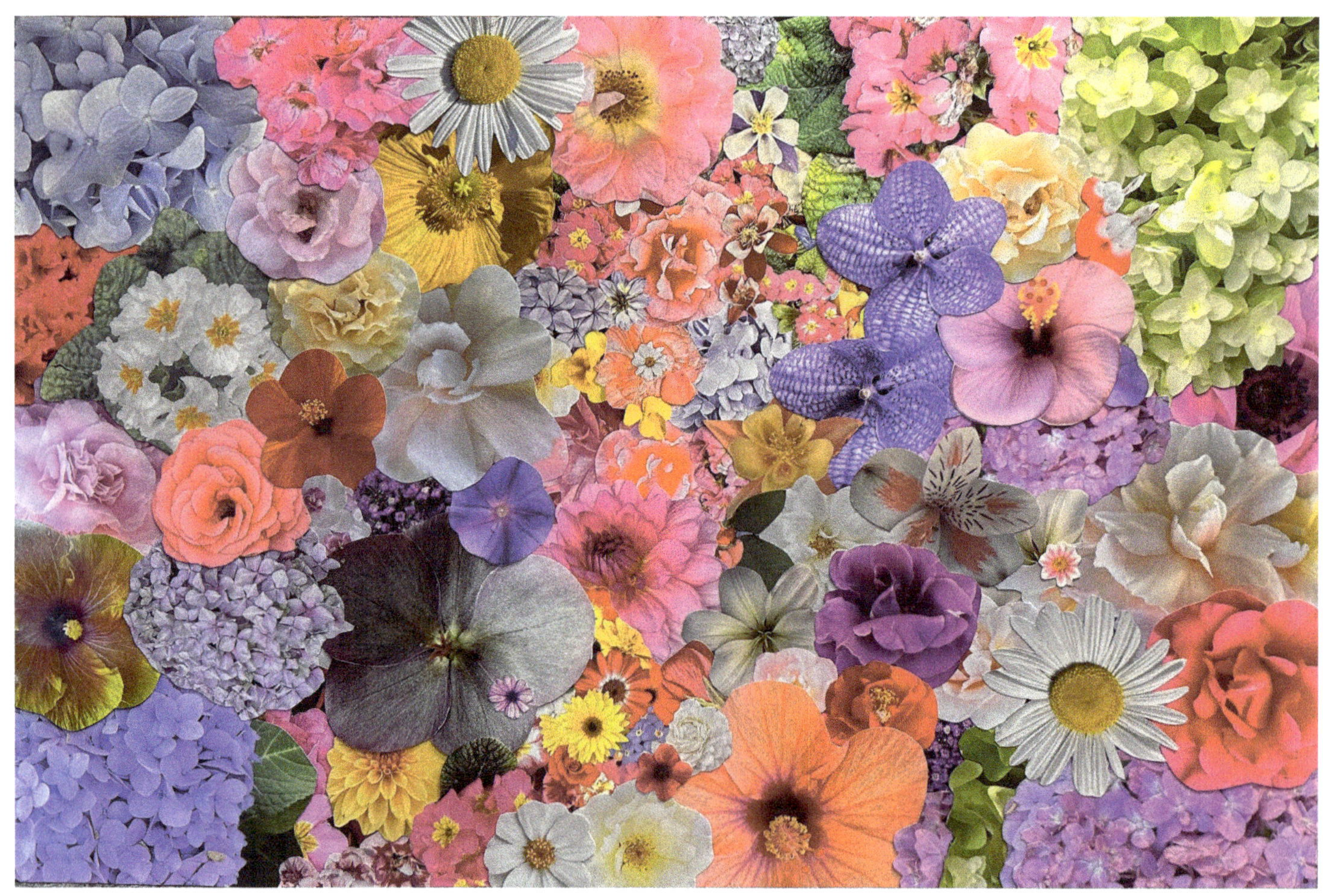

Out Of The Dark

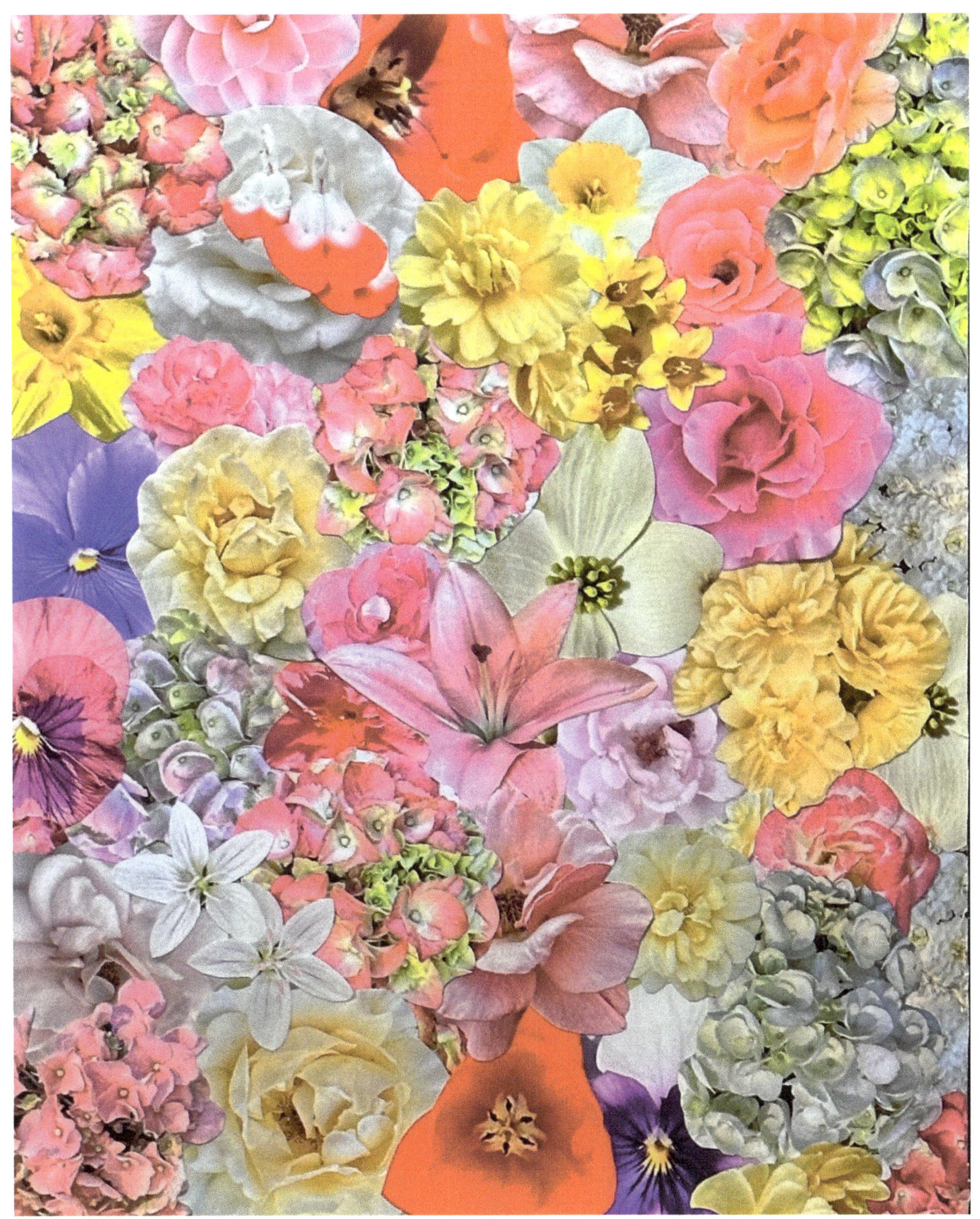

Buttery Bliss

Katja Lührs

katjaluehrs.com

The variety of colors and shapes of flowers, trees and leaves has fascinated me since I was a child. The power of the sun and its play with light and shadow in nature are characterized by: "grace - joy of life - confidence - peace and serenity". With pictures you can capture the beauties of nature. Because what you love, you also protect. That's why my motto for my pictures is: "Save the earth".

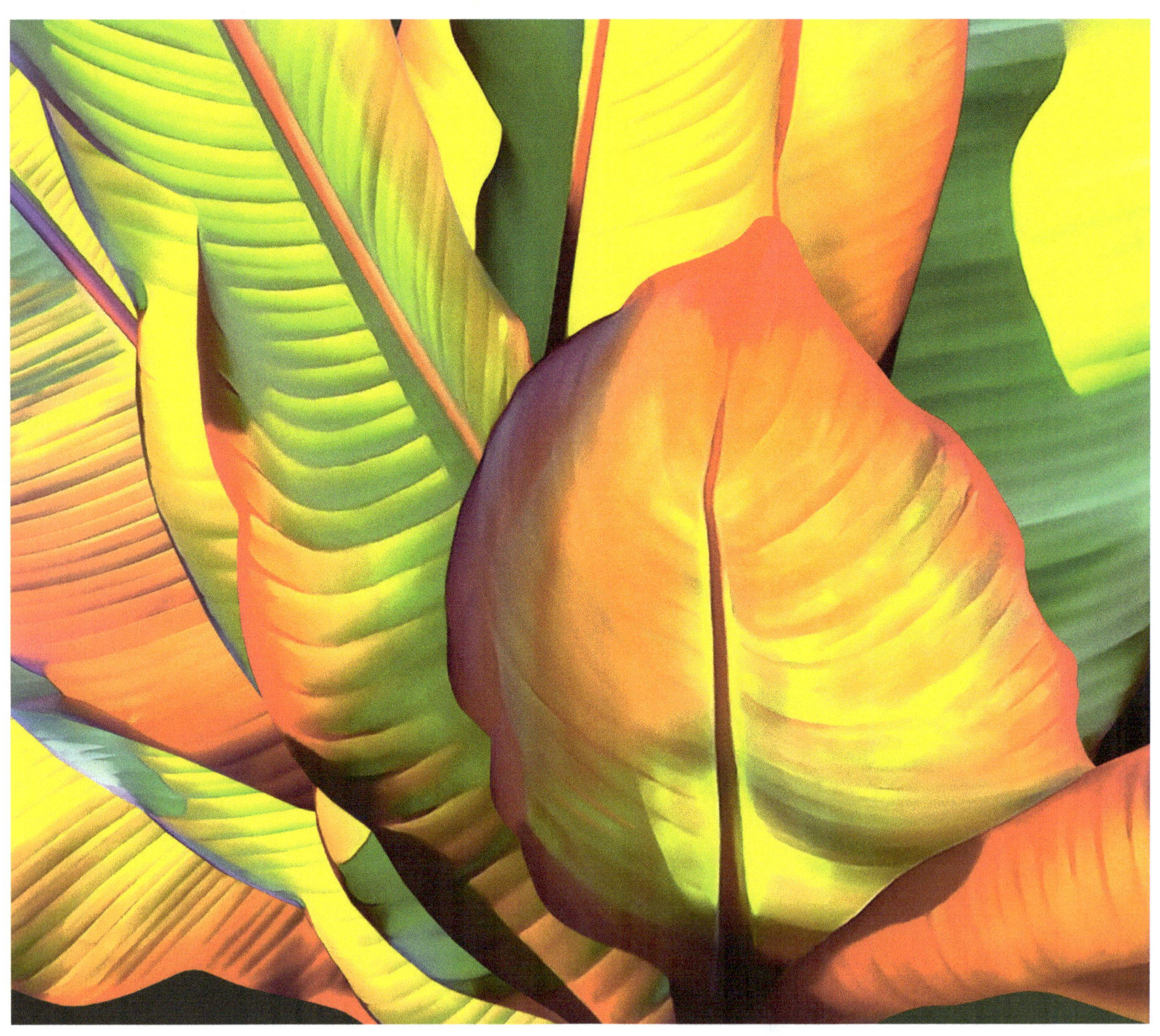

Only for you

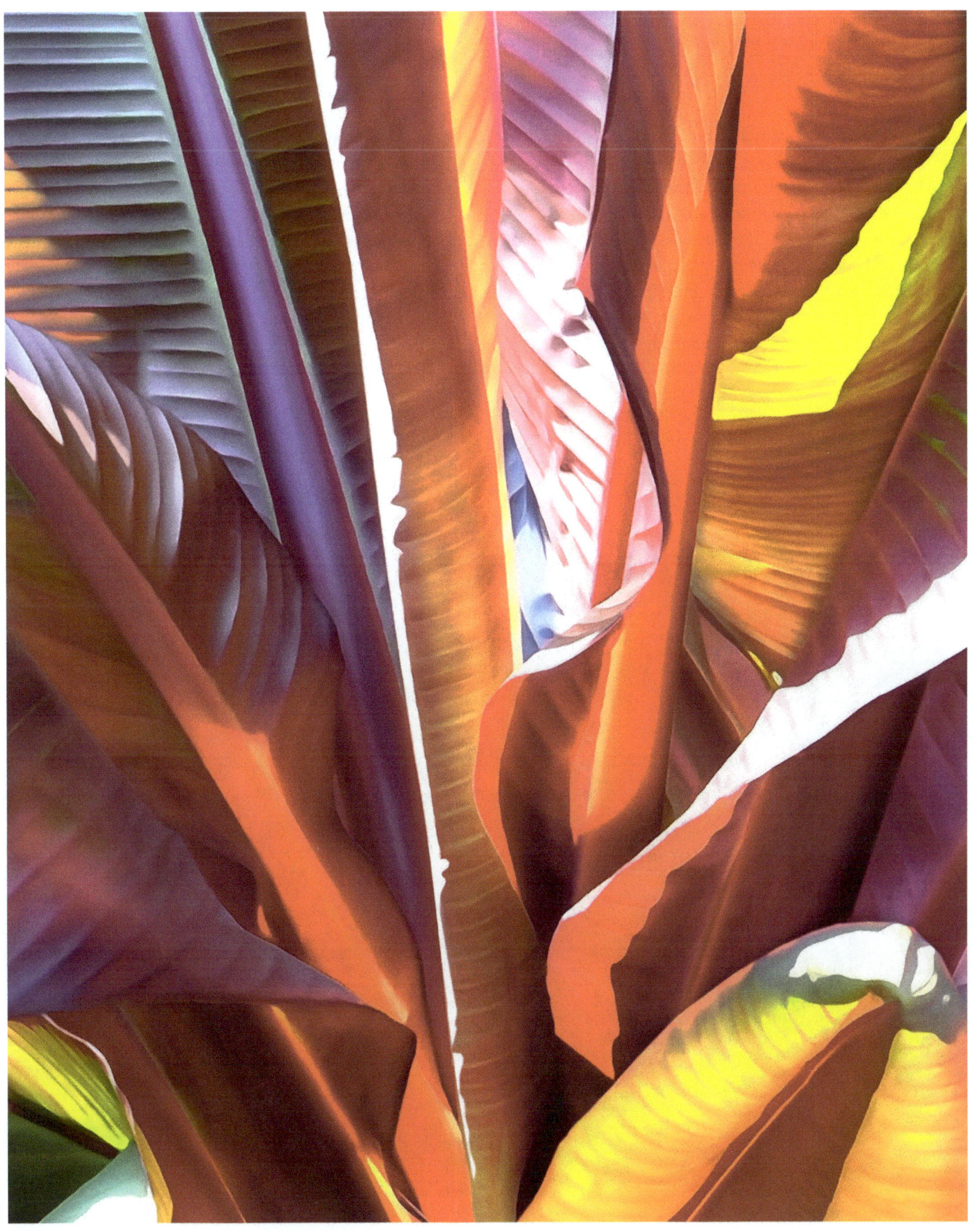

More time for love

Kenan K.

kenank.art

It seems that Life is an illusion to be fulfilled as joy and/or pain in line with an individual's purpose in the World. Then, Art, as a higher level of illusion, should be able to contribute to advance or increase the degree of consciousness for all. In terms of motivation, "Constructive Freedom" is the essence of my works for energy transfer per se, since I believe that destruction is one of the biggest issues to be tackled in today's world. In terms of technique, I try to explore my inner world for the harmony of means and ends, using experimentation through the door of intuition… Since artworks have their own paths while coming to fruition, they become separate and independent entities when completed and/or finished…so giving them an opportunity to express themselves may be desirable. The more you get into them, the more they will communicate. Please let them speak silently and be ready to explore their adventurous music…

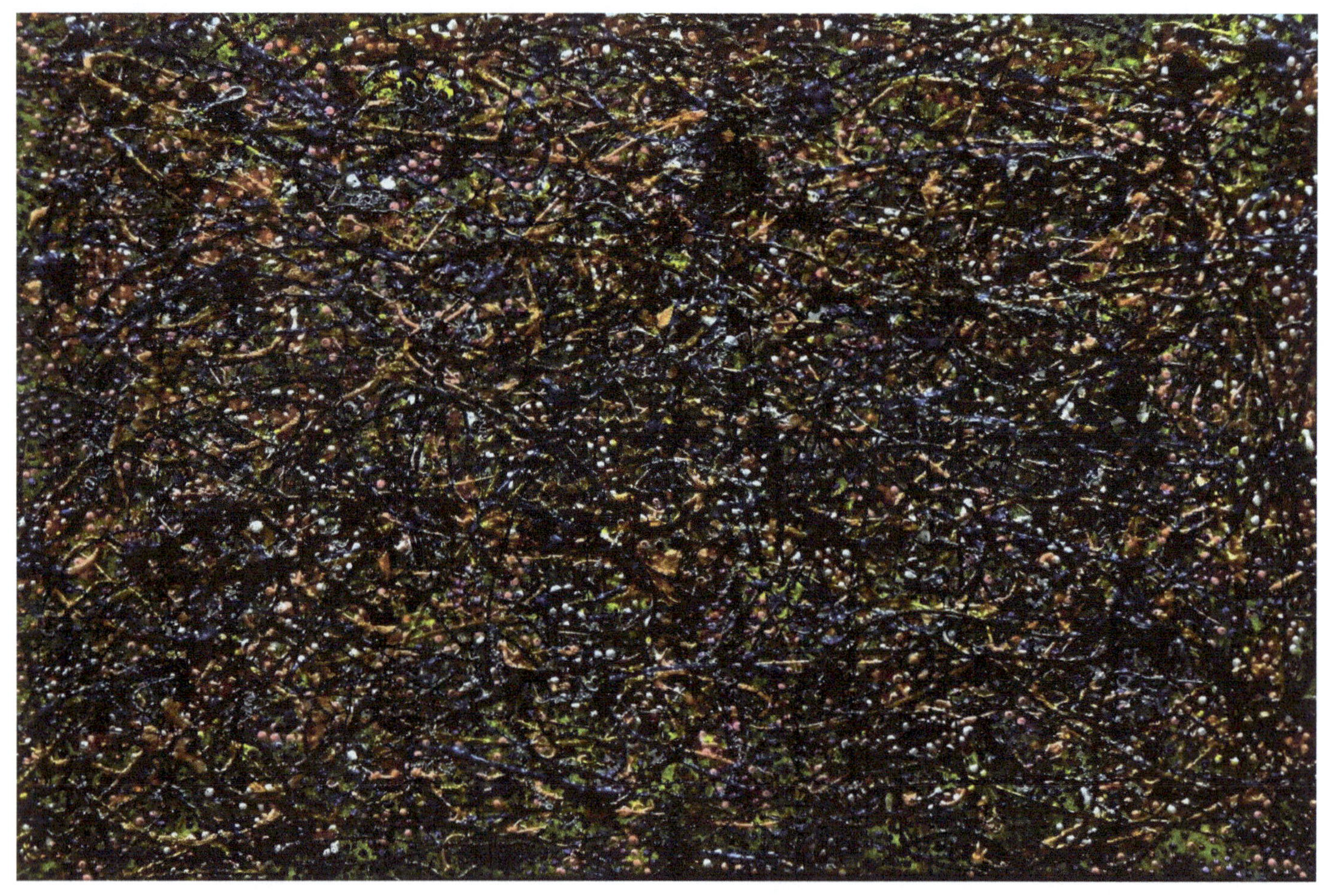

Poetry of the Universe

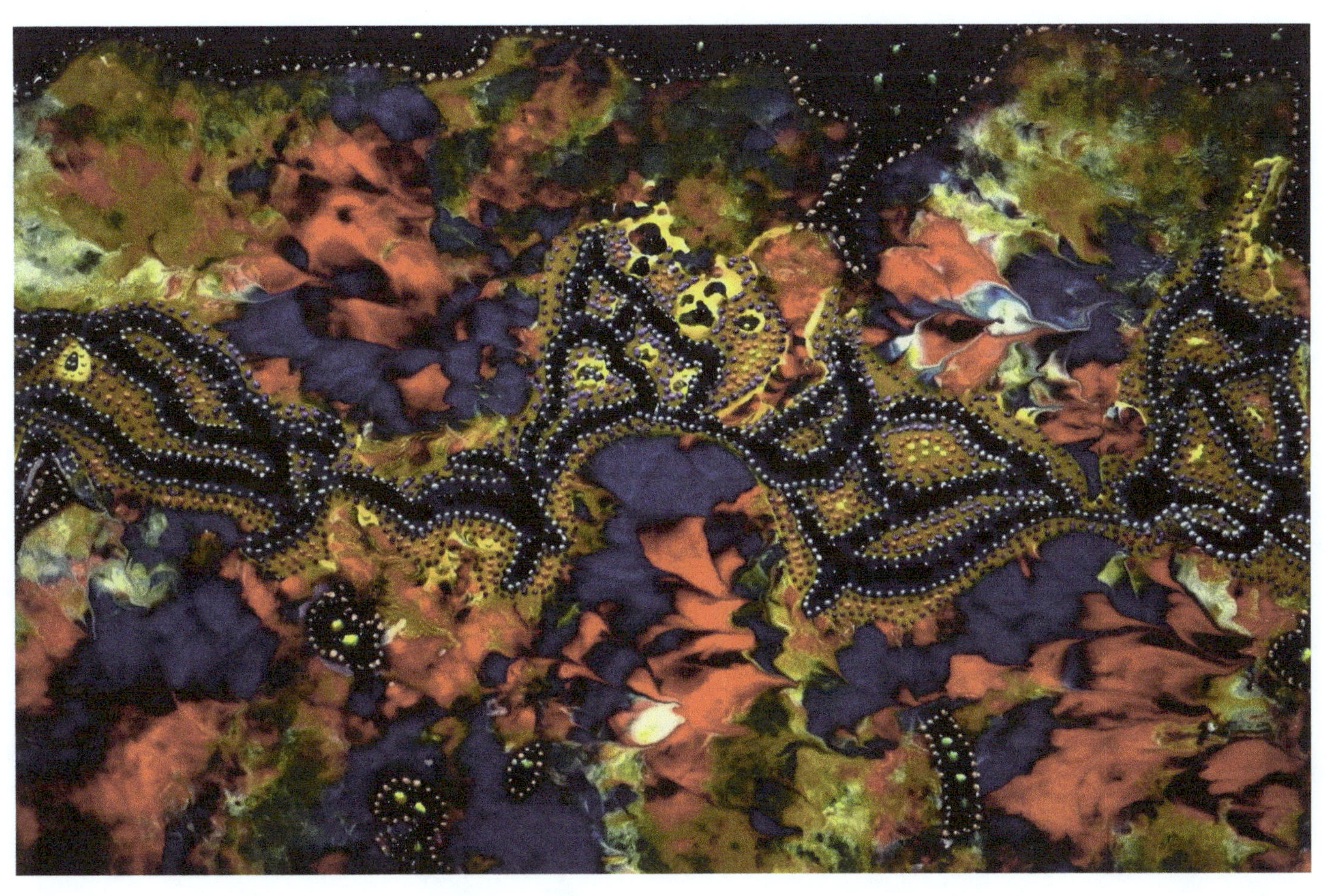

Pastoral Voyage

Kyunghee Lee

lkh.gallery25.co.kr

I deal with various forms of discrimination, violence that occur unreasonably in modern society, human desires and emotions suppressed by them. It is not intended to encourage good and punish evil, but to sublimate it by capturing and expressing the emotions that are suppressed in relationships with others. I think that a peaceful mind can be achieved by consciously expressing the fierce feelings of the unconscious hidden within superficial forms and language. Therefore, to me, work is a kind of meditative act of emptying the mind, and as a result, my work captures Karma's microscopic network of complicated relationships in society.

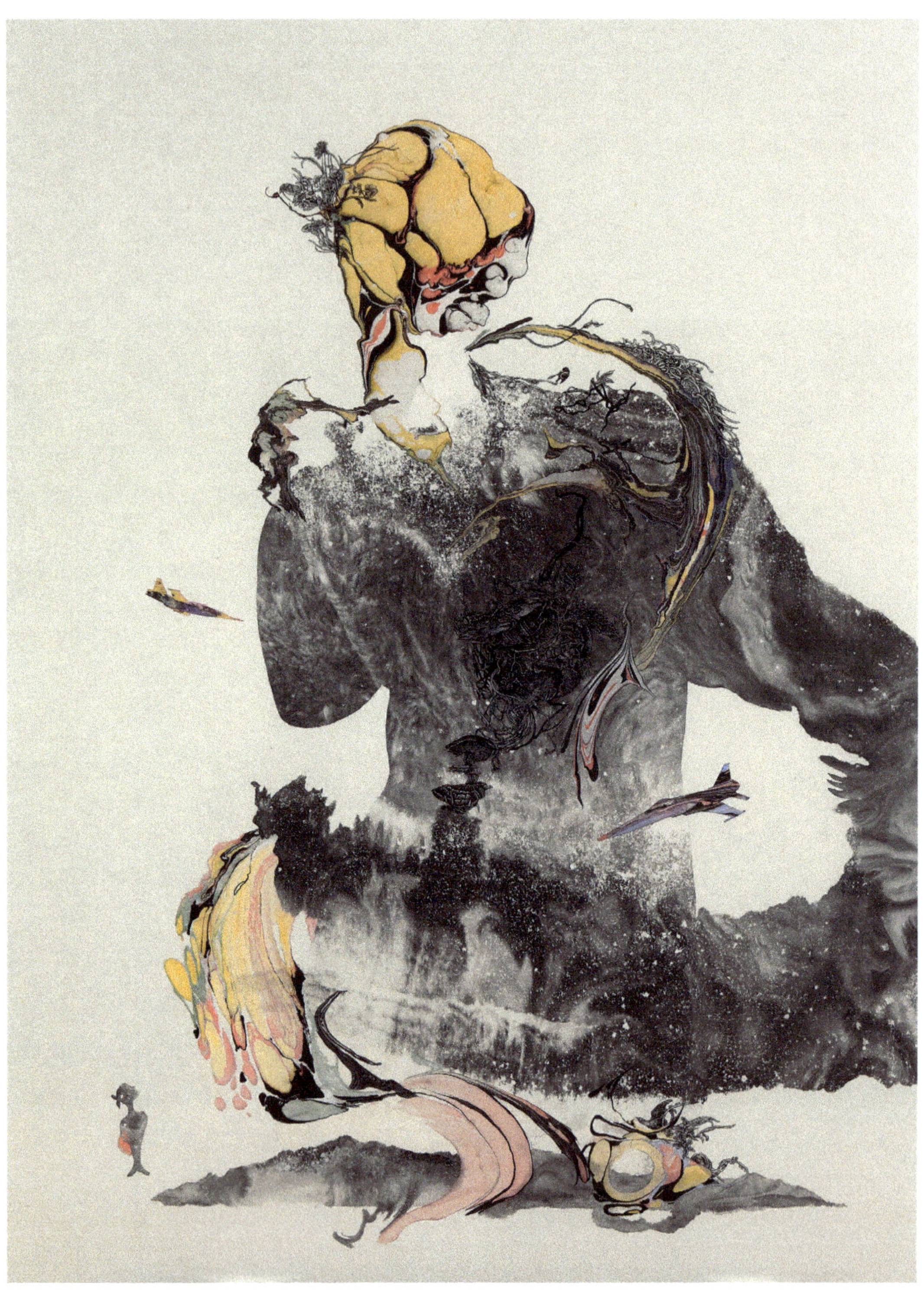

Coincidental Inevitability24109-Void (100.5-72)cm, woodengraving muk collage koreanpaper, 2024

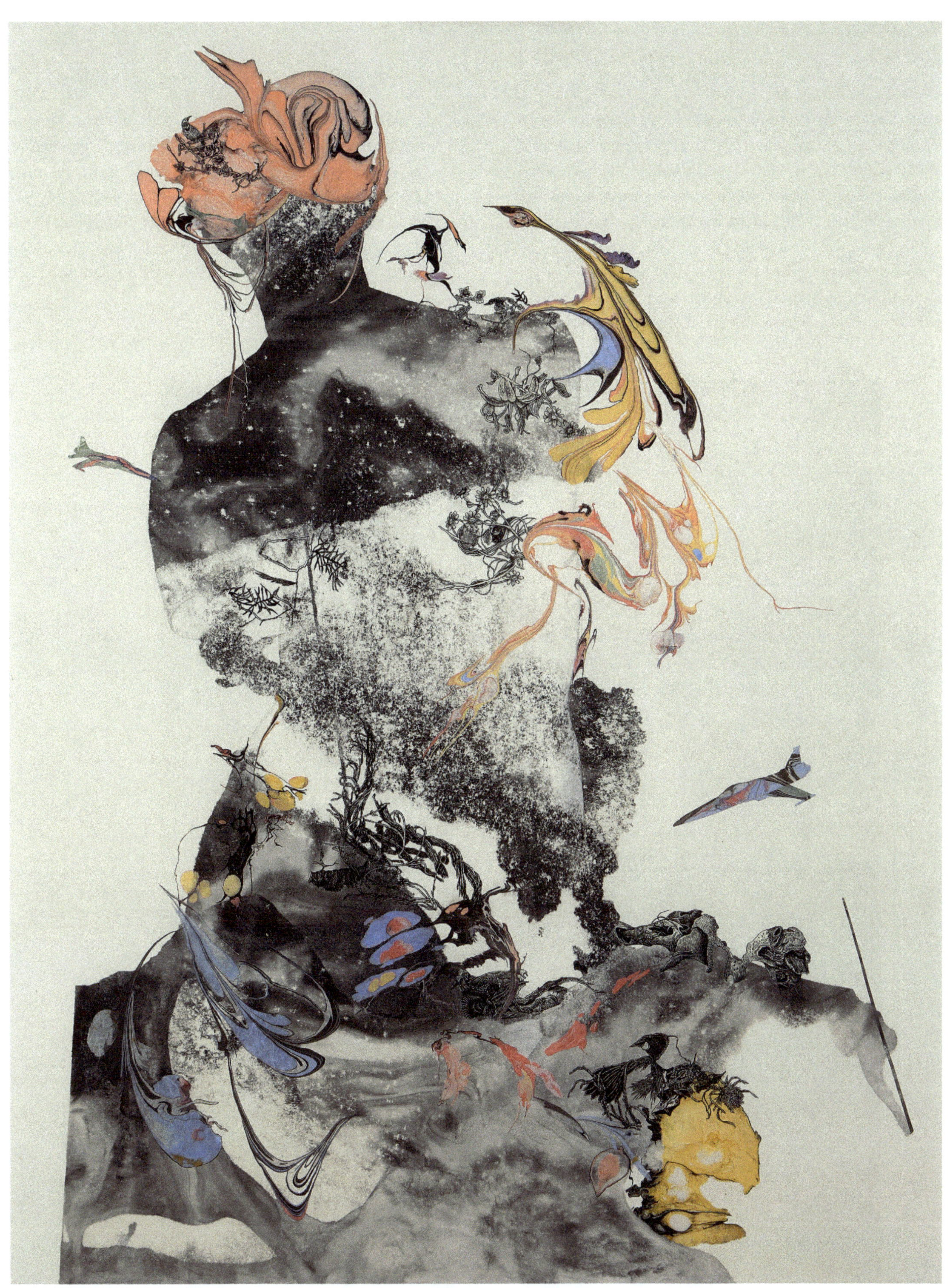

Coincidental Inevitability24110-Void (100.7-74)cm, woodengraving muk collage koreanpaper, 2024

Lode Coen

lodecoen-renaissance.tumblr.com

Lode Coen's art is characterized by an exquisite fusion of elegance and surrealism, resulting in captivating and visually stunning imagery. Within his work, he has crafted a distinct visual realm where beauty, mystery, and the unexpected converge to form extraordinary compositions. While renowned for his mastery of CGI and Special FX, honed in the realms of both Silicon Valley and Hollywood, Coen draws his primary inspiration from the Renaissance era. Most importantly, he wants to share his happiness in creating what he likes, dictated by no one. Notably awarded the First Prize at the Florence Biennale in 2023. Lode Coen's multifaceted talents span the roles of designer, artist, professor, and entrepreneur. He holds educational credentials from the prestigious Royal Academy and his pieces are sought after and showcased on Artsy. Extensive CV and background available on Lode Coen on LinkedIn.

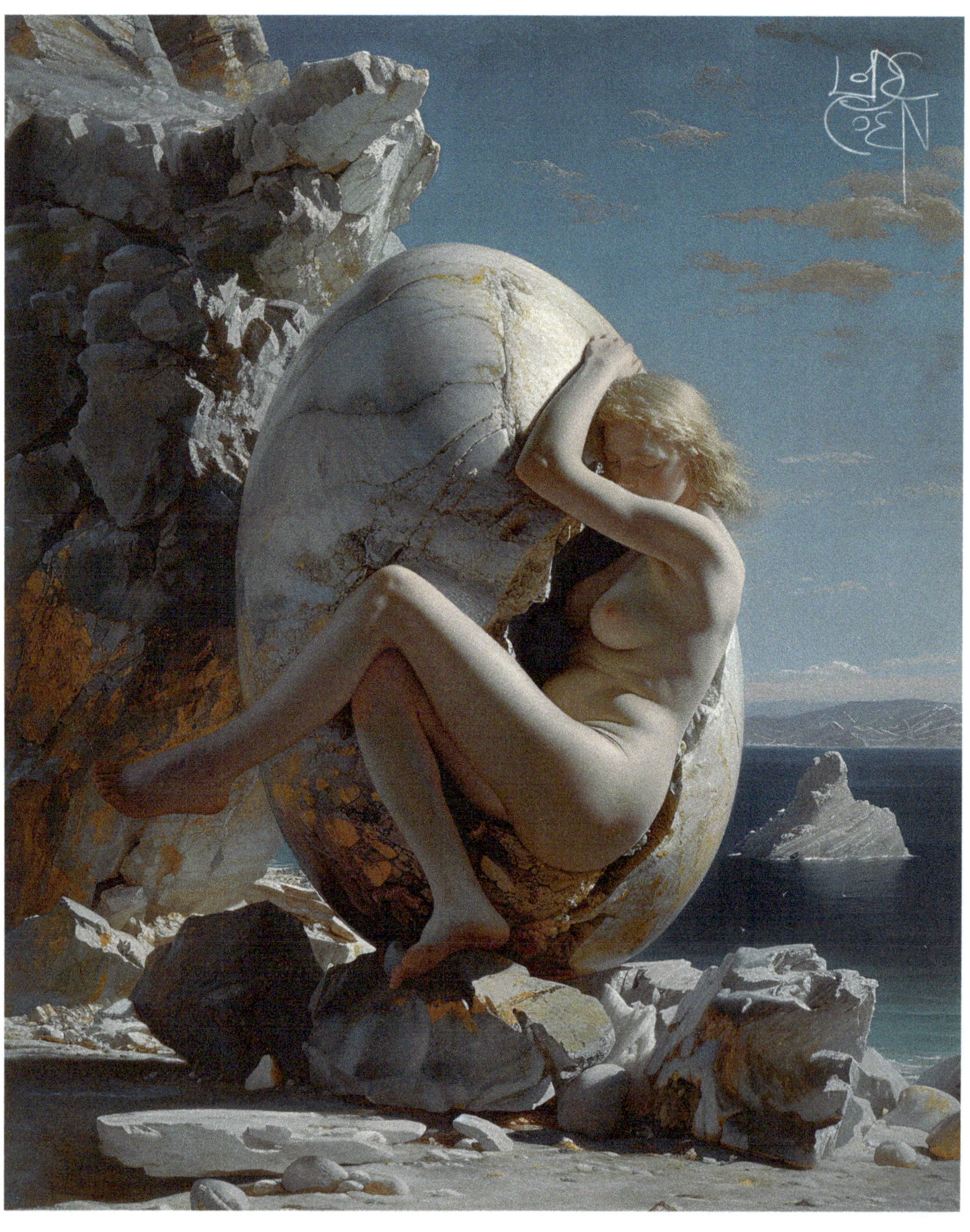

Origin Ovum Venus

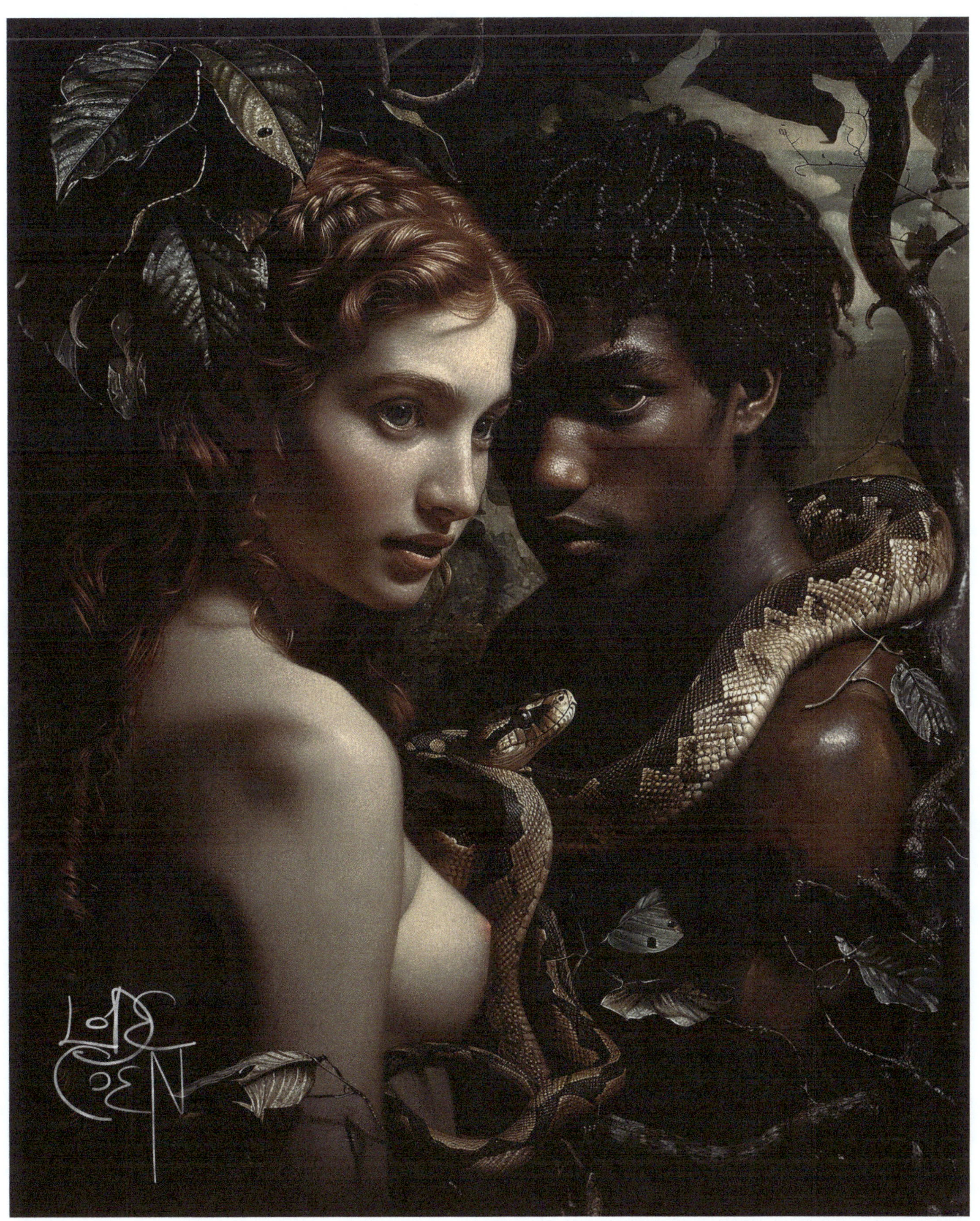

Adam & Eve - A Different Garden of Eden

Marcel Jomphe

marceljomphe.art

Marcel Jomphe studied graphic arts and computer science and worked as a scientific illustrator specializing in botany for a museum and two research institutes. In the 2000s, he became a web designer and then a web development team supervisor. He retired in 2012, and as a freelance artist, developed his personal artistic approach through drawing and photography. His work has been shown in over twenty group exhibitions in Canada, the United States and several European countries. His artistic work has won international recognition and several awards. For over 5 decades, he has meticulously drawn, photographed and intuitively, rather than systematically, observed the world of organic structures. The vital force and unique intelligence of this world, which unfolds in infinite forms, never ceases to fascinate him. These forms are reinvented in his imagination in works of poetic beauty or as a window onto a metaphysical realm.

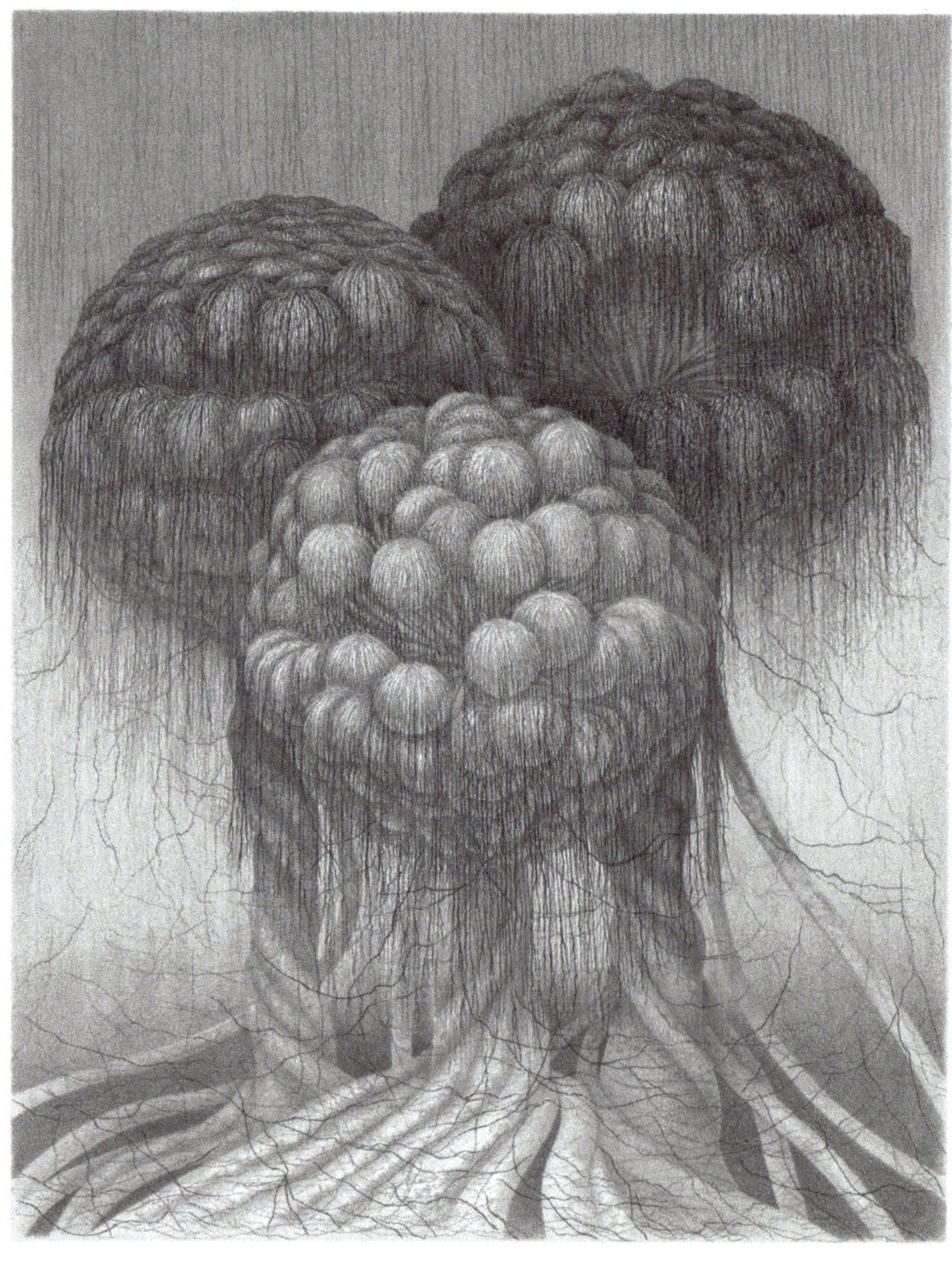

Fragment of an Unknown World, 3

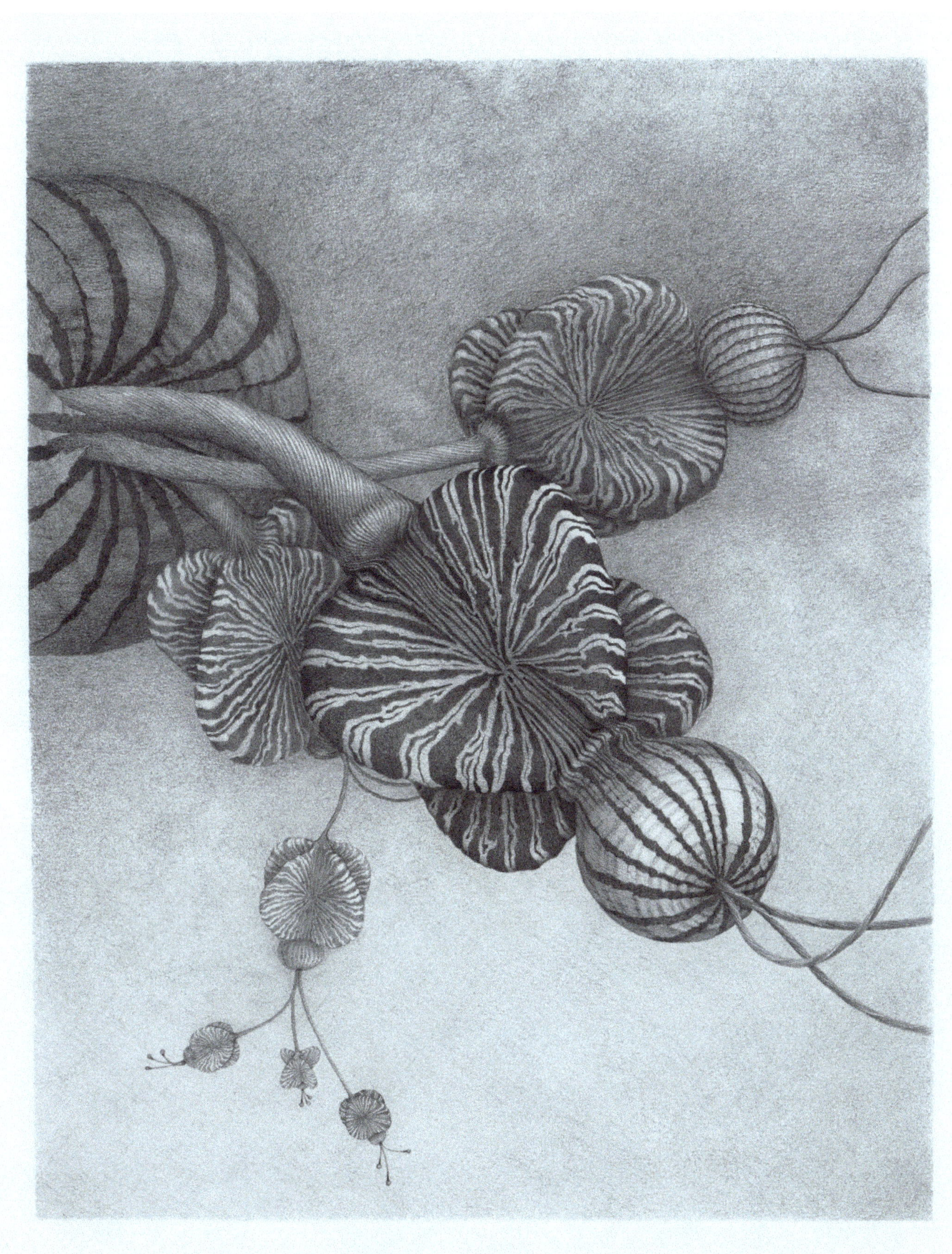

Fragment of an Unknown World, 2

Maurizio D'Andrea

dandreart.info

Maurizio D'Andrea is an international artist deeply inspired by the exploration of the human psyche, drawing influence from the works of Sigmund Freud and Carl Jung. His art delves into the hidden depths of the unconscious, using abstraction to distill the essence of ideas and objects, transcending linguistic and cultural barriers through universal archetypes. His technique is influenced by American Abstract Expressionism, particularly the New York School and artists like Jackson Pollock and Mark Rothko. His creative process, characterized by spontaneous gestures and varied techniques, reflects an intimate connection with his work. D'Andrea founded the "Radical Introversico Artistic Movement" in Turin, a movement that promotes the purity of interiority in art and creative expression free from commercial constraints. His artistic production also includes digital art, exploring the depths of the human mind through software developed by the artist himself, such as "Artetc," which combines shapes, lines, and arcs into new expressive dimensions. His goal is for his art to become a source of connection, contemplation, and inspiration, transcending personal expression to leave a lasting impact on individuals and society. D'Andrea aims to share his art globally, demonstrating that abstract art can overcome cultural and linguistic barriers, touching the essence of humanity. Born in Naples, Italy, the majestic volcano Vesuvio and sea have been endless sources of inspiration for him, shaping his profound artistic journey.

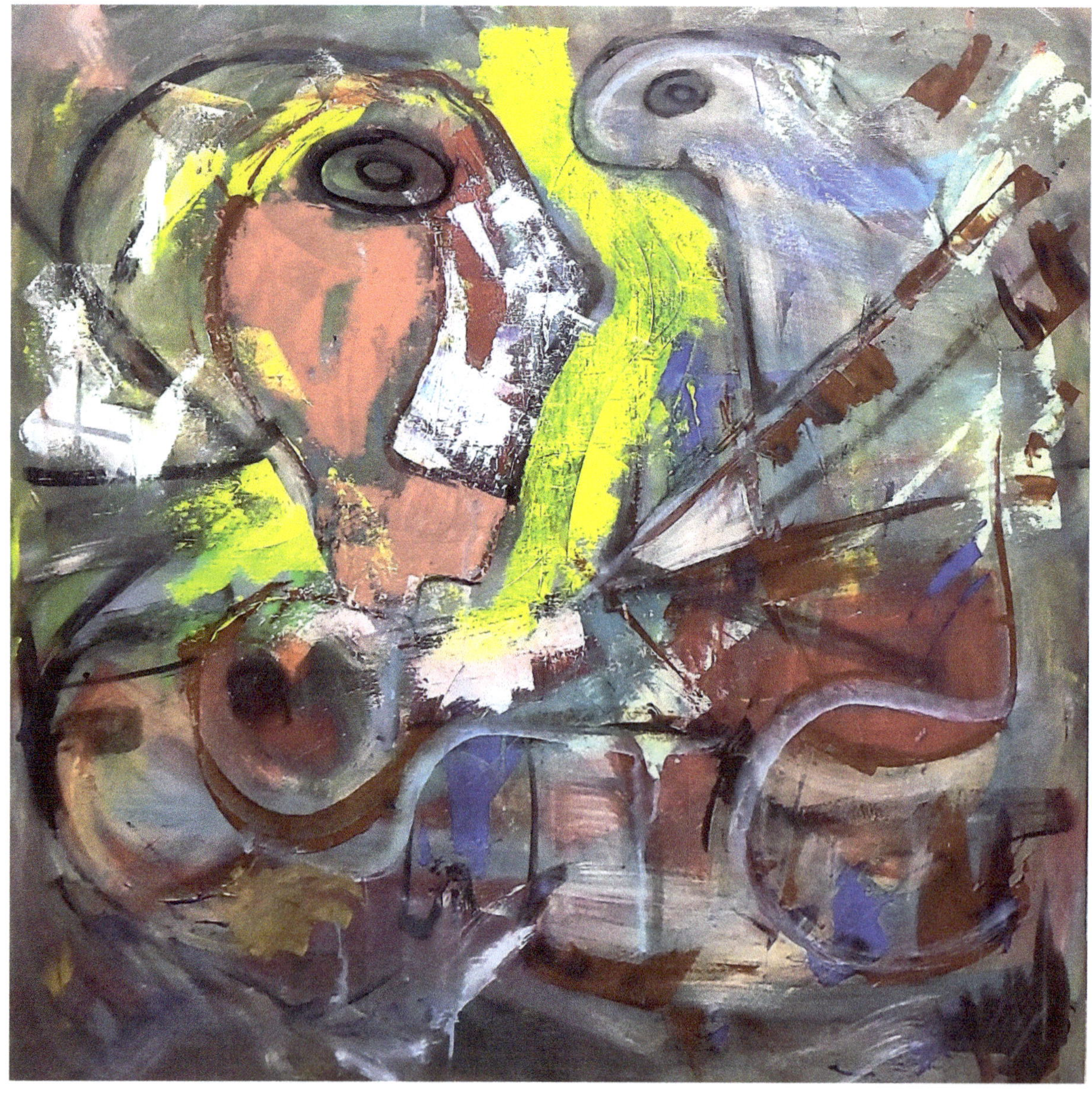

Mi.R bb6o

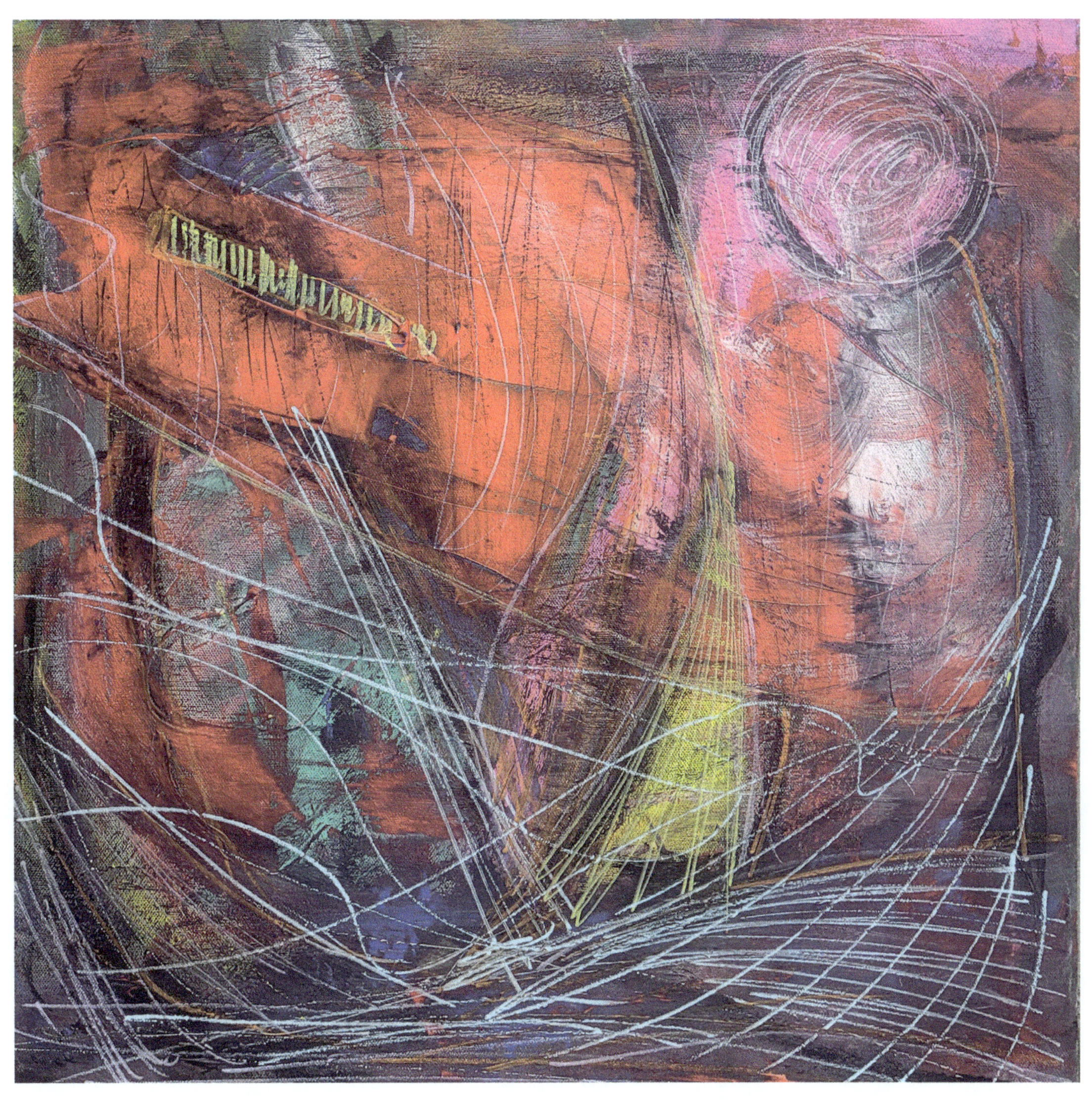

Mi.R bb22

Mari Winkler Solberg

mariwinkler.com

Underneath my career as a graphic designer and lecturer, there has always been a desire for arts and painting. When I finally decided to make the step 5 years ago it fulfilled my life. In front of canvas I let my emotions, beliefs and thoughts guide me, as well as a phenomenological approach - where the canvas, water, pigments and tools at hand also lead me into new dimension. I often paint in layers over time, and very in techniques.

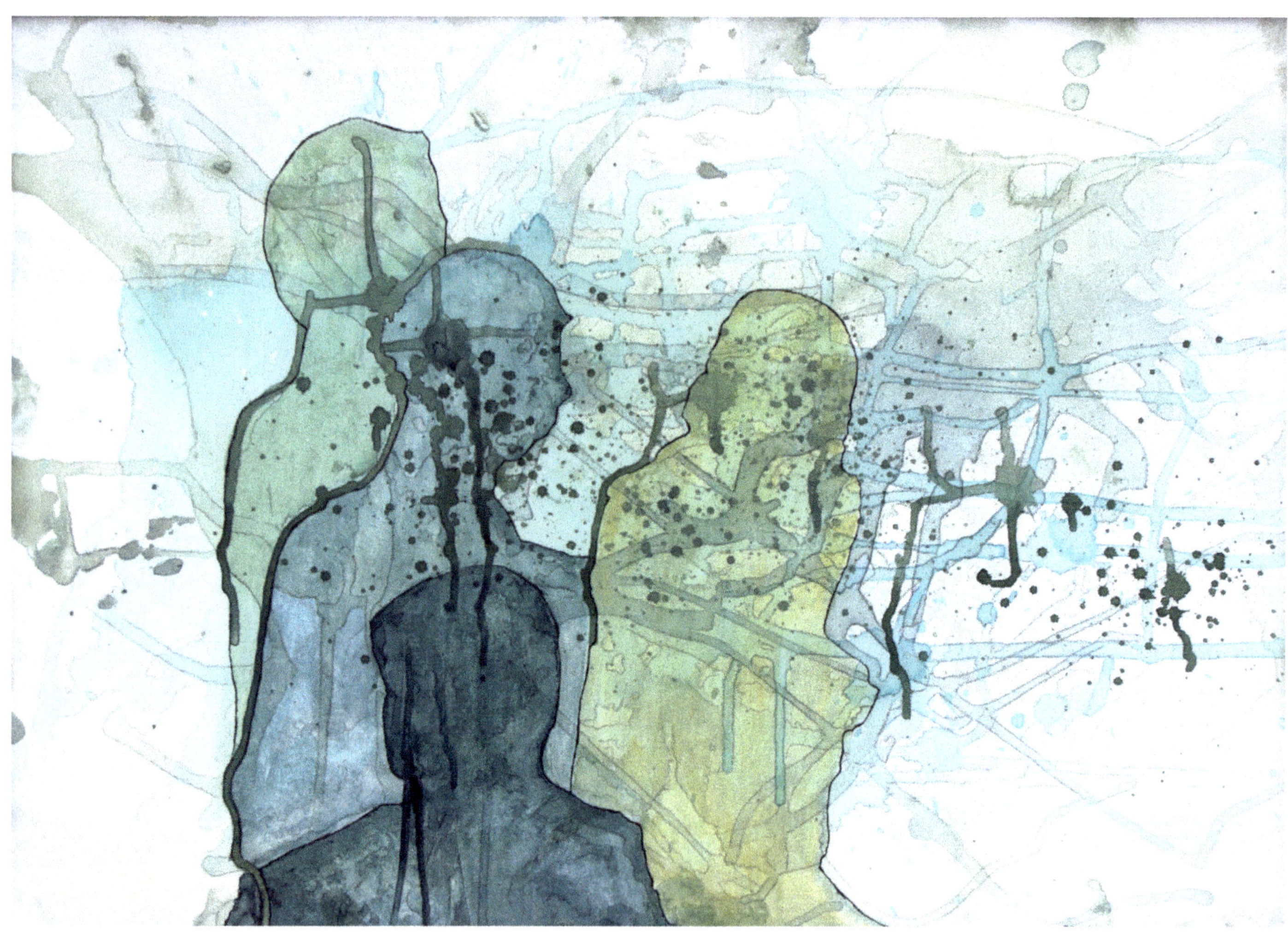

a-social Interactions

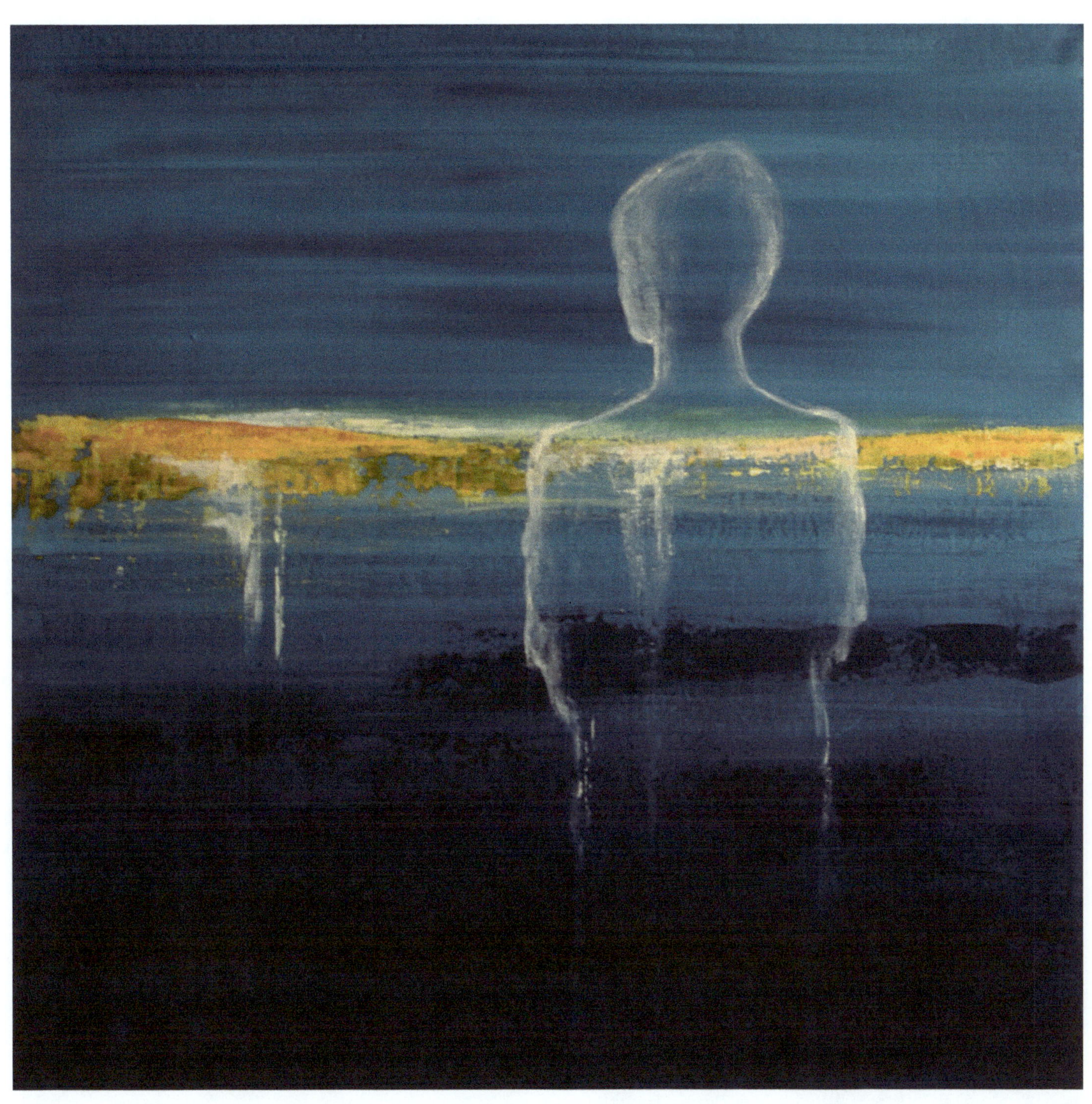

Dimensions

Maria Stella Polce

mariastellapolce.it

Italian artist (and teacher at the Ministry of Public Education), self-taught, she showed her passion for art from a young age, painting in oils with a realistic style. Subsequently, she experimented with other techniques, ranging from pastels to acrylics, tempera, enamels, painting on glass, etc., until she arrived at digital art in the year 2000. With the discovery of fractals (generated by her on the computer) and with the artistic current of Fractalism (Manifesto of the Cultural Movement "Fractalism", by Master Giorgio Orefice, publisched in 1999, considered the protagonist of this avan-garde whichhas had repercussion throughout the world), therefore, Maria Stella Polce has created surprising works that are born from fractals and their modification . With this new genre of digital art, she has been actively participating, since 2015, in collective exhibitions and artistic events in Italy and abroad, has received numerous awards and is featured in magazines and various art catalogs including the Mondadori CAM 54 Modern Art Catalog, the Elite 2019 and 2020, the De Agostini Contemporary Art Atlas 2021, etc.

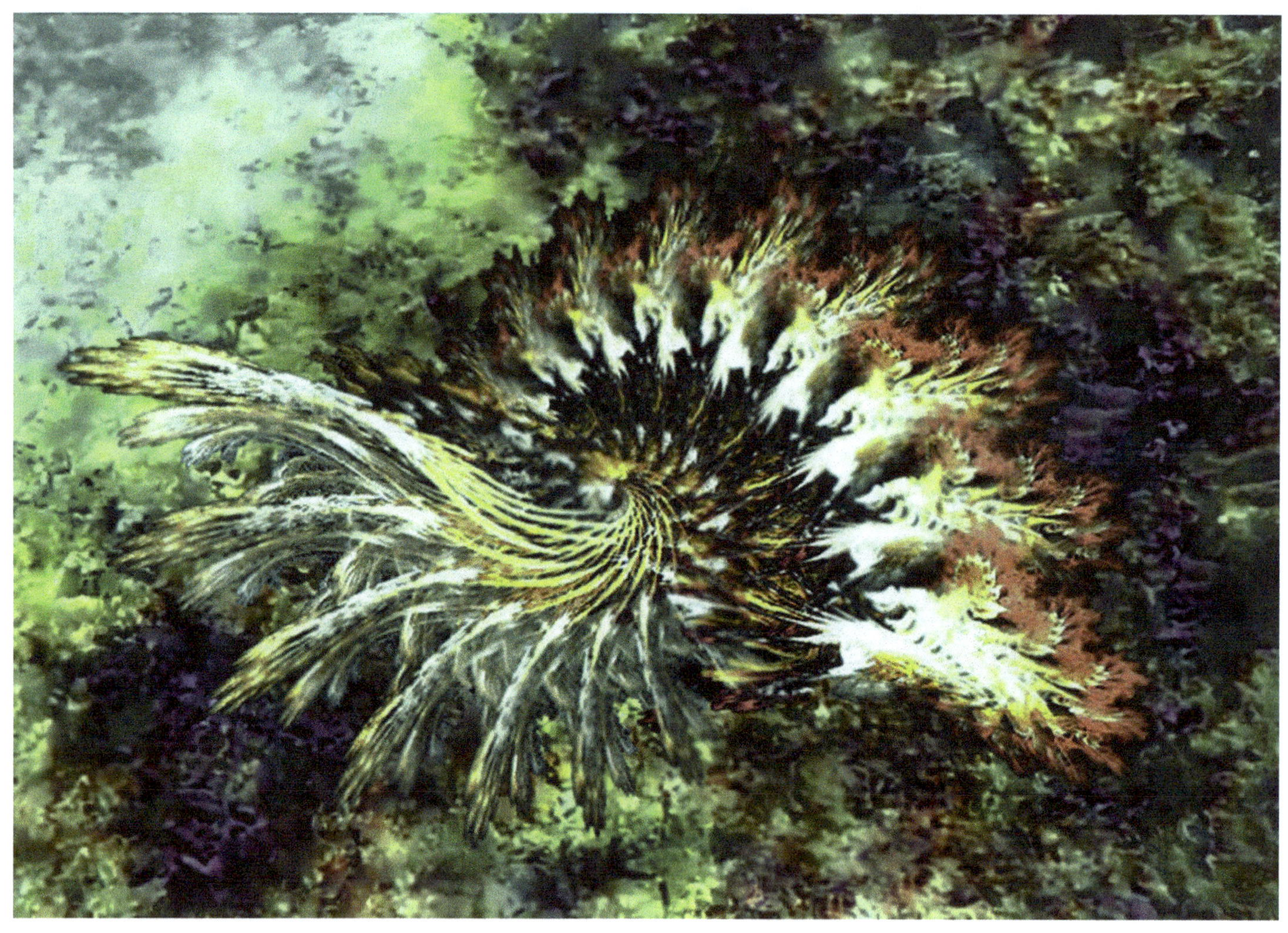

Frattale su Fondale

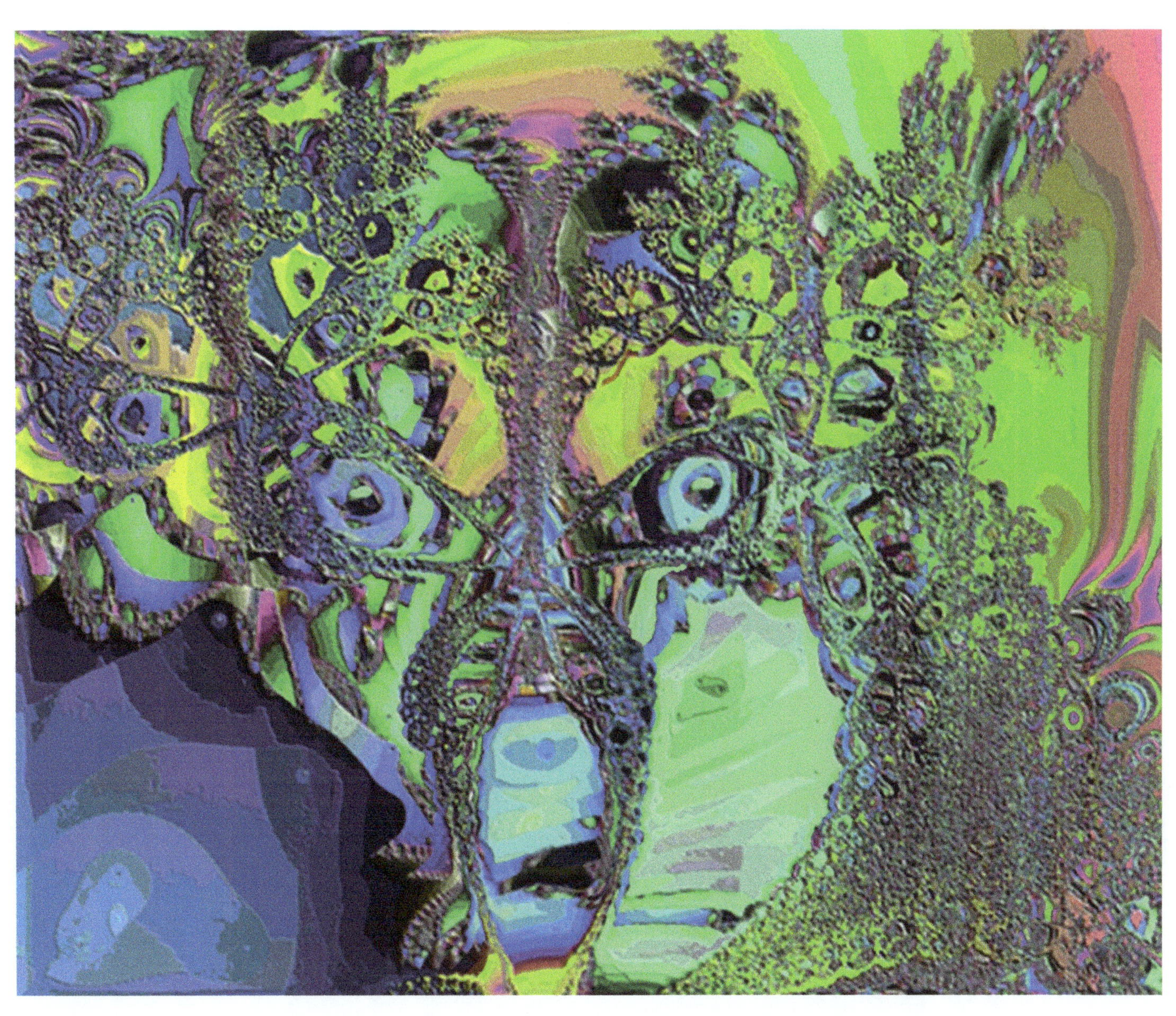

L'urlo del Frattale

Marianne Charlotte Mylonas-Svikovsky

reves-realites.com

Art is my passion joy since I am 12 years,my private personal means to answer my questionings, to come to ends with the constant family's changes of locations, mentalities, languages,cultures and situations all stored in my mind just as are the colors and vibrations I feel. Art has saved me in all situations ,an autotherapy for a mother's deepest griefs with poetry's potential of saying in words what art does in colors composition, gesture and the style determined specific for each image in an alla prima intuitive fashion or mentally matured the time it takes but never imposed nor planned, each image in link with my personal experiences. I want to share, alert on as art has always done : represent emotionally impacting world events,warn about their consequences or just paint our earth's beauties and failures. All means are at disposal chosen intuitively but colors are always the starting point. I nourish myself of others images without ever sticking to a style, of all the happenings in the world of art but I like to stay by myself and paint when I feel that something needs to be fetched from inside me even in the deepest hidden recess of my soul .. pulled out in it's essence in the silence of the night I appreciate for acting out what needs to be said. The best reward is when people understand my meaningful abstractions. Art is a fulfillment, a gift for an inborn creative,a responsibility also and a challenge.

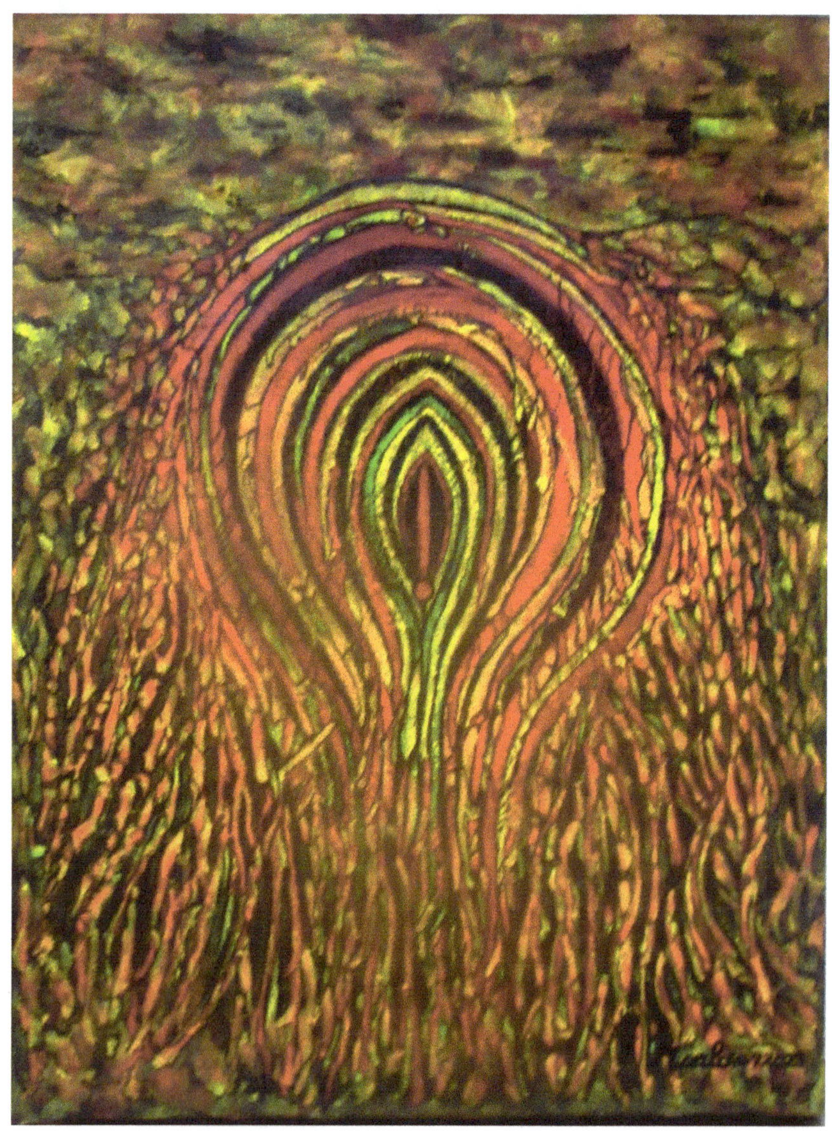

The Core of the question goes way back Israel-Hamas 09.2023. 80 x 60 cm Oil and acrylic

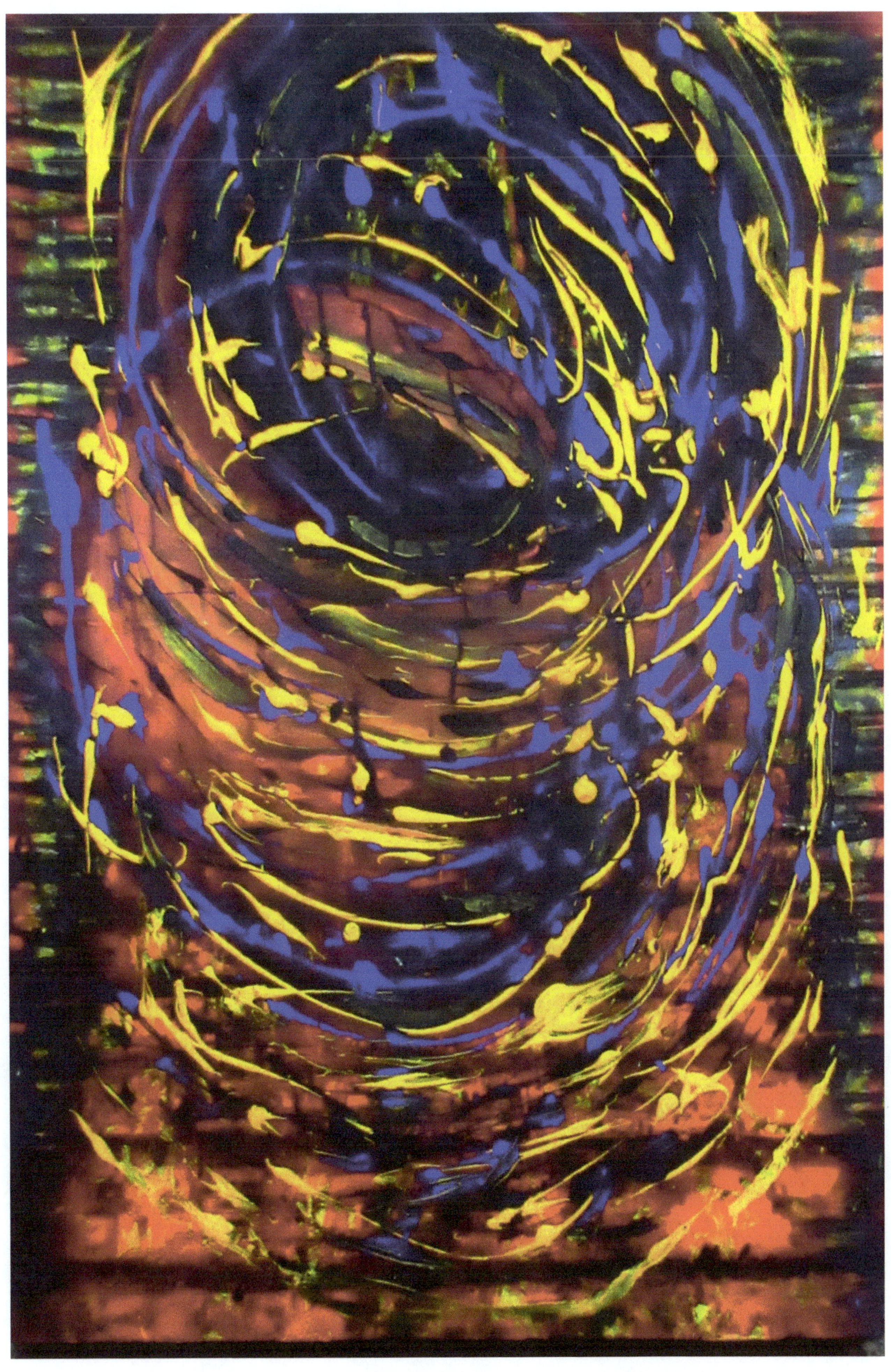

WAR ..It's a never ending story... 90 x 60 cm 24.11.2022. Oil and acrylic on canvas

Marie Ghislaine Beaucé

marieghislainebeauce.weebly.com

Marie-Ghislaine Beaucé, a French artist currently active in London (UK), has from a long time understood the artistic potential of textile fibers, the absolute protagonists of her artwork, which materials of different textures, colors and thickness intertwine and overlap each other, creating a semi abstract and purely geometric lattice, punctuated and delimited by the rhythmic succession of layers of fabrics, making her work a hybrid, a cross between patchwork and plasticism. Marie-Ghislaine Beaucé looks to future without forgetting the past: she actualizes and renews , proposing it in a creative and abstract interpretation, a great artistic tradition: the tapestries.

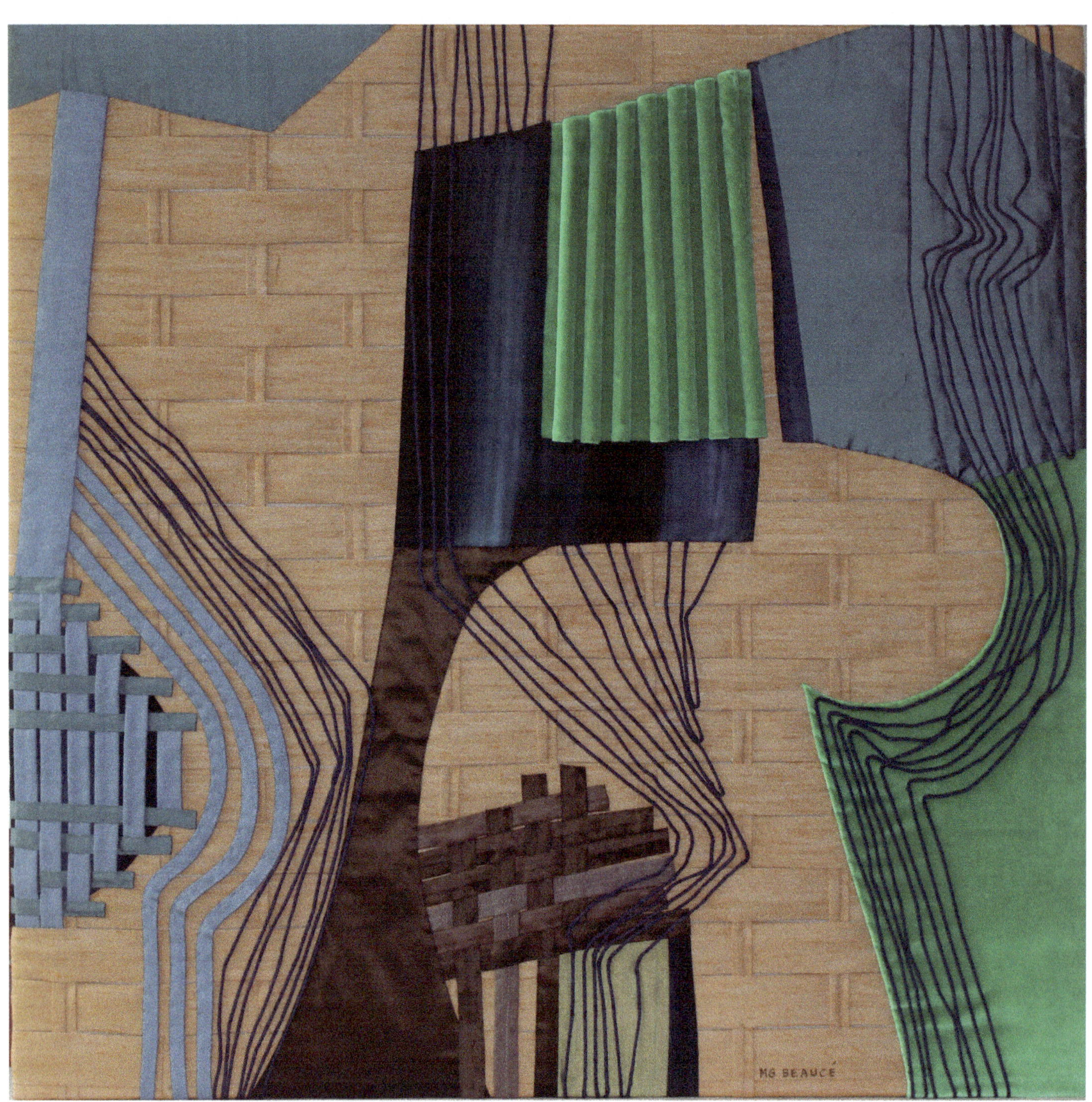

June

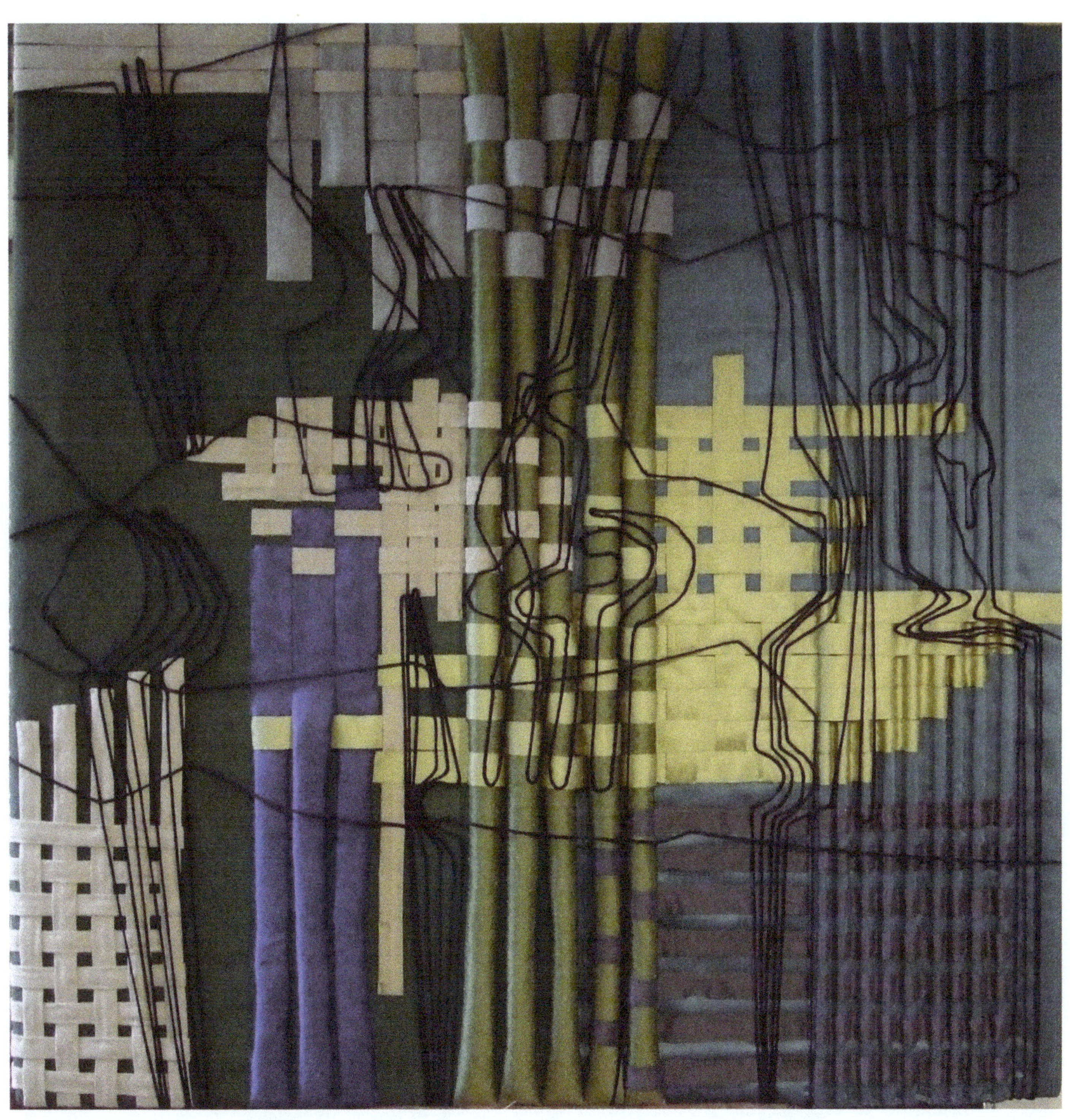

Tissage 4

Marlene Jorge

instagram.com/marlenejorgeartist

My creative process is characterized by impromptu expression and unforced outbursts, resulting in compositions that are akin to a personal diary. My works are inspired by volatile emotions that well up within my inquisitive spirit. To produce unique artwork, I harness my creative urges by drawing from daily emotion-triggering activities as well as the depths of my personal experiences. This allows me to extract all the creative juice necessary to create art that is truly unique and meaningful.

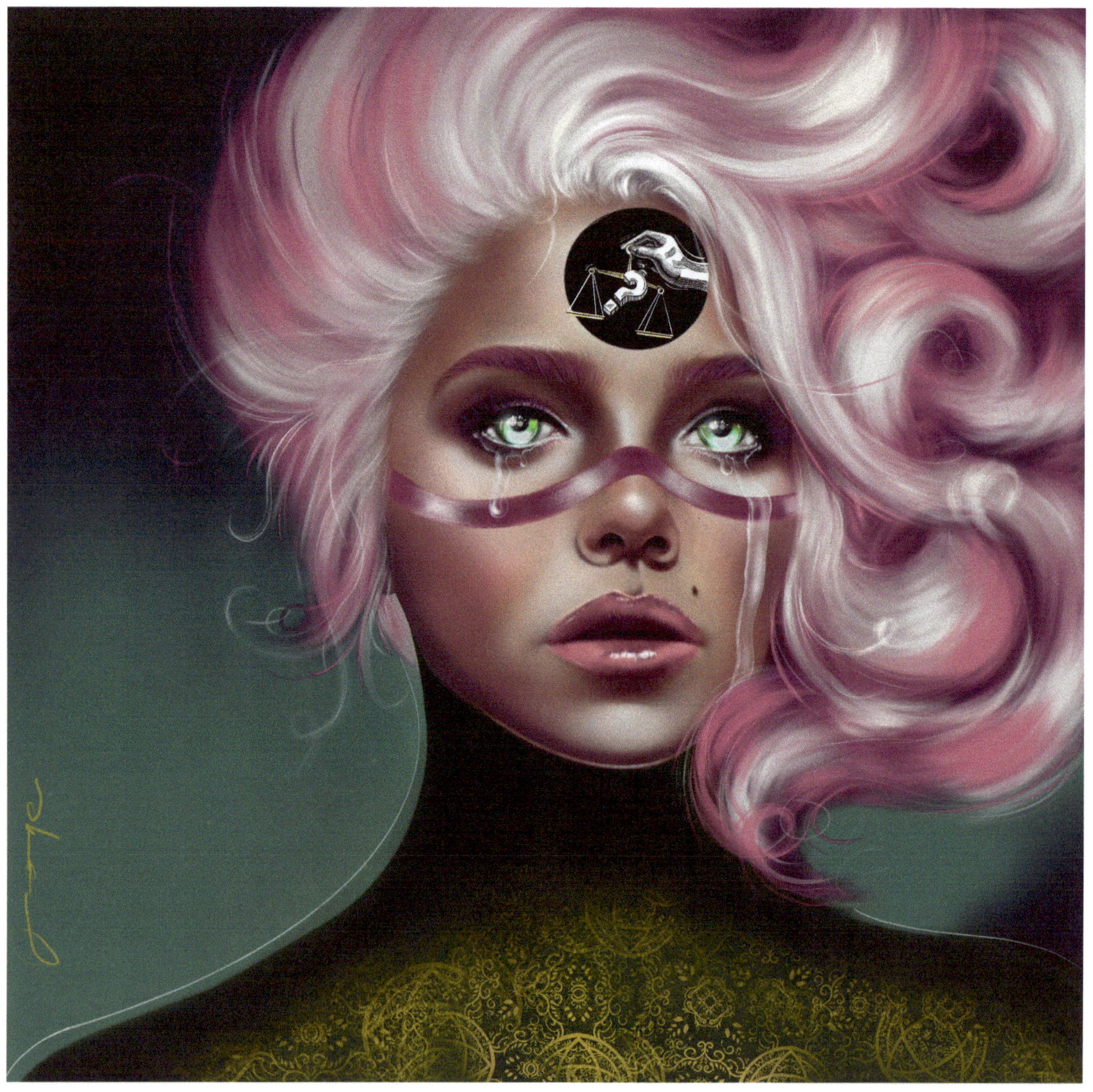

Ambiguedad

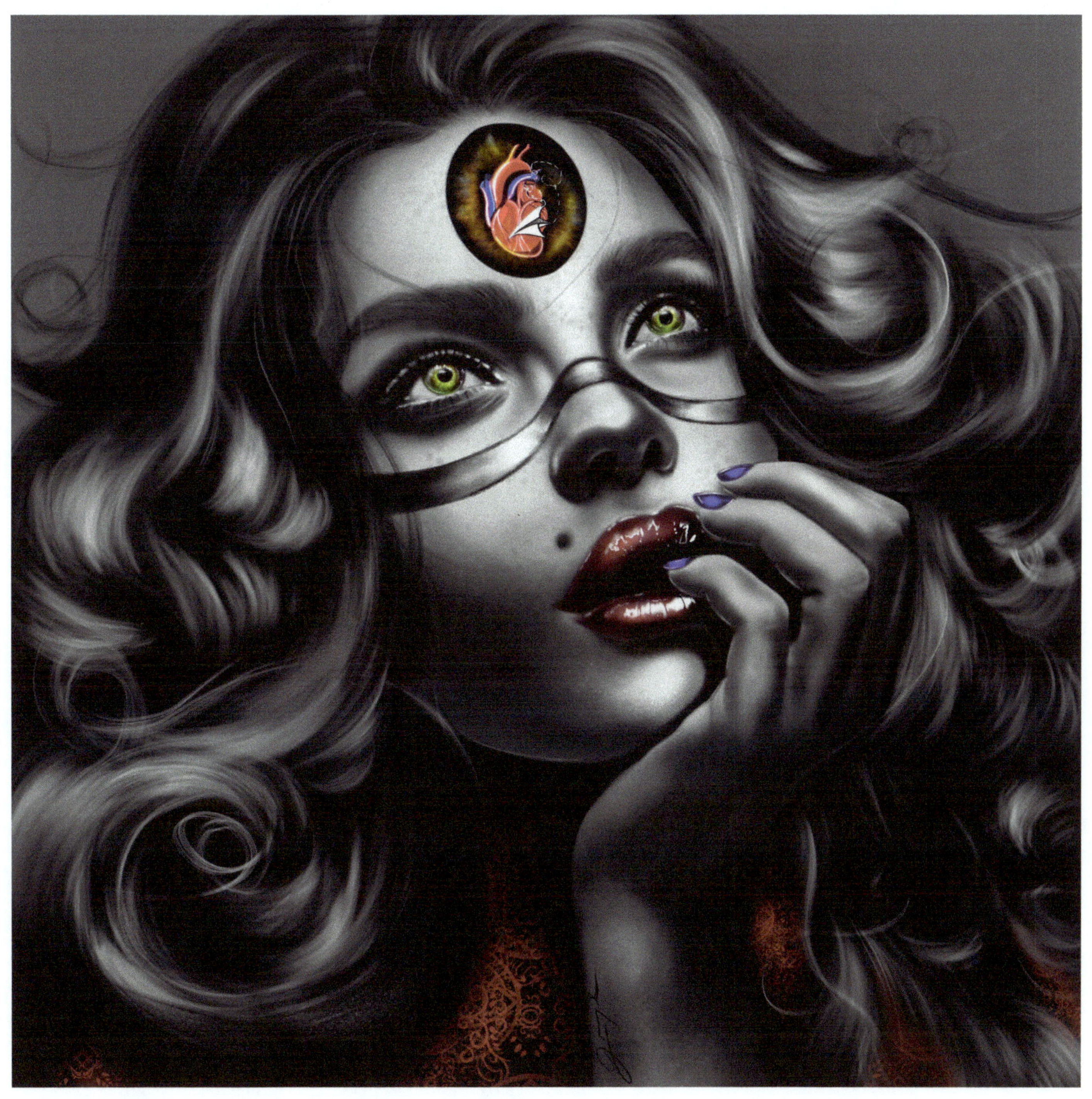

Antologia

Marta Carceller

martacarcellerart.com

My artwork, very far from any trend or fashion, is a testimony of my experiences and my deepest intimacy, and it explains part of my personal history. With the help of paint, brushes, spatulas, canvas, and wood as support I can capture and externalize all of this and transform it into an external to me object lasting over time. My work symbolizes, through scenes that capture everyday moments and lived experiences, the value of family. The family constitutes a universal cultural value that affects all of the Humanity, therefore, my works reflect a concept that for me is one of the most important, and that is also necessary for society in general. Through my work I "speak" about values associated with the family, such as love, generosity, empathy, commitment, trust, respect for others, solidarity, justice, complicity, cooperation, compassion, mutual support, the sense of belonging and tolerance, among others. I am satisfied to be able to transmit to my artworks viewer a minimum part of what I feel when painting involves me in this intimate act of creating what I feel. My technique uses all of this to give a more expressionistic meaning to what is apparent, evoking the most primary feelings.

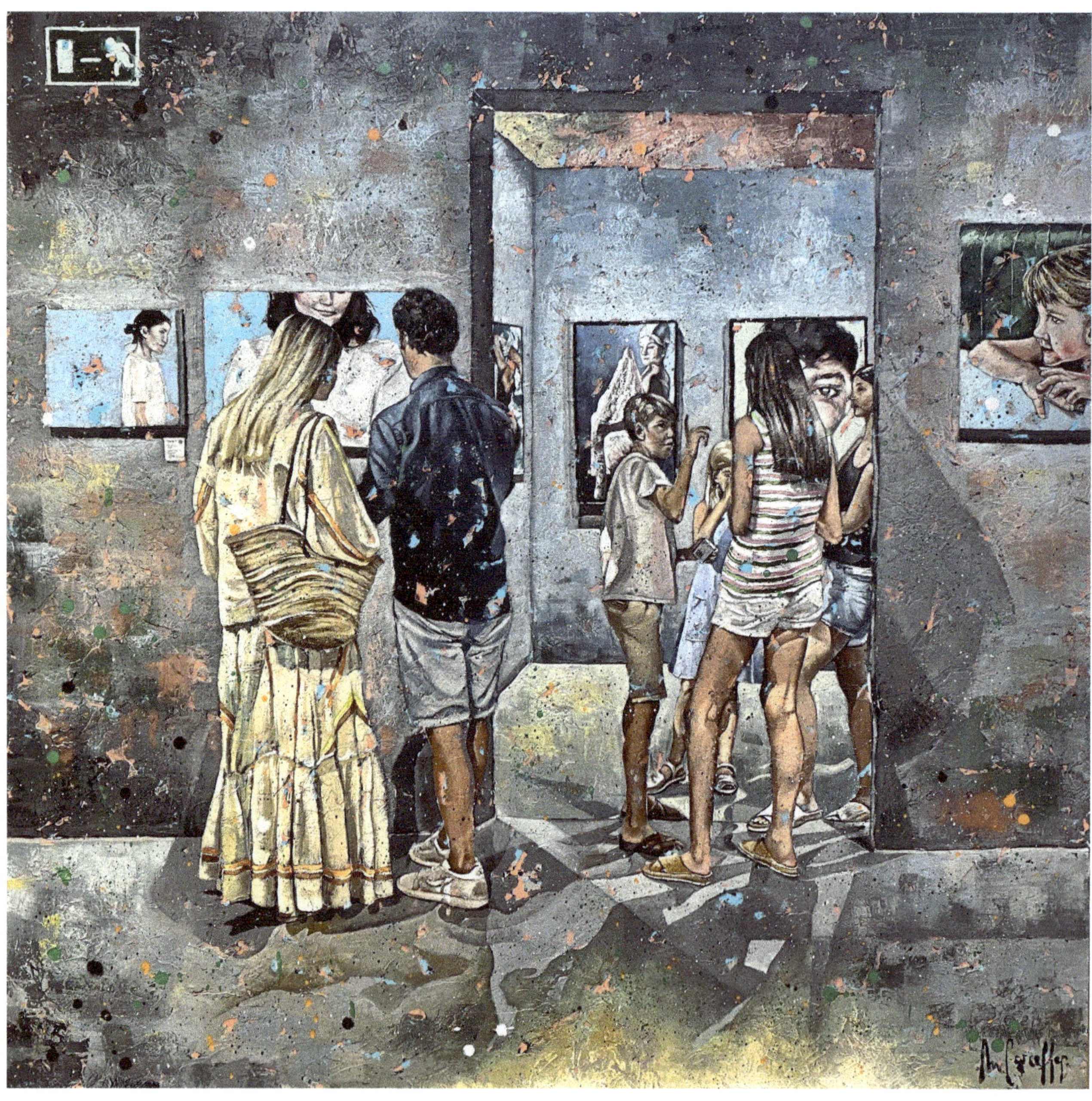

An afternoon at the Museum

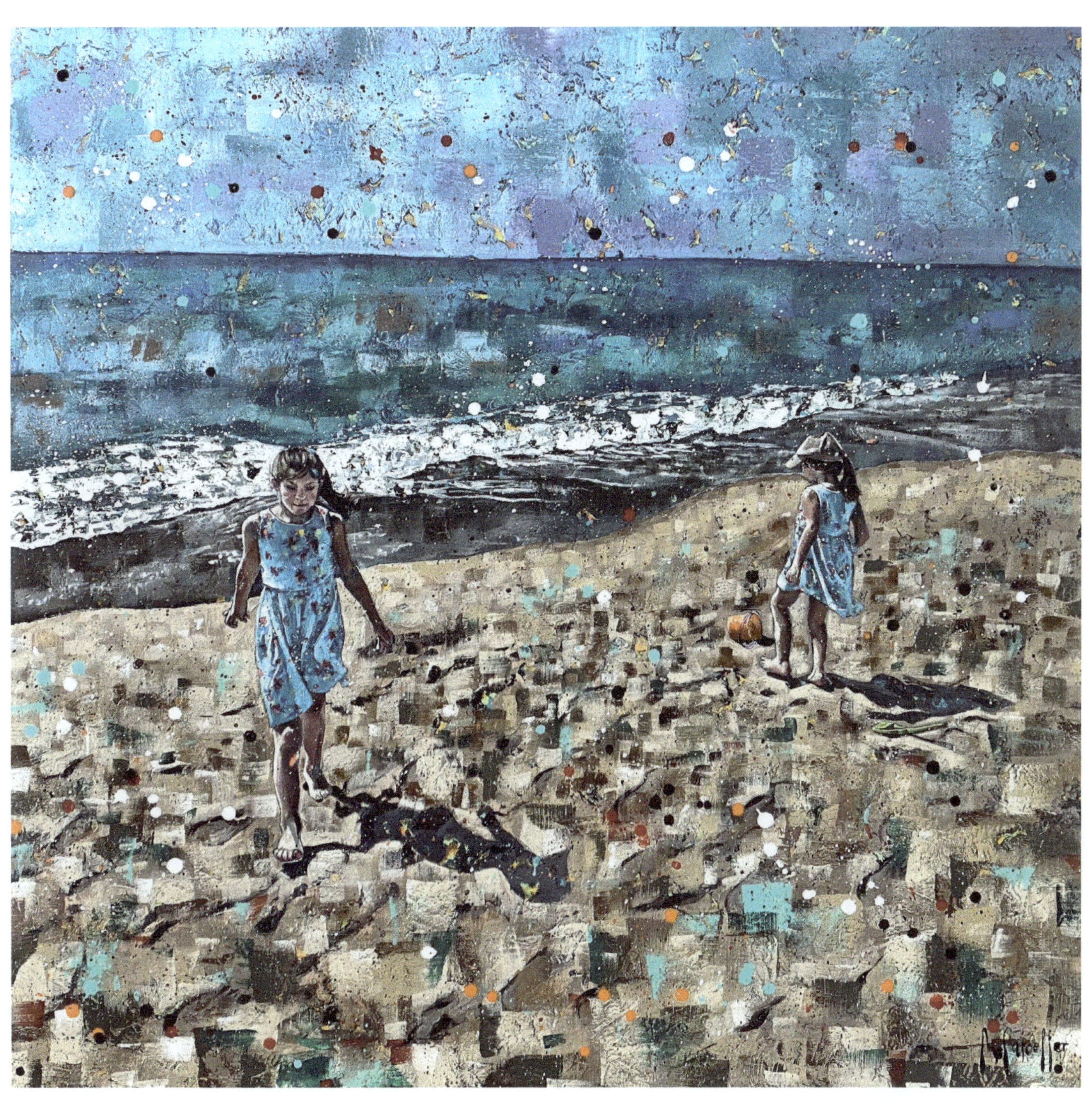

Un matí d'estiu

Michel Audebert

michelaudebert-artphoto.fr

There's such a cohesion and a really interesting duality between energy and reverie, but also a raw stillness, eroticism with almost a contemplative quality that gives his work a haunting quality, I can't think of a single artist working at that level or a similar level... It's so exciting and I think the characteristics of his work will completely catapult his work to the next level... We are delighted to see how strong and amazing her paintings are.
Maria JAMESON
Director of Visual Arts ACCESS ART STUDIO

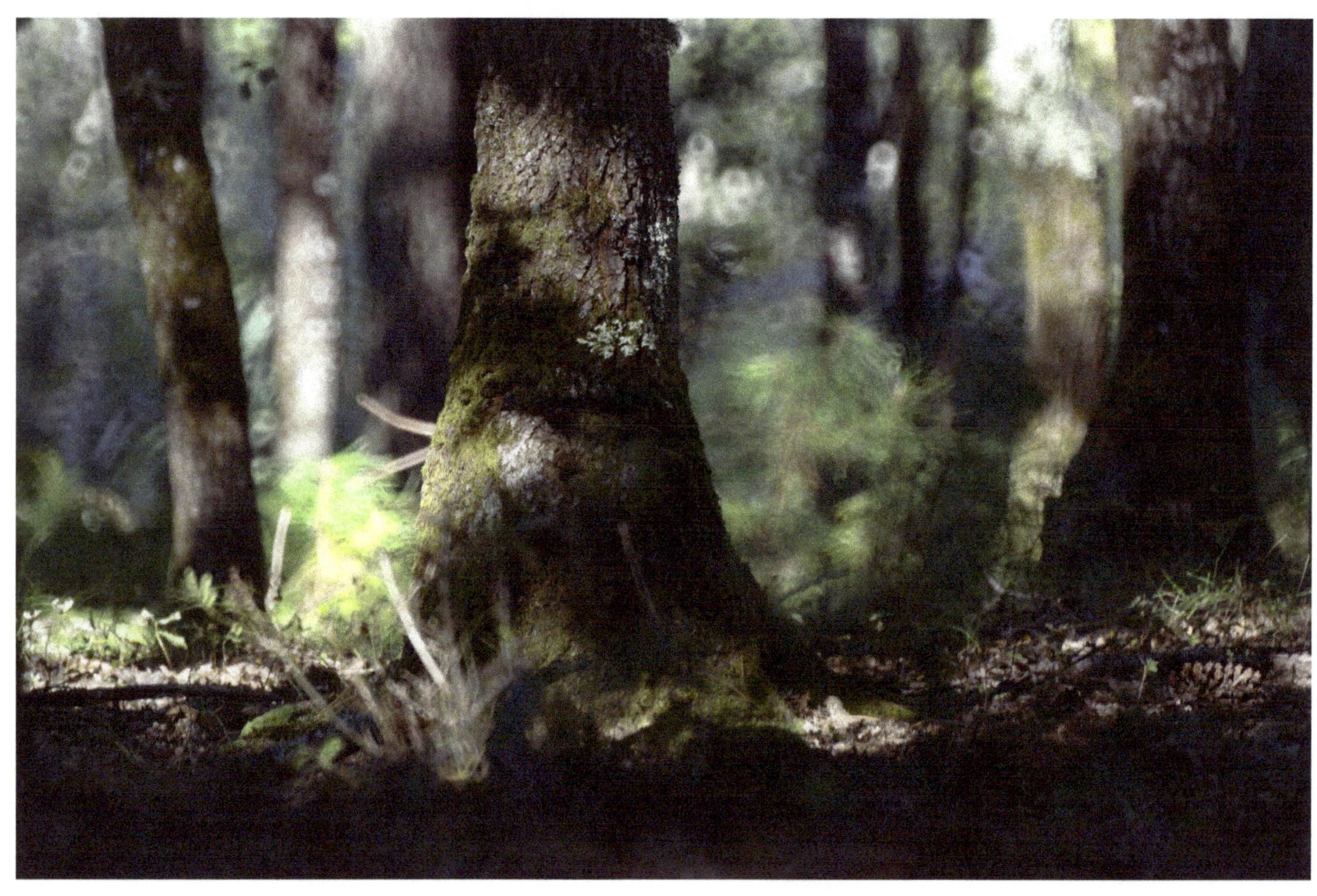

Invitation of the Light...

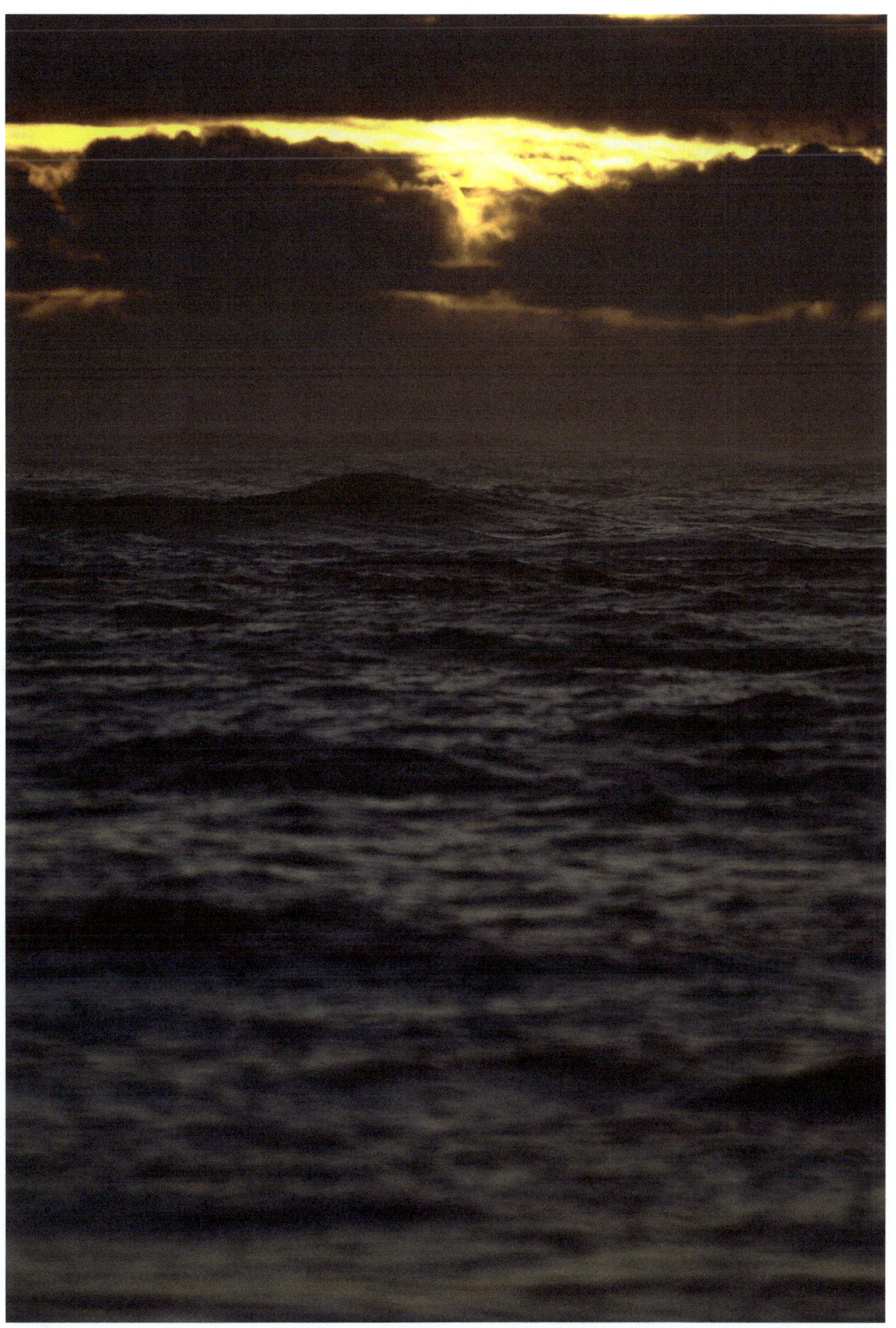

Evening Alchemy...

Misa Aihara

misaaihara.com

My subject is a philosophic exploration of what constitutes the 'reality' within a work of art. I do it with pictorial abstract elements. I want to give an emotional and spiritual impact to a composition on canvas. I want to invite the viewer to the exploration of a deeper dimension of consciousness.

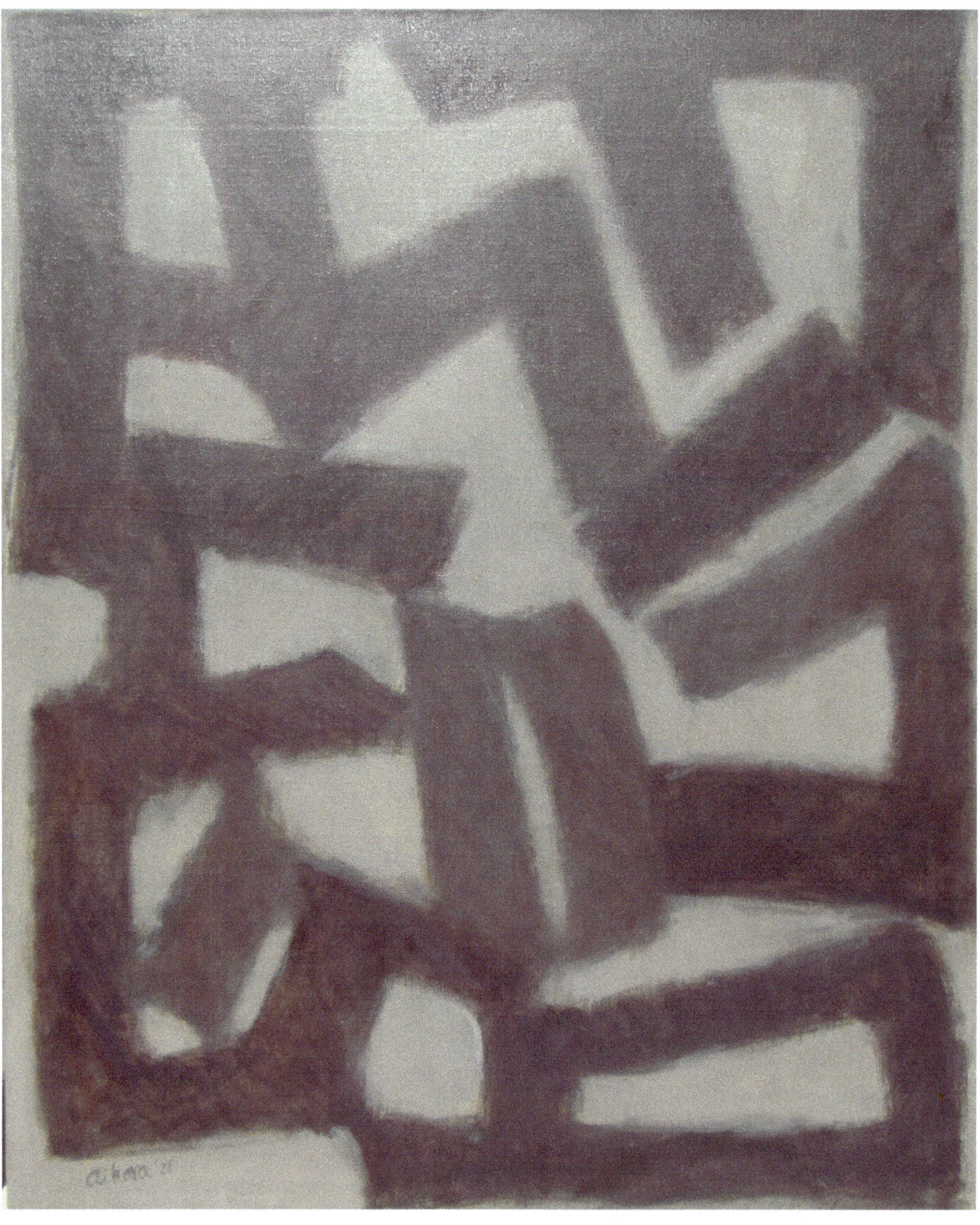

Verko G-11

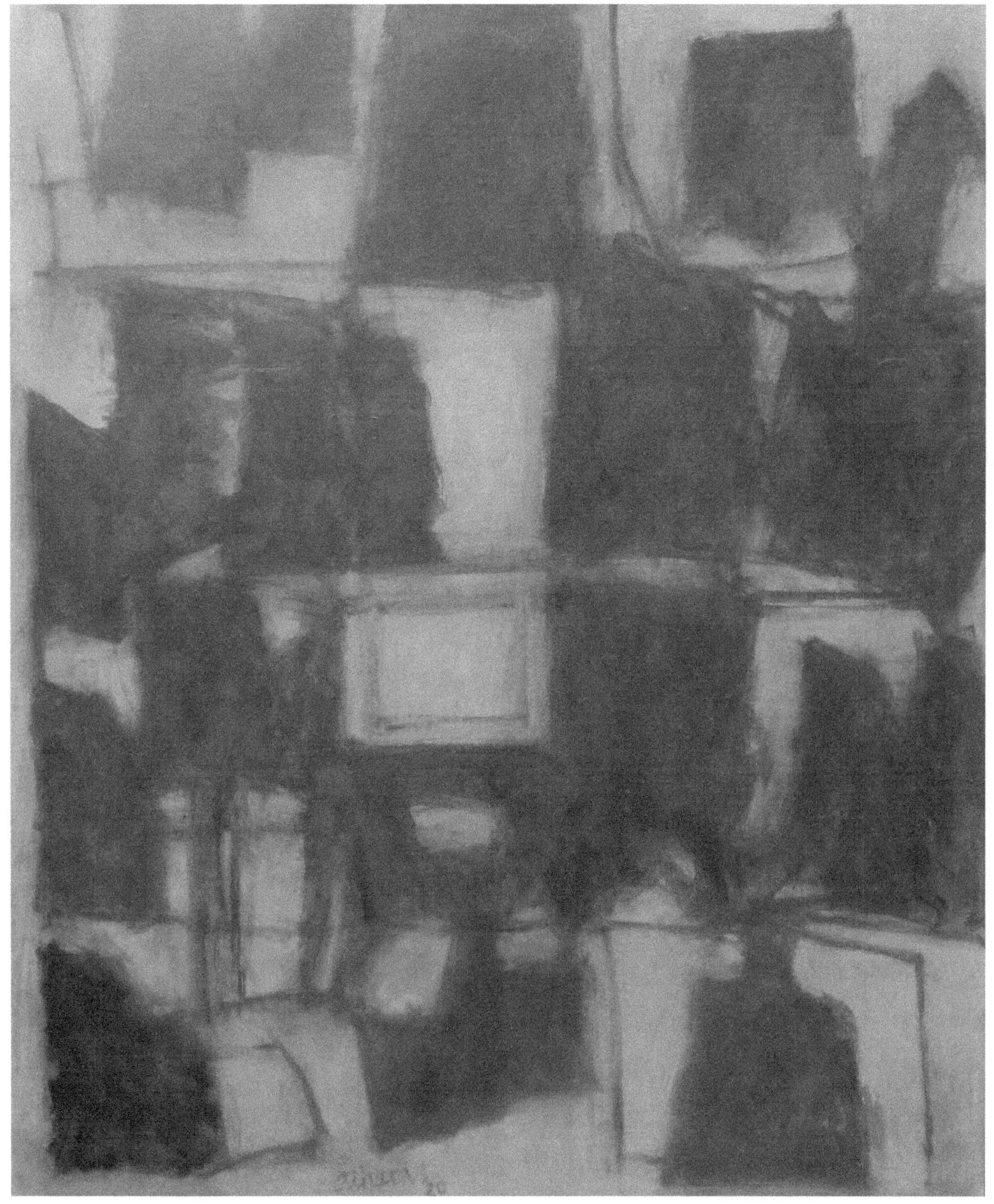

Verko G-5

Mitchell Gibson

Artbymitchellgibson.com

Mitchell Gibson received the Jury Prize for Creativity in a competition at the Museum of Fine Arts in Paris, and his work is published in the Encyclopedia of Living Arts and New Art International listing of World Contemporary Modern Artists, and Miami International. Gibson began painting during his medical residency in 1987. He studied abstract and realistic art forms for over 20 years and he retired from the practice of medicine in 2005 in order to seriously pursue his art. Gibson has sold print and original art pieces to clients all over the world. Gibson displays a number of his original pieces at his private gallery in Greensboro, North Carolina.

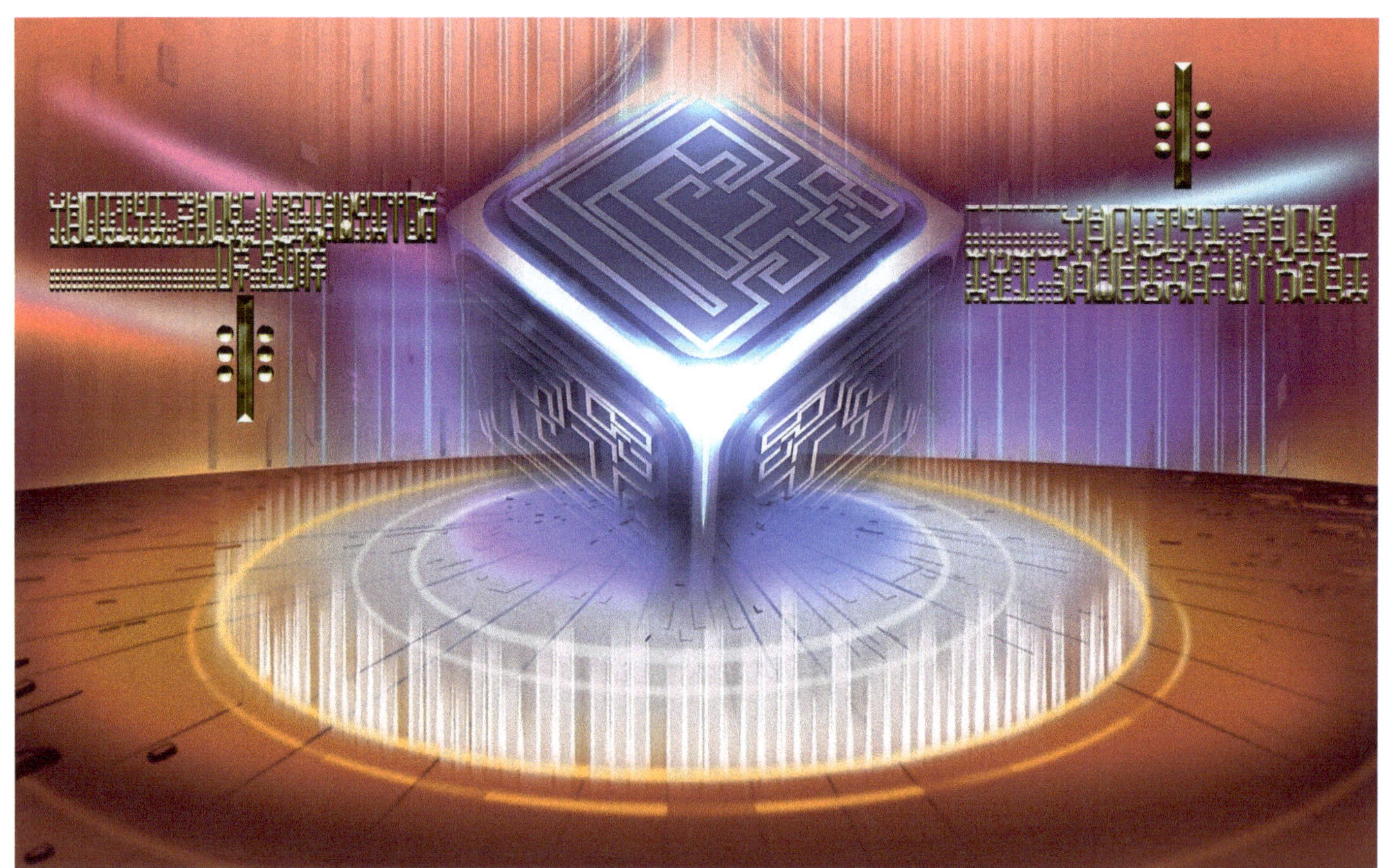

Apotheosis

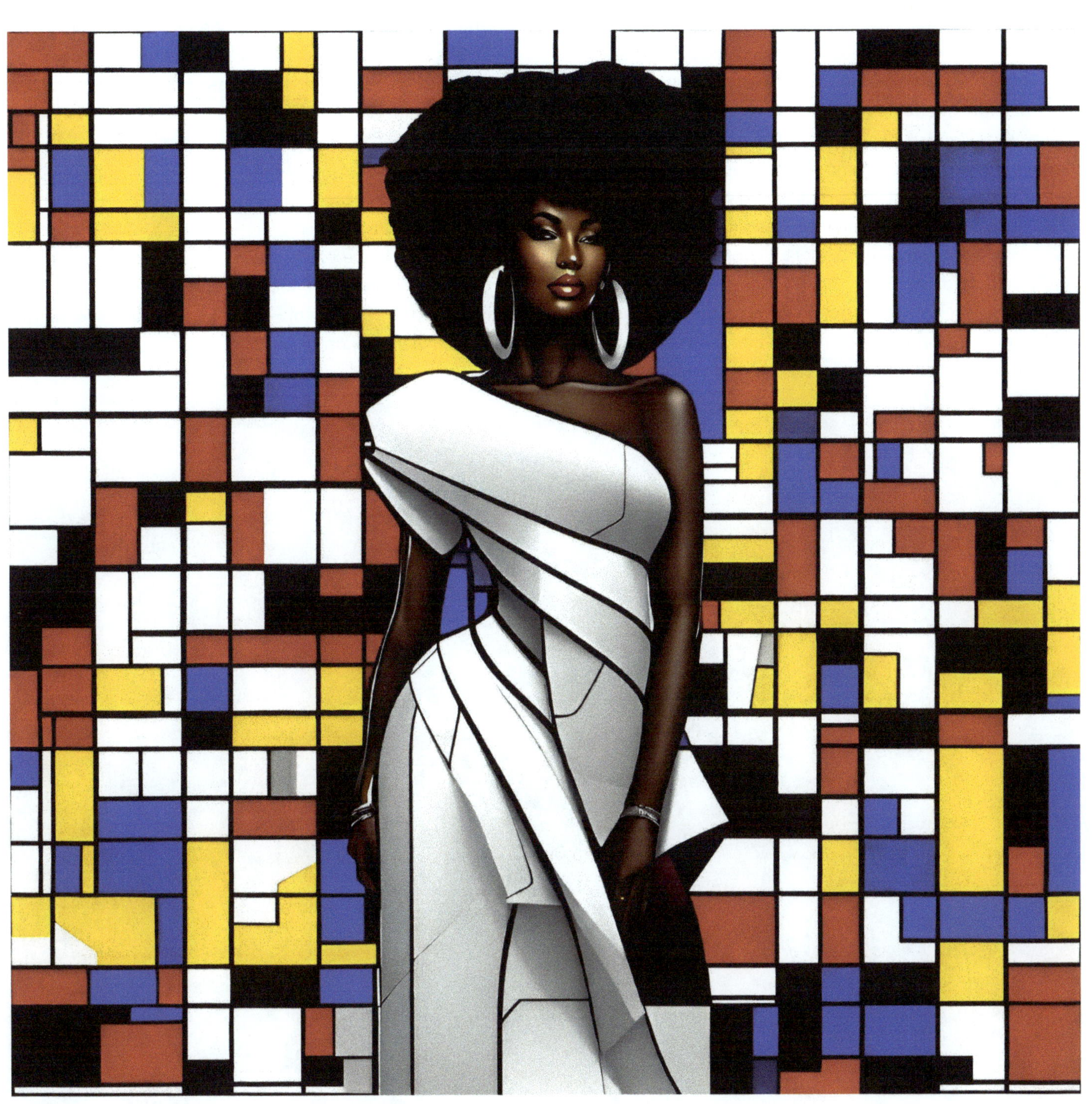

Woman Seven

Nancy Anne Woolf-Pettyjohn
World Master Artist and Illustrator

nancyannewoolf-pettyjohn.com

Nancy Anne Woolf-Pettyjohn is a diversely talented artist born in America, residing in Missouri. She is internationally known both for her accuracy and attention to detail. In the beginning, wanting to be a surgical missionary nurse but having come down with four fatal diseases: (three from a sterile operating room) it was clear God had other plans. Five doctors gave her no chance to survive but God alone healed her. Nancy had a successful antique shop with a vintage clothing museum and did appraisals. After closing her shop to pursue law school she received a degree for Paralegal/Legal Assistant. Working for lawyers and freelancing she was told she was intimidating with her knowledge. She soon found that law came too easy and she needed a challenge. Nancy was born to creative parents both artists and inventors. Her mom always had an appreciation for fine workmanship and lace textiles. Having learned by watching her Mom's artwork all her life and having no formal training she decided to pursue art. This is where she feels the most challenged and satisfied. This was God's plan as he blessed her with a natural God given talent. Her mom once asked, "Can you see it? Then you can paint it". Nancy took it to heart.

Accomplishments include:

Who's Who in Art

Who's Who in America

Who's Who in the World

Only artist in the world to paint museum lace

Nancy is the daughter of Homer & Lucy Woolf and the wife of Matthew Pettyjohn.

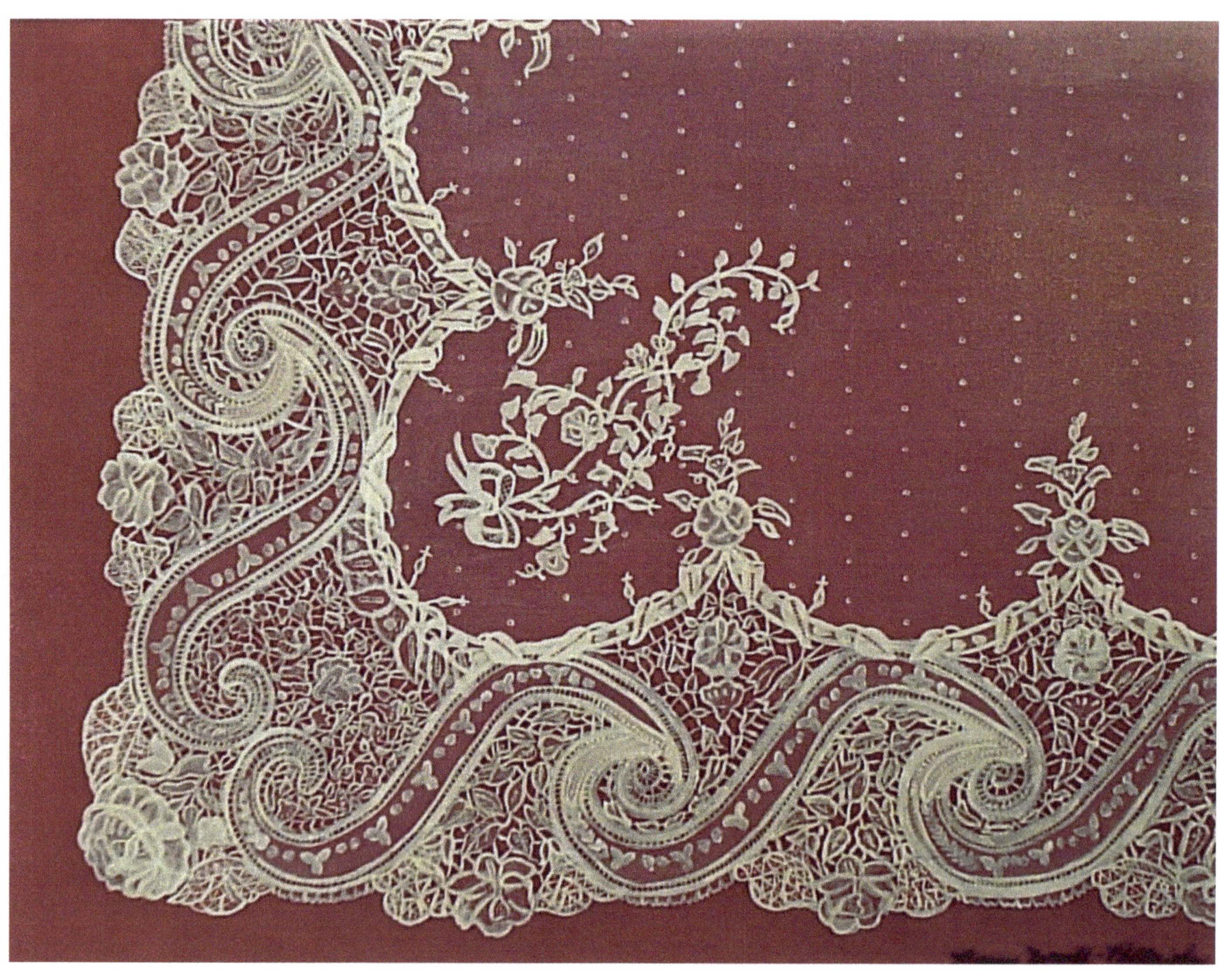

Allhallows Museum Collection #54 Lace Hankie

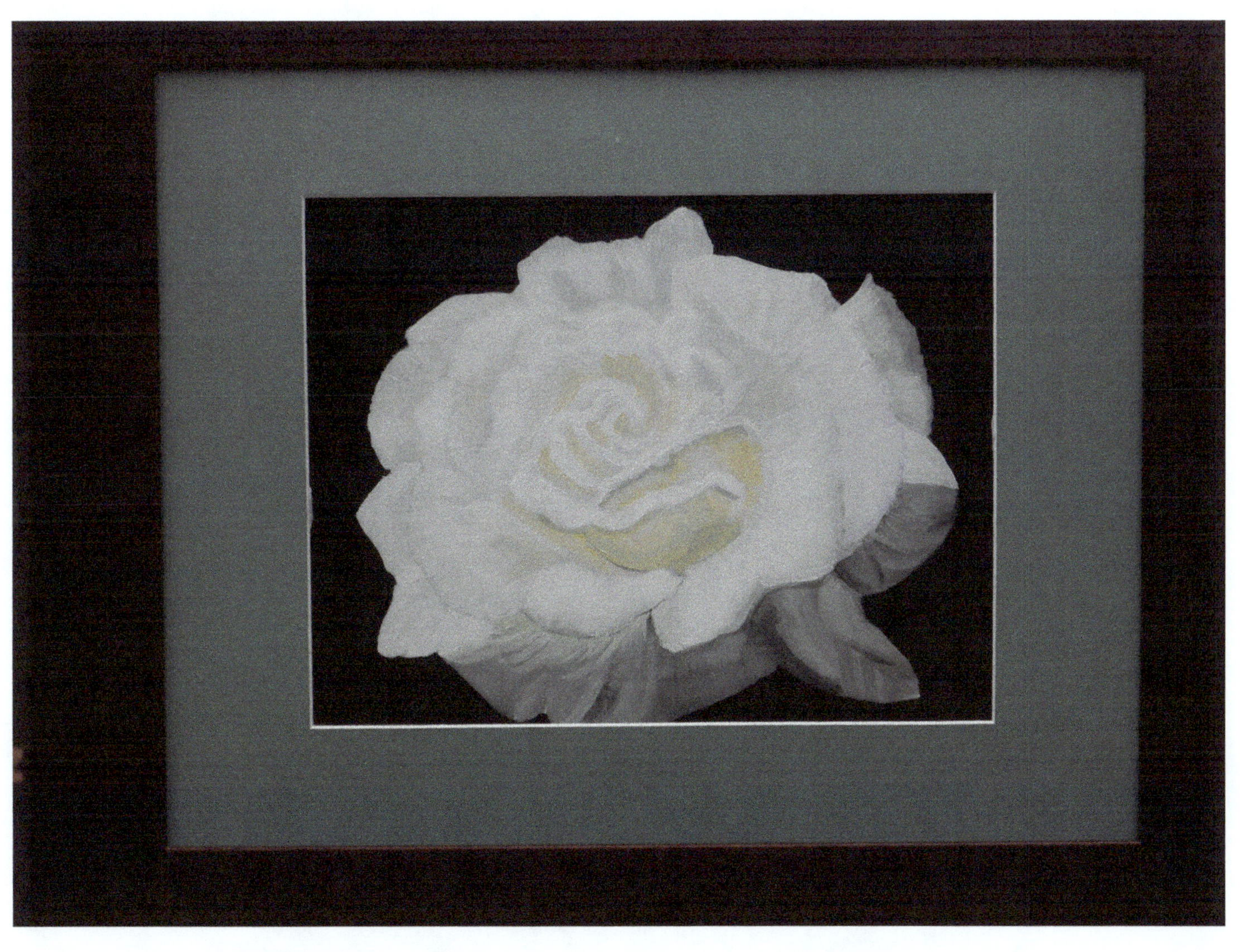

Sugar Moon Hybrid Tea Rose

Nashīnasu ナシーナス

beacons.ai/nashinasu

Rooted in storytelling, my artistic practice draws inspiration from past experiences, timeless images of popular culture, and abstract representations of emotions. While I explore various mediums like pastels and photography, my focus lies in acrylic and oil paintings, as well as graphite pencil sketches, often applied to canvas, medium-density fibreboard (MDF), and paper. Navigating diverse mediums, from the gentle caress of pastels to the stark realism of photography, my true expression finds its home within the realm of acrylic and oil paintings, guided by the meticulous precision of graphite. Each stroke, each shade, meticulously placed upon canvas, medium-density fibreboard, and paper, unveils the profound mysteries of our universe. My distinctive style bears witness to a rich tapestry of influences—from the captivating allure of anime and manga to the enchanting vistas of Disney and Studio Ghibli. It is a narrative that dances between reality and surrealism, influenced by artists including Hayao Miyazaki, Salvador Dali, and Stephen Wiltshire. Yet within the layers of color and form lies a deeper exploration of the human experience. Each creation reflects my evolution—a journey through memory, passion, and curiosity. Inspired by the polka dots artworks of Yayoi Kusama, I infuse my compositions with ethereal light particles, inviting viewers to ponder the enigmatic interplay of shadow and illumination. In a world balanced between the tangible and the intangible, my art urges us to confront the mysteries that lie beyond—to question, to marvel, and to seek the profound truths hidden within ourselves.

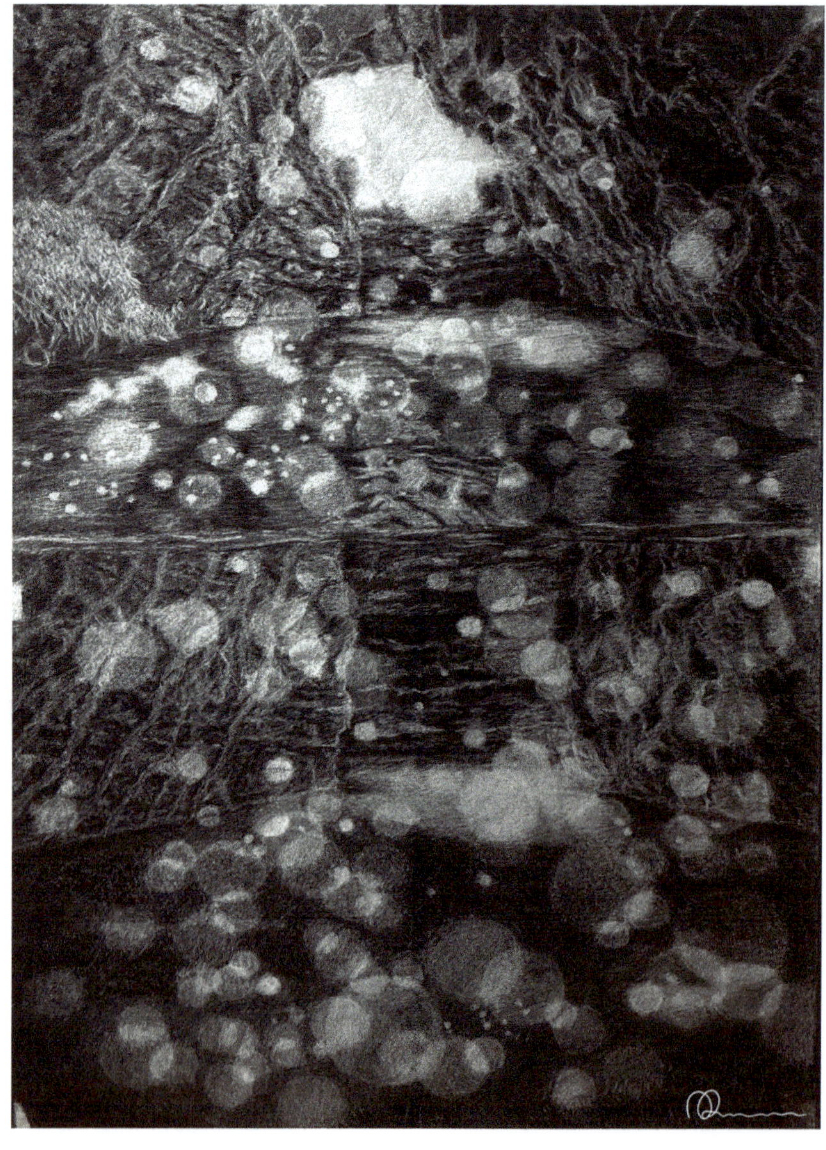

Back to the real world, I guess......

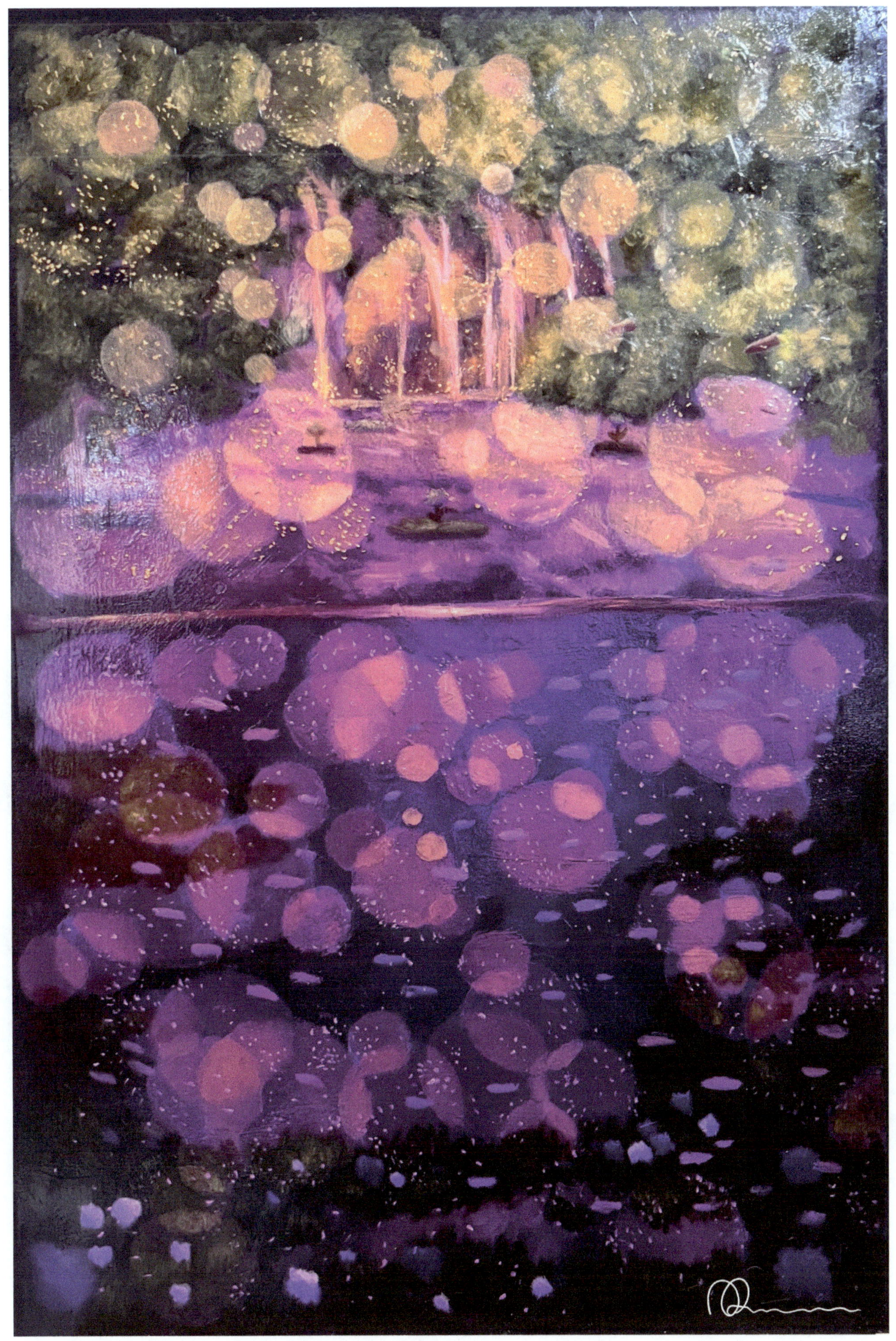

It's Too High

Natalie Egger

unisonart.space

Natalie Egger is an Austrian artist whose vibrant work bridges the realms of digital art and visual arts. Actively engaged in exploring creativity beyond conventional boundaries, Natalie sees the act of creation as a means to discover a unique path that defies rational constraints. Her artistic philosophy resonates deeply with the principles of "l'art pour l'art"—art for art's sake—where the essence lies in the creative process itself rather than the final product.

In her digital artwork, Natalie captures intimate close-ups of serendipitous subjects she encounters during urban explorations and travels. These unexpected moments are transformed into compelling snapshots, which she later deconstructs and reimagines through a meticulous fusion of photographs and pencil drawings. This seamless blend of media allows her to explore and express the intricate layers of her subjects. Her acrylic paintings and pencil drawings reveal a fascination with the human face and body. Through these mediums, Natalie delves into the expressive potential of human features, imbuing each piece with a sense of depth and emotion. Her work invites viewers to engage with the raw and unfiltered beauty of her subjects, offering a glimpse into her unique perspective on the human experience.

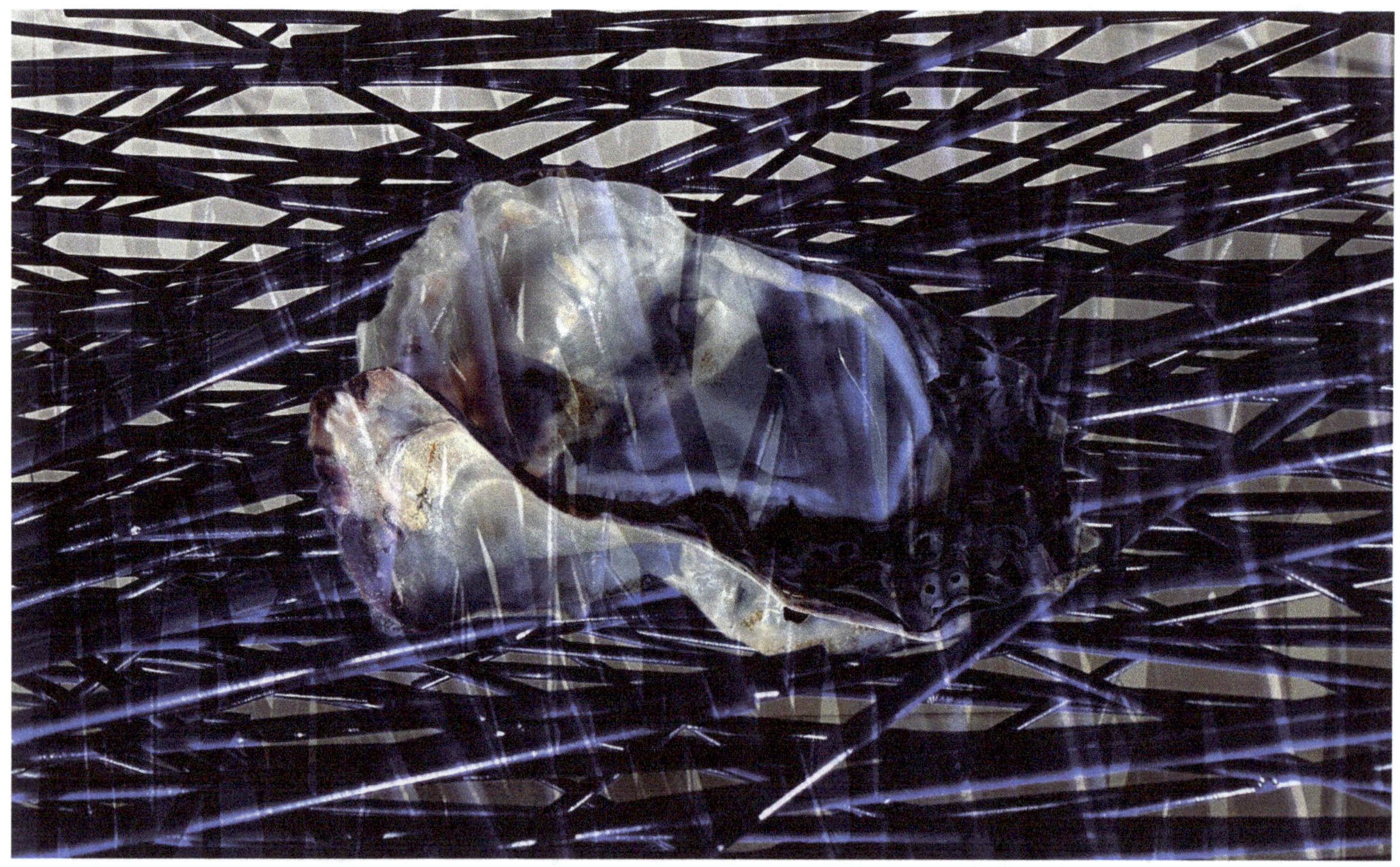

„Ultramarine concha", digital art, photography, 2024

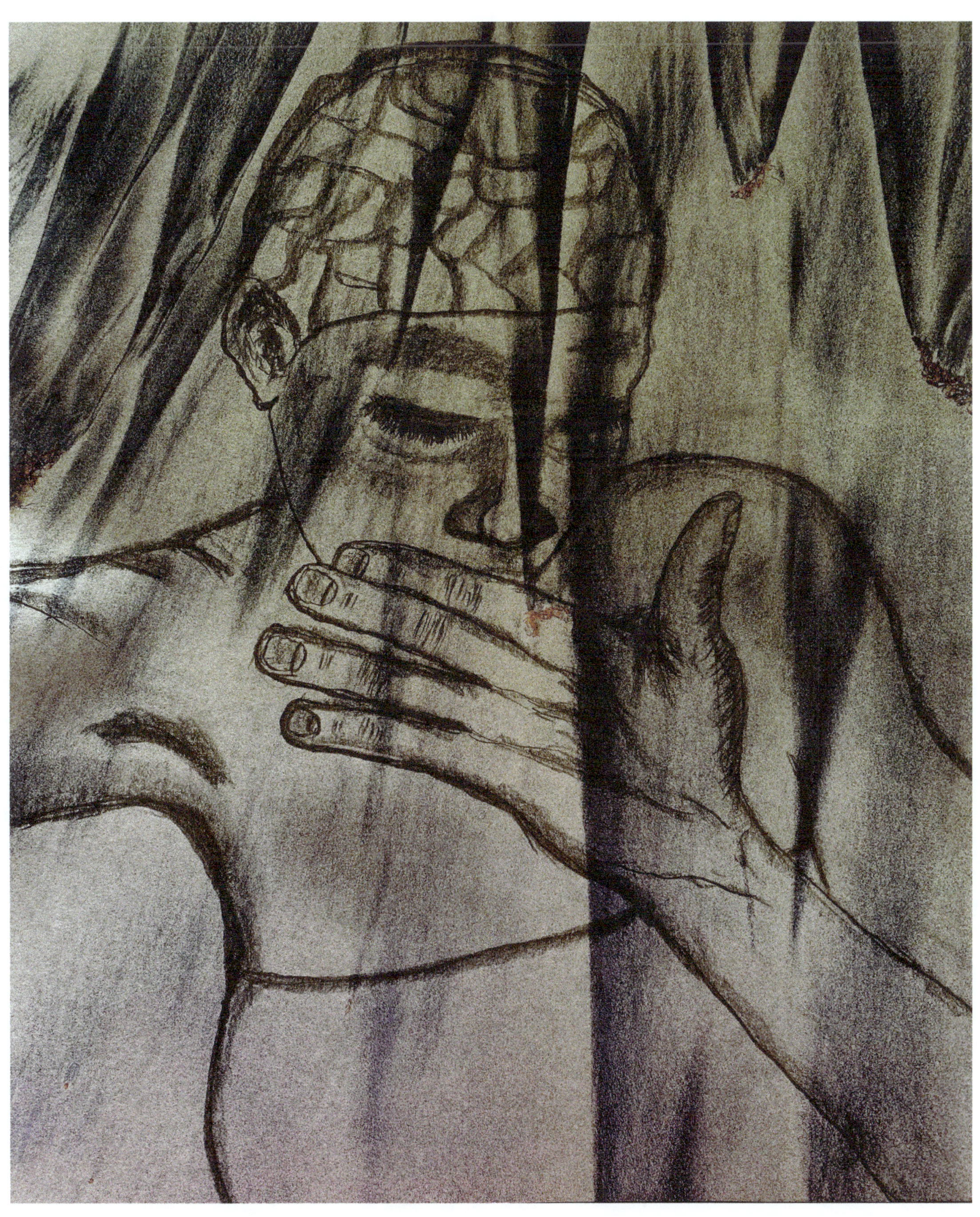

„Nuba de Caldéron Hondo", digital art, pencil drawing, photography, 95x75 cm incl frame, 2024

Paul Hartel

singulart.com/en/artist/paul-hartel-58998

From New York, now living in the West of Ireland, I paint and draw in neo-expressionist and art brut styles with oil, acrylic, oil stick, pastels, charcoal and pencil. I believe in art for art's sake and the veracity of spontaneity. I think of my work as celebrating the spirit of the 'inner child' while commenting on societal issues through an improvisationally eviscerated energy. I believe my work yields a spontaneous truth, not to be mitigated by hesitation. I subscribe to a raw sense of urgency I feel parallels the excitement of life and all its accompanying intellectual, emotional and existential vicissitudes. Only with the viewer's perception, is the artwork complete. In the 'Windows Series,' the paintings are more minimalist but draw on raw emotions and spontaneous gestures. Utilizing vibrant acrylics and bold pastel strokes encapsulated within structured pencil lines, I've explored human differences with each segment portraying a different facet of expression, inviting interpretation and introspection. These pieces serves as a visual dialogue on the spectrum of human feelings and individuality with frenetic strokes and elemental shapes to capture the complexities of human expression and implication of thought. Each face is framed yet fragmented, symbolizing our struggles with identity and self-perception in a world filled with chaos, demanding order. These paintings vibrate with an intensity yet simplicity of feeling.

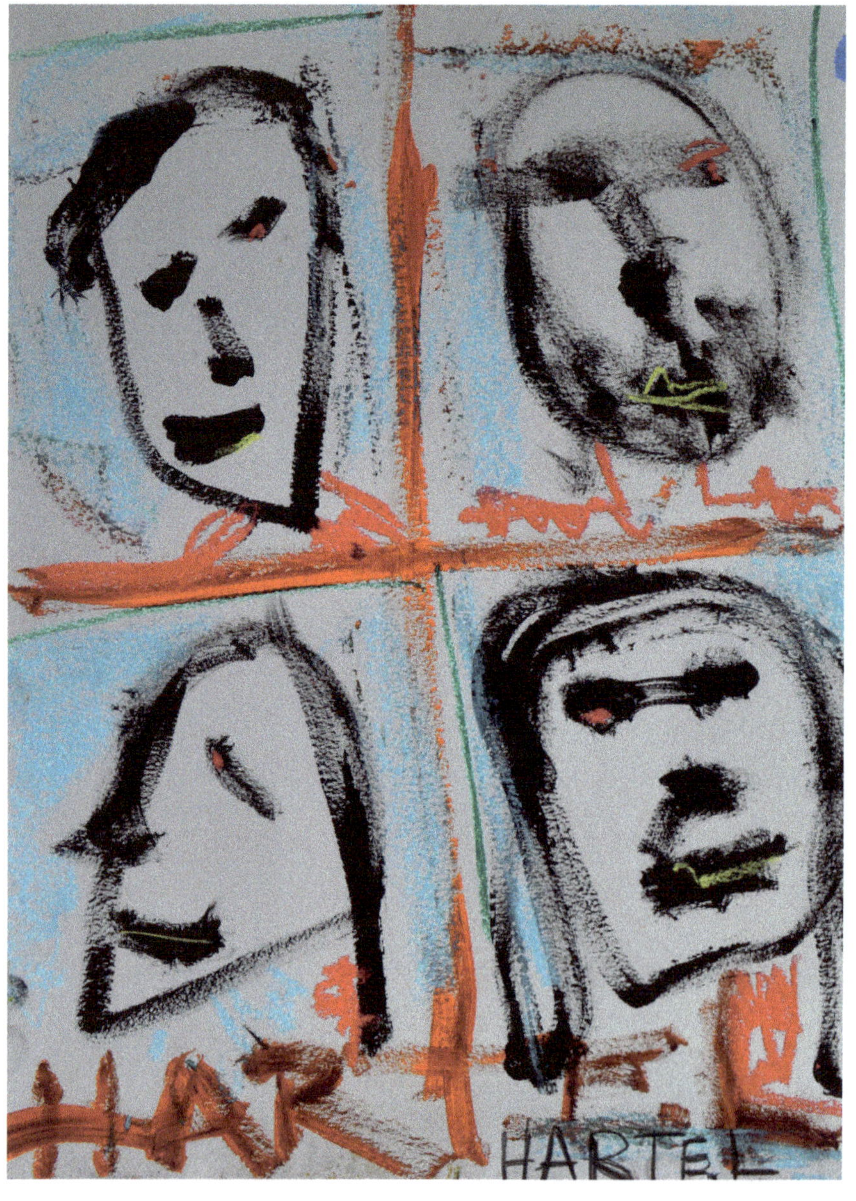

Privacy Windows

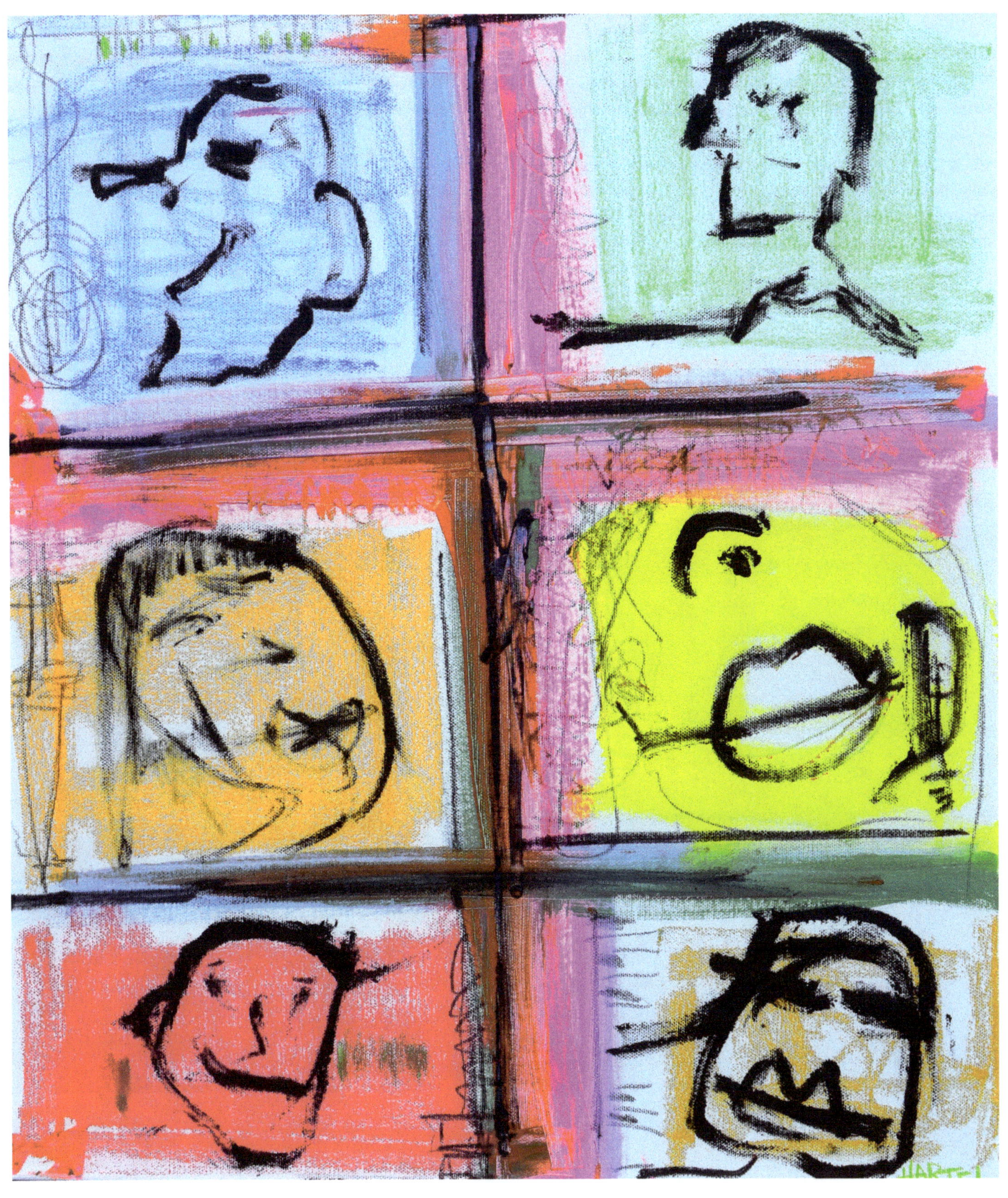

Park Avenue Windows

Peter Wall

picturewall.eu

„Logik bringt dich von A nach B. Deine Phantasie bringt dich überall hin." Dieses Einstein Zitat beschreibt die Richtung meiner Malerei wohl am besten. Mein Ziel ist es, mit meinen Bildern, Spuren zu hinterlassen die über meine normale Existenz hinausgehen. Das Malen ist, seit ich denken kann, so etwas wie ein Verlangen. Dem ich, je nach Lebensumstand nachgab. Schritt für Schritt autodidaktisch bildete sich so die Art und Weise meiner Malerei heraus. Heute lebe ich als Künstler und Illustrator am Malchiner See in Mecklenburg-Vorpommern. Meine

malerische Ausdrucksweise ist gegenständlich und figurativ mit Richtung phantastischer Realismus und Surrealismus – Stilrichtungen in denen sich meine Phantasien so richtig ausleben lassen. In meinen freien Arbeiten verarbeite ich Emotionen, Träume und Empfindungen vielerlei Art. Ich bin mitunter erstaunt und erfreut, über die vielen unterschiedlichen Interpretationen der Betrachter meiner Bilder. Zum Malen bevorzuge ich Acrylfarben auf Leinwand oder Holz.

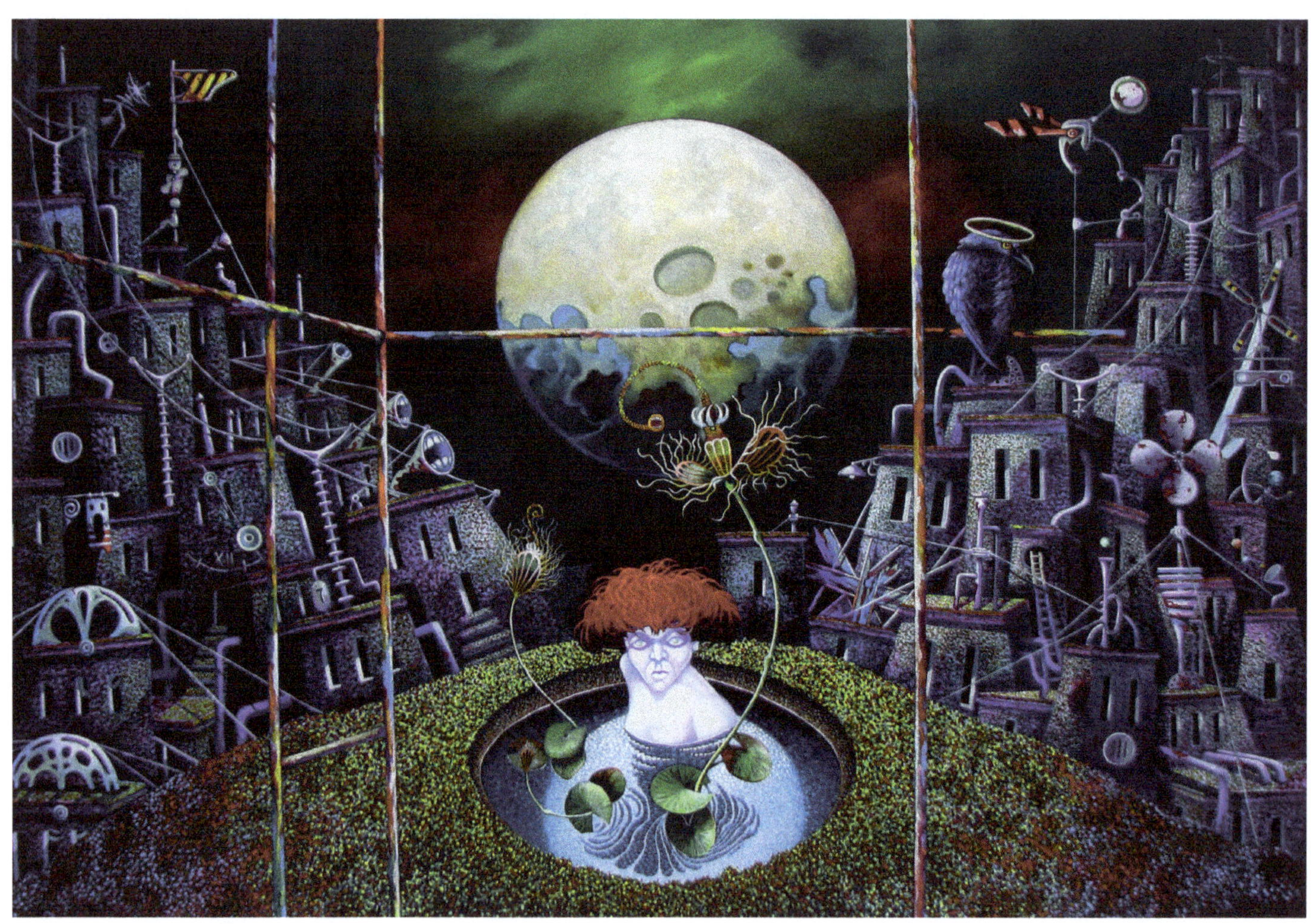

die dunkle Seite des Mondes

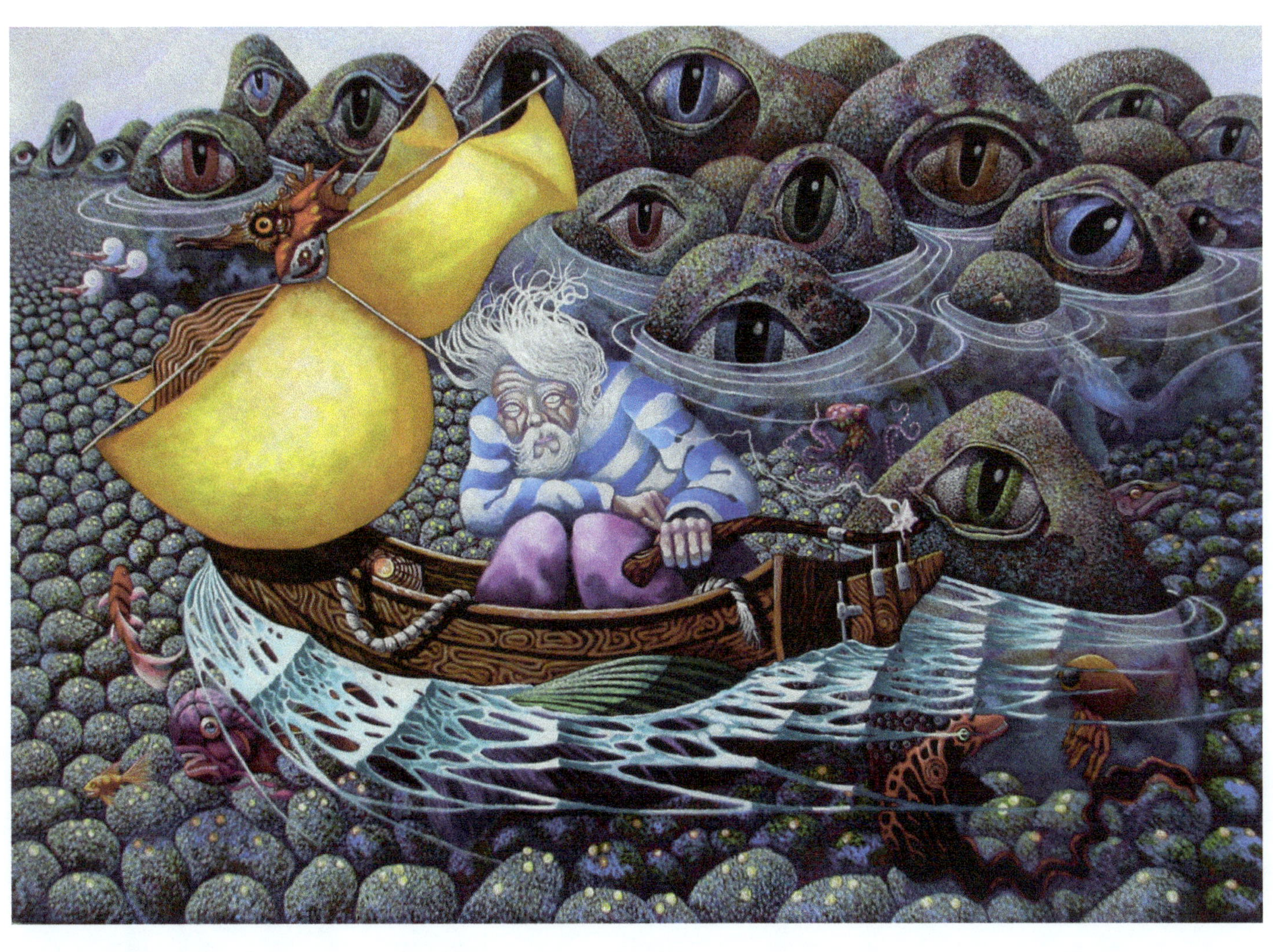

Styx

Pompeyo Curbelo Martin

pompeyocurbelomartin9

Pompeyo Curbelo Martín es un pintor español premiado, nacido en San Sebastián de la Gomera cuyo desarrollo profesional a nivel artístico ha tenido lugar en Viena, Austria. Sus pinturas implican una evolución del arte moderno y conllevan una reflexión de la sociedad actual. Pompeyo cree que el arte debe evolucionar continuamente y no puede quedarse estancado. Sus obras se basan en sus orígenes insulares y en la influencia del entorno donde creció, las Islas Canarias, así como en las preocupaciones de la sociedad actual, explorando "cualquier tipo inquietud", hacienda hincapié en los aspectos socioeconómicos de la sociedad contemporánea. Como artista emergente, sus obras han sido expuestas a nivel nacional e internacional, despertando interés en el mundo, Argentina, Austria, Canadá, Estados Unidos, Eslovaquia, Francia, Italia, Luxemburgo, Japón, Países Bajos, Portugal, Reino Unido y Suiza.

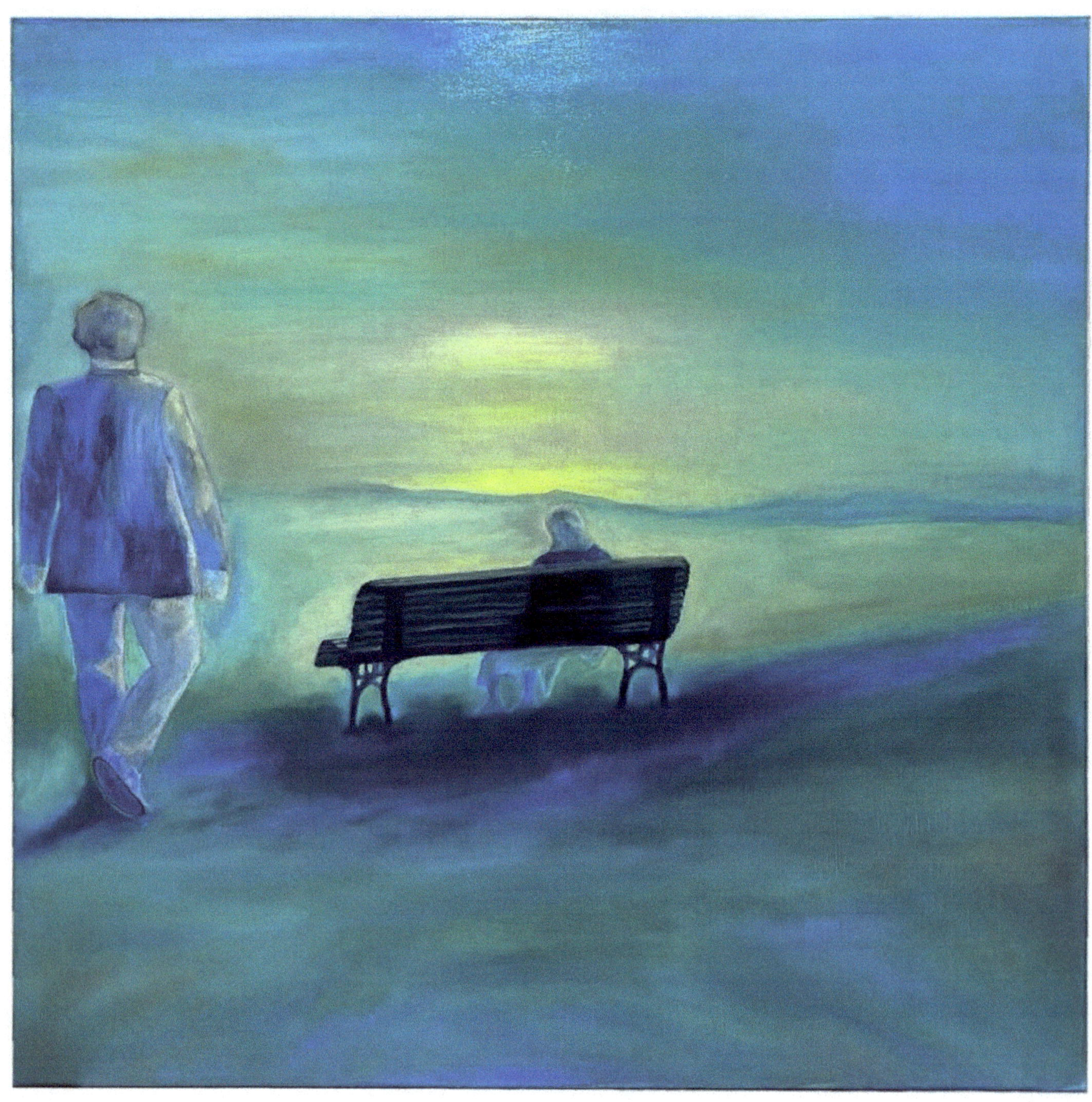

El Cielo. Oleo sobre lienzo, 100x100 cm

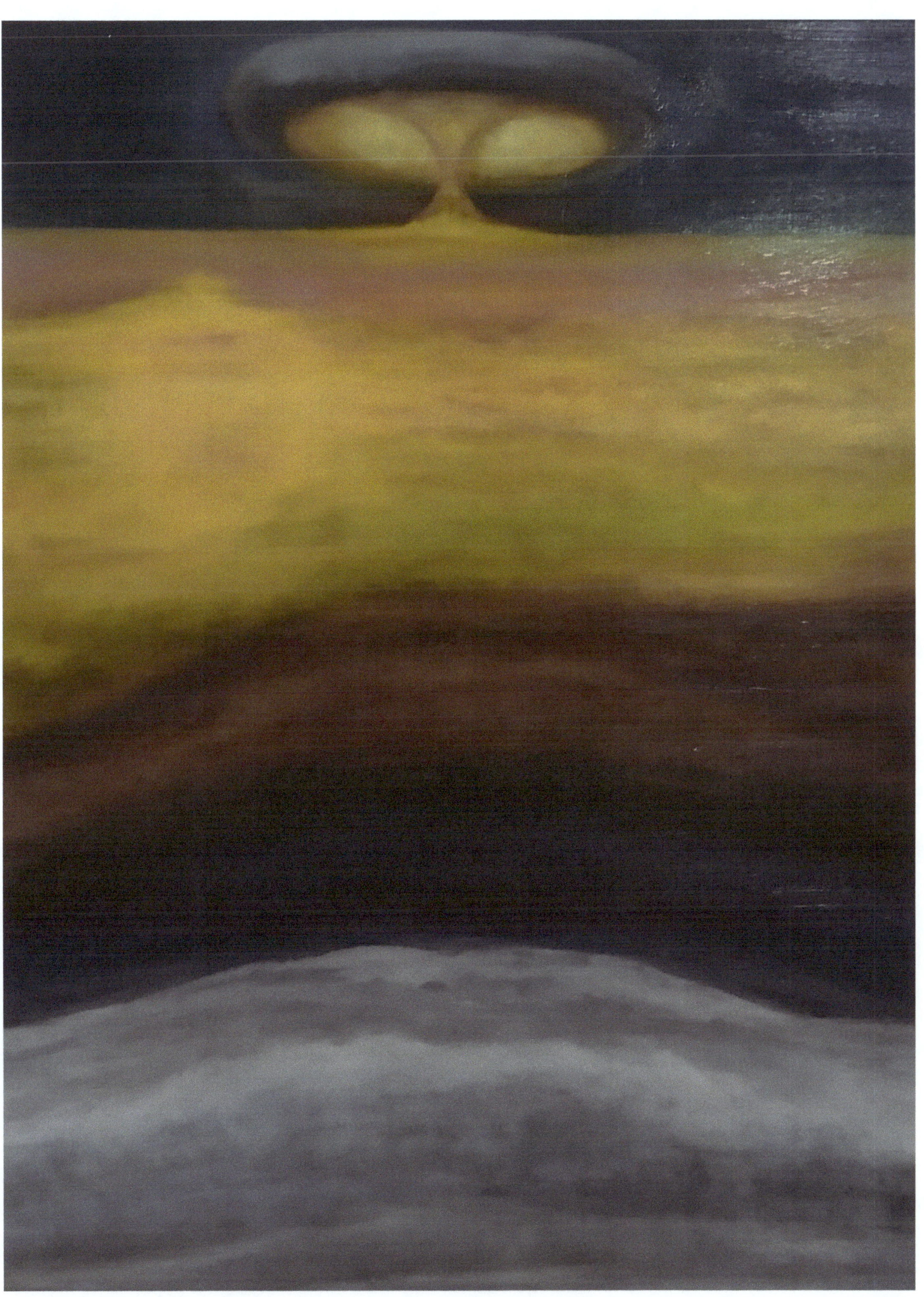

El Trigo del Este, 2023. Óleo sobre lienzo, 100X81 cm

Prudence Au

instagram.com/gallerpru

Prudence is a highly sought-after creations of the Hong Kong artist enjoy worldwide recognition. She graduated as an abstract artist with high acclaims in Fine Art in France & Hong Kong. Colours and textures are two of the main elements with a surging passion and positivity, she sees life filled with colors. She creates vibrant coloring and dynamic rendition to illustrate life's aesthetics and purpose. Articulating the textures of the soul through a vivacious manipulation of ink, oil and acrylic that showcasing her work of obsession in examining the materiality of textures in art. Since 2022, she selected as exhibiting artist to represented in renowned art galleries in Europe. In 2023 - 2024, Prudence has been recognized by a growing number of international institutions that she won various renowned International Artist Awards in Europe such as "Universal Artist Award, Leonardo Da Vinci" Gold Award, "International Award, Michelangelo – The Genius of Italy" and "The Premier Artist Prize" etc. Prudence's work reflects her love for nature and signature artistic vision in matters in its primitive state. Every single line on her artwork is painted free-handed with a high degree of precision to remain grounded to the work of mother nature rather than by objective depiction. Drawn from her unique pursue in abstract art tradition and deep engagement. She excels in the work of a dynamic rendition of vibrant and eccentric coloring and signature contouring layer by layer. Articulating the textures of the soul through a vivacious manipulation of oil, acrylic and ink.

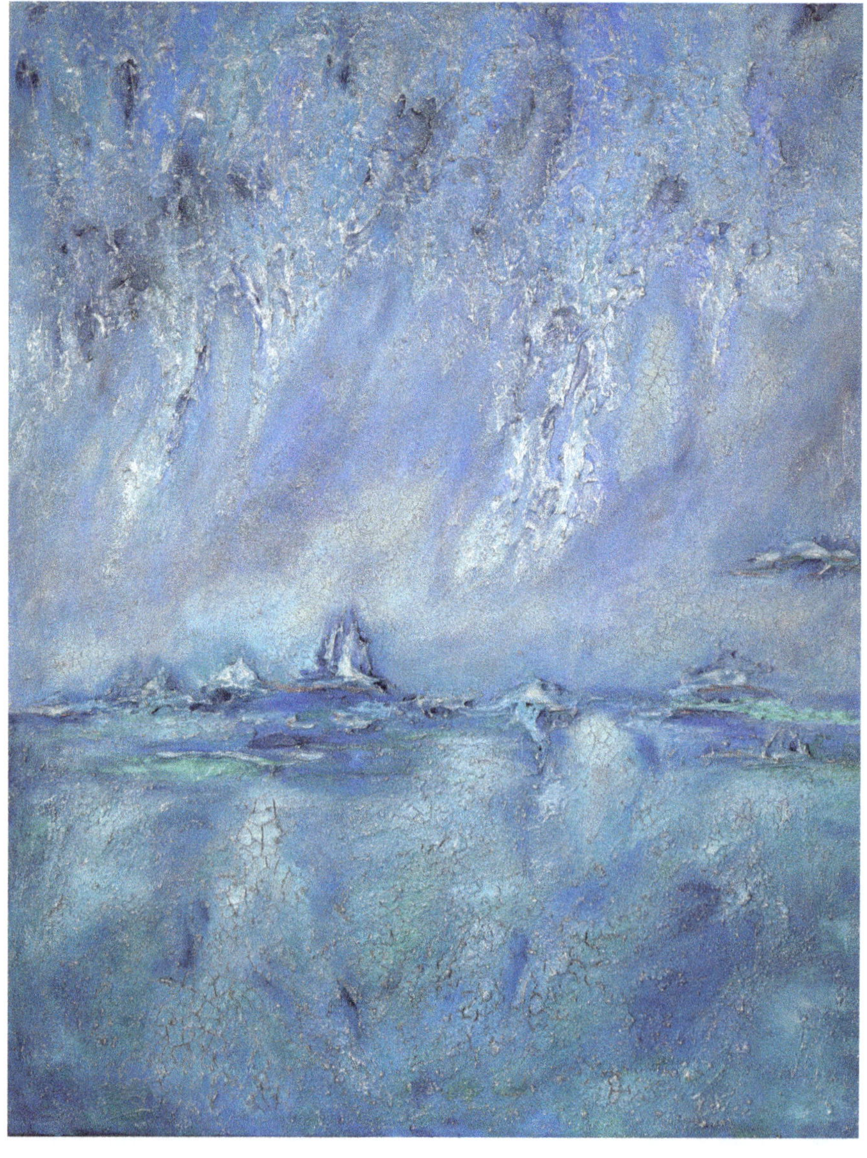

Blue Dremscape

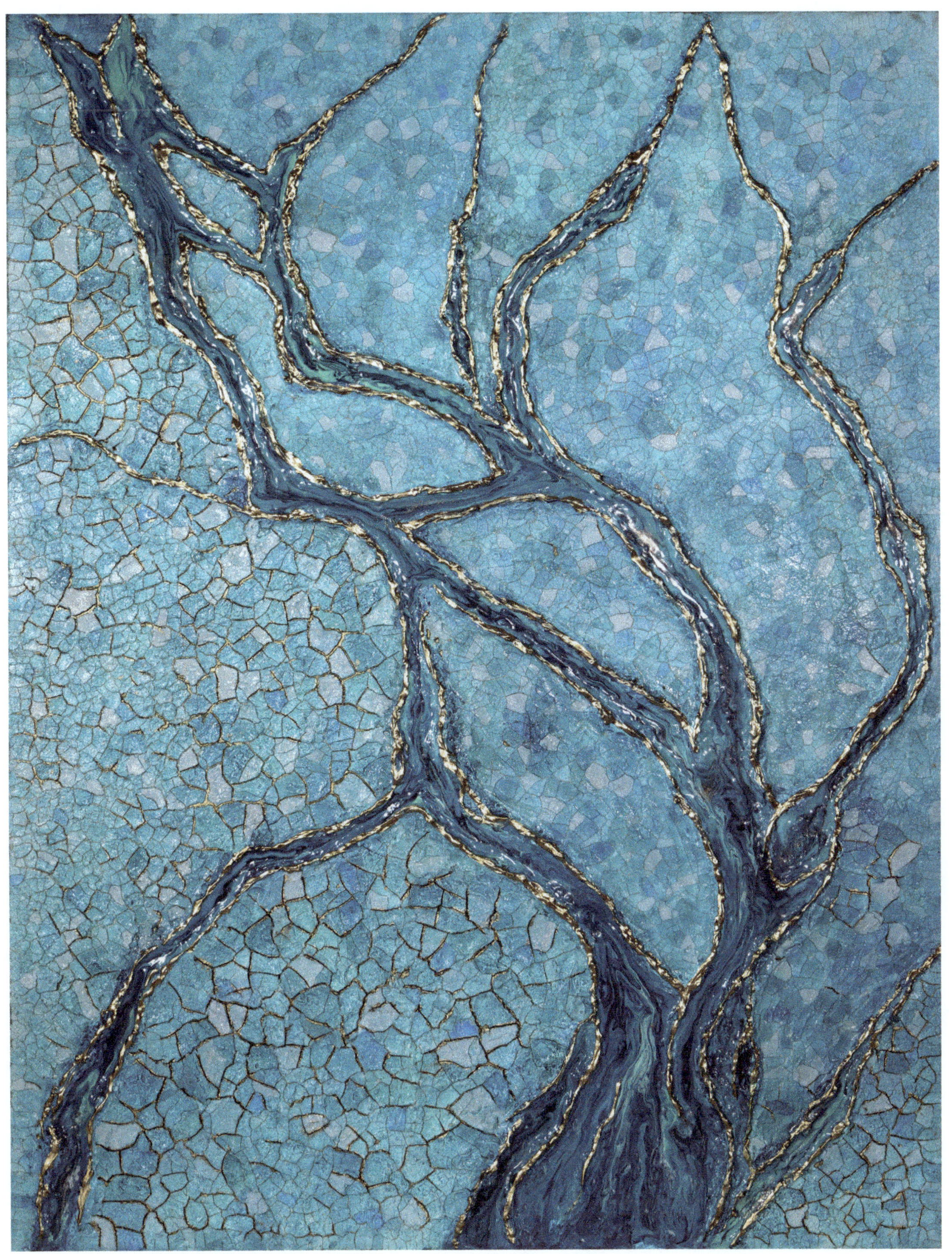

Aqua Glacial Reverie

Ramón Rivas

rivismo.com / instagram.com/ramonrivas_rivismo

His work is rigorously personal, which he applies without limitations through his unique style called Rivismo. He uses his multiple experiences and his creativity to be different and to seek artistic proposals that surprise and excite. His imagination is essential to develop creative and innovative works that interact positively with the viewer. His work is orderly and methodical. He supervises good execution, incorporates scientific themes, balances the composition and makes the painting a transitable space for the viewer. As a result, he creates images with precision work, surprising density and visually captivating depth. His works seek to encourage the viewer to participate and turn him into a creative artist during his visual journey through the scene. Renowned professionals have recognized the exceptional originality and aesthetic appeal of his work, emphasizing his unique vision and exceptional skills that have captivated the public and have contributed significantly to the enrichment of the art world. His art is revolutionary and proves to be a master of linguistic plurality, developing his own unique language. His talent has been recognized through international exhibitions. His artistic contributions have appeared in numerous books, magazines and he has received prestigious international awards, further cementing his reputation as a distinguished artist.

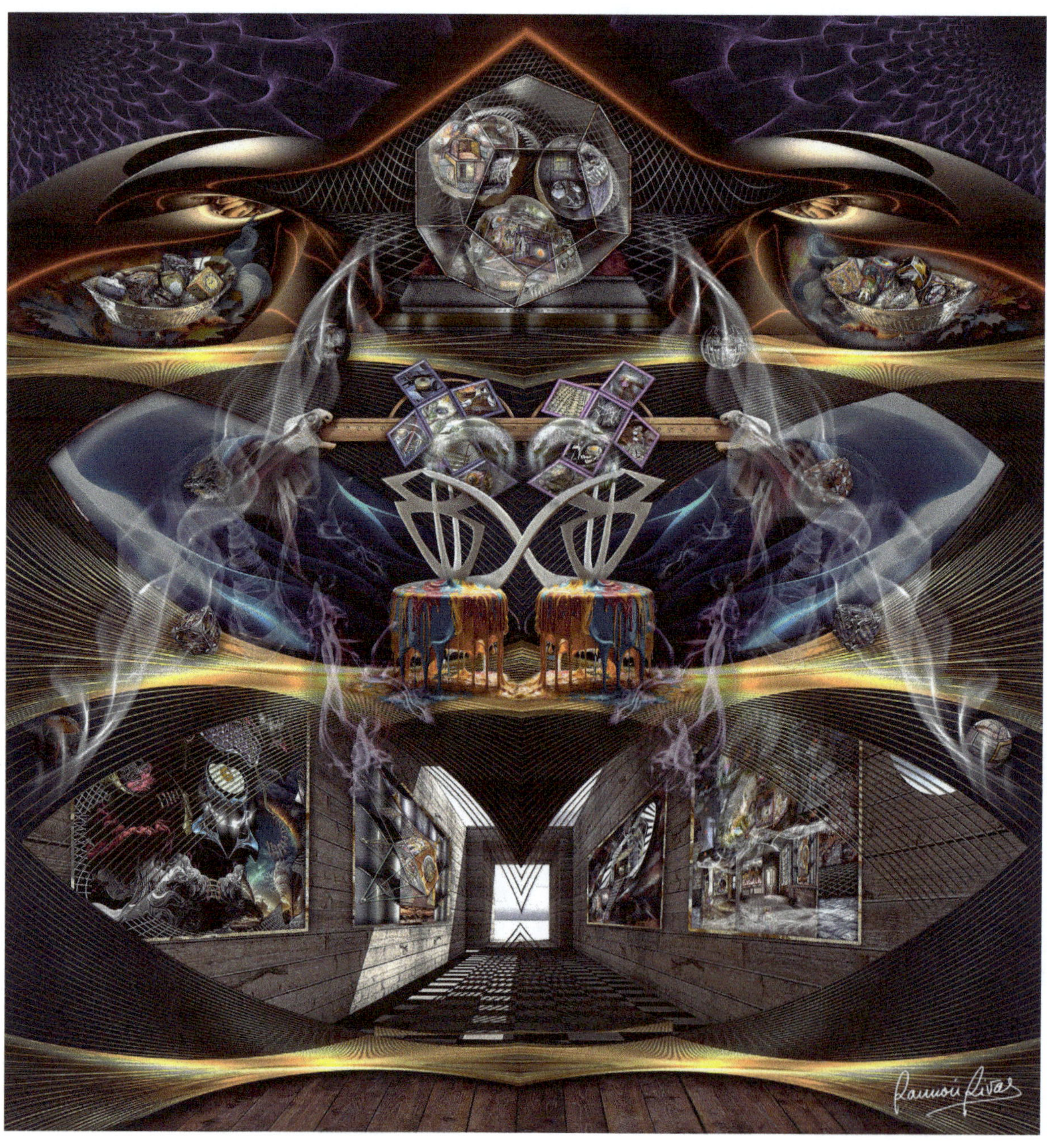

Expo-Park of Experiential Art

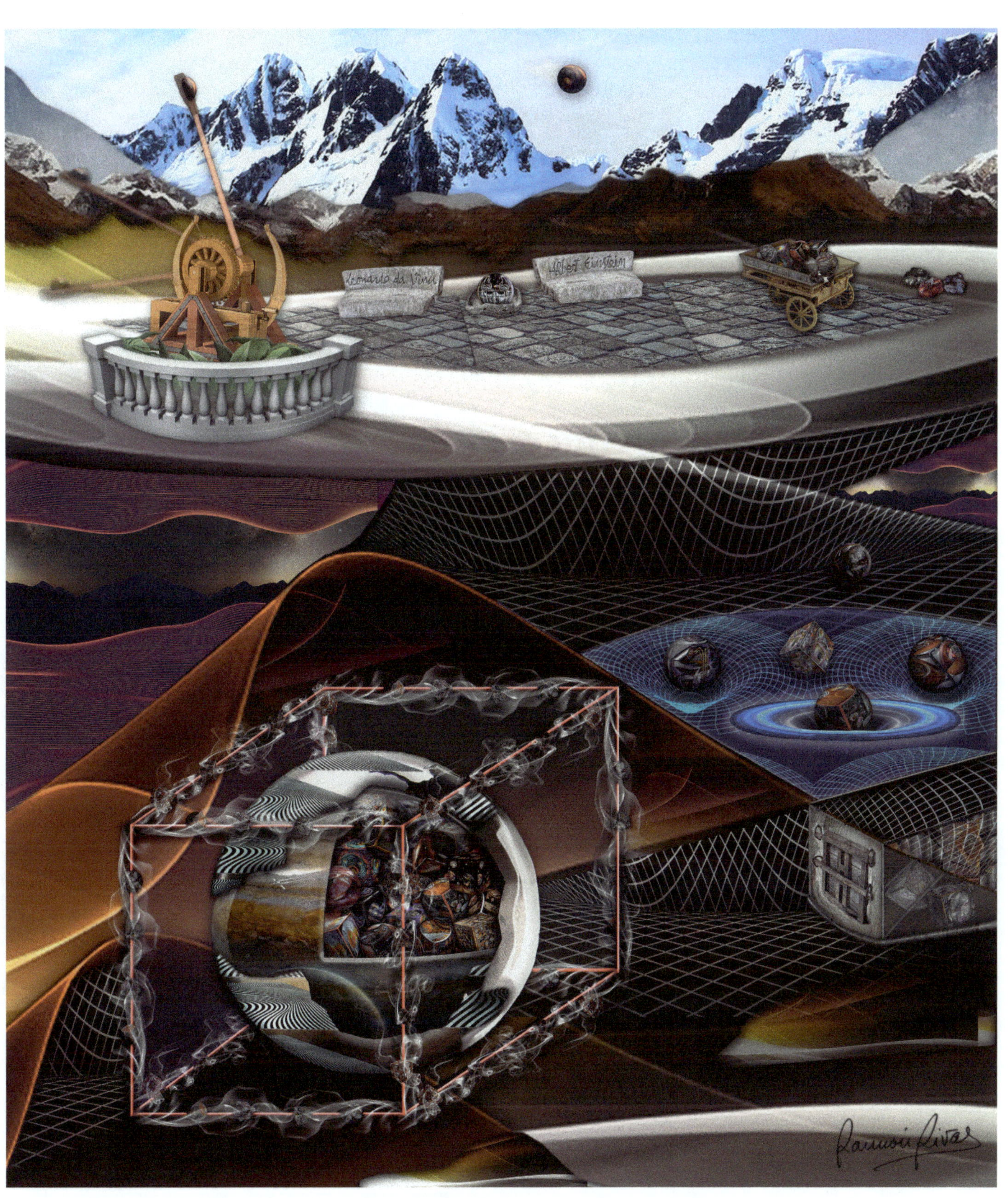

Art between the Catapult and Relativity. Da Vinci & Einstein

Raúl Vega

raulvega.com

II expect a certain amount of randomness in my process. I never quite know how a picture will turn out because each image has a life of its own. My work combines elements of Architecture, cultural iconography, color, textures and the mundane that I see that often goes unnoticed. My work deals with the rainbow of randomness and chaos that is part of our daily lives.

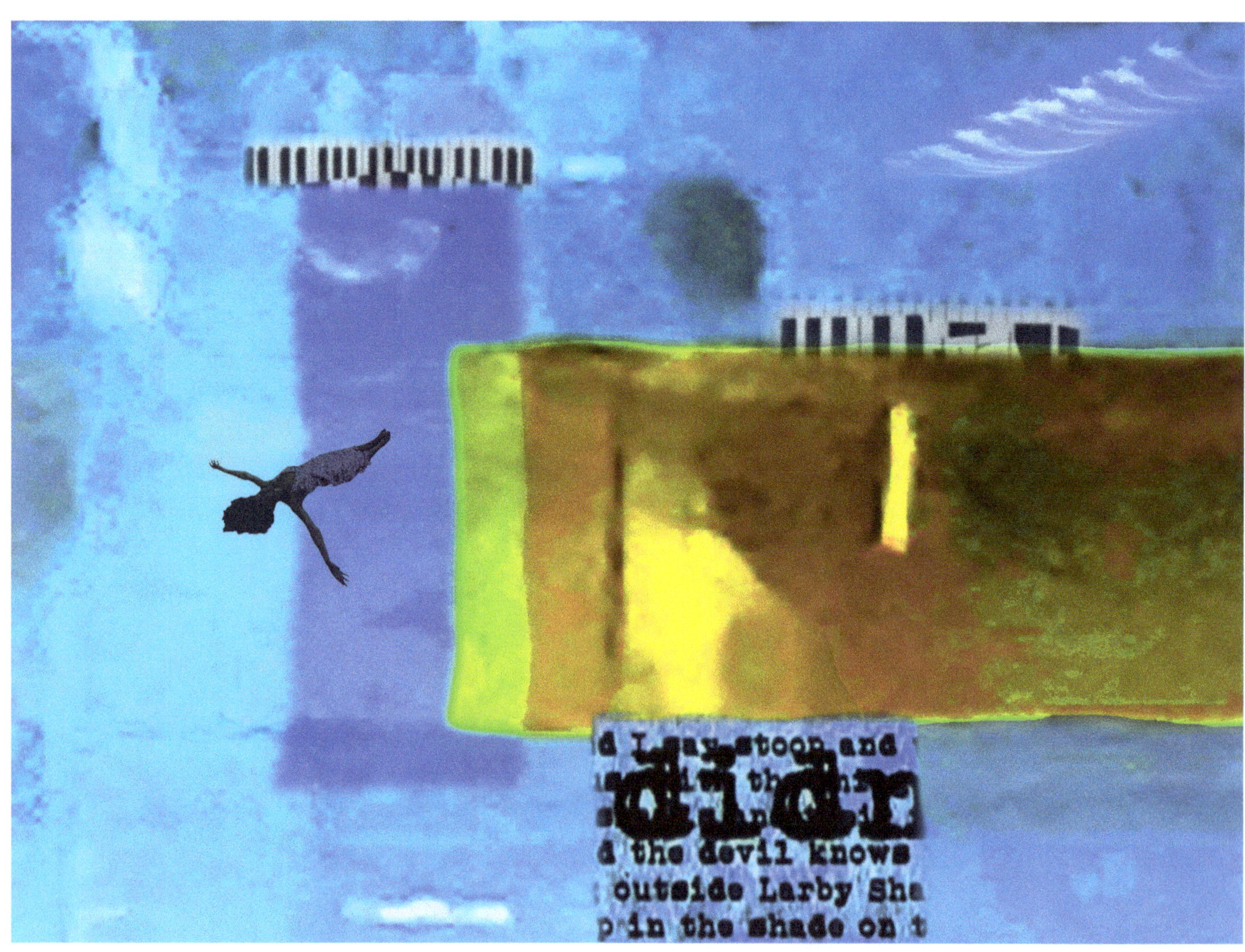

Sontal

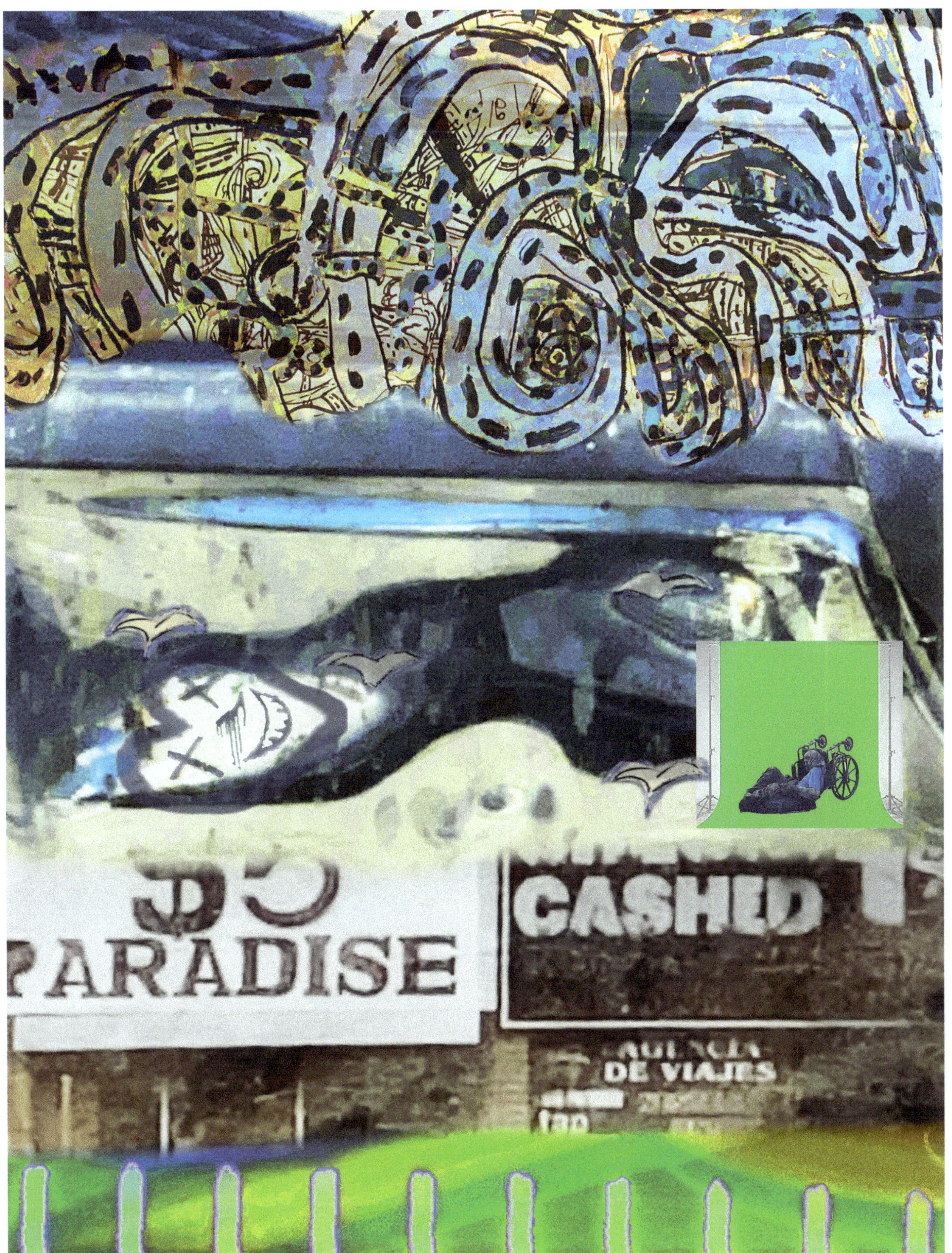

Paradise Cashed

Riitta Hellén-Vuoti

instagram.com/hvriitta

Riitta Hellén-Vuoti (b. 1959) is a Finnish artist, living and working in Kuopio, Finland. By education she is a licensed medical specialist in psychiatry and psychotherapy. She has been artistic since her youth, and started dedicating more time to painting and poetry around the year 2000. Her artistic focuses remain in painting and poetry. Her artworks have been on display in various galleries around Finland since the year 2000 and internationally since 2020. She is now a full – time artist. I am interested in – and inspired by – the human being and the never-ending complexities of life. In art it is possible to deal with all the questions and concepts in a more intuitive way. When I was young, I thought I would grow up to be a painter, and now life has shown me it is possible. At first, I mainly worked with oil paint on canvas, but now I also use mixed media. Paintings and poems are inner images. They can sometimes be the same. Layers, textures and metaphors playing together, creating meaning in varying degrees of abstraction.

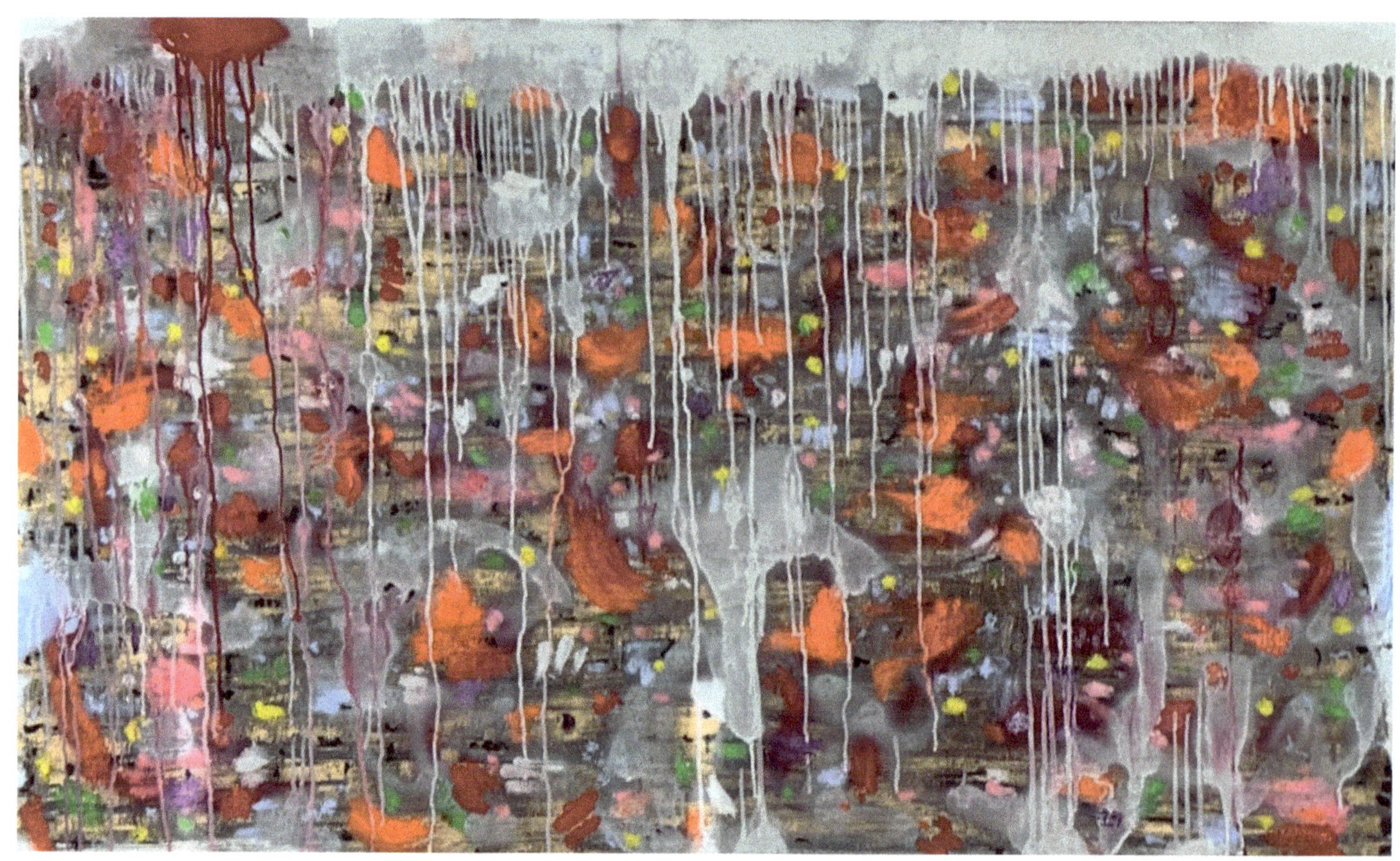

Love is Peace, 2023, Acrylic and oil on canvas, 85 x 140cm

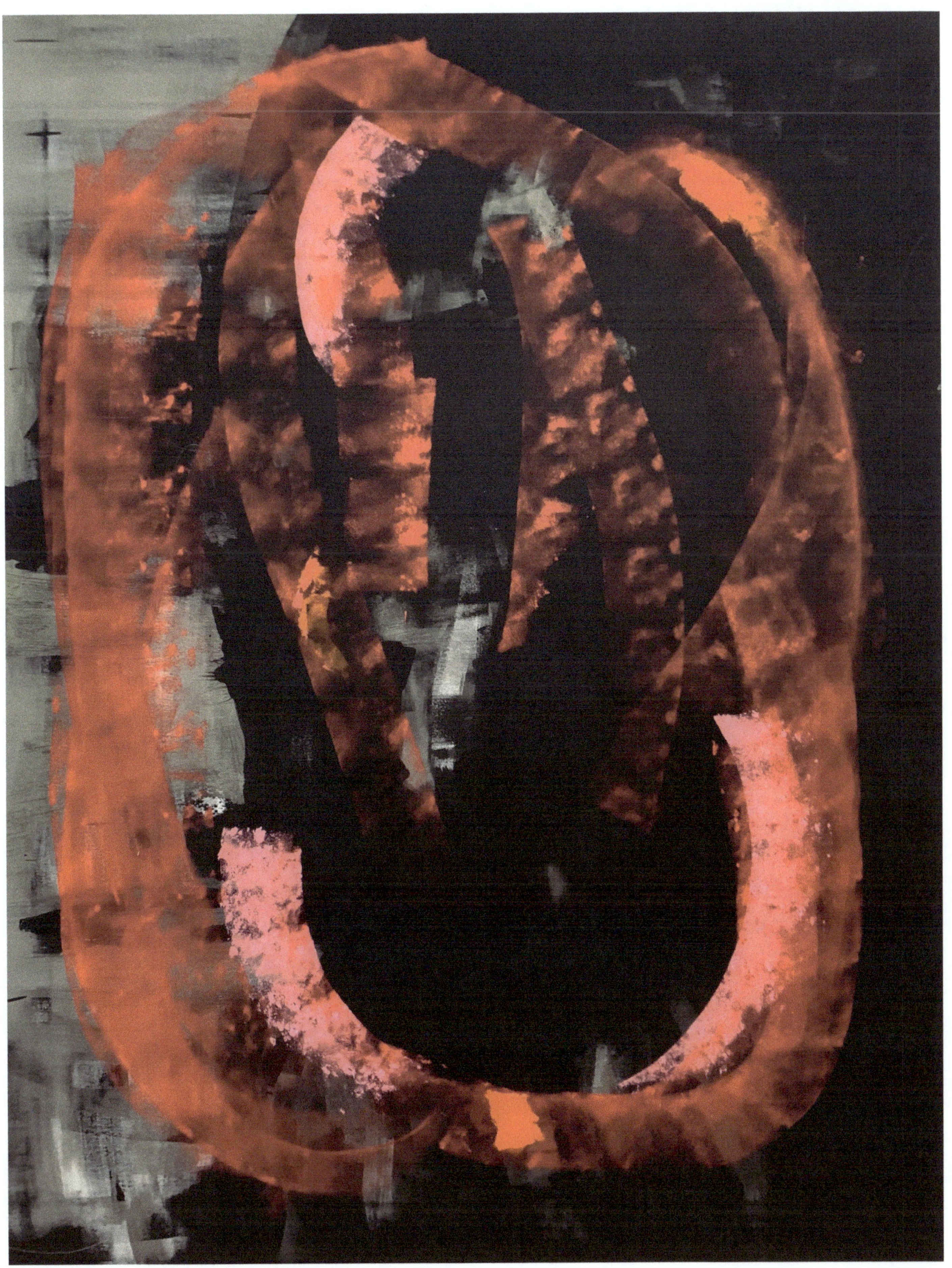

Black Rose, 2023, Acrylic and oil on canvas, 160 x 120cm

Roanne Corteza

instagram.com/paintings_by_roanne

Roanne, a Canadian Contemporary Abstract artist and a proud member of the International Association of Visual Artists (IAVA), draws inspiration from her life experiences and the significant relationships in her life. Her surroundings also influence her artistic vision. Using shapes, patterns, lines, and textures, Roanne transforms these inspirations into captivating works of arts on canvas. Roanne has participated in various individual and.group exhibitions in Canada (Lehang Art Gallery Quebec) Luxembourg (EUPHORIA, International Contemporary Arts Exhibition.- Van Gogh Art Gallery), Germany and Spain (REBELLION- Galeria Azur).

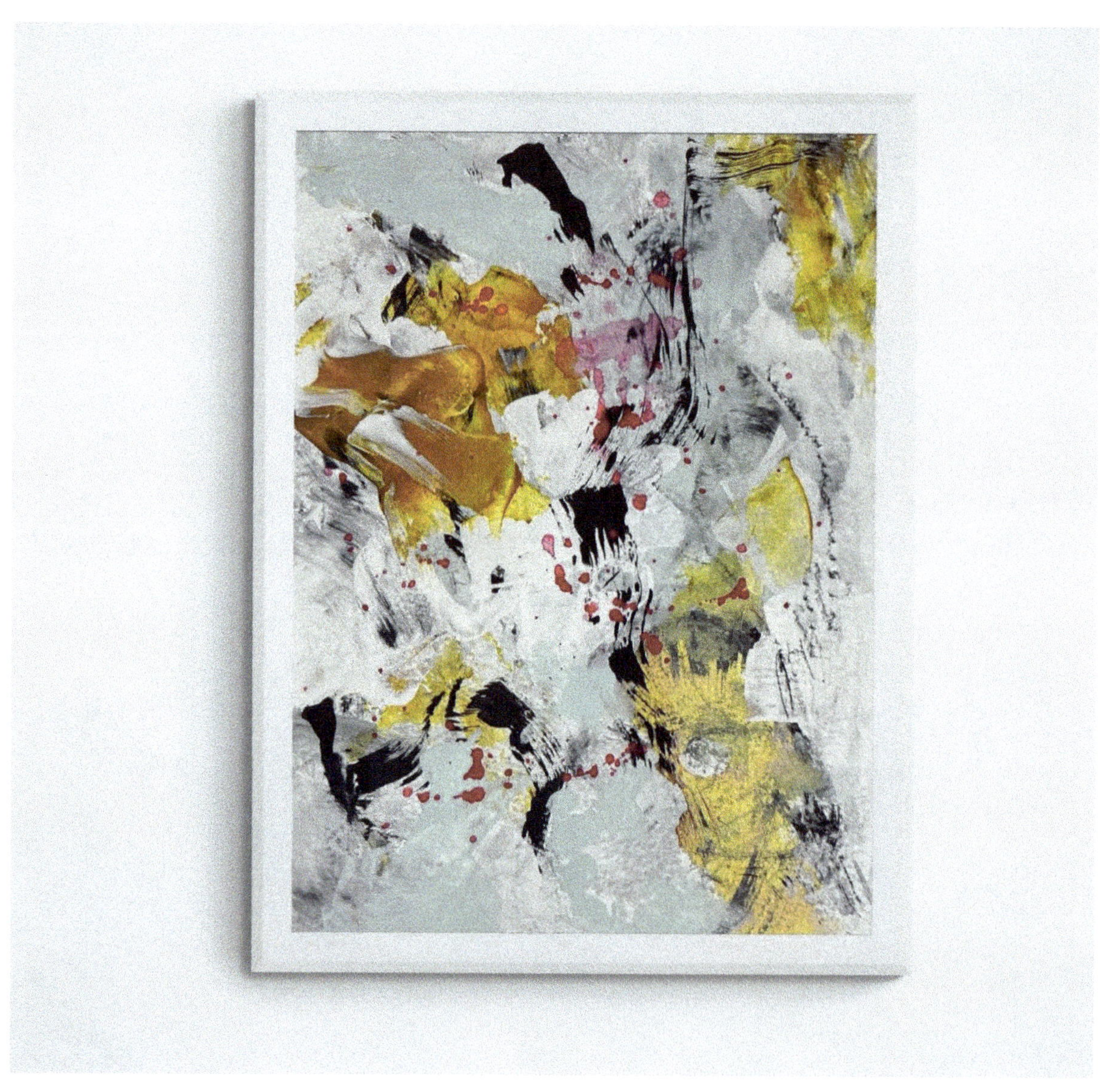

Symphony

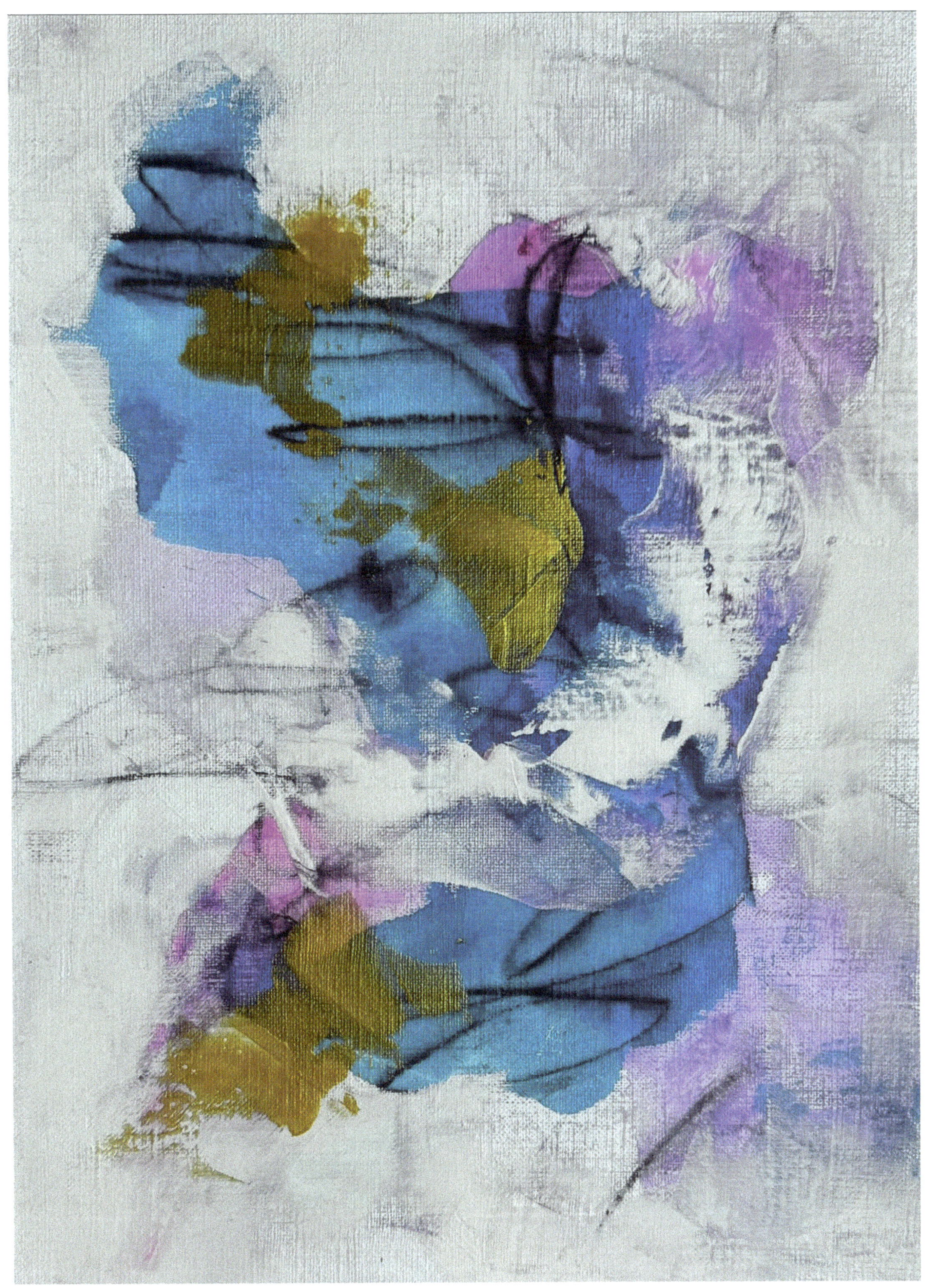

Good Morning Love of my Life

Roxana Werner

roxanawerner.cl

Mi primer acercamiento a las artes visuales fue como diseñadora textil. Trabaje en la tapicería Batik la cual forma parte del Arte Javanés. En la técnica del Batik, se trabaja el color por medio de teñidos sucesivos, lo que imposibilita enriquecer sus tonalidades por medio de los matices. En la búsqueda por ampliar el uso del color y el dibujo, ingrese a la Universidad Católica a estudiar artes visuales. El aprendizaje lo fui enriqueciendo en los talleres de diferentes maestros de pintura. En los primeros años la formación fue académica, muy rigurosa lo que contribuyó a adquirir una base fundamental, lo que me ha permitido incursionar en distintos modos de expresión, técnicas, estilos, etc. El estudio de la Historia y Teoría del Arte en la Universidad de Chile me ha permitido conocer y entender los movimientos que se fueron gestando en el transcurso de las diferentes épocas, todo lo cual ha sido un aporte en mi trabajo. En la pintura es primordial vivenciar "in situ" el espacio en el cual surge la inspiración. Abordar un proyecto, sin la experiencia emocional e intelectual del lugar o el objeto que me cautiva, sería imposible llevarlo a cabo. El momento de conexión, es el primer momento para comenzar a trabajar en un proyecto.

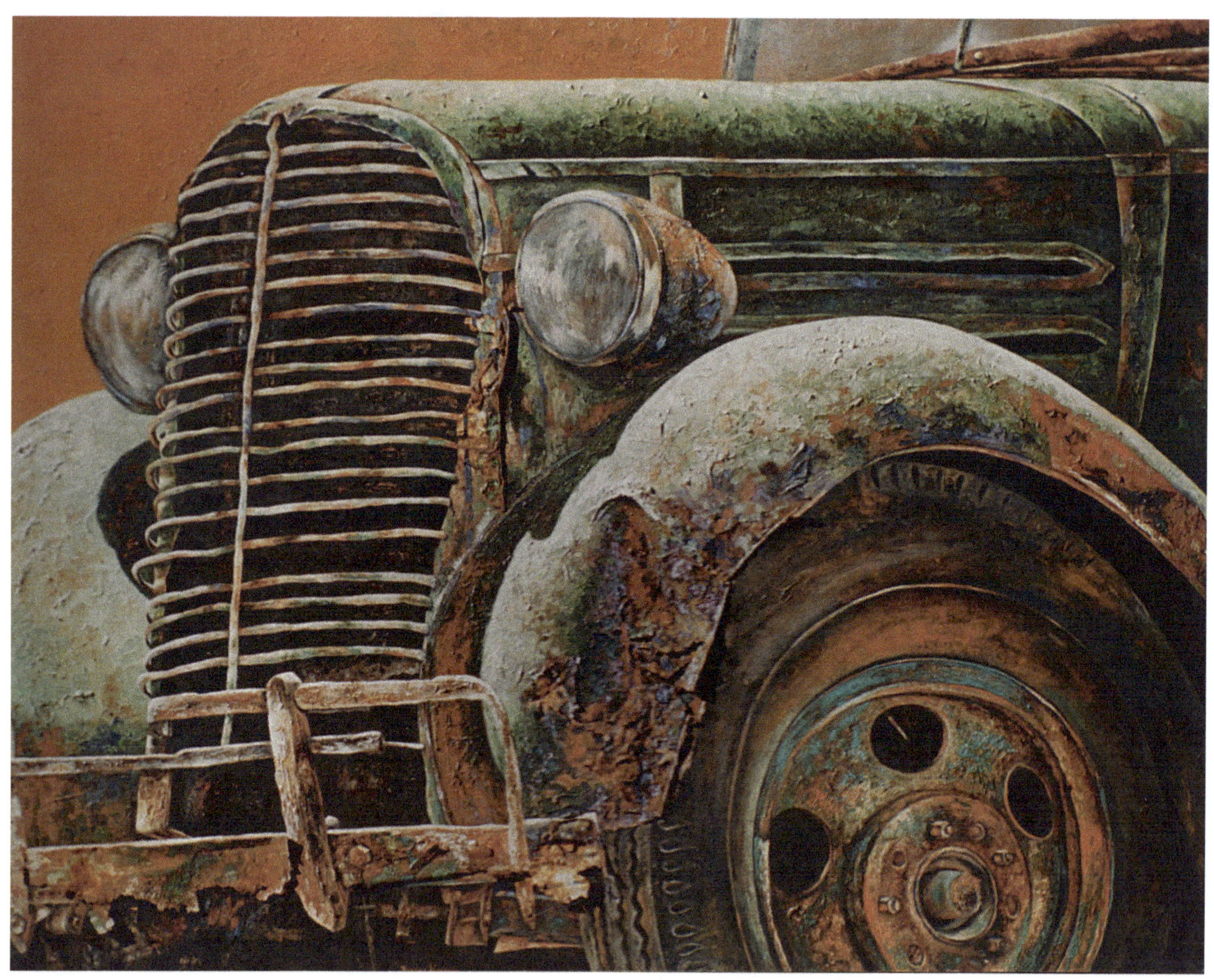

Camion Chilote

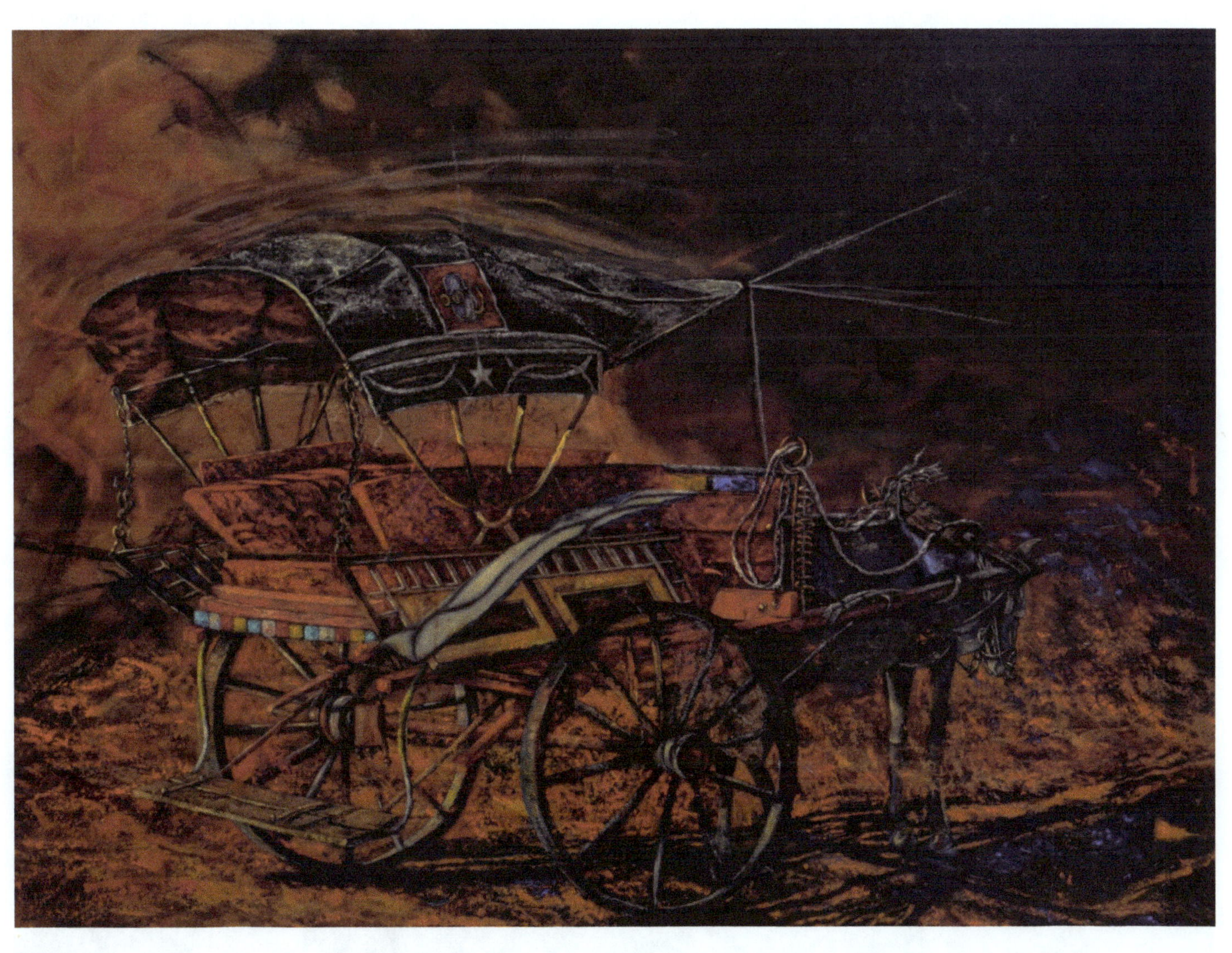

Carreta de Bagan Birmania

Shiri Achu

shiriachuart.com

Shiri Achu was born in Cameroon, West Africa. She and her family immigrated to London, where she lived for many years. Today, she has studios in Cameroon, the UK and the USA, where she is currently based. Shiri Achu's art comes from every day, unsurprising, yet unexpectedly vivid, moments, times, and places. She is reputed to capture the spirit of her subjects and make them come alive through form, color, texture, and tone. One of the aims of Shiri Achu's Art is to showcase the culture of Cameroon and other African countries worldwide. It's also to bring back fond memories to those in the Diaspora. Shiri finds beauty in the woman carrying her child on her back and going on her way. She finds beauty in the African fabrics etc Shiri's paintings reflect the beautiful simplicity of Africa and she offers this to the western world to encourage understanding of the culture and interest in travel to African nations. Shiri is extremely pleased and excited that she is achieving one of her goals of promoting the African Culture worldwide, through her art works, workshops and her annual worldwide InPrint Exhibitions. From 35InPrint:London 2014, then 36InPrint:DC, 37InPrint:Australia, 38InPrint:Jamaica, 39InPrint:Toronto through to 43InPrint:Yaoundé at The National Museum of Yaoundé and the 10th Anniversary Exhibition 45InPrint:DMV in 2024, Shiri Achu's goal is to share/spread imagery of the many beautiful cultures, promoting African Lifestyle and Culture one city at a time. Shiri is honored and grateful for the recognition and awards along the way.

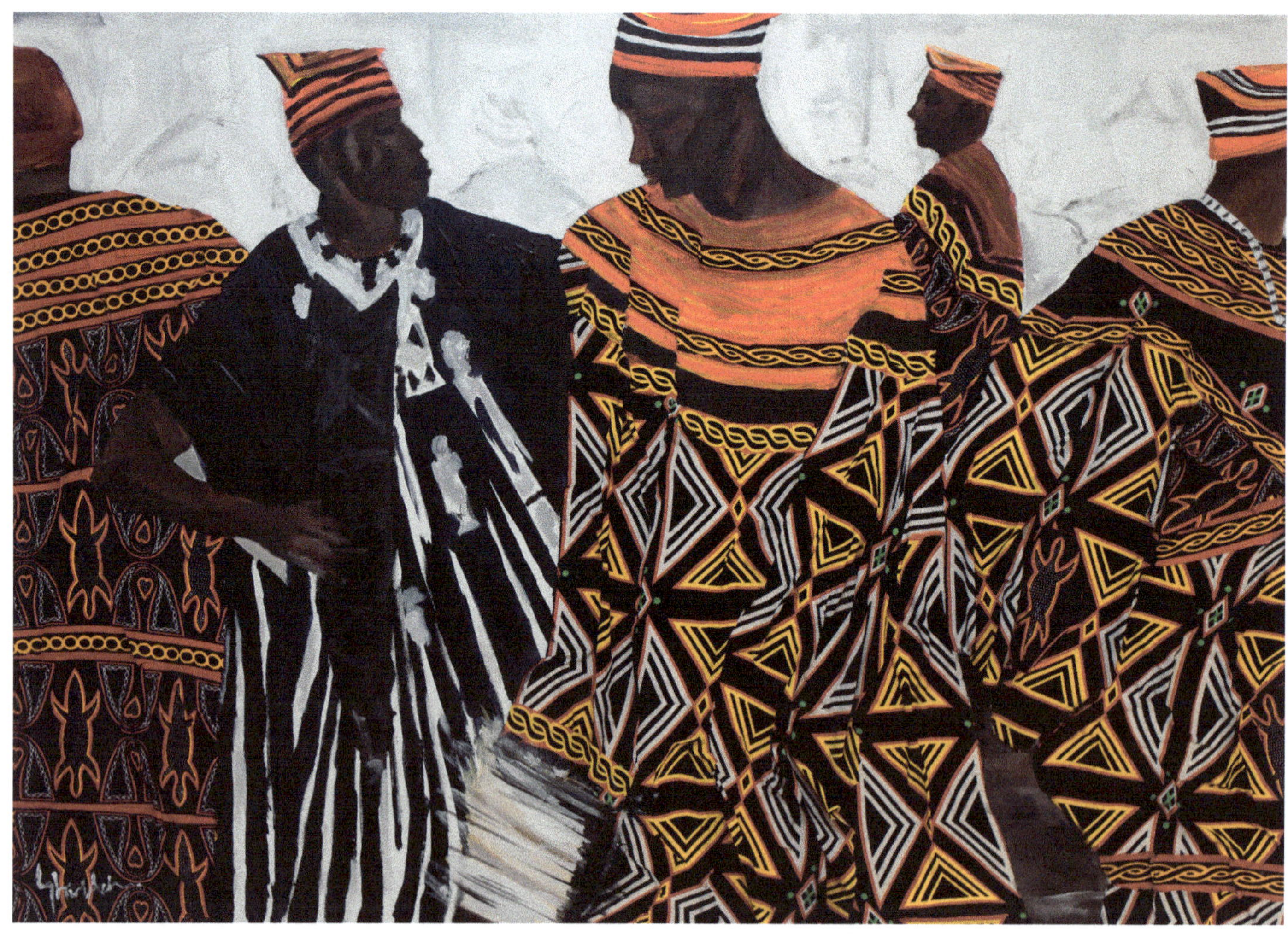

1.1.11 Baforchu Big Men Celebrates

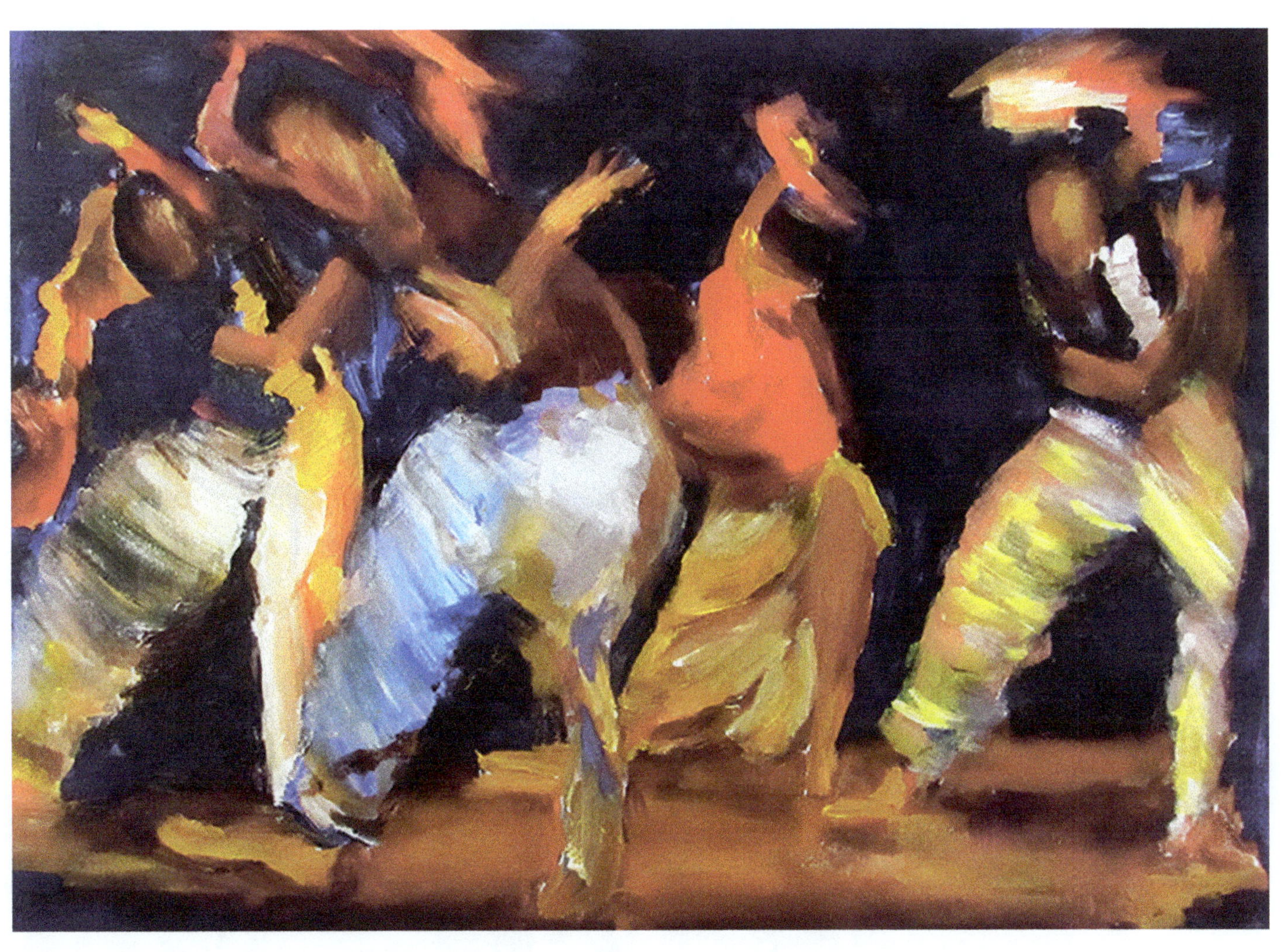

Colours of the Musical Sounds 1

Simon Darling

sdarling-art.com

I'm known for my mastery of deep, obscure portraits that transcend conventional understanding. Through a style I've devised as "Imitated Pragmatism," I explore the intricacies of human emotion, identity, and the enigmatic nature of perception. My work is a reflection of the complexities inherent in the human experience, capturing moments of introspection, ambiguity, and existential questioning. Each stroke of my brush is a deliberate act of excavation, unearthing the hidden truths and contradictions that define our existence. Drawing from a rich array of influences including poetry, psychology, and philosophy, I seek to create art that resonates on a deeply personal level while also inviting viewers to confront universal themes. My portraits, characterized by their depth and ambiguity, serve as mirrors to the soul, challenging viewers to confront their own perceptions and biases. As a multiple award-winning artist, I am driven by a relentless pursuit of excellence and innovation. Each new piece is an opportunity to push the boundaries of my craft, experimenting with practice, texture, and symbolism to create works that are both visually striking and intellectually stimulating. In a world that often privileges surface appearances over deeper meaning, I believe in the transformative power of art to provoke thought, inspire empathy, and foster connection. Through my portraits, I invite viewers to engage in a dialogue with the unknown, to embrace the ambiguity of existence, and to discover beauty in the shadows.

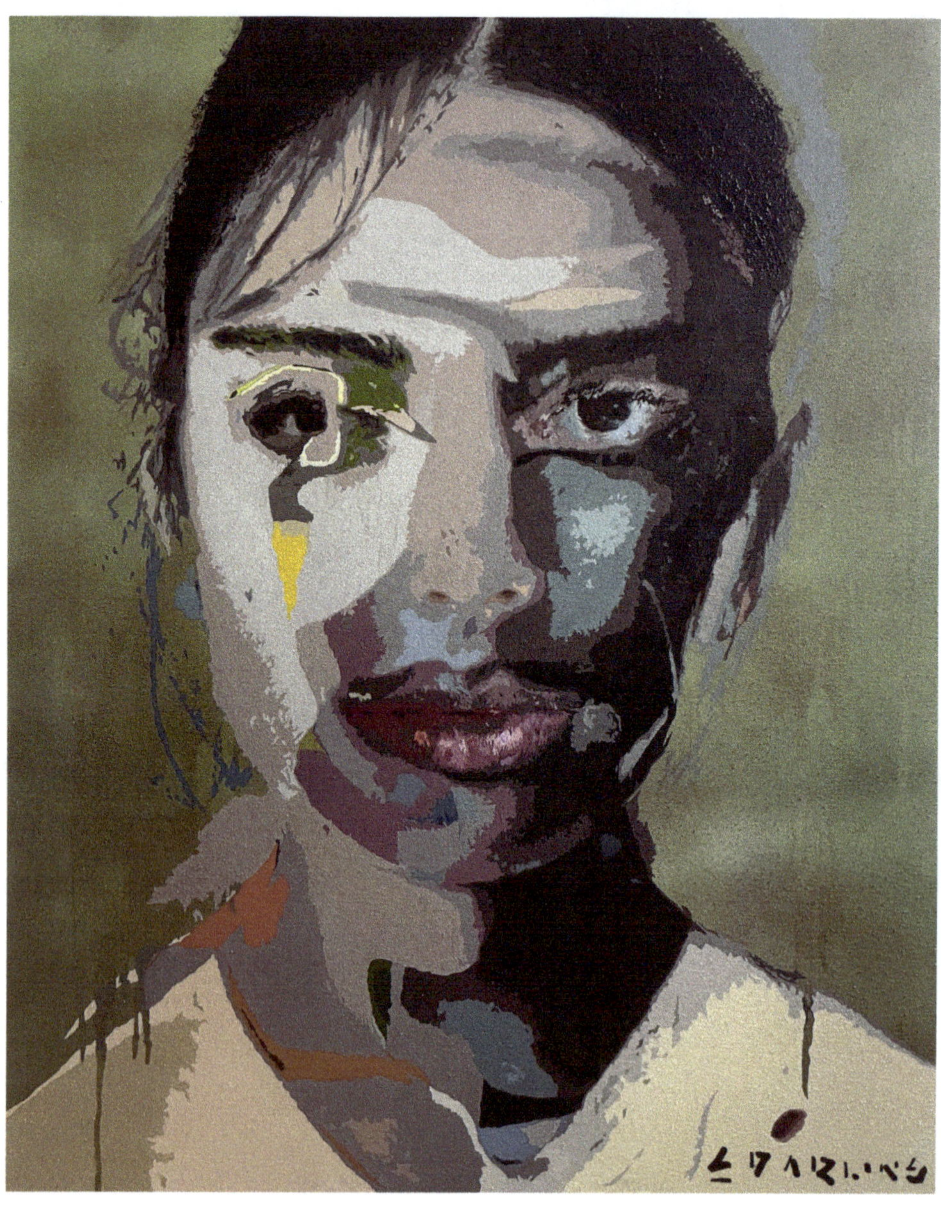

CrypticEchoes_2024_Struc. Acrylic on Canvas_100x80cm

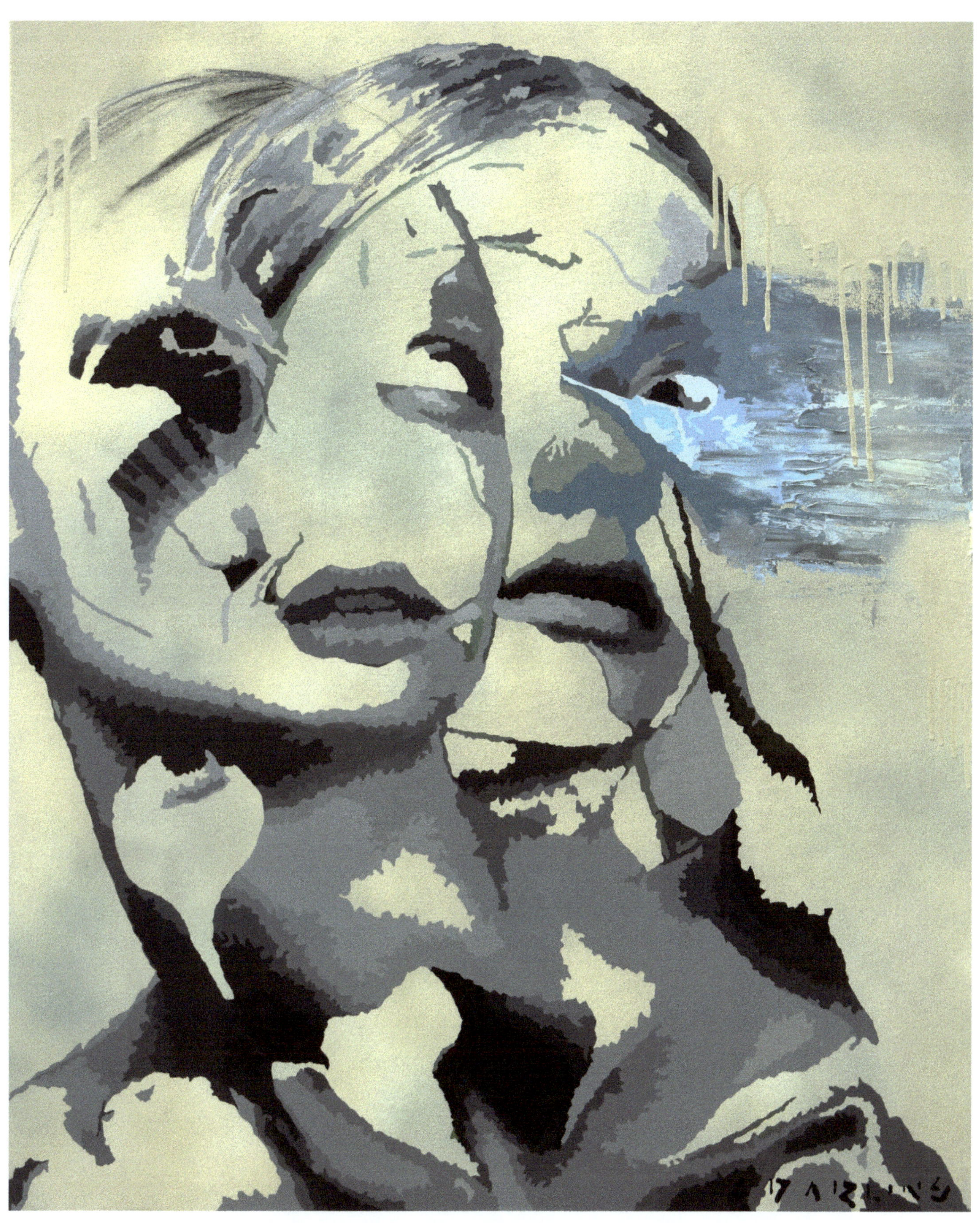

MutedEmotions_2022_Struc.Acrylics on Canvas_100x80cm

Sonia Roseval

soniarosevalartist.net

Japanese ink on paper art, created through freehand drawing and inspired by my meditation, is a captivating expression of the my inner world and my connection to the larger universe. The delicate lace-like patterns, formed by circular and geometric shapes with repetitive lines, symbolize the unity of consciousness. Through my intuitive brushstrokes, these forms come together to represent a harmonious whole, reflecting the interconnectedness of all beings. Japanese ink on paper art serves as a reminder of the profound beauty and unity that can be found through artistic expression and the practice of meditation. It invites viewers to contemplate their own place within the interconnected web of existence and to embrace the conscious unity that binds us all.

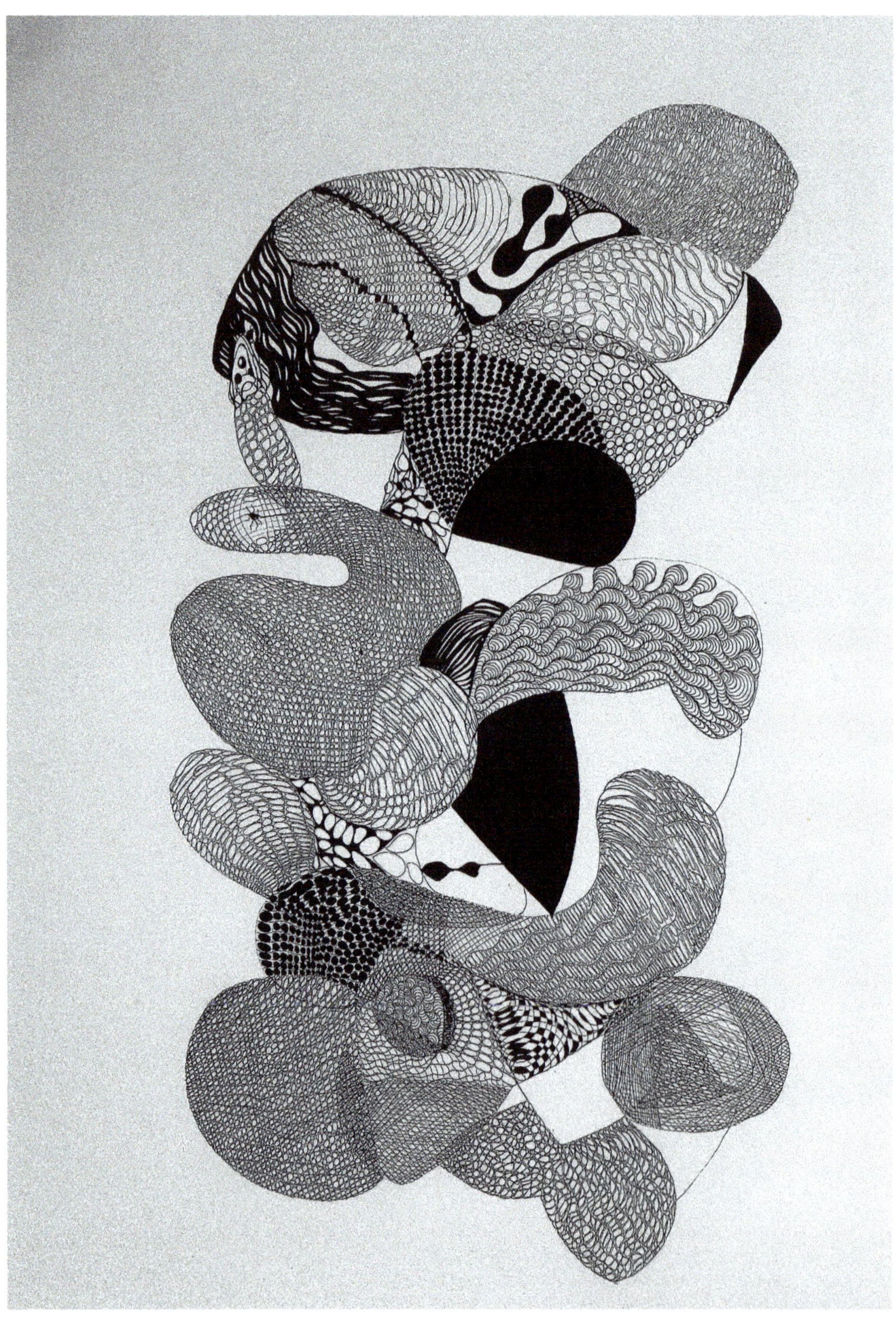

Connections #4

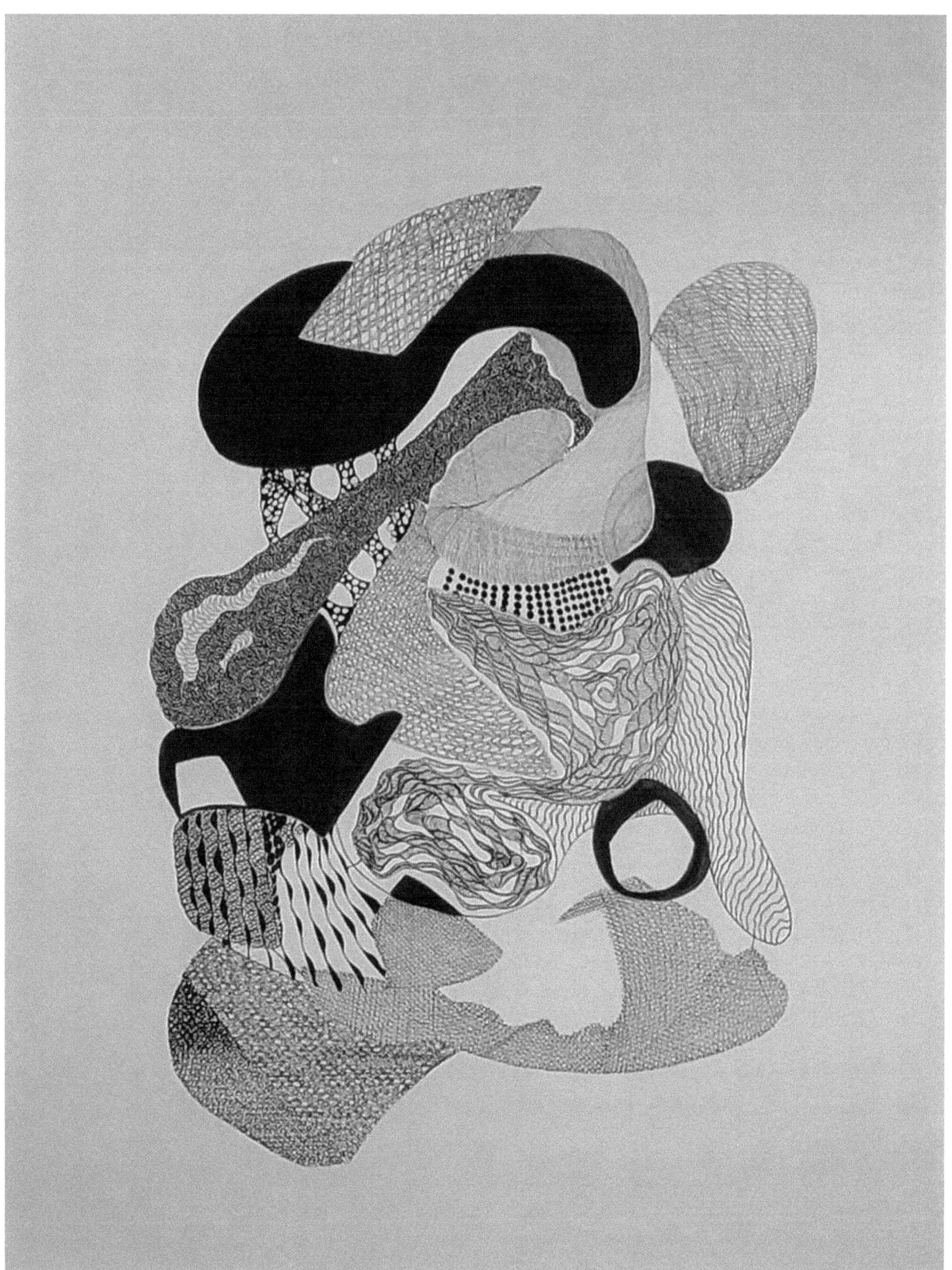

Connections #8

Sotaro Takanami

sotartaro@gmail.com

私の文章も英語表記でお願いします。
大阪□ 島屋史料館はTakashimaya Archive Museum in Osaka
2024年1月6日から2月26日まで大阪□ 島屋史料館で僕の回顧展がありました。多くのメディアと来場者があり緊張し胃腸炎になりましたがとても充実した日々でした。
絵は僕にとって喉が渇いた時に水を飲むようなものです。絵を描く事だけが生きていると感じられます。
この作品は側溝に咲き誇っているツユクサを見つけた時、心打たれ制作したものです。
最初は見える通り写実で描いたのですが枚数を重ねる内に最終的には青いドットになりました。
最後に海外の人々に本を通して僕の作品を見てもらえる事はとても嬉しいことです。

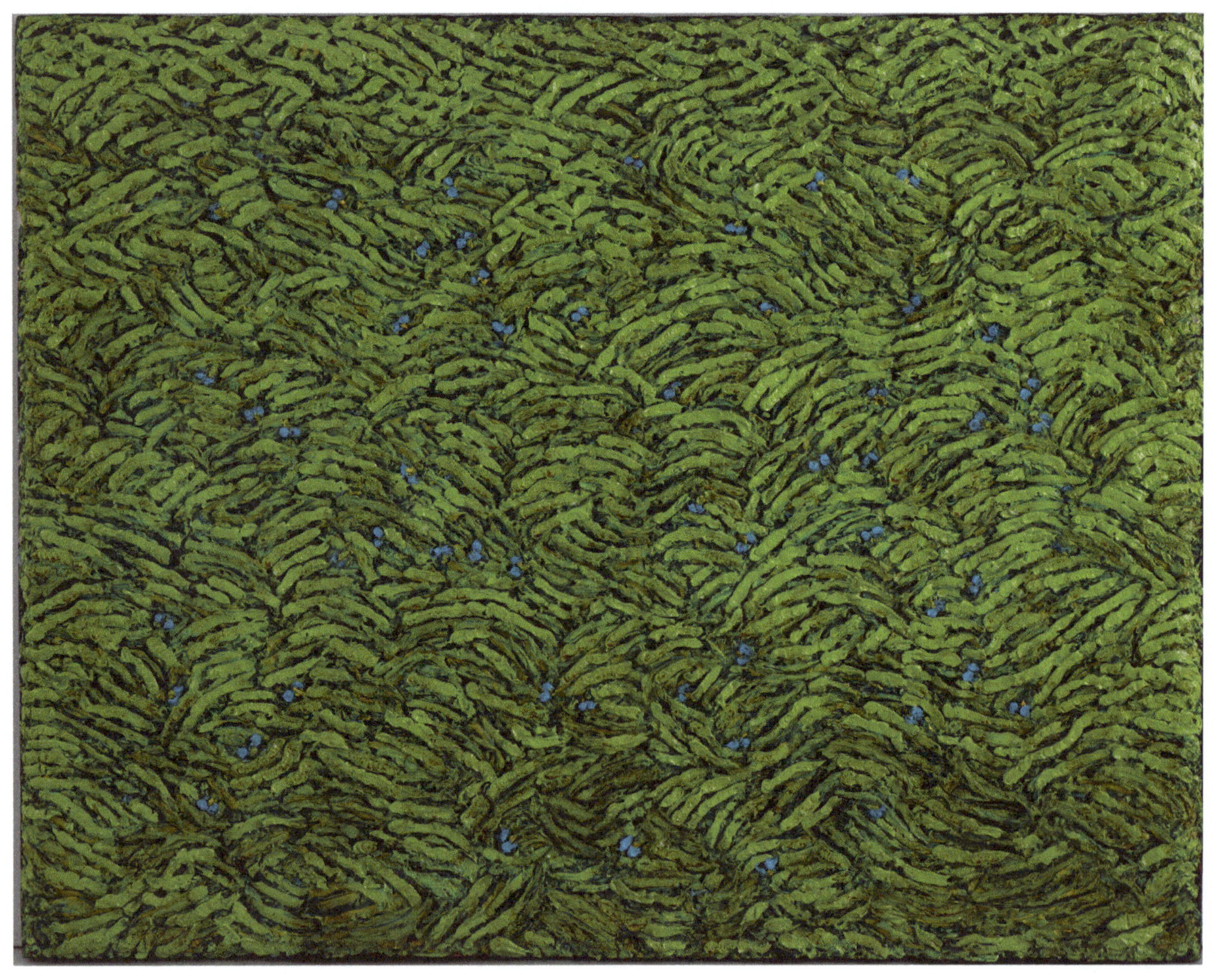

Asiatic Dayflower 73□91cm Oil on Canvas 2008年

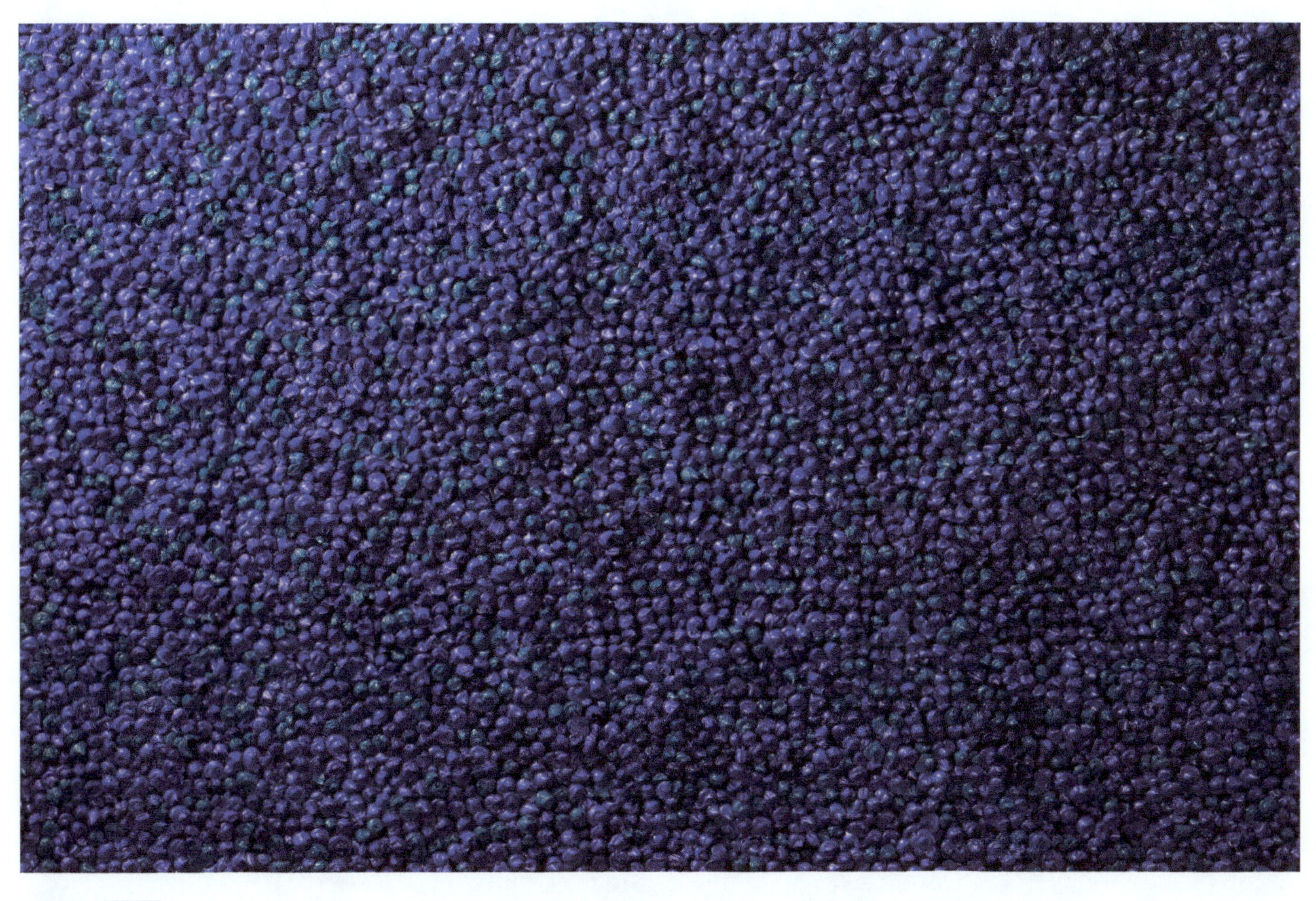

Asiatic Dayflower 73×91cm Oil on Canvas 2008年

Sylvia Kölbl

sylvia-koelbl-ansichtssachen.jimdofree.com

Nature is that artistic that nobody can copy it, nevertheless I make a weak attempt to show some of the wonders around us, which we should protect and be thankful for.

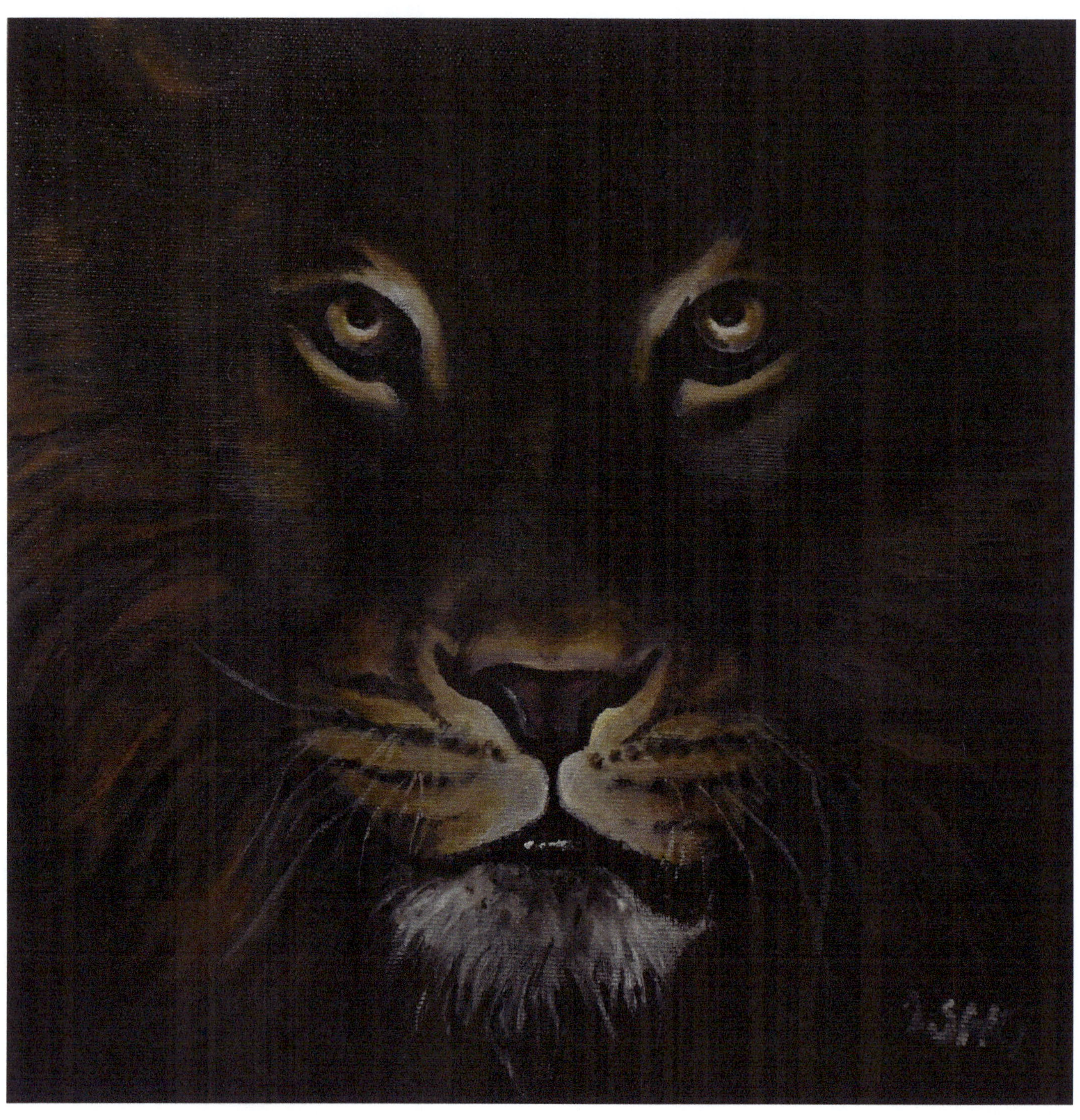

Lost Kingdom

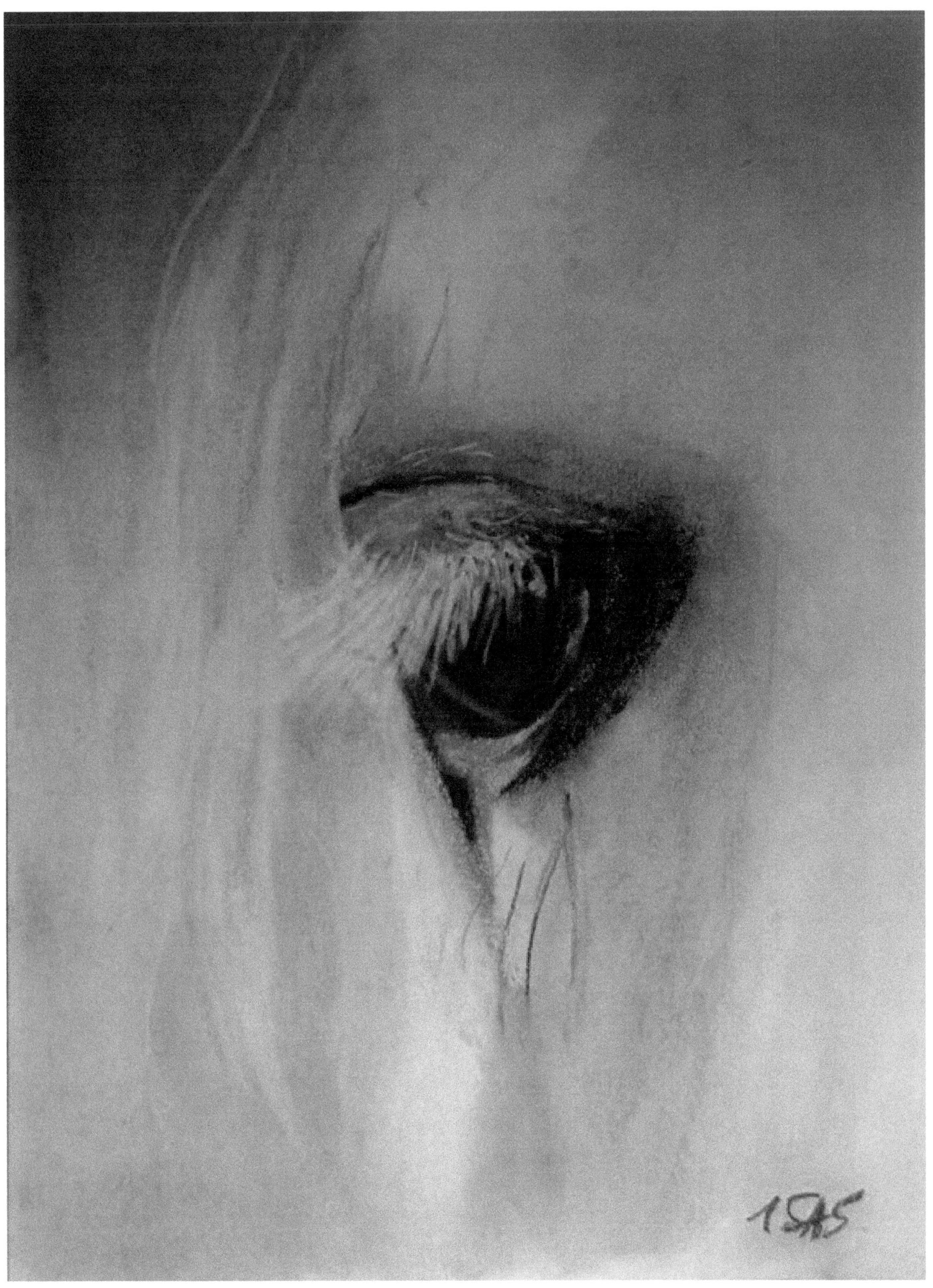

Im Auge des Betrachters

Symona Colina

symonacolina.info

Picking up a brush gives wings to fly with.
Perspectief a wonderful journey
Perspective is a dance with colors and lines that follows a
melody of outspread wings. Perspective is a meeting and
a clash between length, height and width.

Where I see the world inside of me.
Where I see the world outside of me.
Art has many interfaces with existence.
It is all around in its countless disciplines.
And nevertheless unlimited.

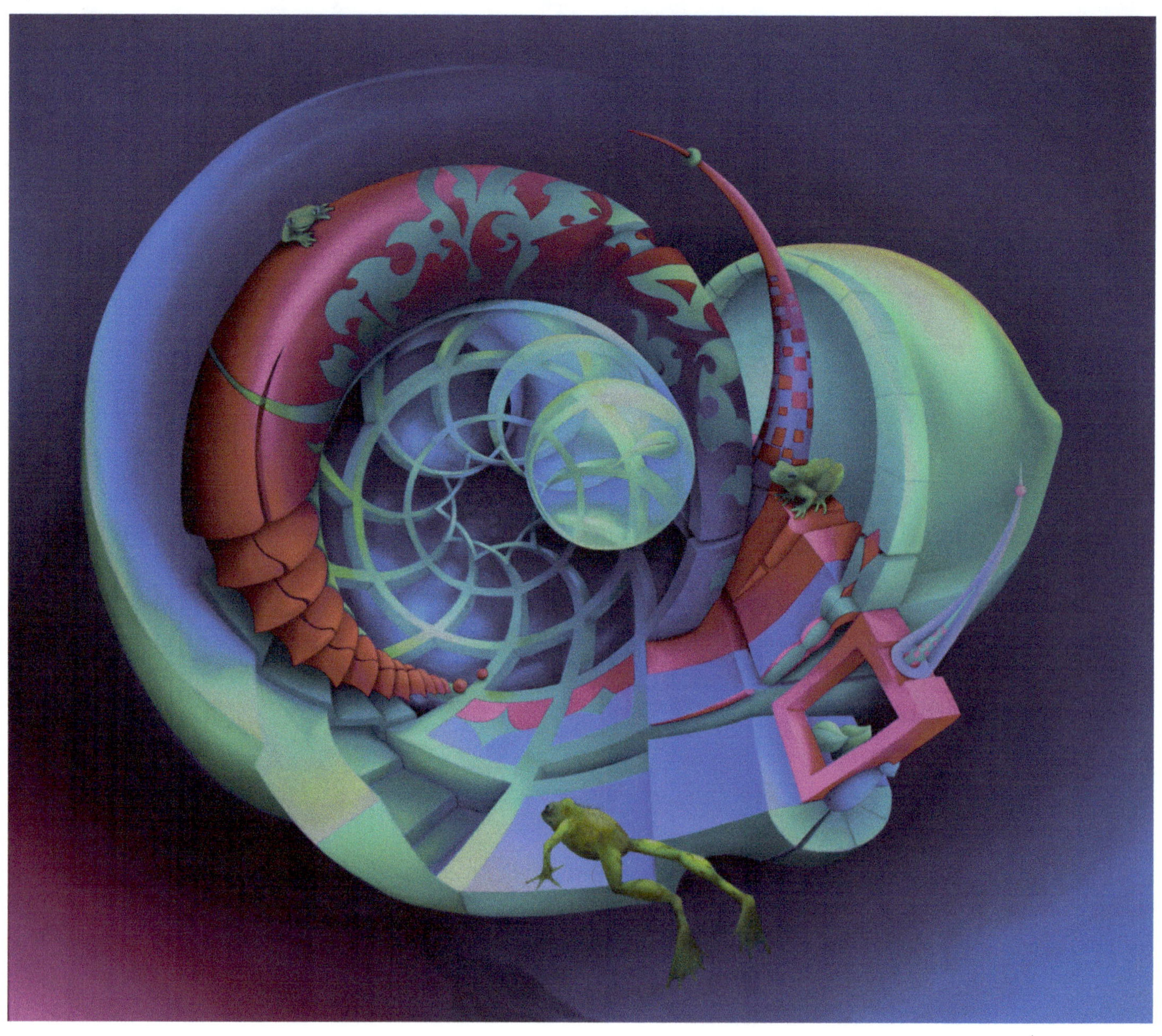

Jumpers - Oil on canvas 80 x 90 cm - 2023

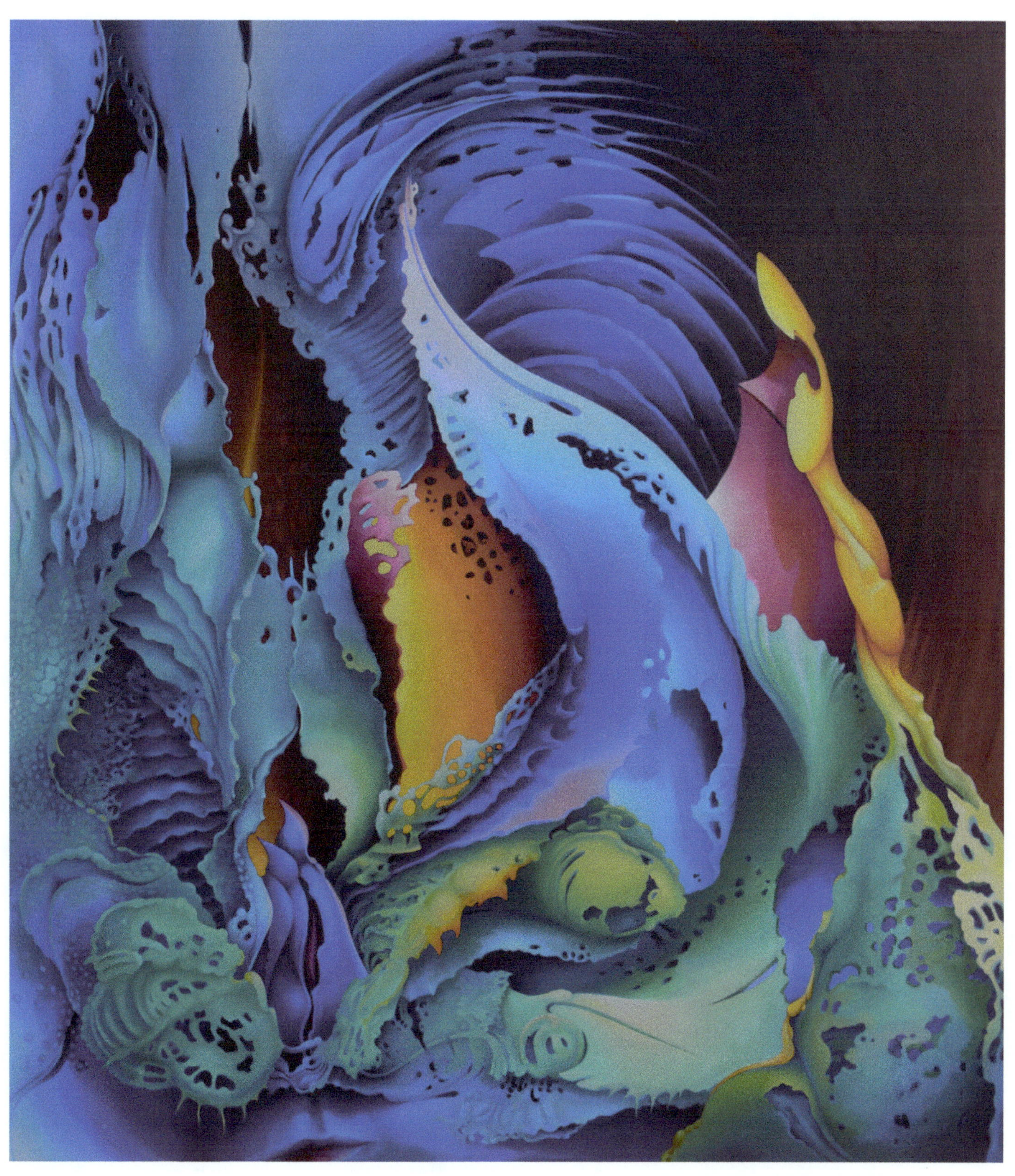

The Breathing - Oil on canvas 100 x 90cm - 2019

Tamara Michel

instagramm.com tamaramichel 1685

Tamara Michel ist in Ukraine geboren,in Moskau studierte und seit 30 Jahren lebt und arbeitet wie Freiberufliche Kunstlerin in Wien,wo sie malt Bilder mit Ol,Aquarell und Acryl Farben auf Leinwand und Papier.Sie arbeitet innovativ ,besonders mit Farbkombinationen und hat ihr eigenes Stiel,gemischt zwischen figurativen und impressionistischen.

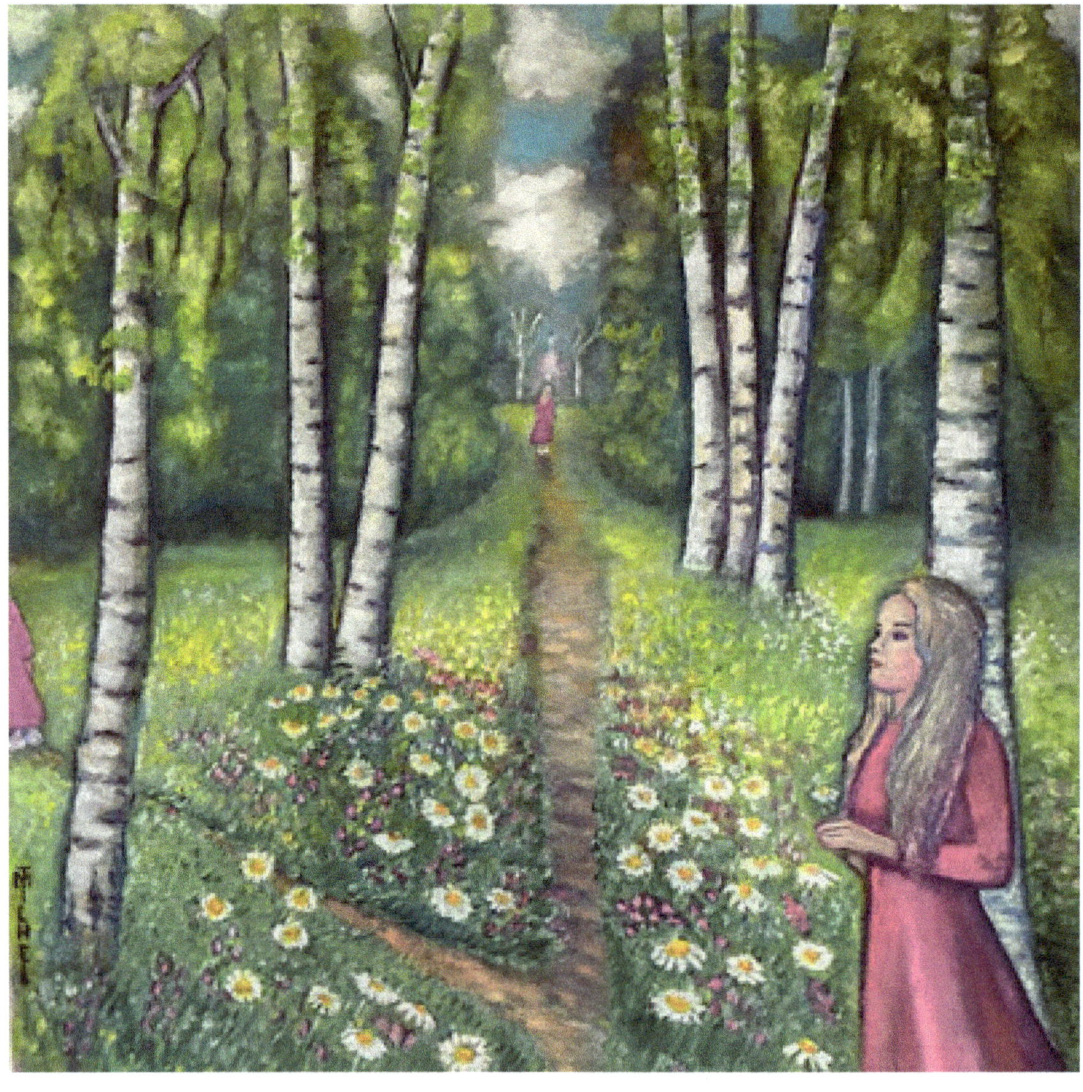

Richtige Weg finden. 100/100.

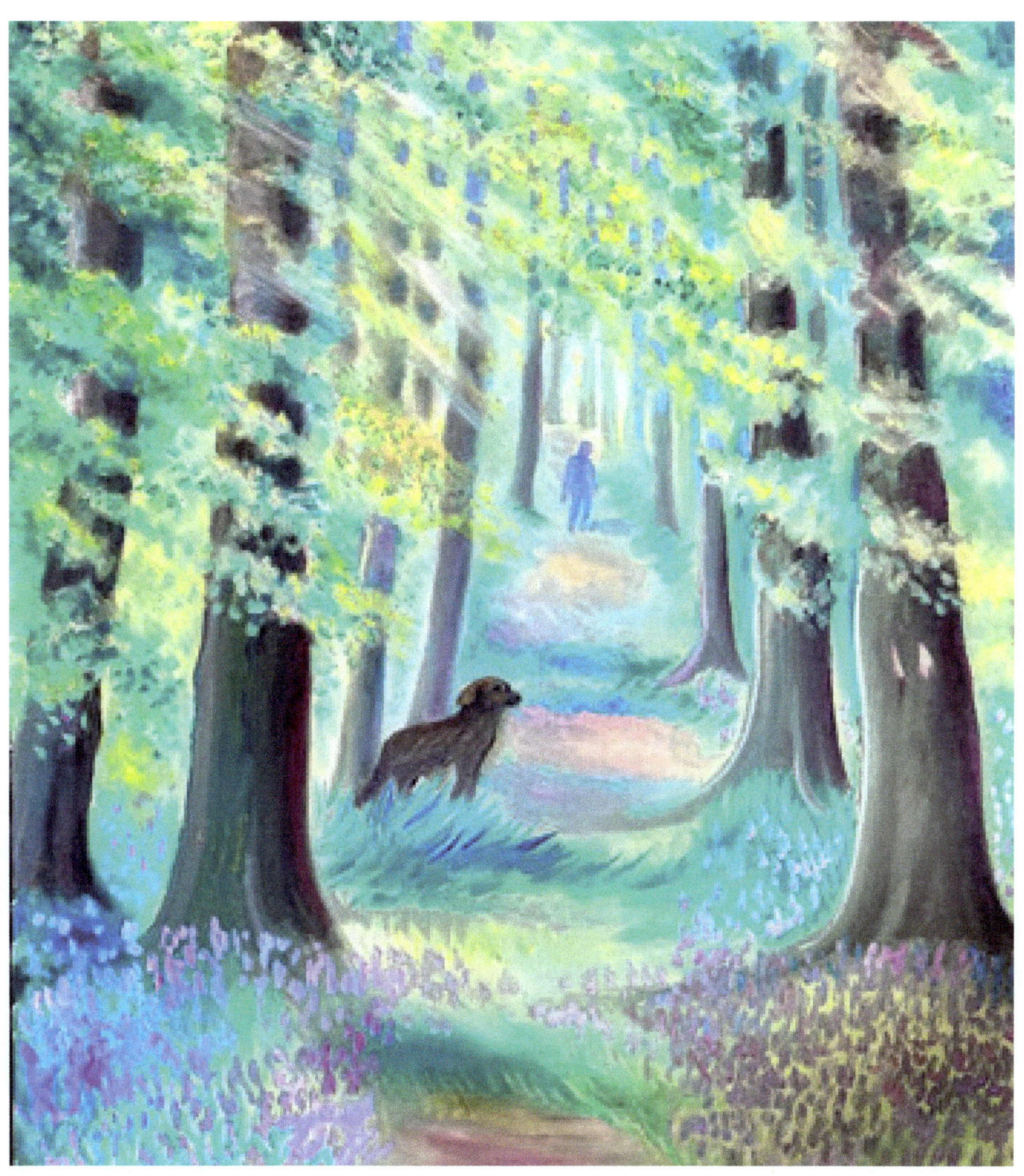

In Wald.100/80.

Toti Cuesta

toticuesta.com

As a surreal portrait artist, I use watercolor to create paintings that merge symbols and vibrant colors, inviting you into a new world filled with light and life. Through these elements, I communicate universal stories that resonate within your subconscious, connecting you with the divine and the eternal. My art offers an alternative view of the world that inspires you to explore more profound levels of consciousness and rediscover human divinity. The female figure, central in my works, symbolizes life, maternity, creativity, resilience, and love. She represents Mother Earth, embodying love and respect for everything around us, including nature and the urban environment, which deserve our care to create a more loving and just world. My colors convey energy and emotion, using a mix of cold and warm tones to symbolize the connection between heaven and earth and arouse emotions. The integration of the female figure into the architecture in my paintings indicates the fusion between humans and their creations, highlighting the often-unrecognized female influence in shaping our world. Through my art, I aim to capture the beauty of the universe and the human experience, prompting reflection on our interaction with the environment and the importance of preserving the natural and cultural beauty surrounding us.

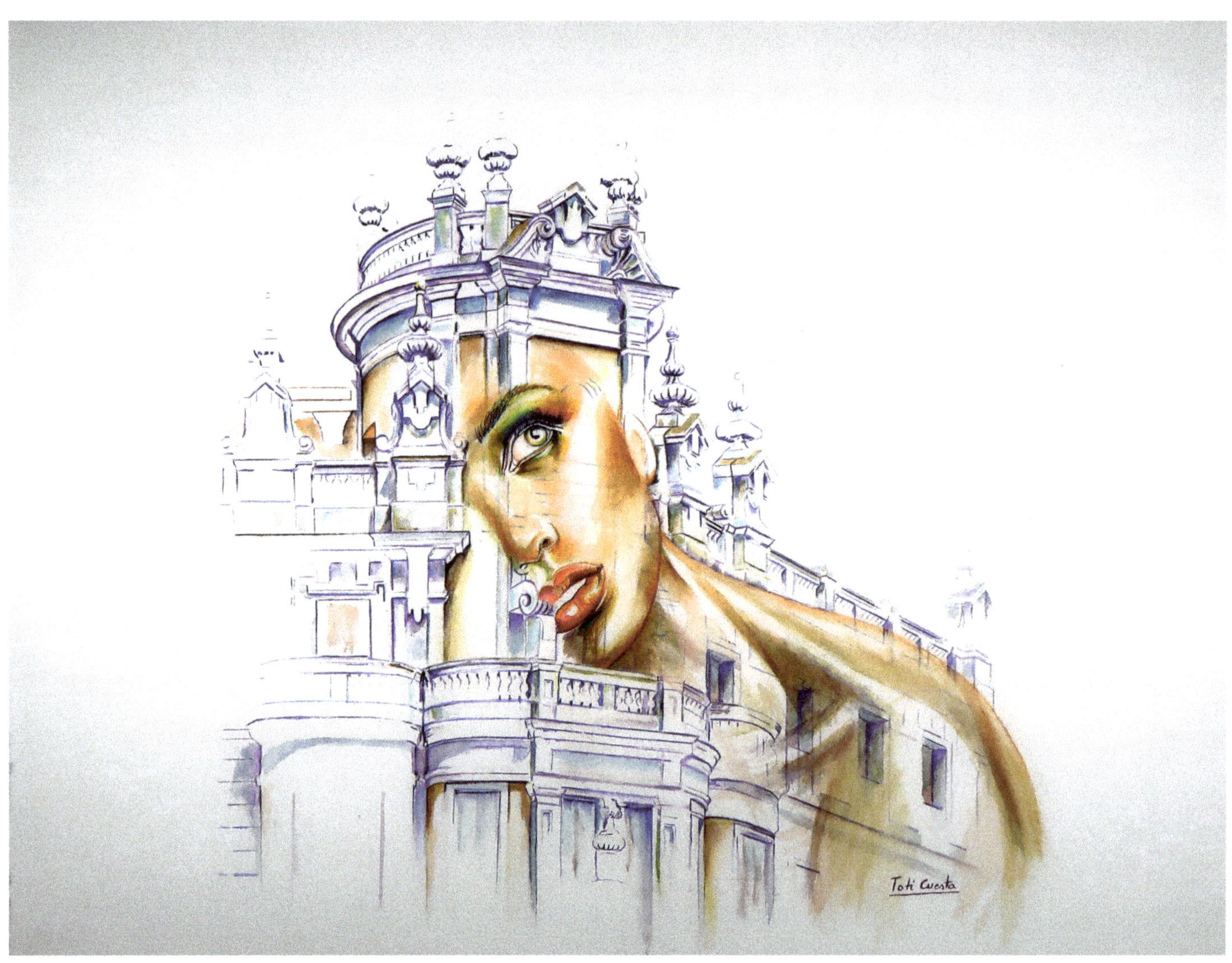

Classical building, Gran Via, Madrid_ watercolor on 640 gr paper_53 x 60 cm

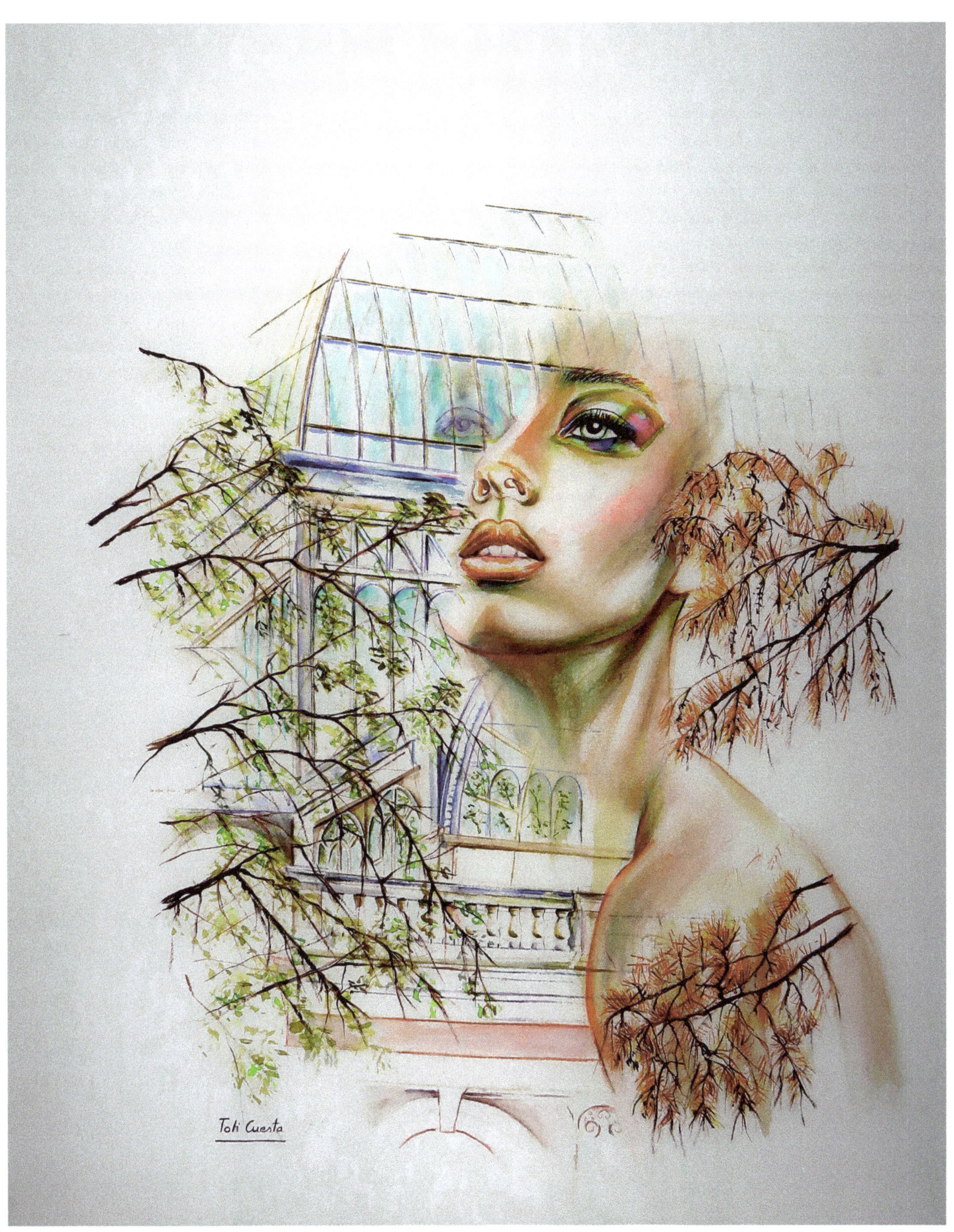

Crystal Palace_watercolor on 640 gr paper_56 x 76 cm

Ursa Schoepper

virtuelledenkraeume.de

Ursa Schoepper first completed her studies in Natural Science with state examination. In addition she completed a study in cultural management, state examinaten, with a concentration in fine arts, new media. In 2001 she was awarded the Media Promotion Prize of German state North Rhine-Westphalia for „Das Museum der abwesenden Bilder". Since 2003 Ursa Schöpper has been working as an experimental photographic artist. Her artwork has been exhibited internationally and she is the recipient of notable awards. Ursa Schoepper lives and works near Bonn. A photography, is an image of divers realities. For me the Experimental Photography is a metapher of Change. My experimental photographic art is the logical departure from reality. It is virtual, so available in possibility. My reconstruction of a digital photograph is an attempt to order the chaos of the world in which we move. Through a transformation of the appearance we can gain new impressions. It is the courage to be free that keeps alternatives open and encourages renewal. It is the courage to break the perception of routine and stands for change in the process. Whoever seizes his chance, like the artist and the strategic genius, risks breaking up the routine of perception. What is it that makes nature appear in such wondrous ways? What ideal formula does it contain? Experimental digital photography gives me the opportunity to research her. As a composer and choreographer, I elicit new Views and perspectives from the geometry of light and colors in their digital appearance.

https://www.contemporaryartcuratormagazine.com/home-2/ursa-schoepper   https://www.contemporary-art-collectors.com/noble-art-conversations/ursa-schoepper

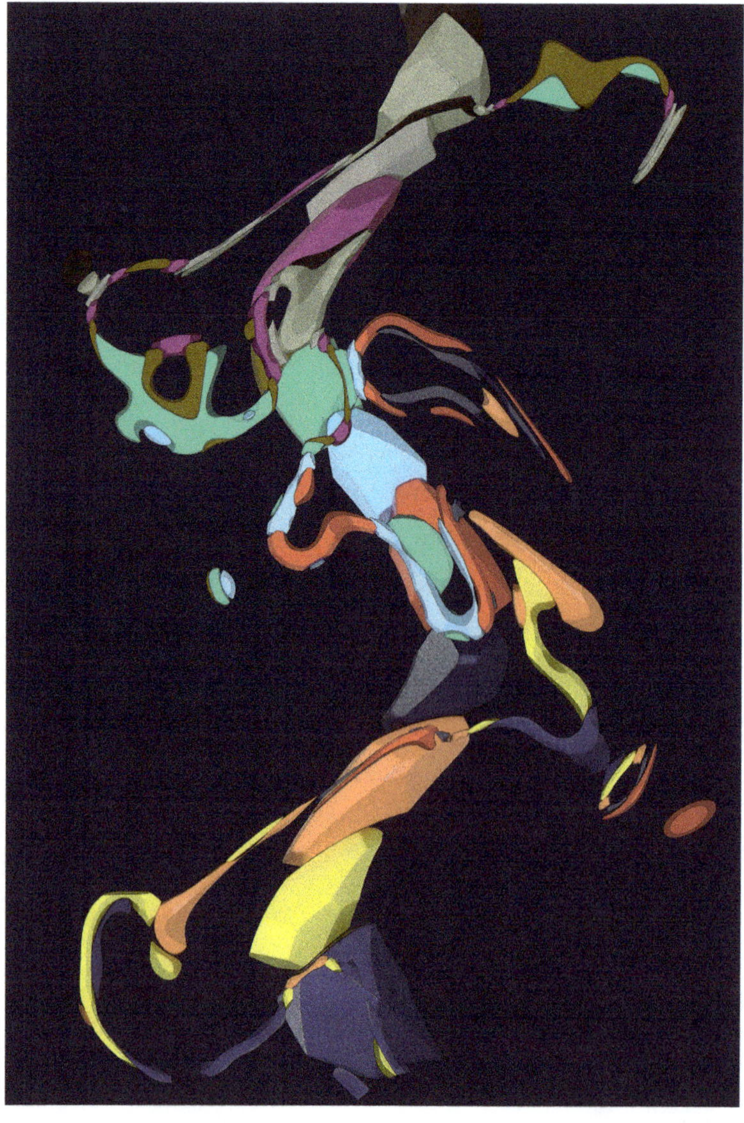

Free Dancing, 2024, Experimental Fine Art Photography, 75 x 50 cm, colorpigment on aludibond, framed und signed on the back

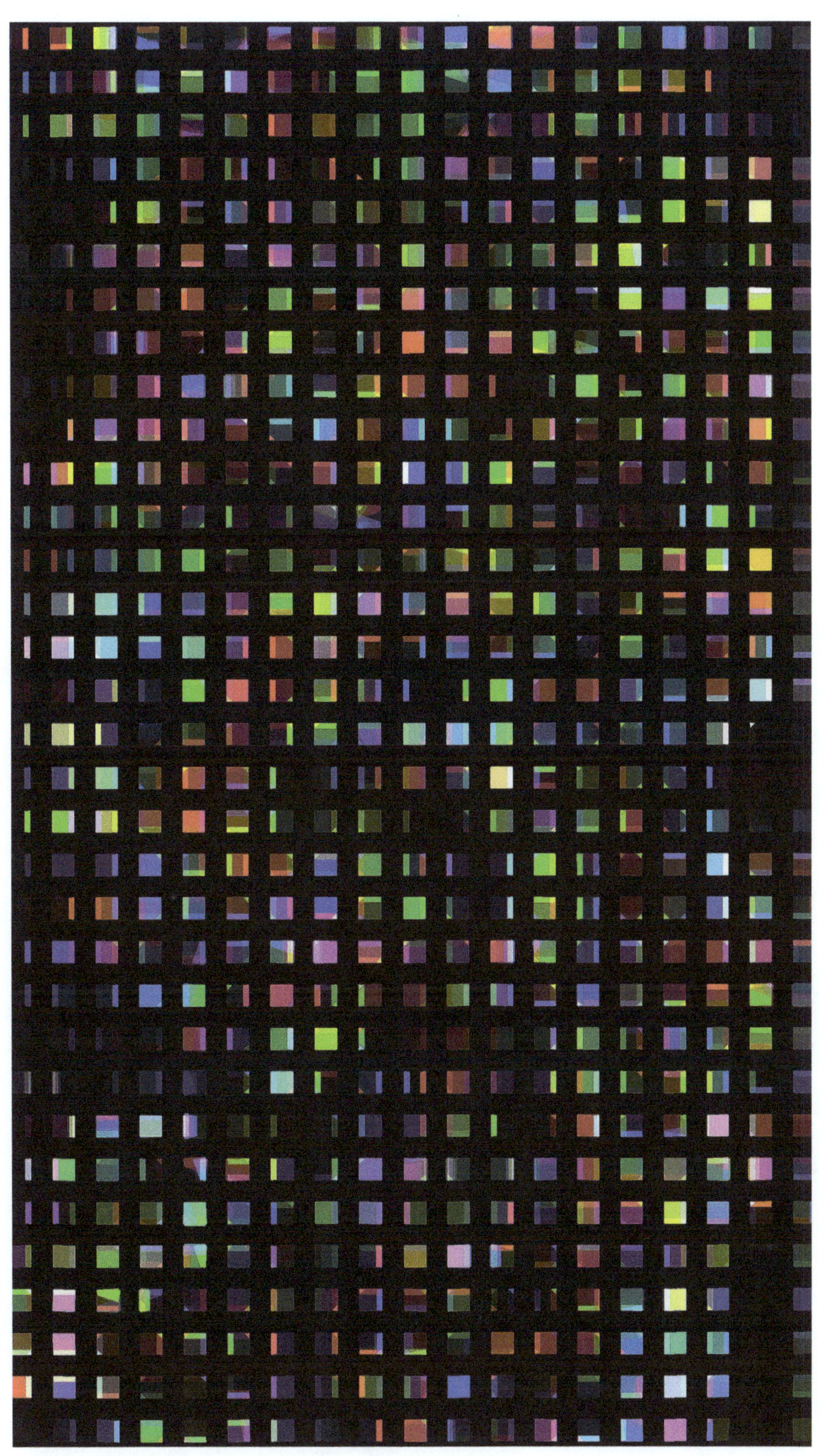

In the grid of nature, 2024, Experimental Fine Art Photography, 90 x 50 cm, colorpigment on aludibond, framed und signed on the back

Varda Breger

vbreger.com

I believe that all our unique planet's inhabitants are parts of a chain, linked together, and dependent on each other, including all varieties of wildlife and plants. We humans have the task of peacefully sharing the planet's resources between us to preserve them for generations to come. According to scientists we are in the middle of the sixth extinction of our planet after the dinosaurs. In my paintings and poems, I want to warn against the inherent dangers, while arousing feelings of wonder on the one hand and anxiety on the other hand. Migrating birds are for me a model of living in peace, without borders. or discrimination of gender, religion, race, or nationality. I convey my philosophy and feelings also as a poet, following are four of my poems:

CIVILIZATION
Ignoring the elegies
Of our planet.
***

Sailing towards Mars,
diving deep into
genomes.
But an olive leaf their bloody
Hands too short to
reach.
***

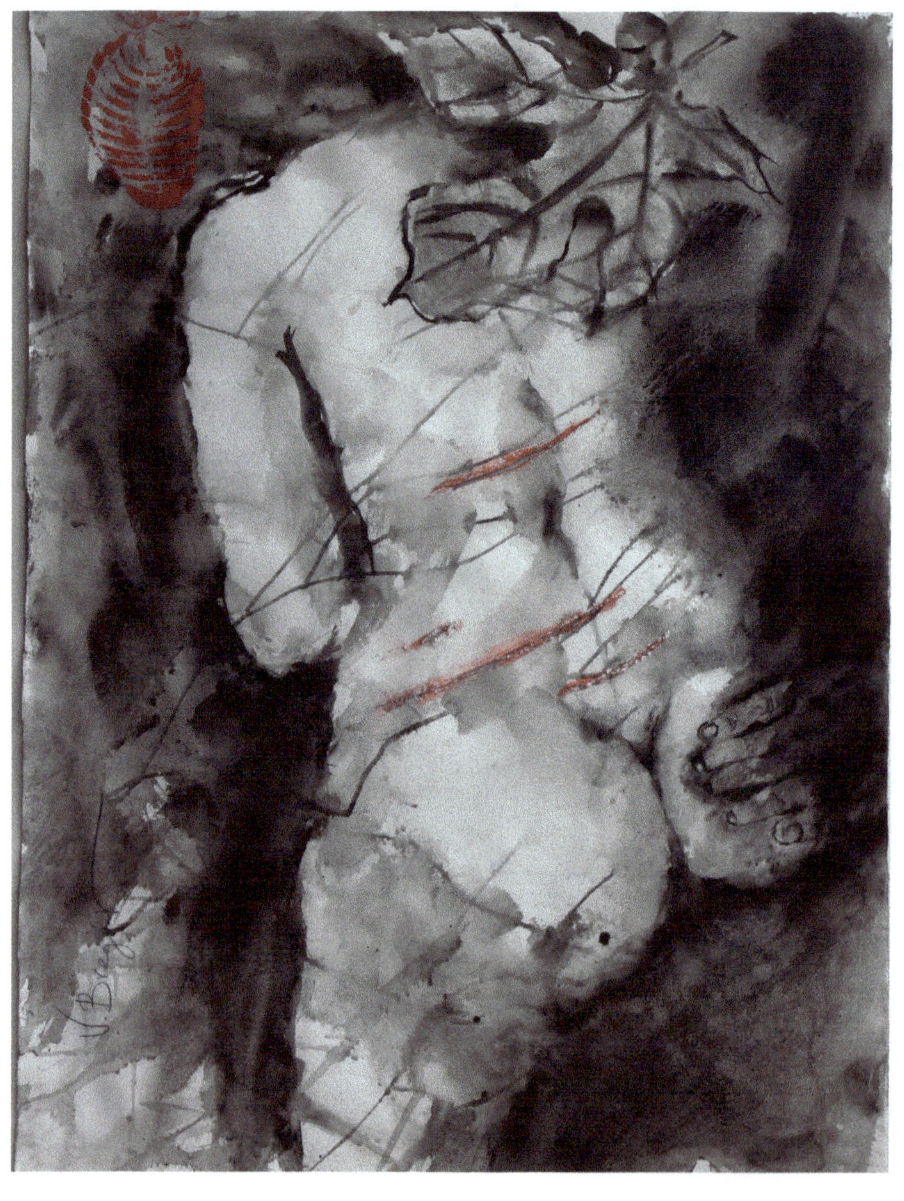

#Metoo 100x70 On Paper Mixed Media

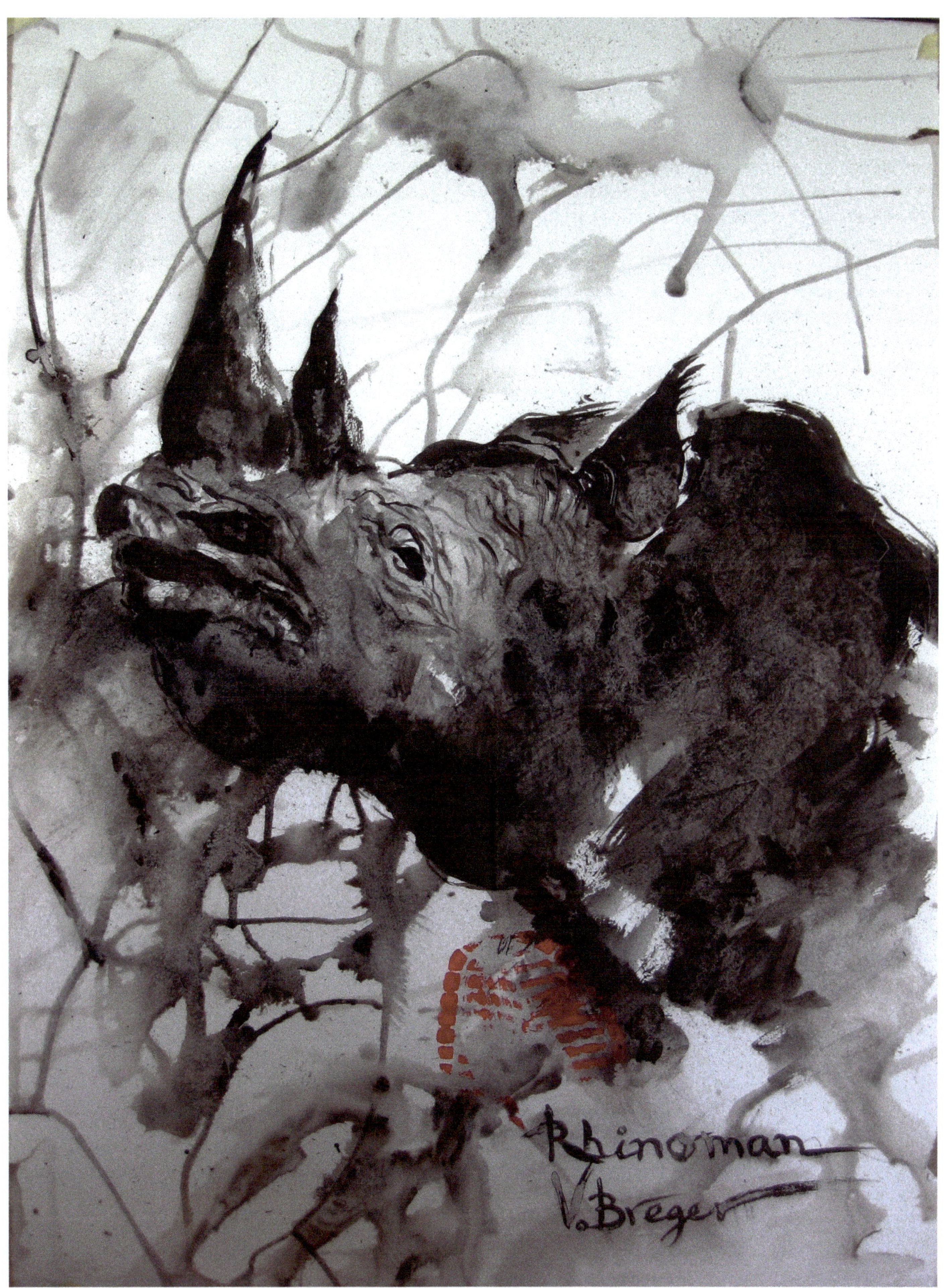

Rhino-Man 70x50 Mixed Mediaon Paper

Vinci Weng

vinciweng.com

I am a practicing artist and professor of fine art. With a rich artistic journey spanning four decades, I have been participating in numerous exhibitions and receive many awards internationally. I have been a gallery artist for YellowKorner Art Photography in Paris, France since 2018. By referencing painting and film, my work is focused on the re-thinking of a 'cinematographic' picture which presents the East-West pictorial concepts; it also associates with the ideas between realism and surrealism. My image can be described as representing a fictitious world of its own, with an intriguing organization of fields, depths, scales and colours which is the central subject to my work. My photograph is fantastic set in a fictional universe, often inspired by our real world; it is without specific place or venue. Specifically, these works have a group of magic events that invites the viewer into the wonder tales of my utopia, in which both natural and artificial realities exist at the same time in the fictitious landscapes. For my digital composite photographs, I do not use AI-generated tools nor stock images, only relying on complex manipulations of my own photographic images captured on locations. My idea, plan, post-production and photographs are all seamlessly connected in order to achieve visual strength of the final result. The working process is painstakingly, and needs to spend several months to produce a large-scale work. My current exploration of work focuses on unraveling surreal vistas and post-photographic aesthetics, masterfully portrayed in my evocative and painterly compositions.

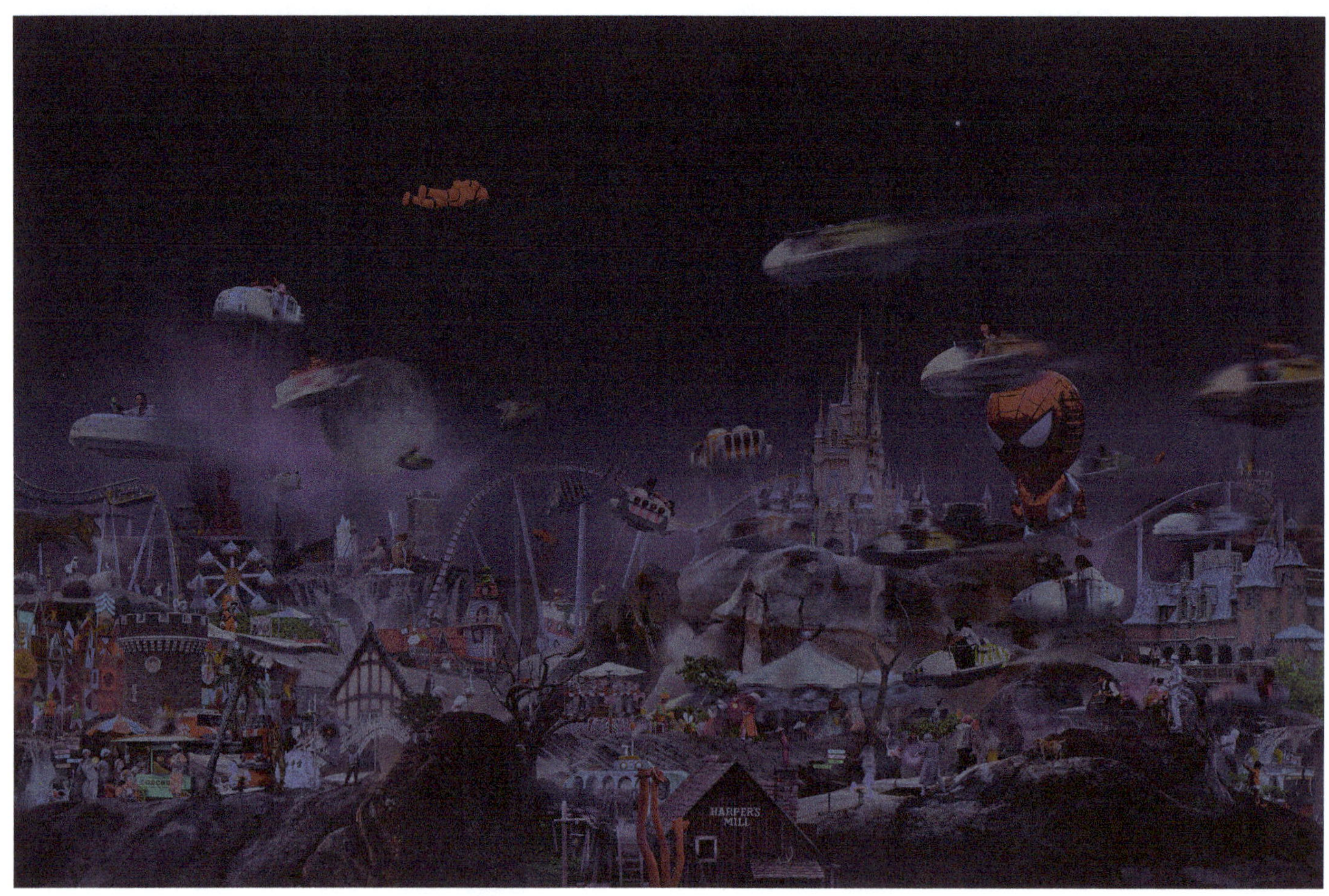

The New Fantasyland

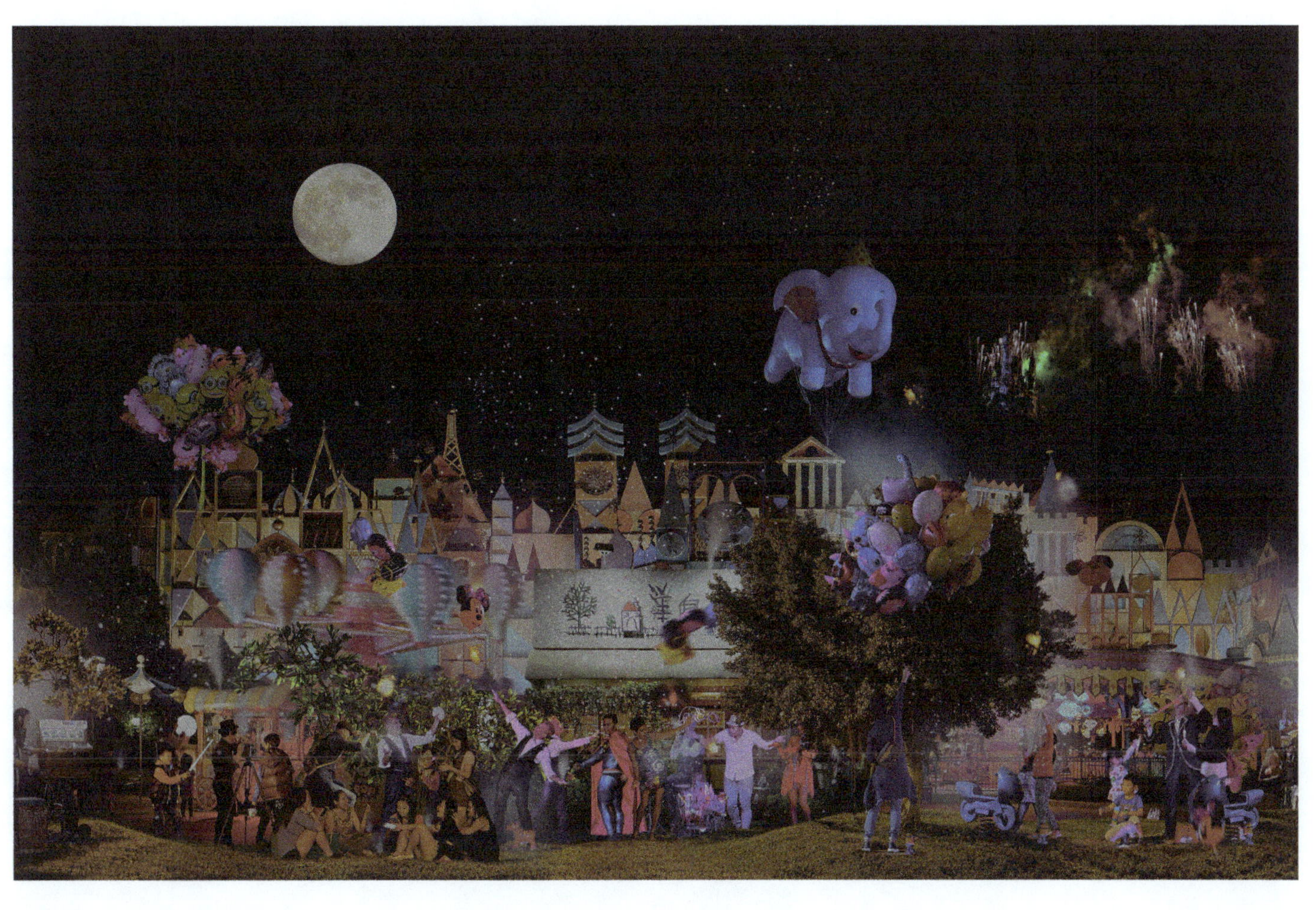

Night Paradise

Wendy Cohen

wendycohen123

Wendy Cohen creates innovative virtuosic mixed media paintings that communicate the harmony and beauty of the world. Incorporating her fascination with abstraction, whether it be a non-objective canvas, juxtaposed with collage elements, Wendy metamorphoses her unique vision by integrating shapes into a cohesive body of colours, lines, and forms. Flowing ideas are manifested that draw the viewer's attention to the brushstrokes, mark-making, and materiality on the surface of each painting. But, the primary focus of Wendy's practice is to invite the viewer to enjoy each painting as she transforms the static space into synchronized, contrasting colours, highlighting its vibrant chemistry and resonance.

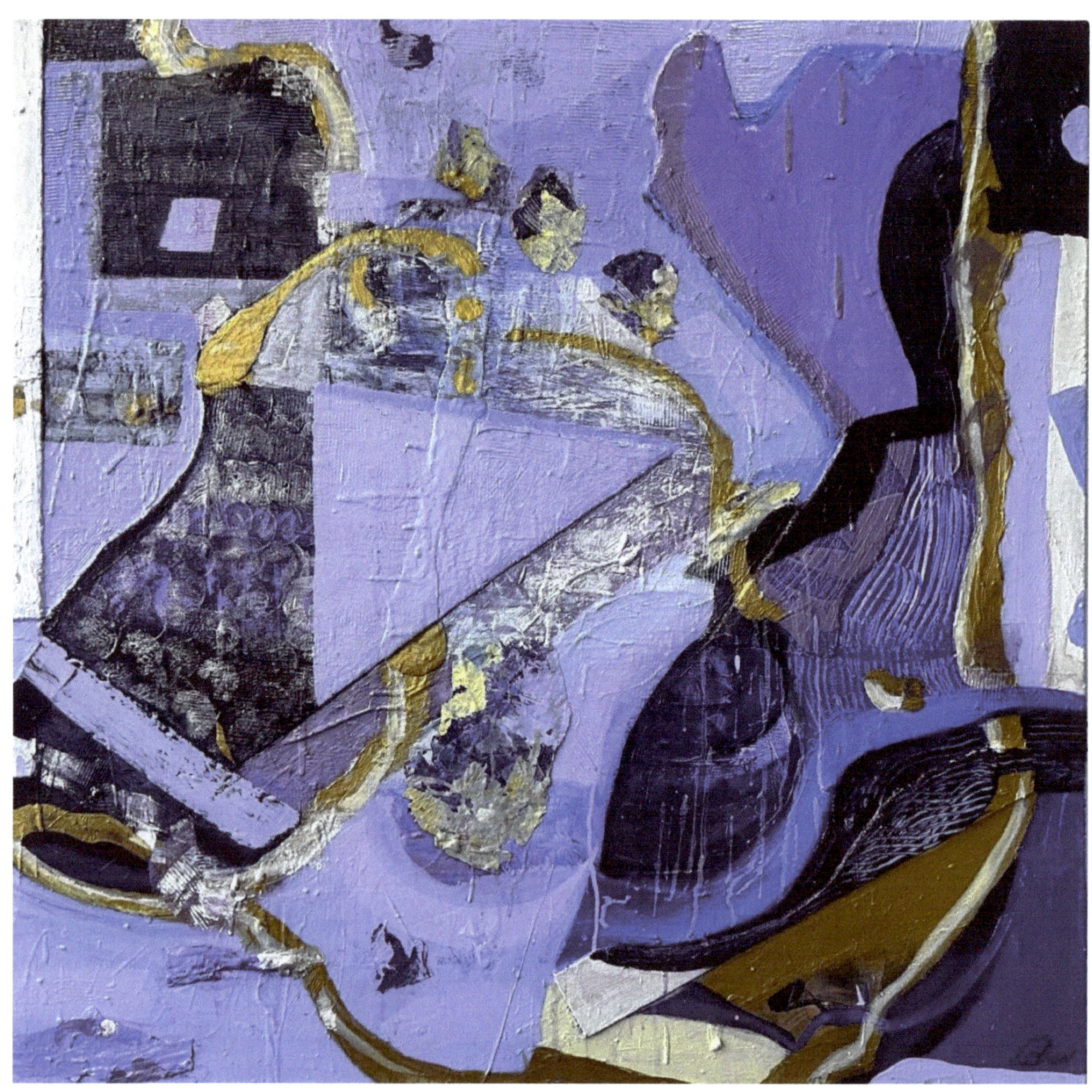

Violet Horizons

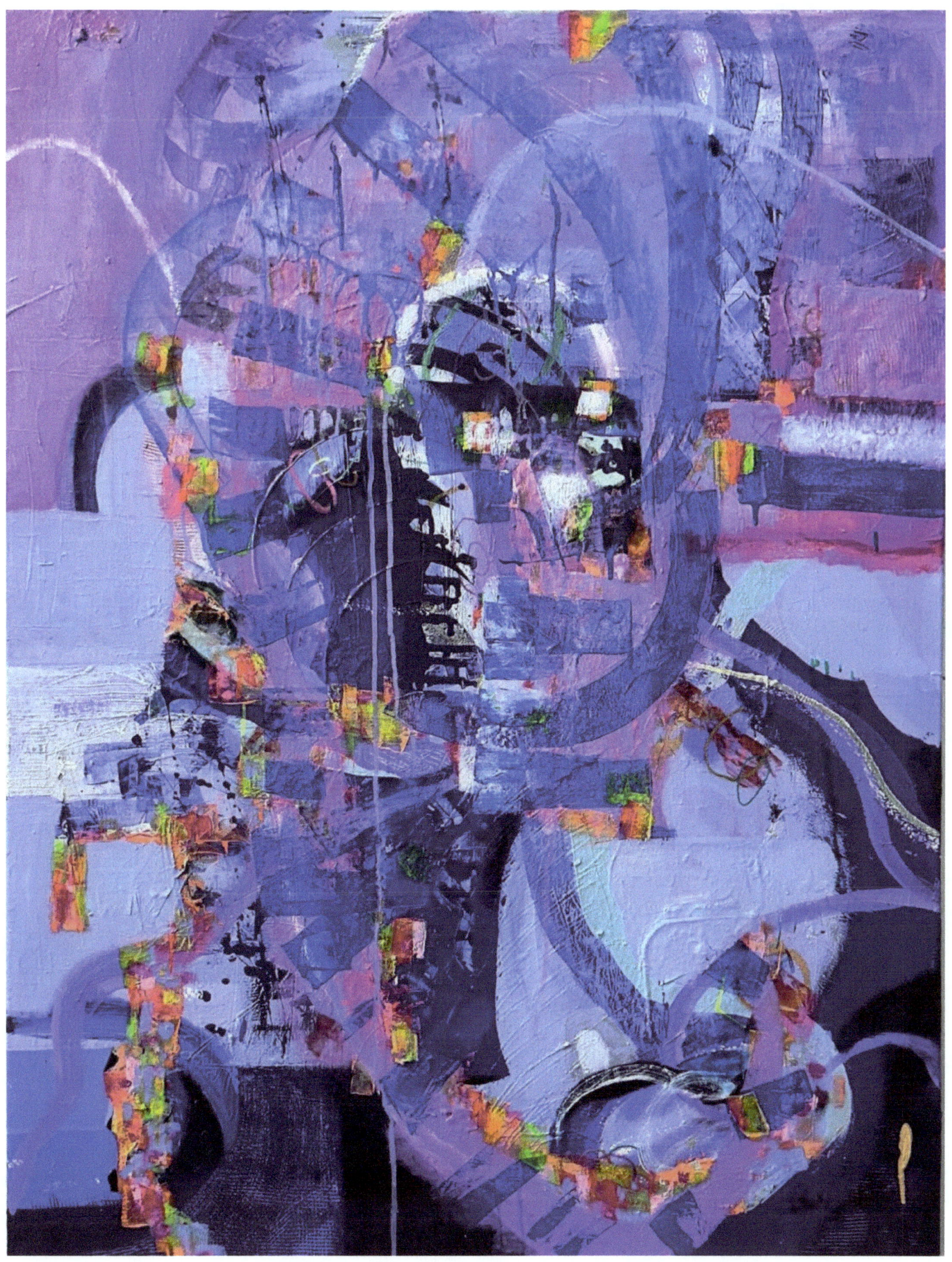

Unfolding Swirl Twirl

Wendy Leyten

wendyleyten.be

In my work, I love to intertwine the mystical, using my camera and light to tell a story that delves deeper than the visible. Inspired by the mystique of the everyday, I evoke emotions that resonate with the hidden layers of existence. Simplicity is key for me. My work serves as windows into a world where the subtle and the elusive converge. Through my images, I aim not only to show but also to invite the viewer to feel and contemplate. Each image captures a moment of deceleration, creating space for introspection. My goal is to create an atmosphere where the viewer embarks on an inner journey, away from the everyday hustle to a realm of contemplation and enchantment. My work is an invitation to get lost in the nuances of the unknown and discover beauty in the seemingly ordinary.

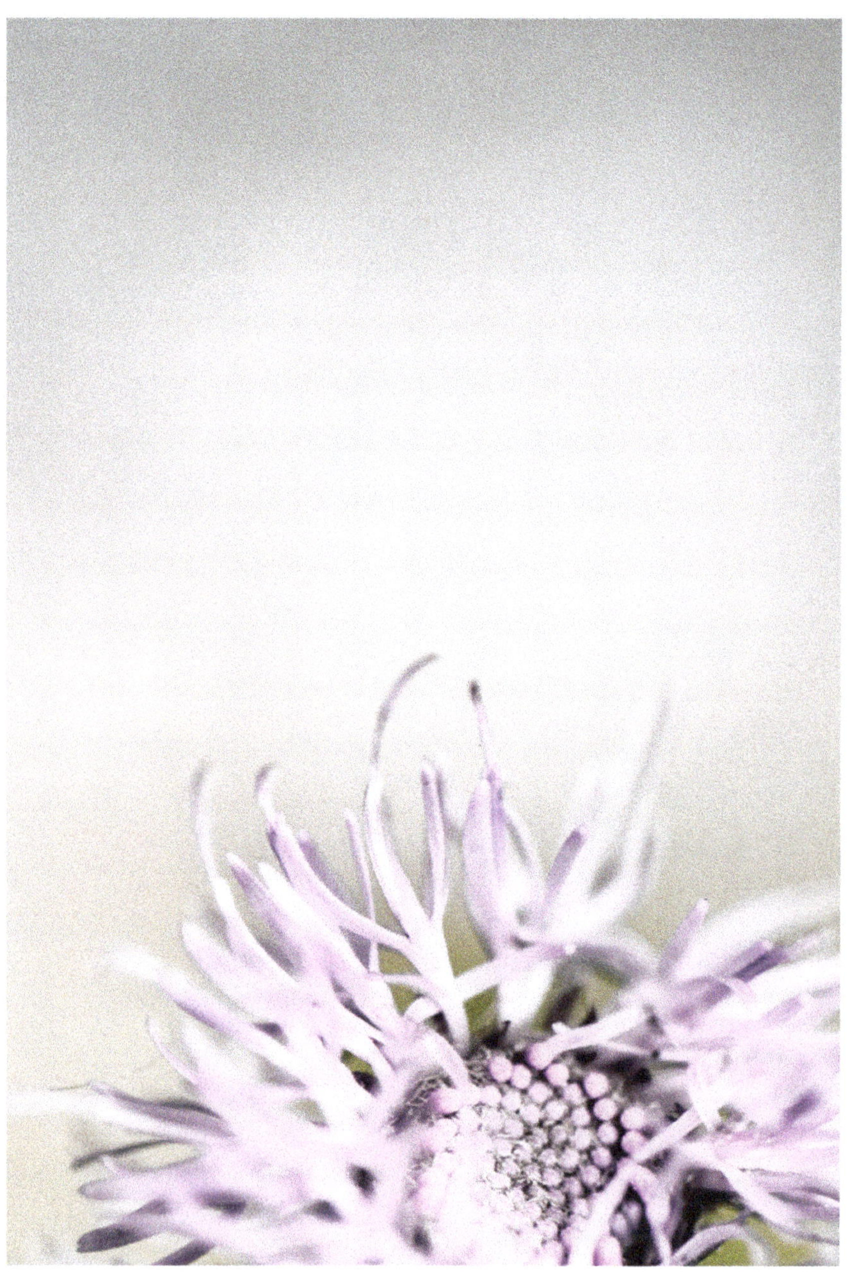

Flower Wisdom

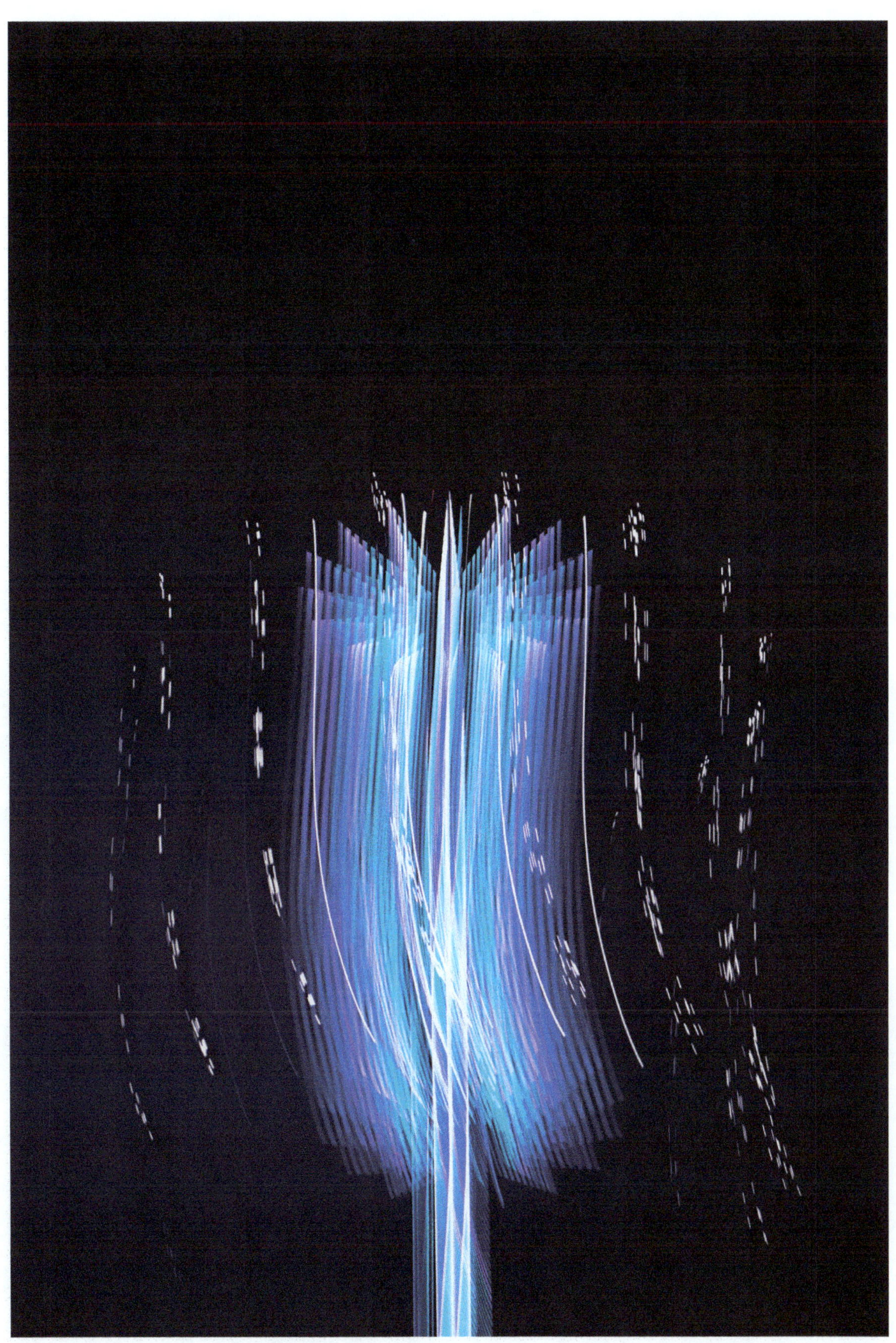

Painting With Light

William Prior

art_by_billprior

My work begins as my original digital, color pencil or digital photography and then is refined by an artificial intelligence;(AI) program. I am interested in imagining the future using AI.

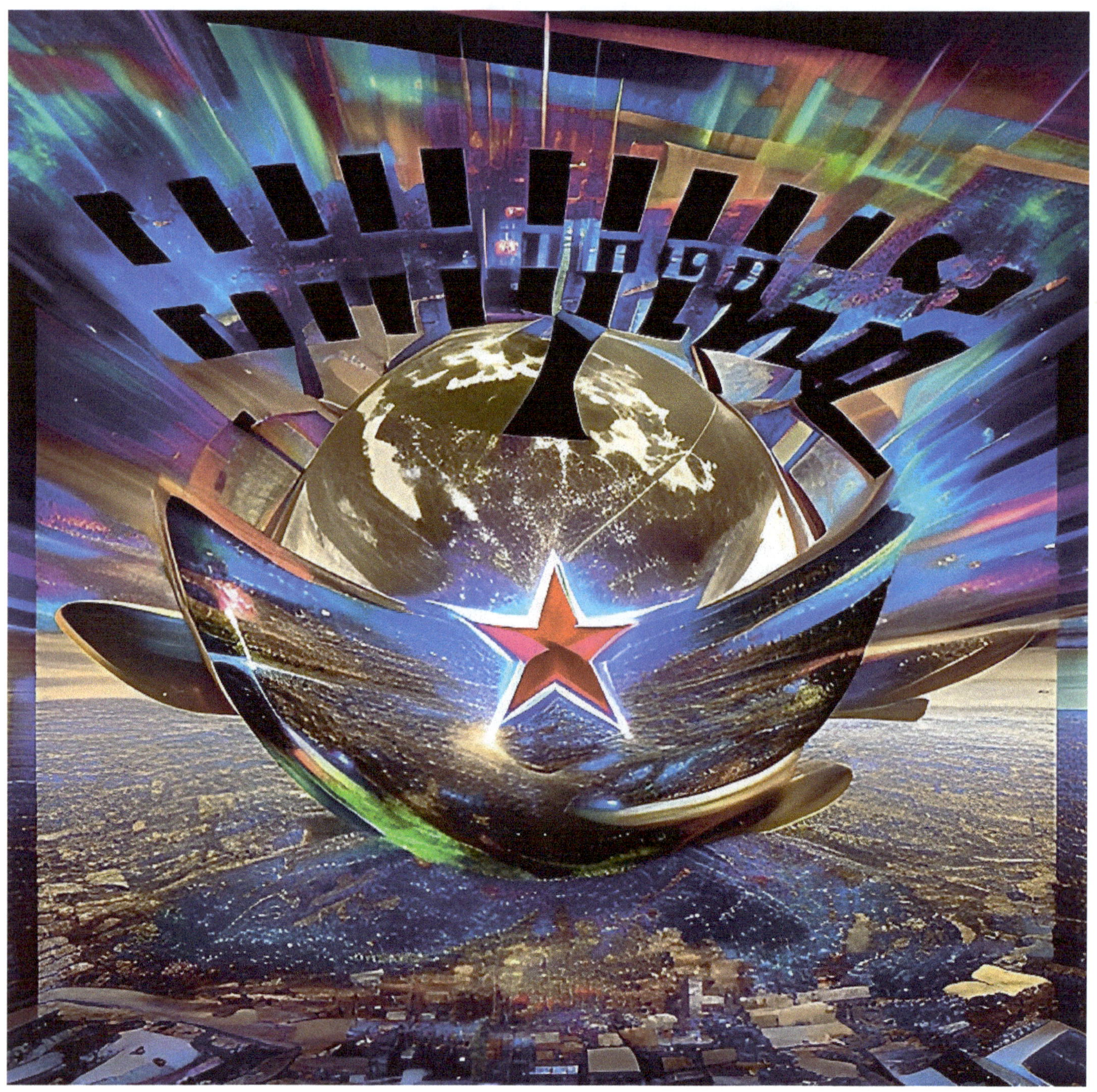

Stargate

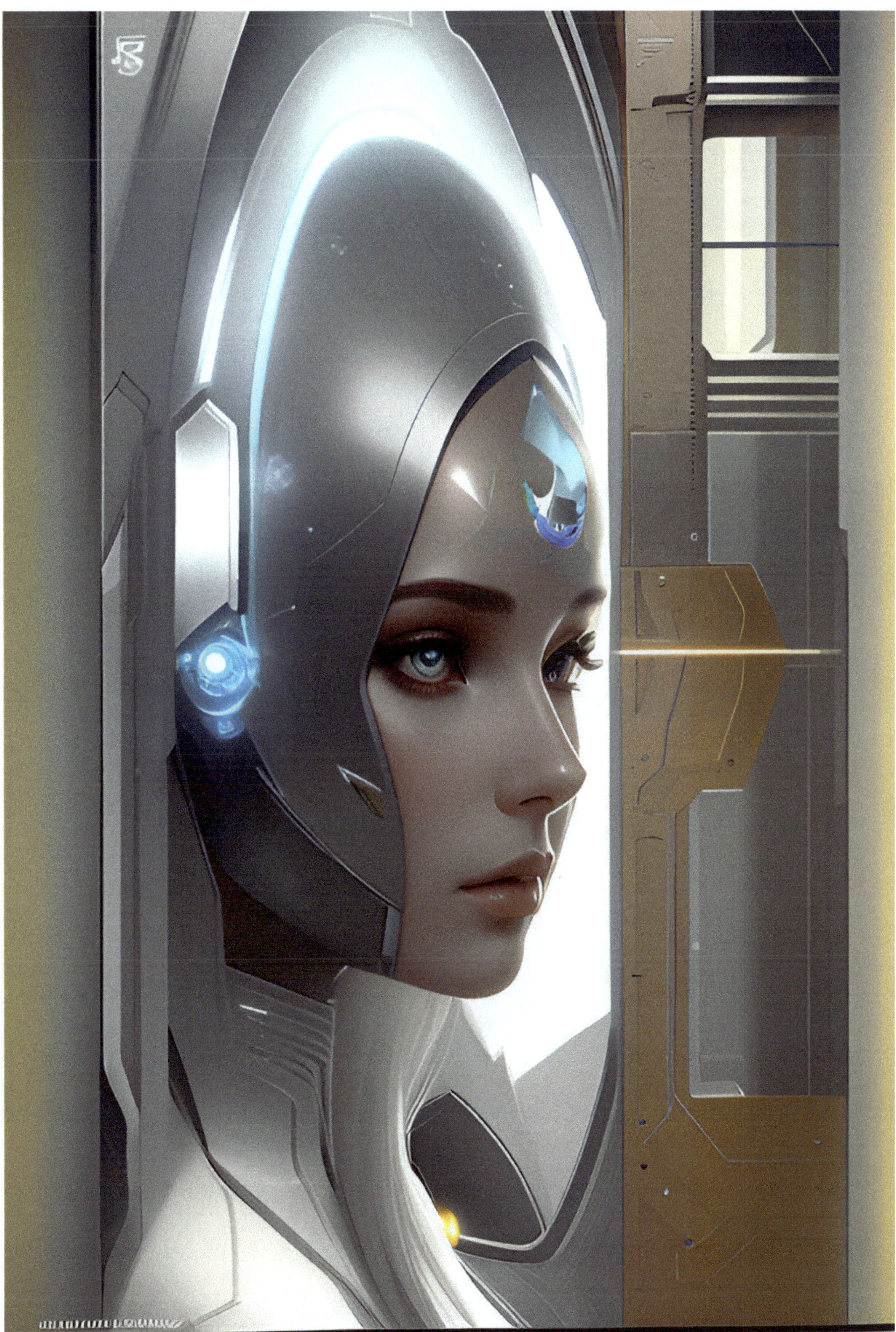

Star Person

Xiaorui Zhong

artstation.com/rzhong

Age 23 (2000), graduated from Ringling College of Art and Design. 3D artist in the game industry. Participated in Halo Infinite (2021) and Forza Motorsport (2022) as the 3D artist. Now as a Senior 3D Environment Artist in an unreleased AAA game project. Focus on 3D rendering art, digital sculpture, concept art.

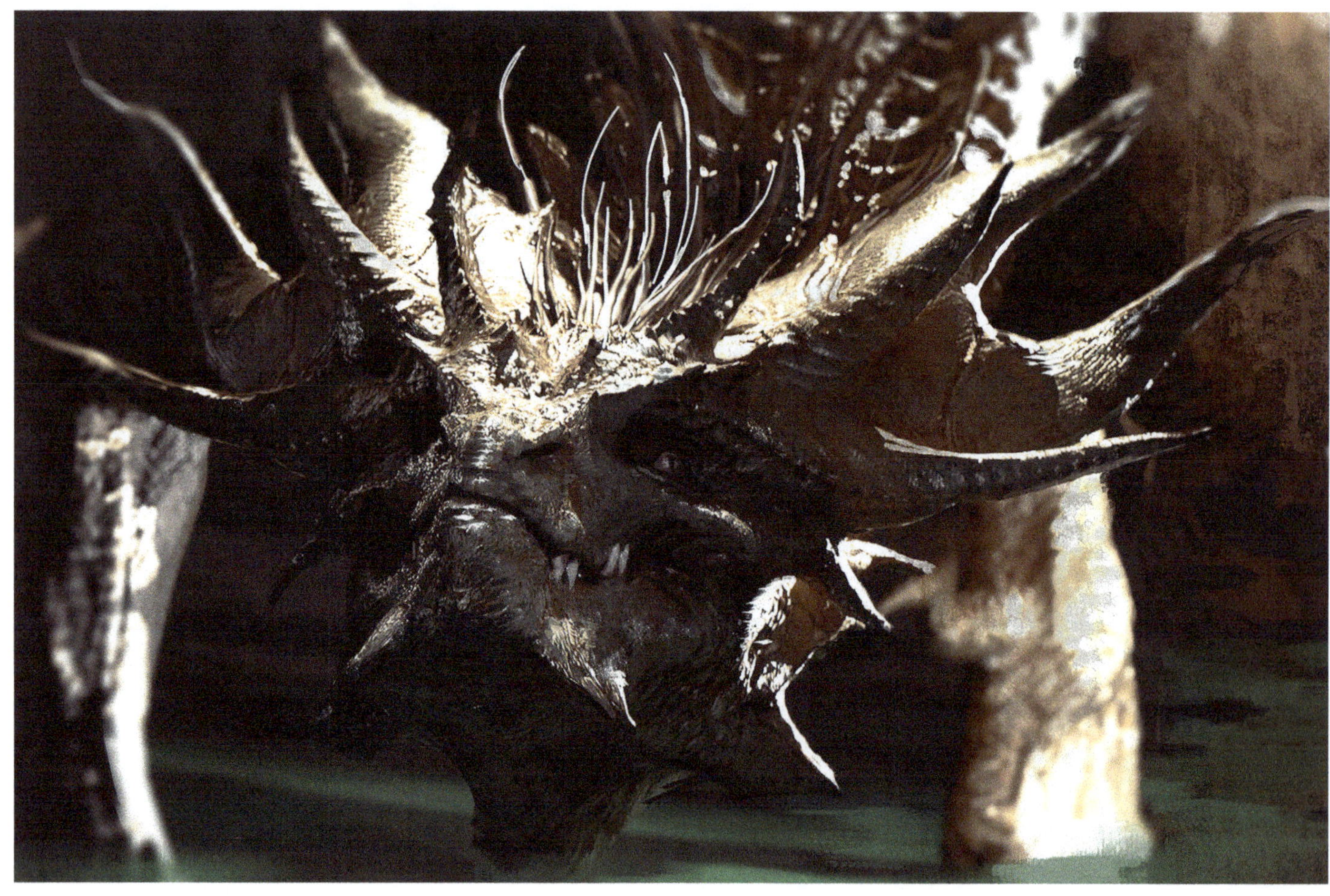

The Haughty Gaze of the Dragon

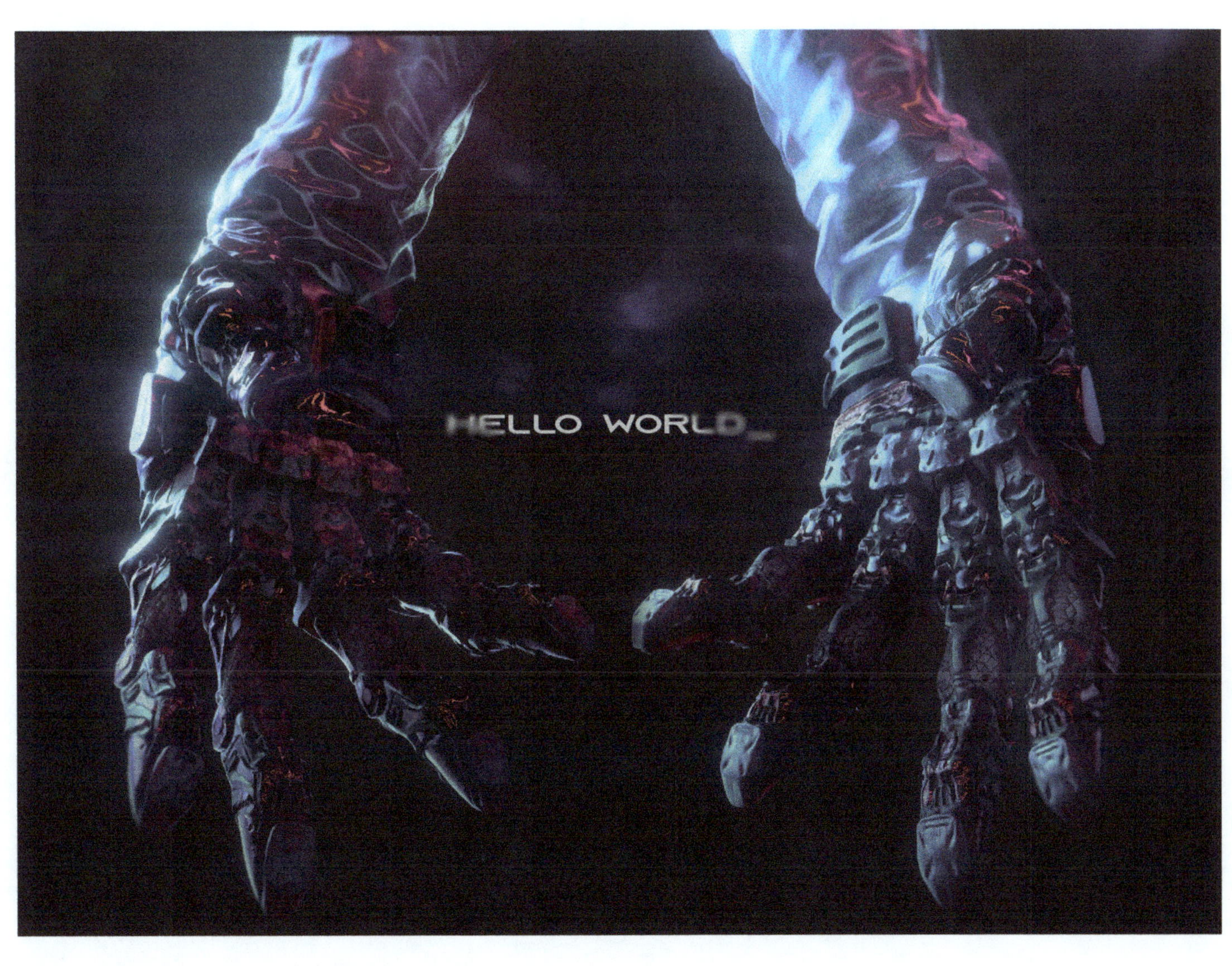

Hello World

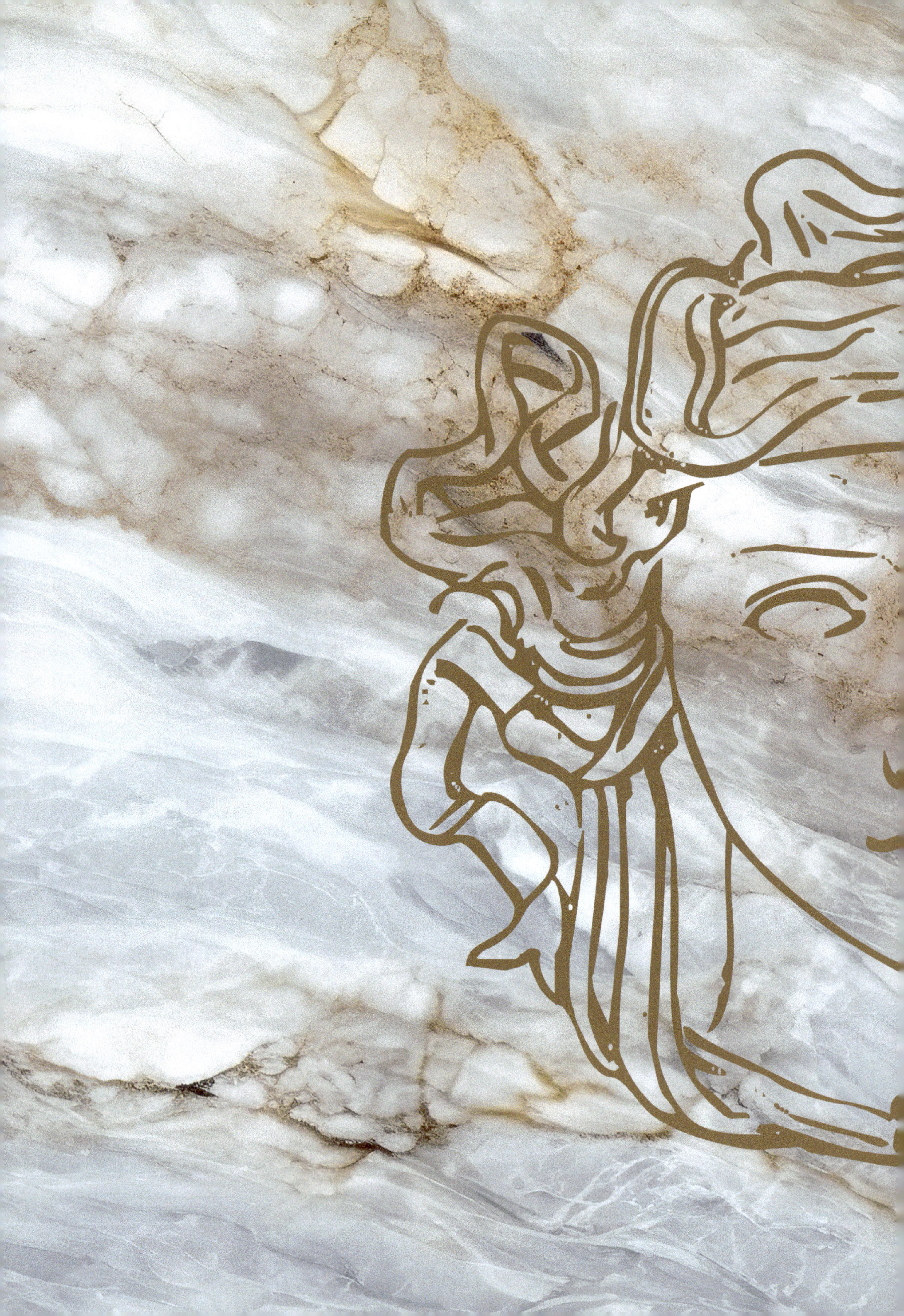

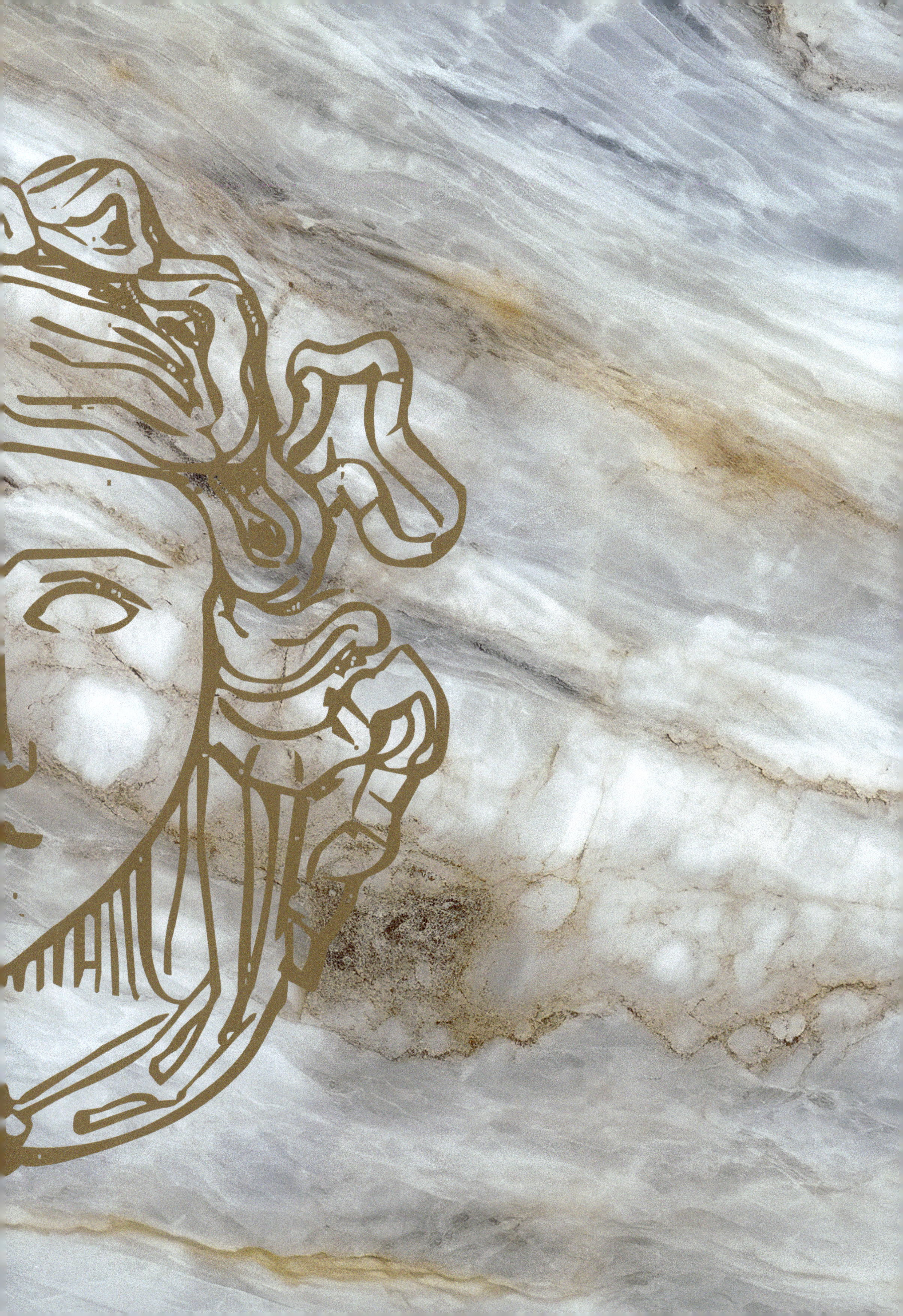

Persona Art Honours
Published by Contemporary Art Station

Publisher
ICM Gestora Cultural, SL
Paseo de Gracia 95, 5º-1ª
08008 Barcelona
Spain

ISBN: 978-84-10291-78-2
DL: GR 1436-2024

Library of Congress Cataloging-in-Publication Data
Persona Art Honours / Contemporary Art Station.
Includes bibliographical references and index.
ISBN 978-84-10291-78-2

Printed in Spain, EU.

First Edition, 2024

Publisher's Contact Information:
Contemporary Art Station
contact@contemporaryartstation.com
www.contemporaryartstation.com

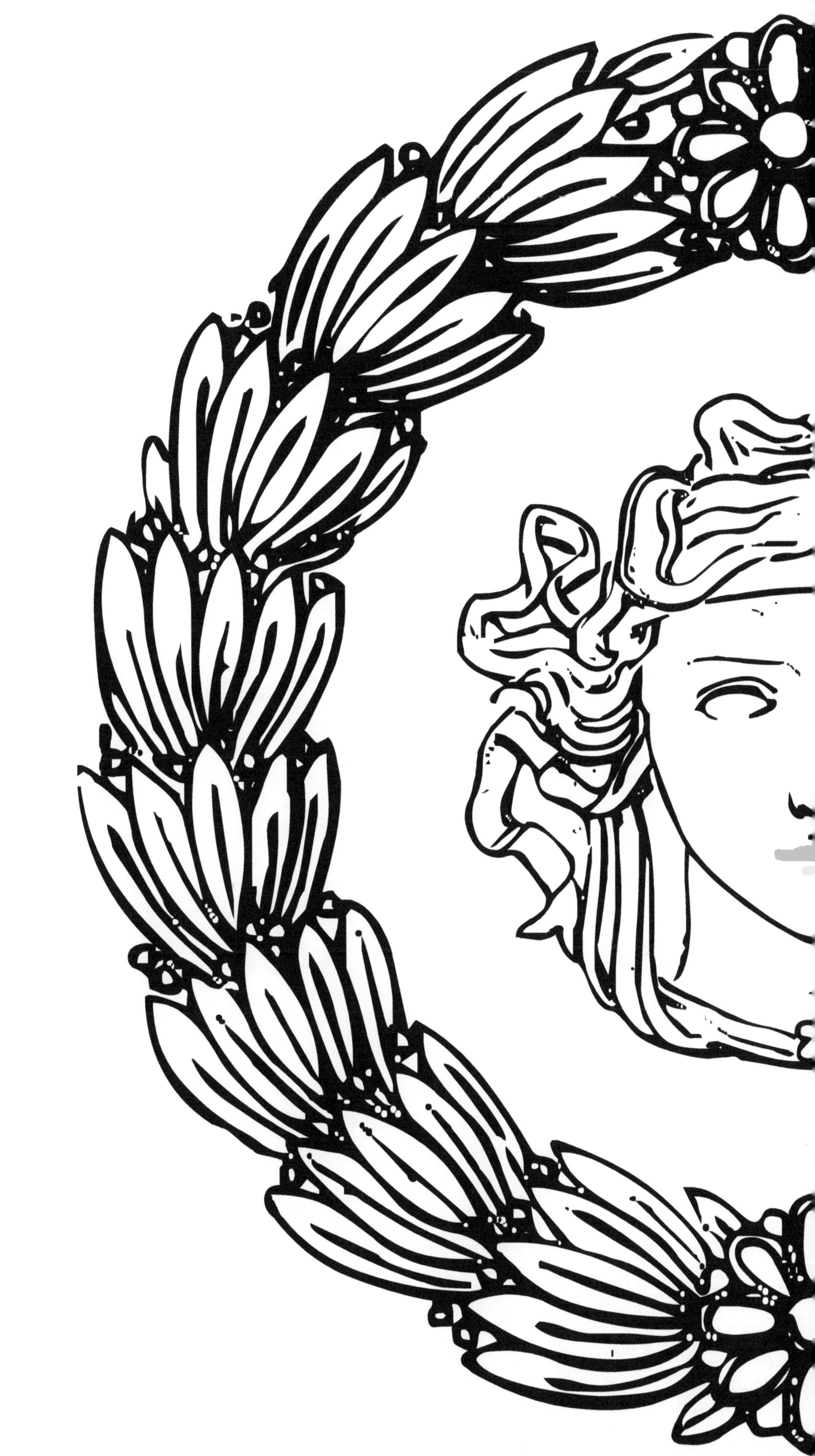

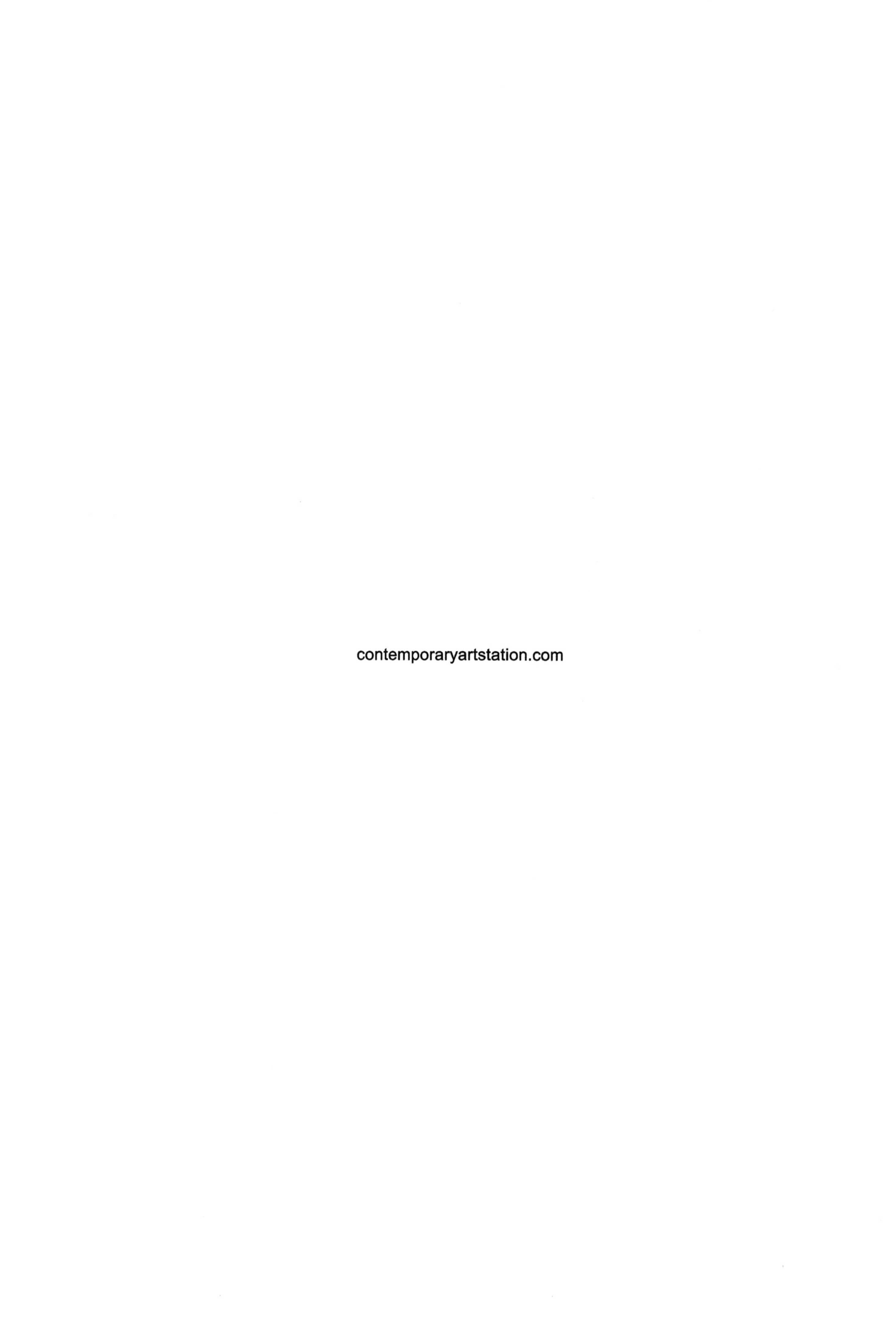

www.ingramcontent.com/pod-product-compliance
Lightning Source LLC
LaVergne TN
LVHW072116180726
843512LV00015B/1192